The
Random House
WRITING COURSE
for ESL STUDENTS

The Random House WRITING COURSE for ESL STUDENTS

Amy Tucker

Jacqueline Costello

both of Queens College
The City University of New York

 Random House • New York

First Edition
987654321
Copyright © 1985 by Random House, Inc.

Library of Congress Cataloging in Publication Data

Tucker, Amy.
    The Random House writing course for ESL.

    Includes index.
    1. English language—Text-books for foreign
speakers.   2. English language—Rhetoric.
I. Costello, Jacqueline.   II. Title.
PE1128.T78   1985   808'.042   84-17875
ISBN 0-394-33807-3 (pbk.)

Text design: John Lennard
Cover design: Jack Ehn
Cover art: John Frederick Peto, *Old Books*, painting
about 1890. Courtesy of Alice M. Kaplan and Langdale
Company. From the collection of Alice M. Kaplan.

Manufactured in the United States of America

Permissions Acknowledgments

Page 10—Cartoon portion of advertisement reprinted by permission of Berlitz Schools.

Page 12—"Ed's Jokes Are Greek to China Visitors" by Arthur Browne from *New York Daily News*. Copyright © 1984 New York News, Inc. Reprinted by permission.

Page 14—Advertisement reprinted by permission of Nichimen Corporation.

Page 15—Excerpts from Ford Motor Company advertisements reprinted by permission.

Page 15—Excerpt from Oldsmobile Omega ES 2800 advertisement reprinted by permission of the Oldsmobile Division of General Motors.

Page 21—Excerpt from advertisement reprinted by permission of Mercedes-Benz of North America, Inc.

Page 43—Adapted from "Brain Damage," *City Life* by Donald Barthelme. Copyright © 1968, 1969, 1970 by Donald Barthelme. Reprinted by permission of Farrar, Straus and Giroux, Inc.

Page 55—"This Is Just to Say," William Carlos Williams, *Collected Earlier Poems of William Carlos Williams*. Copyright 1938 by New Directions Publishing Corporation. Reprinted by permission of New Directions Publishing Corporation.

Page 56—"Pudding Catches Fire at Tower of London," *The New York Times*, December 26, 1983. Copyright © 1983 by The New York Times Company. Reprinted by permission.

Pages 69–70—*New York Times* Best Sellers List, nonfiction and trade paperback, August 15, 1982. Copyright © 1982 by The New York Times Company. Reprinted by permission.

Page 72—WINGO advertisement from *The New York Post*. Copyright © 1982 News Group Publications, Inc. Reprinted with permission.

Page 72—"Insect Troubles" reprinted by permission of C. Z. Guest, noted garden columnist for *The New York Post*, *The Boston Herald*, *The Washington Times* (D.C.), *The Albany Times Union* (N.Y.), *The Farquier Democrat* (Warrenton, Va.) and the *Palm Beach Daily News* (Fla.).

Page 72—"Shoe" cartoon reprinted by permission Tribune Company Syndicate, Inc.

Page 73—"The Marriage Killer" by Jules Feiffer, from *The Village Voice*, July 20, 1980. Reprinted by permission of Jules Feiffer. Copyright © 1980, Jules Feiffer.

Page 73—Selection from Dr. Joyce Brothers' column. Copyright © King Features Syndicate, Inc. Reprinted by permission.

Pages 75–76—Lyrics to "Fifty Ways to Leave Your Lover." Copyright © 1975, Paul Simon. Used by permission.

Page 76—Excerpt from "How to Climb a Staircase," *Cronopios and Famas* by Julio Cortazar, translated by Paul Blackburn. Copyright © 1969 by Random House, Inc. Reprinted by permission of Pantheon Books, a Division of Random House, Inc.

Page 80—"How to Write a Resume" by Jerrold G. Simon. Reprinted courtesy of International Paper Company from their series on the Printed Word.

Pages 81–82—Outline adapted from "How to Write a Business Letter" by Malcolm Forbes. Reprinted courtesy of International Paper Company from their series on the Printed Word.

Page 109—"The House of Chang, 1892" endpaper illustration by Timothy Tsao from *Spring Moon*, by Bette Bao Lord. Copyright © 1981 by Bette Bao Lord. Reprinted by permission of Harper & Row, Publishers, Inc.

Page 112—Adapted "Cats" advertisement reprinted by permission of Fred Nathan.

Page 117—Chart by Robert Conrad from "How the Mind Works," *The New York Times*, January 24, 1982. Copyright © 1982 by The New York Times Company. Reprinted by permission.

Pages 120–121—"Eleanor Rigby" by John Lennon and Paul McCartney. © 1966 Northern Songs Limited. All rights for the United States and Mexico controlled by Maclen Music, Inc. c/o ATV Music Corp. Used by permission. All rights reserved.

Page 125—Advertisement for Weight-Watchers Frozen Meals reprinted by permission of Weight Watchers International. © Weight Watchers International, Inc.

Page 125—Gaines-burgers advertisement reprinted with the permission of General Foods Corporation, White Plains, N.Y. © General Foods Corporation, 1982.

Page 137—Advertisement for Teleplan reprinted by permission of Hilton International Hotels.

Pages 155–159—From *Growing Up* by Russell Baker, Congdon & Weed, Inc., New York, pp. 1–8. Copyright © 1982 by Russell Baker.

Page 192—"The River Merchant's Wife: A Letter" from Ezra Pound, *Personae*. Copyright 1926 by Ezra Pound. Reprinted by permission of New Directions Publishing Corporation.

Pages 193–194—From "CIT Scanners" by David Lampe, *Popular Science*, September 1983, p. 52. Reprinted from *Popular Science* with permission. Copyright © 1983, Times Mirror Magazine, Inc.

Pages 220–221—Illustrations from "The Deranged Cousin," by Edward Gorey, published in *Amphigorey Too*, New York, Putnams, 1975. Reprinted by permission of

To Steve and Ken

Preface

This book is designed to take you through a series of basic writing skills that you can draw on in your college work and in your career. We've called the text a *Writing Course*—rather than a handbook, workbook, or guide—because it incorporates all the elements of a composition course: you will be asked, at various times, not only to practice writing and grammar skills but to read, to respond, to analyze, to edit. Each unit is set up as a kind of classroom workshop in which you have the opportunity to work on your own as well as with classmates in collaborative learning activities. The guiding principle of the book is that writers learn by writing frequently, by listening to the comments of their peers, and by responding to the work of others. Accordingly, we have included many excerpts from the writing of our students—ESL students who, like you, are engaged in the discovery of the writing and revising process.

We have designed our course so that each unit leads logically into the next; however, this sequence is not fixed and inflexible. We have included more lessons, readings, and writing assignments than can be covered in a one- or two-semester course so that the users of this book will have an extensive and varied selection of materials to choose from. Different students and classes have different needs, and these needs will determine how you use the book. Not all members of the class will require practice in the same grammar skills; many assignments can be worked on as either journal exercises or group activities; most important, the order in which you study the units themselves can be shifted. These decisions are left to you and your teacher. We offer the following chapters as guidelines, to encourage you to experiment with the widest possible range of prose techniques and voices.

Acknowledgments

We'd like to begin by expressing our gratitude to our students, whose ideas and essays have had the strongest influence on our way of looking at the process of writing, and whose work is quoted liberally in this text.

We are equally grateful for the generous collaboration and wisdom of our colleagues at Queens College: Nancy Comley, Rosemary Deen, Robert DiYanni, Linda Farhood, Judith Fishman, Marla Garil, William Kelly, Robert Lyons, Donald McQuade, Diane Menna, Susan Mufson, Carmela Perri, Marie Ponsot, Sandra Schor, and Sue Shanker. We thank Marlene Tanzer, as well, for her research.

For their expert guidance, flexibility, and enthusiasm, the editorial team at Random House have our heartfelt thanks: Steve Pensinger, Elisa Turner, June Smith, John Lennard, and Emily Frei. A special note of gratitude must go to our project editor, Cynthia Ward, for her sensitivity and insight into the second-language learning process, and above all for her tact.

In addition, we are indebted to our reviewers, for their valuable criticisms as much as for their plaudits: Tiby Appelstein, Alan Devenish, Tamara Lucas, Debra Deane Matthews, Christine Meloni, Marie Wilson Nelson, Dennis O'Toole, Carol Singley, and Patricia Werner.

Our love and appreciation go to our parents, for their encouragement. Most of all, we thank our husbands, Steve and Ken, who have helped us at every stage of this project. Their suggestions, support, and indefatigable good cheer made our work on this book possible—and pleasurable.

A. T.
J. C.

Table of Contents

Grammar lessons are indicated with a •. Longer reading selections by professional writers are listed at the end of each chapter.

Chapter 7: Writing Fables

Unit 5: Exposition

Chapter 8: Defining, Classifying, Comparing, Contrasting or Four Ways of Looking at a Computer

Chapter 9: Analyzing Causes and Effects

Unit 6: Argument

Chapter 10: Developing an Argument

• Appendices

unit 1 | Communication Up Close

1 Looking into Language

STUDYING A SECOND LANGUAGE

A Note to ESL Students

It has often been remarked that Americans have the unfortunate habit of monolingualism. Consider these items:

- Less than three percent of all American high school students attain foreign-language competence.
- The United States is the only country where you can graduate from college without having studied a foreign language.
- No one in the U.S. embassy in India speaks Hindi.
- In the Soviet Union there are almost ten million students of English, but there are only 28,000 students of Russian in the U.S.
- Luckily, Deng Xiaoping, China's senior deputy prime minister, brought with him an interpreter skilled in English for his talks with President Carter in 1979. The U.S. government, it turns out, does not employ anyone fully qualified to translate simultaneously from Chinese to English.

This linguistic backwardness may be the result of America's geographic isolation or national indifference, or it may be because English has become the primary international language of diplomacy, science, business, and popular music. Whatever the reason, the American educational system runs the risk of turning out students who are, in one educator's term, "globally illiterate."

ESL students have the extraordinary advantage of bilingualism. Over the years we've asked our students to keep notebooks, or journals, in which they record their experiences, observations, and impressions while studying in the United States. Their journal entries show a variety of reasons for learning English and mixed reactions to the problems encountered along the way. Here are a few examples of their comments:

English is an interesting language, and I like it. I think English is basically easier to learn as a first language than Korean. Most of all, I like its pronunciation. It is like a perfectly round pebble in clear flowing water.

But now it is pushing me in the corner. Sometimes I think if I studied all of these college subjects in Korean, there would be nothing to get me in trouble. But it would also make me boring. I like to try something new—I don't care what it is. This English language is something new for me. Even when study is difficult, it reminds me that I am trying something different.

Once upon a time, I was a little kid living with my family in a small village miles away from Athens, the capital of Greece. Now, after many years, I find myself in New York, and my new subject is English. I have to learn English first if I want to do well in my courses. I love this language a lot. Obviously, it is a little difficult for one who starts to learn English at my age, but I think that after a few months I'll be familiar with this language. . . .

Another reason why I like English is that I'll have more opportunities to find a better job in my country than people who don't know English at all.

I studied English for more than five months, trying to learn the basic elements to make myself understood. Anyway, my interest in English is not merely functional. What a pleasure to read Whitman, Joyce, Faulkner, and Shakespeare in their own language. But what a boring process, that of learning. I would like to have pills or something to learn this language.

These writers have taught us a great deal about the nature of English and about the process of acquiring a second language. Their insights have structured the following discussion of language, as they have helped to shape each chapter of this text.

We're grateful to these students for the illuminating journal entries we quote in this chapter: Hi Su Park, Dimos Angelussis, Mauricio Bonnettvelez, Sylvia Torres, Xiao Tian Quian, Haewon Yoon, Anthony Spanoudis, Ko-Ping Tsai, Shahram Haghnazari, Masaaki Ito, Shahram Nabatkhoran, Panayiotis Pantelides, Afshin Mahabadi, Ismail Heikal.

JOURNAL EXERCISE 1.1

Before you continue with this chapter, try writing for fifteen minutes in your notebook about the various reasons you have for studying English. What aspects of your language study have been especially difficult or rewarding?

Comparing Linguistic and Cultural Systems

As our students have pointed out, learning a foreign language usually means acquiring a new range of sounds, writing symbols, and grammatical structures—some easier, some more challenging than those of one's native tongue:

> Portuguese has many words similar to English, but it is very different in the construction of sentences. English is also very hard to pronounce: the sounds I have the most trouble with are the *th* and the *r* sounds. But I still like English a lot; I always liked the way it sounded, even before I knew any English at all.

> Chinese is quite different from English. Our language does not have an alphabet, just words. I think Chinese is not difficult to study for the foreigner. Chinese has hieroglyphics which consist of greatly simplified drawings of the objects that the characters denote. Therefore, by imagination you can figure out the meanings of many words. For example, for "eye" we write 目 . This symbol looks like a person's eye. Also, we write "sun" 日 "moon" 月 , and "umbrella" 傘 , which all relate to what they look like. The pronunciation is also different from English words, which often have several syllables. In Chinese we have only one syllable for each word, so sometimes we are confused by Chinese words which have the same pronunciation but different meanings.
> Another difference is our writing system—we have three kinds of systems. There are top to bottom, right to left, and left to right: each way is acceptable. You just write whatever way you want. However, sometimes I am confused by these writing systems, especially in short sentences, because you can read from right to left or from left to right, but each way has its own meaning.

> Thanks to living here, I can speak two languages, even if I am not fluent. It is interesting to compare Korean and English. They are quite different in sentence structure. For instance, "The boy hit the ball" is composed of subject, verb, and object but in Korean it is subject, object, and verb. This is the simplest sentence. But in a long sentence or to the beginner, this can be very confusing.

> If you ever hear me saying that I love English, don't misunderstand me. I'm talking about speech. But when I say I hate English, be sure that I'm referring to writing and grammar. Oh that grammar. I wish I had never learned this word. If it were possible to erase, banish this word from all English and bilingual dictionaries, I would be the happiest man of all. I hear this word and my hands start shaking, my head's aching, and the beats of my heart tend to the infinite. I'm not kidding. I hate grammar and everything that has to do with it. Verbs—regular and irregular—auxiliaries, passive voice, gerunds, clauses: words that are easy to pronounce but, in the final analysis, more difficult than Rubik's cube.

This last writer, a Greek student, is passionately eloquent on the subject of English grammar. Indeed, learning to manipulate verbs and gerunds is more than just a matter of memorization. Sociolinguists have long observed how different grammar systems reflect variations in cultural thought patterns, and it is these larger thought patterns that you are really absorbing when you study a foreign language.

For example, you have discovered by now that English nouns are not generally classified as male or female. But they are in Arabic and Romance languages: you have to know the sex of a noun to use it properly. English speakers, instead, classify nouns into mass or countable, animate or inanimate. Edward Hall, a renowned anthropologist, notes that this system would no doubt confuse the Trobriand Islander of the Southwest Pacific, who thinks of vegetables as being like animals—able to migrate from one garden to another.

Similarly, you may have trouble with the English verb tense system. The issue becomes especially complex, for example, for speakers of Chinese. Chinese does not inflect verbs for tense or agreement, but instead uses context or specific grammatical markers to indicate these differences. The Hopi Indian of Arizona studying English as a second language would face even greater problems, for his view of time differs drastically from that of the English, European, or Asian speaker. The Hopi language lacks the distinct units of past, present, and future by which most European languages express a linear view of time; for many years, the Hopi lived without clocks, calendars, or written histories. Their culture is primarily organized not in terms of time and space but in terms of events.

In addition to different concepts of grammar and word order, you bring from your native culture certain values, aesthetic judgments, and associations that may not be readily expressed in English:

> I have a very special feeling about my language. When I speak to someone in English, I am able to understand him quite well. However, if I speak to someone in Persian, I feel much better. The words sound more meaningful to me. When I listen to an English song, I cannot fully acquaint myself with it. The only reason I listen to it is that I may like the music, whereas if I listen to a song in Persian, it is more interesting to me. I feel as if the poet is sitting next to me, and every word he sings means memories to me.
>
> When I think about why it was so hard for me to make American friends, I find a good reason for it. I didn't want to speak in their language. However, if I saw two people speaking Persian, I would run to them and start a conversation!

> My native language is Korean, which I love to compare to other languages. Well, I am a kind of native language lover, and I have some special reasons for this. I love to write poetry in Korean. I mean, that's a wonderful feeling that Americans will never understand unless they write a poem in Korean.

This writer goes on to give a second reason for being "a native language lover":

> Korean has a very special distinction between the polite form and the familiar form. So when I have to talk with a person who is older than I, I have to use a polite form without any exception—and this makes people very polite, I believe.

Another Korean student continues the comparison:

> In English we need only one word to address a younger sister, a friend, or an older person. That word is "you" if we do not want to repeat their names. But in Korean we have three different pronouns for addressing people. If I called my father "you," I would be treated as a rotten child.

The distinction between polite and familiar forms of "you" is a feature of many languages around the world, though not of English. Some non-natives find that this informality often extends to the American's *non-verbal* behavior as well. To Asians, for example, Americans may seem aggressive and over-familiar.

The Japanese have a far more formal way of expressing social relationships than Americans do. One Japanese student's discussion of the subject is worth quoting at length:

> When I first came to America, I was puzzled by the differences between Eastern culture and Western culture. It took me some time to get used to the new ways.
>
> First of all, when people meet for the first time, in America they shake hands or just say "Hi! Nice to meet you," but in my country they bow all the time. It is necessary and must be done. The deeper you bow, the better —it means that you are expressing or paying respect to another person. If you don't bow, people think you are very rude and you are stigmatized as an outcast from society. For a while, I kept bowing when I saw Americans because it was a very, very strong custom. So to speak, it is the most important and basic custom in Japanese society.
>
> Second, in Japan we don't believe we should speak up, make demands, or insist on our opinions. It is considered a virtue to keep silent and not express our feelings to others. We have a saying: "The able eagle hides his nails," which is a direct translation. We are also expected to be very generous to others. For example, if you give someone a present, you say, "This is a humble present and it might not please you, but I'd like you to accept it if you can." Everything is done this way.
>
> On the other hand, the American custom is to be very direct and to say what you think very frankly and clearly. But we Japanese try to be ambiguous in every respect so that we don't hurt each other's feelings.

This writer suggests that rituals and manners are a crucial part of any linguistic system. Sociologists have observed that although an individual can stop talking, he or she cannot stop communicating through "body language." Another form of non-verbal communication is physical contact and use of personal space. Hispanics, like Italians, belong to what are known as "contact" or "touch" cultures. Latins touch to say "Hello" or "Thanks," or as a request form meaning "May I see you for a moment?" Similarly, Latins typically converse at a distance of 6 to 18 inches, whereas in the U.S. and most European countries, the personal space distance is 18 to 36 inches. Consequently, Latins are apt to find Americans cold and withdrawn. A young Spanish woman once told us, "When I was a child I used to think that Spanish was the only language in the world," and, in the same way, most of us are inclined to feel that our *body language*, at least, is universally understood. On the contrary: according to Ray Birdwhistell, a pioneer in the study of non-verbal communication, there is no gesture which has exactly the same social meaning in all societies. Even so basic an act as nodding "yes" or "no" varies in significance from one culture to another. Speakers of most European languages nod their heads up and down for "yes," and shake their heads from side to side to signal "no." For the Eskimos, the same motions have exactly the opposite meanings. Sicilians and Greeks say "no" by raising the head and chin—yet this very gesture is used by the Maori of New Zealand to say "yes" and by North Americans to mean "Would you mind repeating that?"

The same kind of variation is found in vocal gestures like crying, giggling, or hissing. In Africa, laughter is not necessarily a sign of amusement: it frequently expresses surprise or embarrassment. Similarly, American speakers addressing a Spanish group are often startled to hear hissing, which is a call for silence rather than an indication of disapproval as it is in the States. This same sound, moreover, is used to show deference in Japan.

The study of non-verbal communication is a fascinating aspect of language learning. Non-native students, consciously or unconsciously, are constantly engaged in decoding the non-verbal messages of the new culture. It is all part of the process of translation from one linguistic system to another.

CLASSROOM ACTIVITY 1.2

In this section, we have discussed how learning a new language often means acquiring new sound patterns, writing symbols, and grammatical structures. To see how the translation process works (or doesn't work), try this informal experiment in class.

Translate the following sentence into your own language:

> The hard-working student typed his English composition on his friend's word processor.

(Your teacher may ask a number of students to write their translations on the blackboard.) Discuss how your language translates these features of the English sentence:

- the recent addition to our vocabulary of the term *word processor*

- the word order (where are the subject [*student*], verb [*typed*], and modifiers [*hard-working, English, his friend's*] placed?)

- the past tense (how is the time of the action indicated?)

- the possessive adjective (*friend's*) and possessive pronoun (*his*)

- the article (*the*) and preposition (*on*)

Compare your sentence with those of your classmates. What differences do you observe?

EXERCISE 1.3

Below are further questions for discussion, suggested by the observations recorded on the preceding pages. You may, in addition, want to write on these topics in your notebook:

A.) A number of students have written about how people in their country show "polite" versus "informal" behavior. Can you think of ways in which a person from your culture uses special gestures or speech patterns to express respect for a new acquaintance, a parent, an older person, or a teacher?

B.) One student calls herself a "native language lover." What special features of your own language or culture would you like to "translate" into English? Are there, for example, particular ways of indicating one's intentions, attitudes, or feelings that American culture doesn't have? Have you noted any differences in "body language" or other forms of non-verbal communication? Which of your culture's customs and holidays have the most meaning for you? What aspects of your culture do you think *cannot* be translated into English?

The Pleasures and Pitfalls of Translation

The cartoon on the next page illustrates the confusion that can arise when language students attempt word-for-word dictionary translation instead of interpreting larger verb structures and idioms.

Of course, one of the joys of learning a new language is finding the precise word or phrase for what you want to say. It is natural that foreign students

depend heavily on their dictionaries, but we do advise you not to use *bilingual* dictionaries. One case will show you what we mean. A Spanish student in one of our classes, wishing to describe a clean, *clear* lake, consulted her Spanish/English dictionary for the English translation of *lucido*:

> **Luciano,** Lucian.
> ✓ **lucido, da,** *adj.* shining, magnificent,
>   splendid; clear.
> **luciente,** *adj.* bright, shining.
> **luciernaga,** *f.* glowworm, firefly, lightning
>   bug.

She then checked the English portion of her dictionary to make sure the word *lucid* exists in English:

> **lucent,** *adj.* brillante, claro.
> ✓ **lucid,** *adj.* luciente, luminoso; claro.
> **lucidity,** *n.* esplendor, resplandor, *m.*
> **Lucifer,** *n.* Lucifer, *m.*; **l—** **(match),**
>   fósforo de fricción.

Thus she produced this incorrect sentence: "The lucid water sparkled in the sunlight."

The entry for *lucid* in a standard, complete English dictionary shows that the bilingual dictionary has left out a lot of important information, and a necessary element of the definition. In English, *lucid* only means "clear" in the sense of "easily understood":

> **lu·cid** (lōō′sĭd) *adj.* **1.** Easily understood; clear: *a lucid speech.*
> **2.** Sane; rational: *a lucid speaker.* [French *lucide* and Italian
> *lucido,* from Latin *lūcidus,* from *lūcēre,* to shine. See **leuk-** in
> Appendix.*] —**lu·cid′i·ty, lu′cid·ness** *n.* —**lu′cid·ly** *adv.*

Occasionally, you may find that English does not possess the term or expression you're looking for. To take just two instances, English has no word or phrase that exactly corresponds to the Spanish/Italian *simpatico* or to the Japanese concept of *hada to hada*—literally, "skin to skin," meaning a mutual willingness to expose one's sincerity. (One Japanese student we know, trying to translate this phrase, combined *skin + kinship* and invented *skinship,* but this expression hasn't caught on yet.) Still, 50 percent of the English language consists of borrowings from other languages, and other cultures will no doubt continue to enrich our vocabulary.

JOURNAL EXERCISE 1.4

You might want to keep a list in your notebook of any words or concepts in your own language for which English seems to have no equivalent—and, by the same token, any English terms for which your language has no corresponding expressions. Can you think of one such word or phrase to begin your list?

We often ask our classes to record funny or frustrating experiences they've had because of misunderstandings in their second language. One student writes:

> It was not that I didn't have any difficulty speaking; rather I was afraid to speak. If I wanted to say something, I would first translate it into my language a couple of times, and then I'd try to say it in English. Of course, I would still make a lot of mistakes and sometimes I wasn't able to express myself. Those embarrassing moments used to make me not talk, but only listen and try to learn.
>
> After a while, I was convinced that this wasn't the right way to go about learning a foreign language. The only way to learn is to practice and to learn from your previous mistakes.
>
> Sometimes the mistakes are funny. I remember what happened to one of my friends. One day he got into a fight with one of his American friends. They were called to the principal's office to settle their fight. My friend was trying to explain that he had been insulted. But what he said to the principal was meaningless in English and very funny to me. In my language, Persian, there is an expression for which the equivalent meaning in English is "to insult." He was exactly translating this expression word by word. He said, "The other guy took the water from my face," but he wanted to say, "I was insulted." That didn't mean anything to the principal, but it sure was a lot of fun for me.

The difficulty this writer and his friend encountered stemmed from their attempts to think in one language while speaking another. Literal, direct translation is usually a futile exercise. With idioms, expressions, arguments, and jokes, something is likely to be lost in the second language. Witness this meeting between two politicians:

Ed's jokes are Greek to China visitors

By ARTHUR BROWNE
City Hall Bureau Chief

Wang Daohan, mayor of Shanghai, met yesterday with Mayor Koch, global diplomat of sorts and New York City's answer to the Cultural Revolution.

The mayor—Koch, that is—was in rare form, even for Hizzoner. He welcomed Wang into his office for a courtesy call and broke the ice with some humor.

"Even in a capitalistic society, we all work," Koch quipped as he provided Wang's interpreter with a chair. No response. "It's a joke," he added, turning to other subjects.

"PEKING DUCK made in Shanghai is better than Peking duck made in Peking," opined Koch, who visited China in 1980. Wang only smiled, and Koch moved on.

"People who live in port cities work faster, talk faster and think faster," Koch declared.

"I guess it's possible," Wang responded quietly. Again Koch changed the subject: He asked for a panda.

"It would have enormous positive impact on the people of the City of New York. They would go crazy," Koch said. Appearing confused, Wang's aides conferred briefly.

"I think it's possible but needs some work," one aide said finally.

Wang then said he was impressed with New York City's buildings, bridges and roads. Koch said that was called "infrastructure." The word didn't translate well, and the topic was dropped.

KOCH'S NEXT question was a bombshell—judging from the way the Chinese journalists accompanying Wang started scribbling.

"What are you going to do with the Gang of Four?" Koch inquired. "Are they still in jail?"

The Gang of Four were subordinates of Mao Zedong who were convicted of inciting rebellion and are blamed for China's Cultural Revolution—the 1966-76 period now regarded with disfavor in China.

After a brief pause, in which no answer was forthcoming, conversation continued, and shortly thereafter the East-West meeting ended cordially. Koch presented Wang with an illustrated history of New York City. Wang gave Koch Shanghai's official medallion.

Mayor Ed Koch is not the first person to have learned that different cultures have different notions of what is amusing or appropriate. We can understand the words of a joke without seeing the humor of it. Here are typical situations described by two students:

I was sitting and talking with some American friends of mine in the Student Union at my college. Suddenly, one of my friends said, "Boys, I'll tell you a very funny joke." We all listened and when he finished his joke all were laughing, including me. You are wondering, of course, what's so strange about this. Nobody can see what's strange about it—except me. I was laughing but I didn't know why I was laughing; I was laughing because that's what was polite, not because I found his joke funny.

Sometimes my friends would watch M*A*S*H on television and laugh; I used to just sit and watch, and it was embarrassing. Other times when I was talking on the telephone, I couldn't express my thoughts because of my lack of English and my fear of making a fool of myself. Some people think you are dumb when you cannot speak. I remember in my math class I used to be afraid to answer questions because I thought the other students would laugh. Also, I remember in a physics exam I couldn't write my idea in English even though I knew the answer, so I answered by drawing pictures, and I got a full mark for that question. Well, as they say, "You learn from experience," and that is true.

One has to be immersed in a culture to understand every nuance of its literature, riddles, jokes, TV shows. As one sociologist puts it, "If you can learn the humor of a people and really control it, you know that you are in control of nearly everything else."

Acquiring a second language, then, is a creative act. If translating from one language to another were simply an automatic activity, sophisticated computers could perform the task. But so far, attempts to perfect a computer translation system have been unsuccessful. According to an often-repeated story, some English proverbs—those wise sayings found in every language—were fed into a computer to be translated into Russian and back into English. The sentence "The spirit is willing, but the flesh is weak" came out "The vodka is good, but the meat is rotten." And the statement "out of sight, out of mind" became "invisible, insane."

Despite all the recent advances in computer technology, machines still produce, at best, rough translations that must be revised by humans. We alone can supply exact shades of meaning and a cultural context for each utterance. Failure to provide this context often results in comically unsuitable statements, as the creators of these advertising campaigns found out:

- In the States, General Motors advertised one of its cars as having a "Body by Fisher" (the name of the designer). This phrase was translated into Flemish as "Corpse by Fisher," which slowed down sales considerably.

- Similarly, when the same automobile company introduced its Chevrolet Nova, no one thought about foreign markets. But folks weren't buying the cars in Spanish-speaking countries, where *no va* means "It doesn't go." The name was quickly changed to Caribe, and sales picked up.

- Schweppes Tonic Water was advertised in Italy as "bathroom water."

- "Come Alive with Pepsi" almost appeared in the Chinese version of *Reader's Digest* as "Pepsi Brings Your Ancestors Back from the Grave."*

---

* These examples come from Paul Simon's *The Tongue-Tied American.*

CLASSROOM ACTIVITY 1.5

A.) Advertisements are rich cultural artifacts; they tell us what a particular society values. Below is an ad for Nichimen Corporation that appeared in an American business magazine. What characteristics does this Japanese company emphasize in order to sell its product to a foreign audience?

"'Even if it's a stone bridge, knock before crossing' is a Japanese proverb. Combining such caution with a dynamic, pioneering spirit is, I think, the secret of Nichimen's success."

Shunji Uyeda, *President*

Global Business Organizer—SOGO SHOSHA

⊗Nichimen Corporation

TOKYO/OSAKA JAPAN   Our extensive network covers 100 key cities throughout the world

B.) Pity the poor advertising executive trying to sell his products abroad. How would you translate the following slogans for automobiles into your native language?

Ford LTD.

The car that holds your family should also hold the road.

Trading Proverbs

Every culture has wise sayings, like the one quoted in the ad on page 14, which teach basic truths about life: they deal with health, love, virtue, wealth. These sayings are meant to be memorable—they are usually brief, occasionally witty, and often make use of repeated sounds or rhymes. Such bits of advice are called proverbs, maxims, or *aphorisms*, a term first coined by Hippocrates, a Greek physician who lived from about 460 to 377 B.C. The first sentence of Hippocrates' book, *Aphorisms*, is a famous example: "Life is short, art is long, opportunity fleeting, experimenting dangerous, reasoning difficult."

Benjamin Franklin, the famous American statesman, author, and scientist who lived from 1706 to 1790, wrote many aphorisms which remain popular today. Look at these examples from Franklin's "The Way to Wealth." What do they mean? Is there a common *theme* in them—a particular set of lessons Franklin wanted to teach about the way to wealth? What similar sayings do you have in your own culture?

The sleeping fox catches no poultry.

He that lives upon hope will die fasting.

Early to bed, and early to rise, makes a man healthy, wealthy, and wise.

For want of a nail the shoe was lost; for want of a shoe the horse was lost; and for want of a horse the rider was lost, being overtaken and slain by the enemy; all for want of care about a horse-shoe nail.

A small leak will sink a great ship.

There will be sleeping enough in the grave.

Here are a few distinctive proverbs our students have brought with them from their native countries:

ETHIOPIA: When spiders unite, they can halt a lion.

RUSSIA: When a wolf shows his teeth, he isn't laughing.

CHINA: When ploughing, look straight ahead.

EGYPT: Small stones move big stones.*

JOURNAL EXERCISE 1.6

Try to recall and translate an aphorism from your native language and write about it in your notebook for ten minutes. Does it remind you of a story you've heard, or of anything you've experienced in your own life? Just put down whatever comes into your head, even if your thoughts seem unrelated to the topic. The important thing is to keep writing. Don't worry about spelling or grammar, and if your mind suddenly goes blank, write "blank" or "nothing" or any other word until something new occurs to you.

The activity you have just engaged in is sometimes called *freewriting* or non-stop writing. It might be compared to the warm-up exercises athletes do before a competition. Its purpose is to loosen up the "muscles" of your

---

* This saying, we're told, refers to the method by which the pyramids were constructed: the great boulders were transported by pushing them on top of smaller, more easily moved stones.

brain, while encouraging you to relax and to see that writing is a process that includes many stages. Most of us become somewhat anxious about putting pen to paper, probably because writing, unlike speaking, seems so formal and demanding. We believe we have to "get it right" the first time. This notion prevents us from using writing to explore what we want to say and often paralyzes our thoughts. Try to consider freewriting as a form of speaking to yourself, a way of thinking aloud. The more freewriting you do, the easier it becomes.

Sometimes, as in Exercise 1.6, you'll start your freewriting with a specific topic: this is called *focused* freewriting. But at other times, you may begin with anything that pops into your mind—a fly buzzing by, a hunger pang, a feeling of fatigue or boredom, an object on the table before you, or the person sitting next to you in the school cafeteria. Anything at all can get you going.

KEEPING A JOURNAL

A Writer's Notebook

All of us have much to discover about ourselves and others, about the world around us and our relation to it. One way to explore the events of our lives is to reflect upon them in a journal. Writing about ideas, emotions, problems, fantasies, dreams, and incidents is often the first step toward understanding them and developing our self-awareness. Keeping a journal also provides an opportunity to experiment with style by trying a variety of prose "voices" and techniques.

Your journal—whether you call it a diary, a notebook, or "letters to myself"—can start out as a simple record of your activities, and eventually become a valuable collection of your thoughts, feelings, and experiences. You can write about anything: let your pen follow the wanderings of your mind and the new paths you may find within yourself. Your journal will undoubtedly reveal something unexpected.

JOURNAL EXERCISE 1.7

You might begin by writing down your thoughts about keeping a journal, as the following people have done—a Dutch teenager, an American writer, and a Russian aristocrat who lived during the nineteenth century:

I haven't written for a few days, because I wanted, first of all, to think about my diary. It's an odd idea for someone like me to keep a diary; not only because I have never done so before, but because it seems to me that neither I—nor for that matter anyone else—will be interested in the unbosomings of a thirteen-year-old girl. Still, what does that matter? I want to write, but more than that, I want to bring out all kinds of things that lie buried deep in my heart.

There is a saying that "paper is more patient than man"; it came back to me on one of my slightly melancholy days. . . . Yes, there is no doubt that paper is patient and as I don't intend to show this cardboard-covered notebook . . . to anyone, unless I find a real friend, boy or girl, probably nobody cares. And now I come to the root of the matter, the reason for my diary; it is that I have no such real friend. . . .

—*Anne Frank*

It is enough if I please myself with writing; I am sure then of an audience.

—*Henry David Thoreau*

What if, seized without warning by a fatal illness, I should happen to die suddenly! I should not know, perhaps, of my danger; my family would hide it from me; and after my death they would rummage among my papers; they would find my journal, and destroy it after having read it, and soon nothing would be left of me—nothing—nothing—nothing! This is the thought that has always terrified me.

—*Marie Bashkirtseff*

Although we often associate journals with professional writers, all kinds of people have found comfort and inspiration in them—scientists, politicians, musicians, painters, prisoners, slaves, businessmen and women, athletes. Perhaps this is because everyone experiences a sense of isolation at times, and journals can be outlets for our pain, our joy, our confusion. They become vehicles for communicating with ourselves: through writing and reading our entries, we both talk and listen to different aspects of this unique "I."

Here are a few students' responses to this activity:

I really enjoy scribbling my thoughts on paper. What's interesting is that when I was younger, I used to love to write in Chinese, anything, anything at all that came into this mind of mine. My mom once said that I alone, in a week, could consume more paper and ink than both of my brothers could in a month or two. The only difference now is that I'm writing in English instead of Chinese. But I like doing it!

I don't know what to write. My head has nothing in it. Nothing, nothing, no thing. No thing. I wonder when those two words got attached. When I was little my sister kept a diary. She locked it up and hid it so I couldn't read it. I wonder what it said. I wonder what I'll say. . . .

I can understand how people like Anne Frank regard their journal as a best friend. Sometimes I have emotions that I can't express to my friends because they are very personal. Ironically, I feel no shame when I write in a journal. The daily pressures of life can overpower you if you keep them bottled up inside. A journal is a kind of self-therapy because the author can be more honest. After she has confided her daily trials in her journal, she may have a clearer outlook on life. Now that I've reflected upon what I've just written, I'm glad about having my own journal. Today I learned something I didn't know before.

After writing I always feel relieved. It's as if I've talked to someone who really cares for me and stays silent so he won't miss any detail. My diary is one of my best friends. Sometimes I open it to an earlier entry and I have the feeling that I'm being transported to that time again. It helps me to understand myself and makes me see the way I am. It's like having a friend that I can always trust and count on.

An important part of this writing course, therefore, will be to keep a journal. Begin by writing for ten minutes four times every week. Subjects will be suggested in each unit, but you are free to choose different ones if you wish. You will also occasionally want to use this "writer's notebook" to experiment with ideas for essays. We encourage you to think of your journal as a *source book* for paper topics. As you will see in each chapter of this text, students' journals frequently provide them with the seed of an idea that eventually grows into a mature essay.

Topics for journals are limited only by your own imagination. Writers often find that re-creating an incident from the past not only allows them to experience it anew, but also to understand that experience in a different way. We continually revise our memories and impressions to accommodate more recent events in our lives and new stages of development; as a result, we are able to organize and interpret these impressions more fully.

Journals can be used for simple descriptions of the world around you:

I was watching a little baby for ten minutes. She was doing very strange things. She was speaking her own language and dancing her own dances. In her right hand she was holding a pen and in her left hand a piece of chocolate. She was trying to write on a piece of paper, but she couldn't do it. Because of that she got angry and started crying.

Journals can also be vehicles for storytelling—for narrating a real or imagined event. Think, for example, about one of your most exciting experiences. What was it like? What does it mean to you now? One student remembers his first kiss:

> One of the most exciting things that ever happened to me was about seven years ago when I was in Iraq. I used to go to a French school there. Most of the students were French, except my brother and me. It was the first time I kissed a girl. She was French, and her name was Magali. She was blond, and she had a nice slim body. I used to see her in the swimming pool wearing her green bathing suit. I can even remember her mother shouting at her when she did something wrong. Her mother was built like a man.
>
> It was a sunny day at the club. Before swimming, Magali and I were sitting on the grass, away from all the people. We were talking about our teacher, and how she was tough and that every day we had a long homework assignment. I started saying romantic things to Magali, in French of course (which I have forgotten). She liked it, but when I tried to kiss her she slapped me on the face. I was mad and she noticed it. We stayed about five minutes looking at each other without talking. All of a sudden I was surprised by her giving me a kiss on my cheek.
>
> I wasn't mad anymore. I was excited, so I suggested we go swimming because it was getting late. I was eleven years old; I didn't know the meaning of what we were doing, but it was fun. All I knew was that it was the end of the school year, and I had to go back to Egypt in a few days. Magali was crying, and she wouldn't even let me talk to her or kiss her goodbye. I guess she thought I was leaving because I didn't love her.

JOURNAL EXERCISE 1.8

Start your journal entry with "One of the most (exciting, sad, embarrassing) things that ever happened to me was . . ." and write without stopping for at least ten minutes.

Or, taking your inspiration from some of the student journals we've quoted in this chapter, write about "one of the (strangest, funniest, most frustrating) experiences I've had with the English language."

CLASSROOM ACTIVITY 1.9

Select a journal entry to read aloud in class. As you listen to your classmates' work, pick out a sentence, phrase, or idea that interests you. Write down any observations you've made about each selection, and ask questions of the author. What would you like to hear more about?

Idiom Review: The *One of* Phrase

In writing about one of your experiences, you may find that you are confused by *one of* phrases. *One of* is one of the most common constructions in English. Look at these statements*:

The Mercedes-Benz 300 SD Turbodiesel is one of the most expensive, least extravagant corporate automobiles you can buy.

"ONE OF THE MOST IMPORTANT BOOKS EVER WRITTEN ABOUT FRENCH CIVILIZATION."
—*Le Monde*

Since 1715. One of the world's more civilized pleasures.

"One of the 100 best new restaurants in America."
Esquire, August 1981

As you can see, *one of* singles out one member of a group. The name of the group completes the *one of* phrase. Usually, the name of the group is a plural noun: *automobiles, books, restaurants, pleasures.* However, there are cases when the name of the group is a singular noun. Look at these sentences:

The cowboy tied up one of the *herd.*

The police arrested one of the *gang.*

Herd and *gang* are singular nouns. They are singular because the members of the herd and the gang make up a *single* unit. Words like *herd* and *gang* are called *collective* or *group nouns.* When they are singular, they refer to *one* collection or group of people or things. When they are plural, they refer to *more than one* collection or group:

---

* Which of these examples is a complete sentence? Can you explain why the others are not? (Chapter 2 will take up the matter of sentence fragments in some detail.)

SINGULAR: One of the *herd* is missing. (*one* herd)

PLURAL: One of the *herds* is grazing in the field. (*more than one* herd)

Note that the plural personal pronouns (*you, us,* and *them*) can also be used to complete the *one of* phrase:

One of the thieves is lying, and one of *them* is telling the truth.

One of our staff is on vacation, and one of *us* is out sick.

The *one of* phrase often acts as the subject of a clause or a sentence. In the following examples, notice what form of the *verb* the *one of* construction takes when it is in the subject position:

One of the staff *is* definitely the thief.

One of the children *was* missing.

Only one of us *wants* to leave now.

When the *one of* phrase acts as the subject of a clause or sentence, it always takes the singular form of the verb. Can you explain why?

EXERCISE 1.10

Choose an appropriate noun or pronoun to complete the *one of* phrase in the sentences below.

1. One of the best _____ is in my home town.

2. When she left the room, one of the _____ began behaving badly.

3. This is one of the most disgusting _____ I've ever eaten.

4. Because there wasn't enough room for all of the children to ride in the wagon, one of _____ had to wait for a turn.

5. The mayor called the snowstorm one of the worst _____

   _____ in the history of the city.

6. My friend belongs to one of the most active political _____

_____ in my country.

EXERCISE 1.11

Correct any errors you find in the following sentences:

1. One of us were guilty.

2. One of the club members have to collect the dues each week.

3. One of the reason for his problem seem to be his carelessness.

4. Which one of these sentences are correct?

5. If you want to be noticed, you can't be just one of the herd.

6. One of the team will win the basketball championship this weekend.

Using Your Journal as a Learning Log

Your journal, as you have seen, can be a useful tool for recording and analyzing your learning experiences and difficulties in English composition. In this sense, your journal becomes a "learning log." Some of your entries might involve concepts or assignments you are having problems with, responses to what is happening in class, questions, comments, suggestions for future classes. You can write stories, poems, plays; discuss the differences between English and your own language; practice areas of grammar or composition; list new vocabulary words and attempt to use them. You may also want to talk about your experiences in other courses, as the following student has done:

During intersession I took a sociology course, and one of the requirements was to hand in a journal at the end. On a number of occasions I found that what I had put down on paper was not what I really wanted to say, or rather, it wasn't what I felt. Realizing this while I was re-reading my entries, I was able to examine what I wrote and how it correlated with my real opinions. I began to see my problems in expressing myself and was able, therefore, to correct them.

Unlike the essays you submit in class, your journal will probably sound more like everyday speech than formal writing. Think of it as a conversation with a friend: we all use sentence fragments, hesitations ("Well, uh, um, I mean . . ."), and casual expressions when we talk. We often change the subject without warning, make grammatical errors, fail to complete sentences or thoughts. Your journal is a playground for your ideas and for the language you are making your own.

JOURNAL EXERCISE 1.12

Throughout this course, try to spend ten minutes each day writing in your journal without stopping. You may simply freewrite, or you may draw upon some of the suggestions made in this chapter.

In addition, using the journal entries you have written in this chapter as a starting point, you might want to keep a "learning log" of your progress (or setbacks) in mastering English — a kind of "Notes of a Non-Native Speaker."

2 | Making Sentences

What Makes a Sentence?

If you look at the table of contents and flip through the pages to come, you'll see that each unit of this book focuses on a particular mode of writing, such as explaining how to do something or developing an argument. You'll also notice that the grammar lessons are closely connected to the reading and writing activities in every chapter. For example, Chapter 6 addresses narrative, or storytelling: you'll be asked to write about events that occurred in the past. At the same time, you'll study the uses of the various past tenses in English as well as methods for combining sentences in a narrative sequence.

For now, however, let's review what you need to begin. Much of what follows will undoubtedly be familiar to you. This chapter is simply meant to summarize the basic grammatical units on which later chapters will build. Since all of the essays you'll be writing will depend on putting sentences together in a variety of ways, this section takes the English sentence as its theme.

The English sentence requires only two elements: a subject and a predicate. The subject is the main character (or characters) of the sentence. The subject may be a single noun or pronoun, or it may include modifying words and phrases: "Robert," "He," and "The most intelligent student in the class" can all act as subjects. The predicate tells something about what that subject *is, does,* or *has done to it.* Like the subject, the predicate may consist of a single-word verb, or it may be expanded in a variety of ways. Most predicates have two main elements: the verb, which tells what is happening, and the predicate *complement* or *completer.* Completers can be nouns, adjectives, phrases, or clauses. (For further discussion of completers, see pages 51–53.)

Sentences come in a variety of shapes and patterns, but they all have a basic subject-verb unit. And because some verb forms must agree with their subjects, it's important to be able to locate the subject of a sentence. Simply knowing that a subject has to be a noun or pronoun often doesn't help, for a sentence may contain several nouns that aren't acting as subjects.

Locating Subjects and X-Words

Subjects do one of three things. They can tell who or what performed an action:

Who spilled the milk?
↕
George spilled the milk.

Subjects can also tell who or what is being described:

What smells so good?
↕
Breakfast smells so good.

Finally, subjects can tell who or what was the receiver of an action:

Who was asked to leave?
↕
I was asked to leave.

So one easy way to locate the subject of a sentence is to ask who or what is doing something, being described, or having something done to it.

There is another easy way to find subjects. First of all, you should know that every complete English sentence will turn into a question that can be answered with *yes* or *no*:

English is difficult.   Is English difficult?

Languages are challenging.   Are languages challenging?

I am studying too hard.   Am I studying too hard?

Notice that each of these *yes-no* questions begins with a form of the verb *be*. The verb *be* belongs to a group known as *auxiliaries* or *X-words*. Here are the most common X-words:

PRESENT	PAST
am, is, are	was, were
do, does	did
have, has	had
will	would
shall	should
can	could
may	might
must	

Watch what happens to the X-word when a statement is turned into a yes-no question:

We *can* leave now.

Can we leave now?

The children *are* ready to go.

Are the children ready to go?

The *subject* of a sentence will always be the word or words the X-word moves around when the sentence is turned into a yes-no question. In a statement, the X-word comes after the subject. In a question, the X-word comes before the subject. What is the subject of each of the above examples?

In negative statements with *not, not* is often joined to the X-word in a contraction (e.g.: *do + not = don't*):

We *don't* want to leave.

They *aren't* leaving yet.

When a negative statement with the contracted form of the X-word is turned into a yes-no question, the entire contraction is moved to the front of the sentence:

Don't we want to leave?

Aren't they leaving yet?

If *not* is used, however, only the X-word moves:

They *do* not know their own names.

Do they not know their own names?

If a sentence has more than one X-word, only the first X-word moves to the front of the sentence to form the yes-no question:

$$\overset{X}{I} \overset{X}{should} \overset{}{have} \text{ paid my bills sooner.}$$

I *should have* paid my bills sooner.

Should I have paid my bills sooner?

EXERCISE 2.1

Convert the following statements into questions and questions into statements. Then circle the X-words and underline the subject of each sentence.

1. You could hire a typist,
an editor, a proofreader,
an accountant, and several consultants,
and pay them to be on call
24 hours a day.

2. **Are you getting the most
from your computer?**

3. YOU WOULDN'T WANT TO DISTURB THE SPIRITS.

4. **A ring must be chosen with care.**

5. Would you
invest $8.97
for a full year
of Success?

6. **NOW MEN WITH
THINNING HAIR
CAN LEAD A
FULLER LIFE.**

7. **Somebody May Be Cheating**

8. **DOES IT PAY
TO START LIFE OVER?**

9. **IMMORTAL MUSIC SHOULDN'T
BE KEPT ON MORTAL TAPE.**

Locating Verbs

As you know, a sentence may have a single verb, or it may have a verb phrase consisting of one or more X-words plus the *main verb*. Verbs can either show an action or link the subject to a description of the subject:

The baby *has been crying* for an hour.

He *seems* hungry.

Being able to identify the verb or verb phrase in a sentence is crucial to understanding English grammar. It helps you to recognize incomplete sentences and to make sure that your subjects and verbs agree.

In statements with a single verb, the verb follows the subject. The verb can be in the present or past tense:

> Every morning, she *walks* the dog.
>
> Yesterday morning, she *walked* the dog.

One way to find the verb is to change the time expressed by the sentence. Because all but a few verbs have different forms for past and present times, you can identify the main verb as the word that changes to express the different tenses.

It's just as simple to locate the main verb in a verb phrase. Once you've identified the subject of a sentence, it's not difficult to locate the verb. You know, first of all, that X-words follow subjects in statements and precede them in questions. The main verb often comes immediately after the X-word (or X-words) in a verb phrase:

>   X   V
>
> Most of my friends are working this summer.
>
>   X V
>
> One of my friends is traveling through Europe.

Watch out for certain words that sometimes occur between the X-word and the verb. These are *not, n't,* and words of relative time such as *never, seldom, frequently, always, often, just,* and *already*:

>   X   V
>
> Children should not play with matches.
>
>   X   V
>
> Most people have never tasted moose meat.

Many sentences contain more than one X-word, but only the *first* X-word in a verb phrase moves to the front of a yes-no question:

>   X   X   V
>
> We should have finished by now.
>
> X   X   V
>
> Should we have finished by now?

When there is more than one X-word in a verb phrase, the main verb follows the final X-word.

EXERCISE 2.2

Use one of these two ways of locating verbs to identify the main verb in each of the following sentences:

1. I'll call you tomorrow.

2. My friend from Hawaii has never seen snow.

3. Because of the extreme cold, one of the water pipes had burst during the night.

4. She has already put the baby to bed.

5. Instead of watching television, he's reading a good book.

EXERCISE 2.3

Now go back to Exercise 2.1 and draw a box around the main verb in each sentence.

The "Hidden X-Word"

You've seen how to form yes-no questions in statements with X-words. But many statements in the simple present and the simple past tenses don't have an X-word. If a statement doesn't contain an X-word, place *do, does,* or *did* in the X position before the main verb, and then turn it into a yes-no question. Again, the subject will be the word that the hidden X-word moves around:

The tail wags the dog.

The tail *does* wag the dog.*

Does the tail wag the dog?

---

* In statements, the auxiliary *do* + the verb implies emphasis:
   Did he really study hard?
   He *did* study hard, and he deserved to pass the course.

The verb *do* acts as a "hidden X-word." The only word you may have to add to turn a complete sentence into a yes-no question is a form of this hidden X-word. In the present tense, the verb *do* has two forms—*do* and *does*. The third-person singular (*he, she, it,* and all singular nouns) form of *do* is *does*. The past tense form of *do* is simply *did*. Notice that when *does* or *did* is placed into a sentence, the main verb shifts to its base form:

He studies on weekends.   He studied hard.

He *does* study on weekends.   He *did* study hard.

Does he study on weekends?   *Did* he study hard?

EXERCISE 2.4

The following statements do not contain X-words. Turn them into yes-no questions by adding *do, does,* or *did*. Then underline the subject.

1. The baby wants more milk.

2. They came home yesterday.

3. Her boyfriend wrote to her recently.

4. The reporters from California arrived on time.

5. One of her younger brothers ran faster than anyone else.

6. The man who lives next door owns a home in Florida.

7. The police caught the thief.

Subject-Verb Agreement

THE SPECIAL X-WORDS: *BE, HAVE,* AND *DO*

You've seen that the X-word *do* has two forms in the present tense—*do* and *does.* When you used *does* with a third-person singular subject—a subject that can be replaced by *he, she,* or *it*—you made the verb *agree* in person and in number with the subject. Most X-words do not change form for singular and plural subjects. But the X-words *be, have,* and *do* sometimes change form to agree with their singular or plural subjects. Whenever *be, have,* or *do* is the first X-word in the verb unit, it agrees with the singular or plural subject:

> He *is* leaving now.
>
> We *are* leaving, too.

Be, of course, is the most irregular English verb, for it has different forms for the past tense as well as the present tense.

PRESENT TENSE

I *am*	We *are*
You *are*	You *are*
He, she, or it *is*	They *are*

PAST TENSE

I *was*	We *were*
You *were*	You *were*
He, she, or it *was*	They *were*

Both *have* and *do* only change form for the third person singular in the present tense: *has* and *does* are used with subjects that can be replaced by *he, she,* or *it.* In the past tense, *have* is simply *had,* and *do* is *did.*

Be, have, and *do* are also the only X-words that can act as main verbs. They can be part of a verb phrase:

> He *should be* home at 7:00.

Or they can stand alone:

> He *is* home now.

When a form of *be* or *have* is the only verb in a sentence, simply move it to the front of the sentence to form the yes-no question:

Most heroes are anonymous.

Are most heroes anonymous?

We have the people to answer your questions.

Have we the people to answer your questions?*

But if *do* is the main verb, add *do, does,* or *did* to form the question. Naturally, when you add *do, does,* or *did,* the main verb changes to its base form:

They did a lot of work for charity.
Did they do a lot of work for charity?

We do our part.

Do we do our part?

REGULAR VERBS

Like *have* and *do,* regular verbs in the present tense only change form (by adding *-s* or *-es*) for the third-person singular:

We *walk* the dog every day.

She *walks* the dog every day.

Here's the spelling rule for the third-person-singular *-s* ending: When a verb ends in *-s, -z, -ch, -sh, -x,* or *-o,* add *-es*: I pass, he *passes*; you buzz, it *buzzes*; they catch, she *catches*; they finish, he *finishes*; I fix, she *fixes*; you go, he *goes.*

If a verb (or a noun) ends in a consonant plus *-y,* always change the *y* to *i*

---

* Most American speakers would probably use the hidden X-word to form this yes-no question: "Do we have the people to answer your questions?"

before adding *-es*: *I cry,* but *the baby cries.* (Notice that *all* third-person singular forms of verbs, whether regular or irregular, end in *s.*)

Problems with subject-verb agreement often occur when the simple subject — the main word or words in the complete subject — is accompanied by modifiers that distract a writer from the true subject of the sentence. Don't be misled by structures that follow the simple subject:

> A *summary* of the debate between the two presidential candidates *is* in today's newspaper.

> Our final *assignments,* including an argument paper, *are* due next week.

> *Many* of the students in our college *come* from other countries.

INDEFINITE PRONOUNS

In Chapter 1, we looked at the *one of* phrase and pointed out that it always takes the third-person singular form of the verb. Before you do Exercise 2.5 in subject-verb agreement, make sure that you're familiar with this list of other words in English that generally take the third-person singular form:

anybody	everyone	each	someone	no one
anyone	everybody	either	somebody	nobody
anything	everything	neither	something	nothing

These words are called *indefinite pronouns*: they usually refer to a single, unspecified person or thing, which is why they take singular verbs:

> None of these answers *is* correct.

> Just about everyone *loves* a parade.

In addition, indefinite pronouns usually take singular possessive pronouns:

> *Each* of my sisters wants *her* own telephone.

> *Did* everyone in this room bring *his* or *her* book?

In this last example, both the masculine and feminine possessive pronouns are used. The reason for this usage is that the English neuter possessive pronoun (*its*) refers to things, not people, and so does not apply. Traditionally, in this case, writers have used the masculine possessive:

> Did everyone in this room bring *his* book?

This usage is certainly correct, and sometimes unavoidable. But writers nowadays are becoming increasingly careful about not using this form to refer to an unspecified person who may be male or female. When possible, use the *he* or *she*, *his* or *her* form. If you are writing a paragraph in which repeated use of this form becomes awkward, try changing the nouns from singular to plural:

> Did all the *students* in this room bring *their* books?

Another problem can arise when using an indefinite pronoun. Occasionally, when the indefinite pronoun clearly means "all" or "many," speakers use the plural pronoun:

> Is *everybody* here?
>
> Yes, *they* are all here.

This usage is acceptable in speech, but less so in written English. In such cases, rewrite the sentence using the plural:

> Are *all* the students here?
>
> Yes, *they* are all here.

OTHER SPECIAL SUBJECTS: COMPOUNDS, UNCOUNTABLES, AND MASS NOUNS

Compound subjects — two or more subjects joined by *and* — take plural verb forms:

> My aunt and uncle *live* in Hawaii.

Uncountable nouns (such as *love, truth,* and *beauty*) and *mass nouns* (such as *salt, sugar,* and *milk*) require singular verb forms. (For a more extensive list of uncountable and mass nouns, see pages 148–149 in Chapter 4.)

> Patience *is* a virtue.
>
> Pepper *adds* flavor to food.

Remember, too, that *collective* nouns like *team, company,* and *family* usually take singular verb forms in American English.

> Our chess club *meets* once a week.

EXERCISE 2.5

Complete the following sentences with present tense predicates. Choose a different verb for each:

1. Anybody who believes in ghosts _____

2. Everyone in my English class _____

3. Everything that I like to eat _____

4. The growth of many modern cities _____

5. Each of my friends _____

6. My family _____

7. Elena's dog and cat _____

8. Either you or I _____

9. Somebody in this room _____

10. No one that I know _____

11. Nothing in that store _____

12. Hamburgers and hot dogs _____

13. Success _____

14. Milk _____

15. The homework assigned in college _____

EXERCISE 2.6

The sentences below were taken from student descriptions of classroom behavior in their native countries. (You'll find their essays on this subject in Chapter 8.) Here, we've used selected sentences for an exercise in subject-verb agreement. Fill in the correct present tense form of the indicated verbs:

1. Soviet students [to spend] _____ only ten years in

school, but when they [to graduate] _____ they [to have]

_____ a much wider education than American students do.

2. In Iran, student behavior [to seem] _____ much more formal than it [to be] _____ in the U.S.

3. Every student [to have] _____ to be in class before the teacher [to arrive] _____. (Greece)

4. A Korean student always [to use] _____ both hands to give a paper to a teacher.

5. No one [to talk] _____ if the teacher is talking. (Iran)

6. If anybody [to talk] _____ or [to laugh] _____ during a lesson, the teacher [to make] _____ him leave the room immediately and he [to get] _____ an absence. (Greece)

7. A student never [to call] _____ a teacher "Tu," which is the familiar form of "you." (Portugal)

8. If someone [to fail] _____ one subject, he or she may have to repeat the whole year. You [to pass] _____ a year, not a subject. (Haiti)

9. Nobody ever [to disagree] _____ with anything a teacher [to say] _____. (Hong Kong)

10. At the end of a class, all of us [to remain] _____ seated until the teacher [to leave] _____ the room. (Israel)

11. It [to be] _____ rude to say that you [not to understand] _____ the lesson because that [to suggest] _____ the teacher is not doing a good job. (Japan)

A FINAL NOTE ON SUBJECT-VERB AGREEMENT: WHEN *THERE*, *HERE*, AND *IT* START A SENTENCE

Although sentences may often begin with *there* or *here*, these words are never subjects. They simply *point to* the subject, which usually *follows* the

There's a reason.

verb. The real subject of a sentence beginning with *there* or *here* is the noun that comes after the verb:

>   V   S
> There is a mouse in the bathtub.

>   V   S
> Here are the mousetraps.

When you are using this construction, check the noun that follows the verb to make sure your subjects and verbs agree.

Similarly, *it*, like *there* and *here*, is sometimes used as a "filler" to replace a subject that comes later in the sentence:

>   S
> It has been a dull *party*.

>   S
> The *party* has been dull.

>   S
> It feels wonderful *to be here*.

>   S
> *To be here* feels wonderful.

In addition, *it* is used as the subject of a sentence in *impersonal* constructions that show weather and time:

> It is very hot—it's 98°!
>
> It is raining.
>
> It is 12:00.
>
> It's too late to start now.

Note that *it*, unlike *here* and *there*, always takes a singular verb, even in impersonal constructions that contain a plural adverb complement:

> It was *ten years ago* that I met her.

This kind of construction is used to emphasize the complement.

EXERCISE 2.7

Complete the following statements and questions with appropriate subjects and verbs:

1. In my country, there are _____.

2. Is there _____ in the house?

3. It _____ getting late.

4. Here _____ the books that you were looking for.

5. It _____ been five years since I last saw him.

6. Here is _____ that I have always wanted.

7. Is _____ going to snow tomorrow?

8. _____ is true that it _____ time to go now.

9. _____ there any _____ in your neighborhood?

Modifying Subjects and Verbs

Modifiers add specific details to the basic subject-verb unit of a sentence. They tell us about the appearance, sound, feel, location, and manner of nouns and verbs. A modifier can be a single word, or, as you'll see in later chapters, a phrase or clause. For the present, we'll look at single-word modifiers.

ADJECTIVES

Adjectives modify nouns, and usually precede the nouns they describe. Many common adjectives are one-syllable words such as *good, bad, slow, fast, old, young.* Many others are formed by adding endings such as *-al, -able, -ful, -ive, -less, -ish,* and *-y* to nouns or verbs: *sensational, agreeable, wonderful, active, useless, foolish, smoky.*

Sometimes more than one adjective is used to describe a noun. Observe the sequence of adjectives in the following sentence (though we don't recommend that you pile on so many modifiers in your own writing):

ARTICLE, NUMERAL, DEMON- STRATIVE, POSSESSIVE, INDEFINITE ADJ.	GENERAL DESCRIPTION OR OPINION	SHAPE, SIZE	AGE	COLOR	ORIGIN	NOUN MODIFIER*	
I own *that*	*gorgeous*	*little*	*old*	*red*	*Italian*	*sports*	car.

Adjectives can also be used as sentence completers, following linking verbs such as *be, seem, appear, look*:

The fender on that gorgeous little old red Italian sports car is *dented*.

Note: The sequence of adjective types is more or less fixed, although adjectives of general description and physical state are sometimes reversed. No commas are required to separate these different *types* of adjectives, but commas are usually needed to separate two or more adjectives of general description: a *clever, obedient* dog. (See Appendix 5 for rules regarding comma usage.)

EXERCISE 2.8

Let's say you are driving a Bentley limousine. It's blue, and very broad. It's brand-new. And of course it's beautiful. Unfortunately, it's also borrowed. In one sentence, say all this while thanking the owner for lending you this automobile.

ADVERBS

Adverbs are modifiers that answer the questions "How," "Where," "When," and "In what manner." They are often formed by adding -*ly* to adjectives. But we cannot depend on -*ly* to identify adverbs: Intensifiers such as *very, quite, too,* and *rather* are examples of adverbs that don't end in -*ly*. By the same token, a number of *adjectives* also end in -*ly*. For example:

brotherly	friendly	lonely
elderly	heavenly	lovely
fatherly	lively	silly

---

* Nouns are sometimes used to modify other nouns: *bus* stop, *summer* day, *math* book.

Adverbs can modify:

VERBS: That gorgeous little old red Italian sports car *rarely* works.

OTHER ADVERBS: That gorgeous little old red Italian sports car rides *quite noisily.*

ADJECTIVES: That gorgeous little old red Italian sports car was *very* expensive.

Or WHOLE SENTENCES: *Really,* I'm sick of that gorgeous little old red Italian sports car.

Notice that adverbs can be placed at the beginning, in the middle, or at the end of a sentence:

FINALLY, you cleaned your room.

You **FINALLY** cleaned your room.

You cleaned your room, **FINALLY.** *

But an adverb *cannot* be placed between the main verb and its object:

You cleaned ~~finally~~ your room.

Do not use an adverb as the complement of a linking verb (such as *be, feel, look, taste, smell, appear, seem, become*):

She felt *glad* about the exam results. (not *gladly*)

The spaghetti smelled *good.* (not *well*)

Good is an adjective, and *well* is almost always an adverb:

Robert is a *good* student; he does *well* in school.

---

* Generally, commas are not used to set off adverbs. But when the adverb acts as a sentence modifier and comes at the beginning or the end of the sentence, a comma is used; similarly, when a *conjunctive adverb* such as *similarly, fortunately, obviously,* etc., comes after a semicolon, it is usually followed by a comma, as in the sentence you are now reading. (For a more extensive list of conjunctive adverbs, see page 62.)

Well is only used as an adjective—with a linking verb—to mean "in good health":

Robert is *well* (i.e., not sick).

Several additional words, such as *hard, straight, high, low, deep,* and *late,* can be used as adjectives or adverbs:

ADJECTIVE: They had a late dinner.

ADVERB: They worked late at the office. (*Lately* means "recently.")

As you have seen in this section, although certain endings sometimes help you to distinguish adjectives from adverbs, the only sure test is to determine how the word functions in its sentence. This next exercise should help you with these parts of speech.

CLASSROOM ACTIVITY 2.9

A.) Working with another classmate, make up pairs of sentences in which you use *hard, straight, high, low, deep,* and *late* as both adjectives and adverbs.

B.) Correct any errors in the following sentences:

1. Although his smile is friendly, he seems unhappily.

2. The food tastes as well as it looks.

3. He feels well about his job.

4. She sings lovely and makes heavenly music.

5. Children often behave silly.

What Else Goes into a Sentence? Function Words

Function words are those English words that have little or no meaning by themselves. These words act as "cement" for putting other words together and building sentences. We've already looked at some of these function words. The list includes:

1. articles (*a, an, the*) and demonstratives (*this, that, these, those*)

2. coordinating conjunctions (*and, or, but, for, nor, so, yet*)

3. subordinators (such as *after, before, while, that, which, although*)

4. prepositions (such as *on, into, under, at, behind*)

5. pronouns

6. indefinite adjectives and adverbs (words like *some, much, very, quite*)

7. X-words

Function words exist chiefly to perform a function: they have no real content. So although function words make up only a few hundred of the more than half a million words in English, they can cause a lot of confusion for non-native speakers.

We'll be providing rules and exercises in Function-Word Reviews throughout this book. The following exercise is to get you started: see how many of these words you already know how to use.

EXERCISE 2.10

In Chapter 1, we referred to the research of several sociologists and anthropologists. In the selection below, author Donald Barthelme gives us a bit of satirical sociology in his comic study of an imaginary tribe, the "Wapituil." We've removed a number of function words in this selection. After you have read the entire piece, go back and fill in each blank with only *one* word.

Monomania

The Wapituil are like us to _____ extraordinary degree. They

have _____ kinship system _____ is very similar

_____ our kinship system. _____ address each other

as "Mister," "Mistress," _____ "Miss." _____ wear

clothes which look much like our clothes. They have a Fifth Avenue

_____ divides their territory _____ east and west. They

have _____ Chock Full o' Nuts and _____ Chevrolet,

one of each. They have _____ Museum _____ Modern Art and _____ telephone _____ a Martini, one _____ each. The telephone and _____ Martini are kept _____ the Museum of Modern Art. In fact they have _____ that we have, _____ only one of each thing.

We found _____ they lose interest very quickly. For instance they _____ fully industrialized, _____ they don't seem interested _____ taking advantage _____ it. After the steel mill produced the ingot [=a metal bar], it _____ shut down. They can conceptualize but they _____ follow through. For instance, their week has seven days—Monday, _____, _____, _____, _____, _____, and Mon-

° **mononucleosis:** A disease that produces abnormally large numbers of white blood cells with single nuclei in the bloodstream.

day.* They have one disease, mononucleosis°. The sex life of a Wapi-tuil consists of _____ single experience, _____ he _____** about for a long time.

—*from* City Life *by Donald Barthelme*

Vocabulary Building: Numerical Prefixes

Can you think of any reason why mononucleosis is an appropriate illness for the Wapituil? Why do you think we've called this excerpt "Monomania"? What does *mono* mean? *Mono* belongs to one group of affixes that are

---

* The missing words in this sentence are not function words.

** This is not a function word. What part of speech is it? How many words can you think of to fill this slot?

called *prefixes*. Prefixes are word elements that are put before a word to change its meaning. The word *prefix* contains a prefix: *pre* means "before" or "in front of." Let's pause here a moment for a brief exercise in vocabulary building, since similar exercises will appear in later chapters.

Among the many useful prefixes English has borrowed from Greek and Latin are those that indicate number. Here are some other words that also use the prefix *mono-*:

monarchy   monochord   monocle   monochrome   monogamy
monolingual   monophone   monopoly   monotheism   monotony

Try to figure out what each of these words means. As you check your dictionary to see how well you've done, mark the stressed syllables in each word to see how the number of syllables affects the pronunciation of that word.

Another prefix that also means "one" is *uni*. What words can you list that use it?

EXERCISE 2.11

Now test your prefix proficiency by answering the following questions:

1. What is the difference between a monologue and a dialogue?

2. How many wives does a bigamist have? A polygamist?

3. Draw a picture of a unicycle, a bicycle, and a tricycle.

4. If your closest friend had quadruplets, how many baby gifts would you have to buy? What about quintuplets?

5. How many years are in a decade?

6. How many legs are there on an octopus? Sides on a hexagon?

Verb Tense Review: The Present and Present Progressive

Being able to control verb tenses is critical to clear writing, so we'll be working with the various English verb tenses throughout this book. Because the first essays you'll be assigned will rely on the present tense, we begin our verb tense reviews with a summary of the ways the simple present and present progressive tenses are used.

The simple present tense has four general uses:

1. To express a habitual or customary action:

   He works at McDonald's five nights a week.

   My alarm clock rings at 7 o'clock every morning.

2. To refer to a future event with the help of a future time word or phrase:

   The meeting is tomorrow afternoon.

   I graduate next month.

3. To indicate situations that are timeless or believed to be always true:

   Water freezes at 32 degrees Fahrenheit.

   The earth revolves around the sun.

   For this reason proverbs — those universal "teaching sentences" we referred to in Chapter 1 — are usually in the present tense: "Experience is the best teacher."

4. To capture a sense of immediacy, particularly in the following situations:
   a) Newspaper headlines are written in the present tense, as though we were actually present at the events described. For example, look at the three headlines on page 54.
   b) We use the present tense to summarize the story of a book, movie, play, or short story. When we *re-tell* the events of a novel, even if the novel itself is in the past tense, we acknowledge that the situations described are frozen in time. Notice that in our introduction of Leo Rosten's story on page 58, we use present-tense verbs (*explains, tells*).

EXERCISE 2.12

Summarize the story of a book you've read recently, or a movie or TV show you've seen.

As you know, the present tense also has a *progressive* or *continuous* form. Most verbs use the *present progressive* form (BE + -ING) to indicate that something is in progress at the present moment:

> My neighbors are shouting.
>
> Their dog is barking.

The present progressive is also used to describe an action taking place over a period of time, though the action may not be taking place at the moment of speaking or writing:

> I'm writing a novel. (But right now I'm talking to you.)
>
> I'm also taking four courses this semester (though I'm on vacation now).

In addition, the progressive can be used to express future action:

> He's getting married next week.
>
> Are you graduating in June?

Certain verbs, however, are not generally used in the progressive verb form:

agree	consent	know
be	contain	like
believe	dislike	prefer
belong	equal	seem
		understand

CAUTION

ESL students are inclined to *overuse* the progressive tenses because they eliminate the need to worry about the different forms of irregular verbs. Native speakers, however, usually use the present progressive tense only to suggest that something is happening or is going to happen, or that something is true for a particular and limited time only.

EXERCISE 2.13

As we've mentioned, Chapter 6 deals with narration of events that took place in the past. But we often narrate events that are taking place in the present—particularly in our letters. Read the following letter, and fill in the blanks with the correct form of the simple present or the present progressive tense:

Dear Avi,

I [to hope] _____ that you [to be] _____

_____ well and happy. I [to miss] _____ talking

to you, which is why I [to write] _____ to you so

soon. Although I've only been in college for two weeks, I [to be] _____

_____ already very busy. I [to take] _____

18 credits, and my professors all [to give] _____ a

lot of homework. In addition to my school assignments, I [to work] _____

_____ as a cashier in a restaurant ten hours a week. Be-

cause I [to speak] _____ _____ English both at school and

at my job, my English [to improve] _____ rapidly.

My roommate and I [to share] _____ the cooking

and the cleaning, but neither of us [to care] _____

much about keeping house. Our meals always [to taste] _____

_____ terrible and the apartment usually [to seem] _____

_____ as though a hurricane hit it. But we both [to agree] _____

_____ that we [to like] _____ living here.

My roommate and I [to study] _____ computer

science, so we [to help] _____ each other with our

homework. Unfortunately for me, he [to marry] _____

_____ his high school girlfriend in a few months, so I [to look] _____

_____ for someone else to share the apartment with me. I

[to pray] _____ that my next roommate [to know]

_____ how to cook and clean.

Write soon and tell me what you [to do] _____.

Sincerely,

Marcos

JOURNAL EXERCISE 2.14

Now write your own letter, and use the various forms of the present and present progressive tenses to tell a friend or a relative what your life in college is like this semester.

EXERCISE 2.15

Chapter 1 included a journal exercise on writing *about* proverbs. At this point, you have all of the materials for *making up* proverbs of your own. Try to come up with some fresh sayings by completing these proverb structures with your own nouns and verbs:

1. _____ the best teacher.

2. Don't   count   your   _____ before   they

_____.

3. Money can't _____.

4. _____ often deceptive.

5. An empty _____ cannot _____.

A Note on the Future Tense

Although both the simple present and the present progressive can be used to express a future action, the future tense is, of course, the most common form for this purpose. It is also the easiest tense to form in English: WILL + BASE FORM OF VERB. Because *will* has only one form, the future tense of a verb never changes: I *will be* home tomorrow; You *will have* a wonderful time in Kyoto; She *will go* to Europe next summer; We *will do* well if we try; They *will see* their families next week.

Will belongs to a group of verbs called *modals*. Modals are one class of *auxiliary verbs* (X-words) that help the main verb in a verb phrase to express a variety of meanings. All modals have a single form; unlike main verbs, they never take an ending. We'll consider the different modals and their special functions in Chapter 7.

JOURNAL EXERCISE 2.16

Another common way to express future time is BE + GOING TO + BASE FORM OF THE VERB.

"For God's sake, Marvin, are you going to live your entire life on the edge of your chair?"°

Drawing by Stan Hunt; © 1983 The New Yorker Magazine, Inc.

° **To be on the edge of [one's] chair or seat:** To be in anticipation of an event; to be *ready* to do something or *just about* to act.

In your journal (or in a letter to a friend), discuss your plans for tomorrow. Use each of the four ways of expressing future time at least once.

Sentence Patterns

Now that we've talked about the elements that go into a sentence, let's consider the ways in which these elements can be put together. Later on in this book, we'll be working with different methods of combining simple sentences to form *compound* and *complex* sentences. So we'll start with a summary of the patterns that simple sentences commonly follow:

Subject + Verb

S   V
Robert ran.

MODIFIERS   S   V   MODIFIERS
My good friend Robert ran happily down the street.

Subject + Verb + Object

An object answers the question "What?" after the verb:

S   V   O
Robert hit the ball.

Subject + Linking Verb + Noun or Adjective

Linking verbs do not express an action, but a state or condition. They must be followed by a noun or an adjective:

S   LV   N
Robert is the class president.

S   LV   ADJ
Robert seems diligent.

In the first example, *Robert* and *president* refer to the same person, and the linking verb acts like an equal sign. In the second example, the predicate adjective *diligent* describes Robert. As mentioned earlier, the most common linking verbs are *be, seem, appear, become, feel, look, taste,* and *smell.*

But note: The various forms of the verb *to be* mean *be located* or *be situated* when they are followed by an adverbial of place:

Robert is at the library.

When a form of *be* is followed by an adverbial of time, it means *happen, take place, begin*:

The celebration was last week.

Subject + Verb + Two Complements
a) SUBJECT + VERB + DIRECT OBJECT + INDIRECT OBJECT

<pre>
 S   V   DO   IO
Robert gave the present to his mother.
</pre>

The *direct object* tells *what* was given. The *indirect object* tells *to whom* something was given.

Indirect objects may also precede direct objects:

<pre>
 S   V   IO   DO
Robert gave his mother the present.
</pre>

When the indirect object comes before the direct object, the preposition is dropped. Thus, *to* is omitted in the above example.

b) SUBJECT + VERB + OBJECT + OBJECTIVE COMPLEMENT

An *objective complement* is an object that follows the direct object and has the same identity as the direct object:

<pre>
  S   V   DO   OC
The students elected Robert president.
</pre>

Occasionally, adjectives act as objective complements:

<pre>
  S   V   DO   OC
The students consider Robert brilliant.
</pre>

In addition, subjects, verbs, complements, and modifiers in each of these sentence patterns can be multiplied by using *and, or (nor)*, and sometimes *but*:

SUBJECTS: The President or the Vice President will attend the ceremony.

VERBS: The audience cheered and clapped wildly.

MODIFIERS: They were poor but happy.

EXERCISE 2.17

Obviously, people don't write sentences by following a list of patterns, but it is useful to know how to manipulate these structures. To practice these simple sentence constructions in English, try composing a sentence or two for each of the following patterns:

1. Subject + Verb

2. Subject + Verb + Object

3. Subject + Linking Verb + Noun

4. Subject + Linking Verb + Adjective

5. Subject + Verb + Direct Object + Indirect Object

6. Subject + Verb + Indirect Object + Direct Object

7. Subject + Verb + Object + Objective Complement

Active and Passive Constructions

As you work your way through the chapters ahead, you'll discover that verbs are not only fundamental to English grammar but to energetic writing as well. Because verbs and the words derived from them provide the *action* in any piece of writing, they are among the writer's most powerful tools. As you improve your command of verb tenses and forms, you'll also want to use the two basic sentence "voices" of English — the *active* and *passive* constructions — to their best advantage.

Writers generally prefer the active construction because it expresses an action more directly. It calls attention to the *agent* of the action: in most cases, the subject performs the action, and the object receives that action. In this sense, subjects are "doers" and objects are "receivers." For instance, we took these typical sports headlines from one Saturday's newspaper. They show three different ways of announcing the victory of one baseball team over another:

Yankees Pound Angels

Mets Top Giants

Orioles Turn Back Royals

This is what happens when we change a sentence from active to passive in the present and past tenses:

ACTIVE: The Yankees pound the Angels.
$\qquad$ S $\qquad$ V $\qquad$ O

PASSIVE: The Angels are pounded by the Yankees.
$\qquad$ S $\qquad$ V $\qquad$ AGENT

ACTIVE: The Orioles turned back the Royals.
$\qquad$ S $\qquad$ V $\qquad$ O

PASSIVE: The Royals were turned back by the Orioles.
$\qquad$ S $\qquad$ V $\qquad$ AGENT

As you can see, the original subject—the performer of the action—now follows the verb and becomes the object of the preposition *by*. The original object—the receiver of the action—moves to the subject position.

In the passive construction, the verb is some form of the verb *to be* + the *past participle*. In the present passive, you use *am, is,* or *are* + the past participle; in the past passive, you use *was* or *were* + the past participle. Remember that the past participles of regular verbs end in *-d* or *-ed*: live, *lived*; walk, *walked*. The past participles of irregular verbs are listed in Appendix 1.

Although the active voice is more dynamic, there are several instances when the passive construction is a more suitable choice. The passive voice is useful when the agent—the performer of the action—is unknown or unimportant, or when the speaker wants to emphasize the receiver of the action:

The Eiffel Tower was erected for the Paris Exposition of 1889.

The scientists were universally praised for their discovery.

The witness was asked to describe the theft.

Thus, you can use the passive voice when you want to eliminate a vague pronoun subject:

VAGUE: In college they expect you to write developed essays.

BETTER: In college you are expected to write developed essays.

The passive voice also comes in handy when you want to avoid blaming someone, or when you don't want to take responsibility for something:

> Remember those delicious plums you were saving for breakfast? They were eaten.

JOURNAL EXERCISE 2.18

Here is a famous poem by the American poet William Carlos Williams. It is written in the form of a brief note, with no punctuation, such as you might hastily scribble and tack on the refrigerator. Part of the charm of the poem is that the speaker apologizes for something he is obviously glad he did. What would be the effect of the poem if it were written in the passive voice?

This Is Just to Say

I have eaten
the plums
that were in
the icebox

and which
you were probably
saving
for breakfast

Forgive me
they were delicious
so sweet
and so cold

Compare the advantages and disadvantages of the active and passive voices by composing two notes in your journal. In the first note, apologize for something you're secretly happy you did. In the second note, inform someone of what you've done, but don't admit responsibility for the act (use the passive voice). Example: "Dear Mother — I hope you had a wonderful trip. By now you have probably noticed the mess in the kitchen. Dirty dishes *were left* in the sink. . . ."

EXERCISE 2.19

Here's a news story from London. Pick out the passive constructions and explain why you think they were used.

> ### *Pudding Catches Fire*
> ### *At Tower of London*
>
> LONDON, Dec. 25 (AP) – A Christmas pudding burst into flames at the Tower of London today, sending firetrucks racing to the medieval fortress on the Thames.
>
> More than 20 firemen were called out when the pudding caught fire inside a microwave oven, a spokesman for Whitechapel Fire Station said.
>
> No one was hurt, and no serious damage was done. But the pudding, destined for a Christmas dinner for the tower's guards, the Beefeaters, was reduced to a "black, shriveled lump," the spokesman said.

EXERCISE 2.20

We've made up a news story of our own. You'll notice that our paragraph sounds dead because all of the sentences are passive constructions. Give it some life by rewriting it with active constructions wherever they seem appropriate (though you may want to leave a few sentences in the passive voice).

Dog Is Bitten by Man

A two-year-old French poodle was bitten in the leg yesterday by a man dressed up as a Siamese cat. The man was picked up by the police after the incident was reported by a neighbor. The man was identified by the police as Felix Smythe, 36, of Rock Ridge. The police were informed by

several of Smythe's neighbors that local dog owners were often threat-
ened by Smythe. They were warned, police were told, to keep their dogs
indoors. Apparently, Smythe's Siamese cat was frequently chased by the
French poodle, and revenge was sought by Smythe on behalf of his pet.
Mr. Smythe was charged with disturbing the peace, and he is being sued
by the owner of the injured dog.

EXERCISE 2.21

Here are five more sentences from students who wrote about classroom
behavior in their own countries. These examples have been written in the
passive voice, although, as you'll notice, *no agent* has been mentioned. Your
job is, first, to fill in the passive form of the indicated verb. Afterwards, try
to rewrite the sentences in the active voice. (*You* have to supply the agent.)
In which sentences is the passive form a better choice? Why?

1. Whenever a teacher [to enter] _____ a classroom,

   the students [to be + expect] _____ to stand up.
   (India)

2. In Cyprus, all students [to be + tell] _____ to

   wear uniforms and girls [not to be + allow] _____
   to wear make-up or jewelry.

3. When we [to be + speak to] _____ we look
   down. It is very rude to look directly at the teacher. (Spain)

4. Every morning, classes at preliminary and high schools [to be +

   begin] _____ with religious worship. (Ceylon)

5. If you want to ask a question, you raise your hand and quietly wait for

   your name [to be + call] _____. (The Philippines)

How to End a Sentence

Since we've been discussing what goes into a sentence, we should take time to review the three marks of punctuation with which we can end a sentence. Each indicates a different tone of voice or type of emphasis:

(.)   The period is used after a statement.

(?)   The question mark is used for asking questions.

(!)   The exclamation point indicates that the sentence would be spoken with force or strong emotion.

A story told by Leo Rosten, a well-known humorist and linguist, illustrates how these marks are used. In his book, *The Joys of Yiddish*, Rosten explains that the best way to make a point is often through a humorous story. Yet translating the joke from speech to writing is a tricky matter, as Rosten tells us:

> But *writing* jokes proved far, far more difficult than I ever anticipated. (Think how much you are aided, in telling a joke, by tonal variations and strategic gestures; by artful pauses and inflections; by the deliberate camouflage of chuckles, dismay, smiles, murmurs.) And certain stories, gorgeous in the telling, just cannot be put into print without suffering. . . . As good an example as I know is this classic:
>
> During a giant celebration in Red Square, after Trotsky had been sent into exile, Stalin, on Lenin's great tomb, suddenly and excitedly raised his hand to still the acclamations: "Comrades, comrades! A most historic event! A cablegram—of congratulations—from Trotsky!"
> The hordes cheered and chortled and cheered again, and Stalin read the historic cable aloud:
>
> JOSEPH STALIN
> KREMLIN
> MOSCOW
> YOU WERE RIGHT AND I WAS WRONG. YOU ARE THE
> TRUE HEIR OF LENIN. I SHOULD APOLOGIZE.
> TROTSKY
>
> You can imagine what a roar, what an explosion of astonishment and triumph erupted in Red Square now!
> But in the front row, below the podium, a little tailor called, "Pst! Pst! Comrade Stalin."
> Stalin leaned down.
> The tailor said, "Such a message, Comrade Stalin. For the ages! But you read it without the right *feeling*!"
> Whereupon Stalin raised his hand and stilled the throng once more.
> "Comrades! Here is a simple worker, a loyal Communist, who says I haven't

read the message from Trotsky with enough feeling! Come, Comrade Worker! Up here! *You* read the historic communication!"

So the little tailor went up to the reviewing stand and took the cablegram from Stalin and read:

JOSEPH STALIN
KREMLIN
MOSCOW

Then he cleared his throat and sang out:

YOU WERE RIGHT AND I WAS *WRONG*? *YOU* ARE THE
TRUE HEIR OF LENIN? *I* SHOULD APOLOGIZE??!!..
TROTSKY!

This story, of course, makes its point through exaggeration. As you can see, *underlining* (which is printed as *italics* in books) is used to *emphasize* a point. But we caution you not to overuse this helpful device. Similarly, multiple end marks (??!!..) are used here, incorrectly, for comic emphasis. Please use only *one* mark of end punctuation per sentence!

We'll deal with colons (:), commas (,), and quotation marks (" ") in later chapters. For a review of all punctuation, you may refer to Appendix 5.

EXERCISE 2.22

We have mentioned that the present tense is used for summarizing events in a short story. Above, Rosten tells an anecdote that takes actual historical figures and places them in a fictional story. Using the present tense, can you state the point of the story, and summarize the events in a few sentences?

What's *Not* a Sentence?

Once you have become familiar with sentence elements and patterns, you can correct three of the most common grammatical errors in student writing: *fragments, comma splices,* and *run-ons.*

SENTENCE FRAGMENTS

You now know that every complete sentence can be turned into a yes-no question. Using the yes-no question test is the most efficient way to determine if a group of words can stand alone as a sentence. Any word group that won't turn into a yes-no question is an incomplete statement—a *sentence fragment.* Can the following examples be turned into yes-no questions?

Tiny Spider Discovered In Panama

IN AN AGE WHEN CARS CAN TALK

Because stone-age man didn't know
there was such a thing as salt.

Although sentence fragments are commonly used in advertisements, news headlines, and everyday speech, they are to be avoided in formal writing. It's also true that professional writers sometimes use fragments for particular effects, but wise student writers will make every effort to correct any fragments in their papers. Become familiar with the following types of common sentence fragments, and remember to use the yes-no question test whenever you're in doubt about a sentence:

Phrases

A phrase is a group of closely connected words that does not have a subject-verb unit.

A *noun phrase* includes a noun and its modifiers:

Book Publishing Around the World

A *verbal phrase* consists of a *gerund* (the *-ing* form of a verb when it is used as a noun), a *participle* (the *-ing* or *-ed* form when it is used as an adjective), or an *infinitive* (*to* + verb) and its objects and modifiers:

KEEPING COOL AT THE NORTH POLE

NO STRINGS ATTACHED

A *prepositional phrase* contains a preposition (a word like *at, on, by,* or *for*) and its object:

FROM THE DIRECTOR'S CHAIR

Subordinate Clauses

A clause is a group of words that has a subject-verb unit. Subordinate clauses have subjects and predicates of their own, but they begin with a subordinator—a word such as *after, although, because, before, since, who, which, that.* These words make a clause *dependent,* so it cannot stand alone. Subordinate clauses must be attached to an *independent clause*—a group of words that can stand alone as a complete sentence.

If at first you don't succeed .

Some sentence fragments have no subject, or an incomplete predicate. Remember that the *-ing* verb form can never stand alone as a complete verb. It must be combined with an X-word, which carries both tense and agreement.

Announcing the end of the isolated employee.

U.S. Donating Food To Hurricane Victims

EXERCISE 2.23

Make each of the ten sample fragments above and on pages 60–61 into a complete sentence. Then use the yes-no question test to check your answers.

COMMA SPLICES

What's wrong with this headline?

THE ROOM SAYS LUXURY, THE PRICE SAYS ECONOMY.

Here we have a good example of a common error called the *comma splice.* Comma splices occur when two or more simple sentences (independent clauses) are joined—spliced—with *only a comma.* A comma splice can be corrected by using a comma *plus* one of the *coordinating conjunctions:*

The room says luxury, and the price says economy.

The room says luxury, but the price says economy.

This error can also be corrected by separating the two independent clauses with a period, or by connecting them with a *semicolon*. The semicolon (;) joins two independent clauses, and is especially useful when the independent clauses are closely related in meaning:

The room says luxury. The price says economy.

The room says luxury; the price says economy.

Another comma splice occurs when two independent clauses are joined by a comma + one of the *conjunctive adverbs*—words such as *moreover, also, consequently, furthermore, then,* and *therefore,* or a transitional expression such as *for example, as a result, in addition, on the contrary,* or *that is.* This error can be corrected by placing a semicolon or a period before the conjunctive adverb or transitional expression:

INCORRECT: The room says luxury, however, the price says economy.

CORRECT: The room says luxury; however, the price says economy.

           The room says luxury. However, the price says economy.

EXERCISE 2.24

Use what you've learned about comma splices to correct the following errors:

1. I went to bed very late last night, consequently I overslept this morning.

2. I dressed quickly and rushed to school, however, I missed my first class.

3. I went to the chemistry lab to work on an experiment, then I had lunch with some friends.

4. My last class was over at 3 o'clock, therefore, I had time to go to the library.

5. I found the books I needed for my sociology report, in fact, I finished my research.

6. The day started badly, it ended well.

7. I got most of my work done, I arrived home early enough to enjoy the evening.

RUN-ON SENTENCES

Another sentence error occurs when two independent clauses have no connecting word or punctuation between them:

The stars were shining the moon was bright.

A sentence like this is called a *run-on* because its independent clauses simply run into each other. Run-ons can be corrected in the same ways as comma splices. You can check for both comma splices and run-ons by using the yes-no question test: any sentence that will turn into two (or more) yes-no questions needs (1) a comma + a coordinating conjunction, or (2) a semicolon, or (3) a period between its independent clauses. If we take the sample run-on above, we see that it turns into two yes-no questions: Were the stars shining? Was the moon bright? There are three possible solutions:

The stars were shining, and the moon was bright.
The stars were shining. The moon was bright.
The stars were shining; the moon was bright.

EXERCISE 2.25

We've taken the following paragraph from a student's description of class-room regulations in Greece, but we've changed the punctuation. See if you can repair the damage we've done to this paragraph by correcting the fragments, comma splices, and run-on sentences we've created:

The Board of Education in Greece still maintains certain rules for

students' behavior, these rules are very strict. Although we live in

times when feminism has had a great impact on society. There is still a distinction between the sexes in my country. Girls have to obey the dress code, boys have no such obligation. Other rules are also strict, students must enter the classroom. Before the teacher does. Failure to do so is considered an absence. If a student is caught smoking. He or she may be thrown out of school temporarily. On days of religious and national feasts. Pupils must be present at the ceremonies.

EXERCISE 2.26

If your sentence skills are proficient, you can probably write grammatically correct sentences without much thought or difficulty. What we're about to ask you to do, then, may seem as unnatural to you as trying to sing off-key: write a paragraph in which you deliberately include sentence fragments, comma splices, and run-ons. Then exchange papers with a classmate and edit each other's work.

EXERCISE 2.27

Below are sentences that were written by students in response to the above exercise. Identify the type of error in each example and then correct it:

1. Many teenagers would be lost without the telephone they wouldn't know what to do with their spare time.

2. Although we often disagreed and argued. I still wanted to be friends with her.

3. My room isn't large or luxurious, it's still the only place where I can find peace and privacy.

4. After many hours of traveling, I finally arrived in London. To find that nobody was waiting for me.

5. I wanted the job, in fact, I needed it badly.

6. Because I studied very hard, every single night, even on weekends and during vacations when other people were having fun.

7. The tall blond man who was wearing a tan raincoat, carrying a large black umbrella, and hurrying toward me.

8. I screamed, my mother jumped, the baby started to cry.

9. We looked all over, however, we couldn't find the missing wallet anywhere.

10. Going off to work in a place where everyone was much older and more experienced than I was.

We'll continue our discussion of sentence fragments, comma splices, and run-ons in Chapter 5.

unit 2 | Process Analysis

3 | How to Write a How-to Essay

The Process Essay

What do the starred book titles on these best-seller lists have in common?

Best Sellers

This Week | NONFICTION

* **1** **LIFE EXTENSION,** by Durk Pearson and Sandy Shaw. (Warner, $22.50.) Ways to add years to your life and life to your years: a popularly written medical-science book.

* **2** **JANE FONDA'S WORKOUT BOOK,** by Jane Fonda. (Simon & Schuster, $18.95.) An exercise book for women, seasoned with the film star's philosophy of physical well-being.

3 **WHEN BAD THINGS HAPPEN TO GOOD PEOPLE,** by Harold S. Kushner. (Schocken, $10.95.) Comforting thoughts from a rabbi.

4 **LIVING, LOVING & LEARNING,** by Leo Buscaglia. (Holt/Slack, $13.50.) Inspirational talks by a University of Southern California professor.

* **5** **RICHARD SIMMONS' NEVER-SAY-DIET COOKBOOK.** (Warner, $15.95.) More than 100 recipes by the Hollywood television personality and exercise guru.

* **6** **NO BAD DOGS: The Woodhouse Way,** by Barbara Woodhouse. (Summit, $12.50.) Advice on training dogs by a British expert: tie-in to a television series.

7 **A LIGHT IN THE ATTIC,** by Shel Silverstein. (Harper & Row, $12.45.) Humor in cartoons and verse.

8 **AMERICA IN SEARCH OF ITSELF: The Making of the President, 1956–80,** by Theodore H. White. (Harper & Row/Cornelia & Michael Bessie, $15.95.) A summing-up by the historian of the modern Presidency.

9 **EDIE,** by Jean Stein, edited with George Plimpton. (Knopf, $16.95.) Edie Sedgwick, minor celebrity of the 60's, remembered by friends and acquaintances.

Paperback Best Sellers

TRADE

Trade paperbacks are soft-cover books usually sold in bookstores and at an average price higher than mass-market paperbacks. This listing is based on computer-processed reports from 1,600 bookstores in every region of the United States.

1 **REAL MEN DON'T EAT QUICHE,** by Bruce Feirstein. (Pocket, $3.95.) Macho humor, with drawings.

* **2** **THIN THIGHS IN 30 DAYS,** by Wendy Stehling. (Bantam, $2.95.) How-to.

3 **THE ELFSTONES OF SHANNARA,** by Terry Brooks. (Ballantine/Del Rey, $7.95.) A fantasy sequel to "The Sword of Shannara": fiction.

* **4** **COLOR ME BEAUTIFUL,** by Carole Jackson. (Ballantine, $8.95.) Beauty tips for women.

5 **GARFIELD WEIGHS IN,** by Jim Davis. (Ballantine, $4.95.) The latest adventures of the gluttonous feline: cartoons.

6 **CHOCOLATE: The Consuming Passion,** by Sandra Boynton. (Workman, $4.95.) A celebration of chocoholics in words and drawings.

7 **GARFIELD BIGGER THAN LIFE,** by Jim Davis. (Ballantine, $4.95.) Cartoon humor.

* **8** **WHAT COLOR IS YOUR PARACHUTE?** by Richard Nelson Bolles. (Ten Speed Press, $7.95.) Guide for job hunters and career changers.

* **9** **NEVER-SAY-DIET BOOK,** by Richard Simmons. (Warner, $7.95.) A regimen by the Hollywood television personality.

10 **GARFIELD GAINS WEIGHT,** by Jim Davis. (Ballantine, $4.95.) Cartoon humor.

11 **GARFIELD AT LARGE,** by Jim Davis. (Ballantine, $4.95.) Cartoon humor.

10 A FEW MINUTES WITH ANDY ROONEY, by Andrew A. Rooney. (Atheneum, $12.95.) Reflections on contemporary life by the journalist and television commentator.

11 THE FATE OF THE EARTH, by Jonathan Schell. (Knopf, $11.95.) Essays on the dangers to life on earth from nuclear weapons.

12 PRINCESS, by Robert Lacey. (Times Books, $16.95.) The life of the Princess of Wales in words and pictures.

* **13** HOW TO MAKE LOVE TO A WOMAN, by Michael Morgenstern. (Clarkson N. Potter, $10.95.) A lawyer tells men "what women want."

14 THE UMPIRE STRIKES BACK, by Ron Luciano with David Fisher. (Bantam, $12.95.) Memories of the oddball baseball umpire.

* **15** WEIGHT WATCHERS 365-DAY MENU COOKBOOK. (New American Library, $14.95.) A compilation of more than 500 new recipes.

12 ONCE IN A LIFETIME, by Danielle Steel. (Dell, $6.95.) A young woman copes with the problems of widowhood and motherhood: fiction.

* **13** PERSONHOOD, by Leo F. Buscaglia. (Fawcett, $5.95.) A prescription for becoming one's individual self.

* **14** THE JOY OF SEX, by Alex Comfort. (Simon & Schuster/Fireside, $8.95.) With illustrations.

* **15** THE OFFICIAL M.B.A. HANDBOOK, by Jim Fisk and Robert Barron. (Simon & Schuster/Wallaby, $4.95.) How to behave like an M.B.A. without attending business school: humor.

All of these books, of course, explain how to do something. They appeal to our desire to improve ourselves, to develop our self-confidence, and to become well-rounded, successful individuals. When we have questions or problems, many of us seek the advice of experts. Instead of paying professional fees for such advice, we can now refer to books written by psychiatrists, physicians, dieticians, stockbrokers, cosmetologists, and millionaires. The how-to books range from the practical to the ridiculous, but certain subjects—such as how to lose weight or succeed in business—appear on the best-seller lists week after week. The reading public, it would seem, loves advice and is willing to pay quite a bit for it. So, if you want to know "How to Get Rich Quickly," think about writing a how-to book.

One of our students, Marla Stern, has researched this modern-day sociological phenomenon. Her findings:

Looking through a library card catalogue, you will find hundreds of How-to books. They are written in varying styles—serious, funny, satirical, sarcastic, and so on. You can find a book suitable for every age group, every craft or hobby, and every life situation. If you are about to become a mother, for example, you'll find some of these titles appropriate: *How to Be a Mother, How to Raise Your Child, How to Care for Your Sick Child, How to Educate Your Child*, and finally, *How to Marry Off Your Child*.

Anyone can attempt to become an expert in any field by following a few helpful guidelines. The average How-to book is entitled "How to _____," and the blank is filled in by the subject the book investigates. The table of contents usually serves as a summary of the step-by-step instructions for how to master the desired subject. The language is simple so that anybody can read and understand it. The chapters are short and concise. Specific points are emphasized by diagrams or cartoons. These visual devices are used to bring additional information to the reader. Occasionally, short quizzes are included at the end of a chapter to test your progress. By the time you have completed your book, you will have acquired a store of knowledge that can help you to fix a pipe, lose ten pounds, have a baby, be your dog's best friend, be your own best friend, or decide to forget the whole thing.

People are continually giving or receiving directions: following a recipe, learning to play a game, programming a computer, taking an English composition course, telling a friend how to get to the airport, trying to figure out the instructions for assembling a child's toy the night before Christmas. Everywhere you look in newspapers and magazines you'll find advice. A variety of examples from the newspapers follows on pages 72 and 73.

Giving Directions

Notice that one common way to give directions or analyze a process is to use the imperative sentence. As you know, every English sentence must have a subject and a verb, and the imperative sentence is no exception— though the subject is usually "hidden." The imperative sentence gives an order or a command. Its subject is always *you* whether the *you* is actually stated or not. Most often, *you* is implied or understood:

(*You*) Put the eggs and milk in a blender.

The imperative construction uses the base form of the verb. Four other words, commonly used when giving directions, also act as base form signals: *have* (when it means "to urge someone to do something"), *let*, *make*, and *help*. These words are usually followed by a noun or object pronoun + the base form of the verb:

Have your boss *call* me in the morning.

Let me *do* my homework.

Make Lisa *stop* teasing the cat.

Help him *wash* the dishes.

Have, let, and *make* are never followed by the infinitive. But *help* may be followed by either the base form of the verb or the infinitive:

This exercise will help you *understand* the imperative.

This exercise will help you *to understand* the imperative.

HOW TO:

MAKE A MILLION

MAKE A MESS

AROUND THE GARDEN with C. Z. Guest

Insect troubles: why not get them juiced?

THE SUMMER season subjects your plants to all sorts of crawling, creeping, flying, jumping and burrowing pests — all bent on one thing: destruction.

And some of these chewing, sucking demons (snails, slugs, cockroaches and crickets) are clever at hiding and come out only at night to feast. We all have our favorite remedies to combat this problem. My favorite is the potent "bug juice cocktail."

Collect the annoying insects which are ravaging your garden and mix them in a blender with water.

Strain the mixture and spray a diluted solution on your flowers and vegetables.

I have had tremendous success with this method. Let me know how you make out.

SHOE

1. Put eggs and milk in blender.

2. Sift in flour
3. Add vanilla
4. Add ½ cup sugar
5. Turn on blender

Careful not to get your tie caught in blender.

MURURDER A MARRIAGE

THE MARRIAGE KILLER *By Jules Feiffer*

Groom-to-be has 2d thoughts

DEAR DR. BROTHERS: I asked a girl to marry me three months ago and ever since I proposed, I've had a pain in my back, shoulders and neck. It got so bad, I had to take time off from my job to see a doctor. He couldn't find anything wrong, but it's getting worse and worse the nearer I get to marrying.

I didn't think my pain had anything to do with my proposal until recently, but now I'm sure they have a lot to do with each other.

Knowing this doesn't help me. Her parents have gone to a lot of ex-

DR. JOYCE BROTHERS

pense and they'd go through the wall if I canceled out on this. I feel like running, but I don't know what to do. — **J.Y.**

DEAR J.Y.: Your body is sending you a powerful message. Listen to it. Your anxiety about the marriage is undoubtedly causing this muscular tension and unless you do something about it, it's only going to get worse.

Everyone experiences a certain amount of anxiety before making any major life change, but what you describe is excessive. This doesn't mean that you shouldn't marry this young woman, nor does it necessarily mean that she isn't "right" for you, but it does mean that you should put on the brakes

(regardless of the money that may have been spent).

Surely her parents would rather alter the wedding plans now than have their daughter enter into a marriage that would begin with instability because of your misgivings.

It's going to take a lot of courage and maturity on your part, but take the giant step now before it's too late. Talk with your fiancee and her parents. Don't go through with something that is creating this much anxiety and pain.

EXERCISE 3.1

Locate all of the imperative verbs in the how-to samples on pages 72–73.

EXERCISE 3.2

Advertising slogans frequently use imperative sentences:

SEIZE THE MOMENT
TASTE THE MAGIC
BREAK TRADITION

Using this pattern, write an advertising headline for a car, a resort, a packaged food, a cleaning product, and a magazine.

Here's another common verb construction used for giving advice or directions:

should
must } + base form

ought to
have to } (these modals, too, are used to show obligation or necessity)
need to

This verb construction should come in handy in the next exercise.

JOURNAL EXERCISE 3.3

Imagine for the moment that you write an advice column called "Dear Akim," and you have received these three letters. Answer them, explaining in each reply what you think the writer should do about his or her problem. Use the imperative and the modal + base form constructions whenever appropriate.

Dear Akim:
I'm having a problem with my father, who smokes three packs of cigarettes a day. I've been begging him to quit for the past year, but he only gets annoyed with me when I tell him how bad it is for his health. Last

week, I tried a new tactic: whenever he lit a cigarette, I plucked it out of his mouth and broke it in half. Now he's so angry with me he won't let me use the car or go out with my friends on weekends.

I was just trying to help my dad, and I think he overreacted. Was I wrong?

—A Burnt-Out Case

Dear Akim:

My sister recently got a dog. She insists on bringing him to my apartment when she visits, even though she knows I'm scared to death of it. Akim, this is a large dog with sharp teeth, and he's not too crazy about me, either. I've asked my sister to leave Brutus home, but she just laughs and tells me I'll get used to him because he's really very sweet and gentle.

My sister and I have always been close, so I want to handle this situation tactfully. What should I do?

—Katy

Dear Akim:

I am a foreign student in my first year at an American high school, and I'm having some difficulty adjusting. Here's an example: today my history teacher called me over after class and asked me why I haven't been participating in classroom discussions. I think she doesn't believe I've been doing my homework. To make matters worse, while she was speaking to me, I lowered my head (this is a sign of respect in my country) and she asked, "Why don't you look at me when I'm speaking to you?" How can I make my teacher understand that I am a serious student who does not mean to be impolite?

—Troubled

Even popular songs are full of advice: a process can be described in rhyming verse as well as prose. In his song "50 Ways to Leave Your Lover," Paul Simon passes on some advice, not to the lovelorn, but to the "love-worn":

"The problem is all inside your head," she said to me.
"The answer is easy if you take it logically.
I'd like to help you in your struggle to be free—
There must be fifty ways to leave your lover."
She said, "It's really not my habit to intrude;
Furthermore, I hope my meaning won't be lost or misconstrued.
But I'll repeat myself, at the risk of being crude—
There must be fifty ways to leave your lover
Fifty ways to leave your lover"

. . . Just slip out the back, Jack
Make a new plan, Stan

You don't need to be coy, Roy
Just get yourself free.
Hop on the bus, Gus
You don't need to discuss much
Just drop off the key, Lee
And get yourself free.

EXERCISE 3.4

"Fifty Ways to Leave Your Lover" gives gleefully idiomatic ways to tell a boyfriend (or girlfriend) that you're no longer interested in continuing the relationship. Try to think of five new ways to "leave" a boyfriend or girl-friend. Remember to use an imperative sentence for each line and to rhyme the last word of the command with the name of the person to whom it's addressed.

As some of these books, cartoons, and songs illustrate, one popular approach to the how-to essay is to give a humorous description of an everyday process. Indeed, even the simplest, most familiar procedure can be made to seem absurd if its steps are analyzed in maddening detail. Argentinian author Julio Cortázar once composed an entire "Instruction Manual" offering directions for "How to Cry," "How to Sing," "How to Be Afraid," and, in the following excerpt, "How to Climb a Staircase":

> . . . You tackle a stairway face on, for if you try it backwards or sideways, it ends up being particularly uncomfortable. The natural stance consists of holding oneself upright, arms hanging easily at the sides, head erect but not so much so that the eyes no longer see the steps immediately above, while one tramps up, breathing lightly and with regularity. To climb a staircase one begins by lifting that part of the body located below and to the right, usually encased in leather or deerskin, and which, with a few exceptions, fits exactly on the stair. Said part set down on the first step (to abbreviate we shall call it "the foot"), one draws up the equivalent part on the left side (also called "foot" but not to be confused with "the foot" cited above), and lifting this other part to the level of "the foot," makes it continue along until it is set in place on the second step, at which point the foot will rest, and "the foot" will rest on the first. (The first steps are always the most difficult, until you acquire the necessary coordination. The coincidence of names between the foot and "the foot" makes the explanation more difficult. Be especially careful not to raise, at the same time, the foot and "the foot.")
>
> Having arrived by this method at the second step, it's easy enough to repeat the movements alternately, until one reaches the top of the staircase. One gets off it easily, with a light tap of the heel to fix it in place, to make sure it will not move until one is ready to come down.

You can see that how-to essays need not be serious. You may, like Cortázar, want to write a *parody* of a process—that is, to make fun of a how-to essay by imitating its characteristics in an exaggerated way. One student, for example, noticed the popularity of diet books on the best-seller list and decided to poke fun at these plans for weight loss. Here are the final days of her "guaranteed" one-week scheme for success:

The fifth day (Friday):   Pay no attention to classmates who say that you look as if you've been starving. Keep going! Beauty needs victims.
Breakfast (10 a.m.)   A glass of water
Lunch (1 p.m.)   3 strawberries
Dinner (6 p.m.)   3 more strawberries
Supper (9 p.m.)   A glass of water

The sixth day (Saturday):   Wake up and sing if you are still able to make human sounds. Today is going to be the last day of your diet! That's why you won't have any breakfast, lunch, dinner, or supper at all!

The seventh day (Sunday):   Cremation.

P.S.   Our booklet can be helpful to rejected lovers and budget-conscious shoppers as well.

—*Marina Berkovich*

JOURNAL EXERCISE 3.5

In your notebook, try composing a brief entry that parodies a familiar process such as the above example does. Some suggestions: How to Win Friends and Influence People; Improve Your Looks; Train a Pet; Conquer Depression; Build Your Self-Confidence.

Alternately, try writing a page describing a nonsensical or absurd process. For example, a well-known comedian recently invented a "Book Club" featuring such titles as *How to Filet a Panda, How to Turn Unbearable Pain into Extra Income*, and *Cooking with Heat*. Write a set of instructions for a comparably silly process—but remember that your directions (however bizarre) should be clearly defined and convincingly ordered.

CLASSROOM ACTIVITY 3.6

If a set of directions is clearly and logically presented, the reader should be able to figure out what that process is without being told. This exercise, in fact, is a handy way to test the effectiveness of a how-to essay. Your teacher will divide the class into small groups, assigning each group a process to work on together ("How to Fail Your English Course," "How to Lose Your Best Friend," "How to Murder a Marriage" are possibilities). After you have agreed upon the steps involved and their sequence, compose a paragraph with the members of your group but do not name the procedure you are describing until the final sentence. If the rest of the class can quickly guess your topic, your paragraph is sufficiently clear. Read the following example of one such paragraph written in class. (The last sentence has been omitted.) What was this group's task?

> First, make sure that you always enter through the window, not the door. Then, after arriving ten minutes late, greet your fellow classmates noisily. Take the bottle of wine out of your schoolbag and distribute the paper cups. After a few shots, take out that cute little computer game from your jacket pocket and start playing. If your teacher asks you a question, yawn loudly. When she begins to write on the board, pull out the left-over ketchup packet from lunch and smear it on her seat. You'll get a kick out of it when she sits down. Next, make sure you have some chalky erasers nearby so that you can get chalk powder all over her back. It will stick nicely to the ketchup. Then, the one time you do make it to class early, throw all the chalk in the garbage and loosen the screws on the blackboard screen so that when she pulls it, it'll fall on her head. If all of this doesn't work, call us for more advice.

These students clearly relished their topic. See if your group can write a paragraph as lively as this one. When all the paragraphs are finished, have one person from each group read the paragraph to the entire class, leaving out the last sentence. Have you made your description specific enough for the rest of the class to guess what your task was?

Following Directions

In the preceding classroom activity, you experimented with one method of making sure your instructions are clearly written. Another way to test the effectiveness of many process essays is to see whether your reader can actually follow your advice and perform the task you describe. In this section, you'll be asked to read two sets of directions—a developed essay and an outline—and to try following the directions in both. The subject of this section is a task that concerns most of us at one time or another:

HOW TO GET A JOB

STEP 1: THE RESUME

The first step in getting a job is to write a resume showing your work background and your qualifications for employment. Here's an example:

Elena Heraclides
8809 Cromwell Road
Ft. Lauderdale, Florida 33313
(305) 739-1176

WORK EXPERIENCE
October 1983–present. Part-time cashier at Jimmy's Place, a restaurant. Responsibilities include checking receipts and keeping accounts.

December 1982–September 1983. Part-time waitress at Jimmy's Place.

Summers, 1978–1981. Junior clerk at pharmacy in Athens, Greece.

EDUCATION
1982–present. State College, second year. Major not yet decided; probably either Computer Science or Accounting. Grade point average to date: 3.0.

1978–1982. Athens High School, Greece.

PERSONAL DATA
Age: 20   Marital Status: Single
Health: Excellent   Hobbies: Photography, camping, writing my own software for computer games.
Languages: Fluent in Greek and English; some French.

ACTIVITIES
Member, Photography Club and Greek Students' Organization. Helped organize International Students' Day at State College, June, 1983.

REFERENCES
Jimmy Dionides, owner   Prof. Susan Marks
Jimmy's Place   Computer Science Dept.
1278 Lacosta Blvd.   State College of Florida
Ft. Lauderdale, Fla. 33313   Ft. Lauderdale, Fla. 33313

EXERCISE 3.7

Using the sample resume as a model, see if you can come up with a brief set of instructions to follow in writing your own resume. Quickly jot down a list of possible steps for this procedure. When you have finished, compare the items on your list with those found in the following reading selection. How is each item developed into a paragraph or paragraphs in the finished essay?

How to write a resume

by Jerrold G. Simon, Ed.D.
Harvard Business School

If you are about to launch a search for a job, the suggestions I offer here can help you whether or not you have a high school or college diploma, whether you are just starting out or changing your job or career in midstream.

"What do I want to do?"

Before you try to find a job opening, you have to answer the hardest question of your working life: "What do I want to do?" Here's a good way.

Sit down with a piece of paper and don't get up till you've listed all the things you're proud to have accomplished. Your list might include being head of a fund-raising campaign, or acting a juicy role in the senior play.

Study the list. You'll see a pattern emerge of the things you do best and like to do best. You might discover that you're happiest working with people, or maybe with numbers, or words, or well, you'll see it.

Once you've decided what job area to go after, read more about it in the reference section of your library. "Talk shop" with any people you know in that field. Then start to get your resume together.

There are many good books that offer sample resumes and describe widely used formats. The one that is still most popular, the *reverse chronological*, emphasizes where you worked and when, and the jobs and titles you held.

How to organize it

Your name and address go at the top. Also phone number.

What job do you want? That's what a prospective employer looks for first. If you know exactly, list that next under *Job Objective*. Otherwise, save it for your cover letter (I describe that later), when you're writing for a specific job to a specific person. In any case, make sure your resume focuses on the kind of work you can do and want to do.

Now comes *Work Experience*. Here's where you list your qualifications. Lead with your most important credentials. If you've had a distinguished work history in an area related to the job you're seeking, lead off with that. If your education will impress the prospective employer more, start with that.

Begin with your most recent experience first and work backwards. Include your titles or positions held. And list the years.

Figures don't brag

The most qualified people don't always get the job. It goes to the person who presents himself most persuasively in person and on paper.

So don't just list where you were and what you did. This is your chance to tell *how well you did*. Were you the best salesman? Did you cut operating costs? Give numbers, statistics, percentages, increases in sales or profits.

No job experience?

In that case, list your summer jobs, extracurricular school activities, honors, awards. Choose the activities that will enhance your qualifications for the job.

Next list your *Education*—unless you chose to start with that. This should also be in reverse chronological order. List your high school only if you didn't go on to college. Include college degree, postgraduate degrees, dates conferred, major and minor courses you took that help qualify you for the job you want.

Also, did you pay your own way? Earn scholarships or fellowships? Those are impressive accomplishments.

No diplomas or degrees?

Then tell about your education: special training programs or courses that can qualify you. Describe outside activities that reveal your talents and abilities. Did you sell the most tickets to the annual charity musical? Did you take your motorcycle engine apart and put it back together so it works? These can help you.

Next, list any *Military Service*. This could lead off your resume if it is your only work experience. Stress skills learned, promotions earned, leadership shown.

Now comes *Personal Data*. This is your chance to let the reader get a glimpse of the personal you, and to further the image you've worked to project in the preceding sections. For example, if you're after a job in computer programming, and you enjoy playing chess, mention it. Chess playing requires the ability to think through a problem.

Include foreign languages spoken, extensive travel, particular interests or professional memberships, *if* they advance your cause.

Keep your writing style simple. Be brief. Start sentences with impressive action verbs: "Created," "Designed," "Achieved," "Caused."

No typos, please

Make sure your grammar and spelling are correct. And no typos!

Use 8½″ × 11″ bond paper—white or off-white for easy reading. Don't cram things together.

Make sure your original is clean and readable. Then have it professionally duplicated. No carbons.

Get it into the right hands

Now that your resume is ready, start to track down job openings. How? Look up business friends, neighbors, your minister, your college alumni association, professional services. Keep up with trade publications, and read help-wanted ads.

And start your own "direct mail" campaign. First, find out about the companies you are interested in—their size, location, what they make, their competition, their advertising, their prospects. Get their annual report—and read it.

No "Dear Sir" letters

Send your resume, along with a cover letter, to a specific person in the company, not to "Gentlemen" or "Dear Sir." The person should be the top person in the area where you want to work. Spell his name properly! The cover letter should appeal to your reader's own needs. What's in it for him? Quickly explain why you are approaching *his* company (their product line, their superior training program) and what you can bring to the party. Back up your claims with facts. Then refer him to your enclosed resume and ask for an interview.

Oh, boy! An interview!

And now you've got an interview! Be sure to call the day before to confirm it. Meantime, *prepare yourself*. Research the company and the job by reading books and business journals in the library.

On the big day, arrive 15 minutes early. Act calm, even though, if you're normal, you're trembling inside at 6.5 on the Richter scale. At every chance, let your interviewer see that your personal skills and qualifications relate to the job at hand. If it's a sales position, for example, go all out to show how articulate and persuasive you are.

Afterwards, follow through with a brief thank-you note. This is a fine opportunity to restate your qualifications and add any important points you didn't get a chance to bring up during the interview.

Keep good records

Keep a list of prospects. List the dates you contacted them, when they replied, what was said.

And remember, someone out there is looking for someone *just like you*. It takes hard work and sometimes luck to find that person. Keep at it and you'll succeed.

EXERCISE 3.8

What kind of job would you like to have this summer, or after you have finished your education? Using the guidelines in the essay, write the resume you might submit when you apply for the position.

As Jerrold Simon points out, you need to send your prospective employer a cover letter along with your resume. Simon gives a few pointers regarding this next step in the process of applying for a job (see his section on "No 'Dear Sir' Letters"), but you're going to need a more detailed set of instructions to accomplish this task successfully.

STEP 2: THE BUSINESS LETTER

We have outlined here an article on "How to Write a Business Letter" by Malcolm Forbes, publisher of *Forbes* business magazine. We write business letters for a number of reasons—not just to introduce a resume, but to set up an interview, to request information, to complain about a product, or to explain why we haven't paid a bill on time. Forbes's advice applies to all of these situations, and, indeed, to many of the assignments you will be asked to submit in college.

Most formal letters and essays consist of:

I. The introduction—this is the "hook" that grabs your reader's attention, draws him into your letter or essay, and announces the main idea that will be discussed in the rest of your paper.

II. The body, or center, of the letter or essay—here you offer specific details, examples, or reasons to support or develop the main idea you have announced in your introductory paragraphs.

III. The conclusion, or "wrap-up" of your letter or essay—here you summarize your main ideas by restating them in a new way. In your concluding paragraph you emphasize the points you want your reader to remember.

Here, then, are Forbes's guidelines for writing the introduction, body, and conclusion of a successful business letter. After you've read them, we'll ask you to test their usefulness by composing a business letter or two of your own.

I. Introduction
   A. Tell what your letter is about in one or two sentences—for example, if you're applying for a job, mention the job you desire and where you heard about it.

    B. If you're answering a letter, refer to the date it was written.
  II. Body
    A. Write so the reader will enjoy it.
      1. Be positive.
      2. Be nice—even when you're disagreeing with your reader.
      3. Be natural—read the letter aloud to make sure it doesn't sound stiff or unnatural.
      4. Have a sense of humor, but don't be cute or disrespectful.
      5. Be specific—give facts to support what you say.
      6. Use the active instead of the passive voice whenever possible—it's stronger.
    B. Give it your best effort.
      1. Make the letter appetizing.
        a. Type it on good-quality 8½ × 11 stationery.
        b. Keep it neat.
        c. Use paragraphing that makes the organization of your letter easier to follow.
      2. Make it perfect—no typographical errors, misspellings, or factual errors.
      3. Don't exaggerate: be honest.
      4. Edit ruthlessly: cut out unnecessary words.
  III. Conclusion
    A. The last paragraph should tell the reader exactly what you want: "May I have an appointment? Next Monday, the 16th, I'll call your secretary to see when it will be most convenient for you."
    B. Close with something simple like "Sincerely."
    C. Sign your name legibly: an illegible signature is an "ego trip."

As you can see from this outline, one of the rules for writing a business letter—especially a job request—is that the writer's tone should be respectful, serious, and sincere. *Tone* in writing refers to the "tone of voice" that an author employs in a particular piece of writing; in place of vocal inflection, a writer uses word choice and sentence structure to communicate his or her attitude toward the material and the audience. The tone you use on paper, like the tone you use in conversation, can be sarcastic, solemn, casual, humorous, and so on. Adopting the wrong tone can produce catastrophic results, as the following business letter illustrates.

EXERCISE 3.9

Using the resume printed on page 79, we've invented a letter requesting an interview for the position of computer operator. It's awful. Try rewriting it using Forbes's advice, as well as specific information from the resume.

To Whom It May Concern:

Unfortunately, college does not last forever. It is a fact of life that sooner or later, everyone must get a job. I am writing to you because it occurs to me that since summer is not far away, I should be sending out letters and seeking some means of employment. Consequently, copies of this letter and resume are being forwarded by me to a number of businesses, including yours.

I forget whether I saw your advertisement in the paper or whether a friend told me about it. Anyway, I think I might possibly have some of the qualifications your company requires of applicants for this job. I certainly hope you think so too—otherwise, I'll starve!

But permit me to be serious for a moment. My last employer, Jimmy, who was not exactly the most generous boss in the world, said I was the smartest and hardest-working employee he had ever known. I was asked to perform many duties at my job, and I was successful at every single one of them. I'll tell you about my work esperience when I meet you. I can provide references from other employers, too.

So how about an interview? I ~~can't~~ can only come on Monday mornings between 9:00 and 10:00.

Best Regards,

[signature]

EXERCISE 3.10

Below, we've posted a selection of "Help Wanted" ads that are similar to those found in the Sunday newspaper. Select a job that interests you, and write a cover letter introducing yourself and stating your qualifications for the position.

Alternatively, you may want to write the cover letter for the "ideal job" you had in mind when you wrote your resume in Exercise 3.8. Begin by writing a "job wanted" ad, describing the job you'd love to have. These examples from the "Positions Wanted" column of a newspaper will help you compose your ad:

Then write the letter you would submit to request an interview for this job.

Before you go on to the third step in the process of getting a job—the interview—one more "how-to" needs to be covered. After you have written down on paper all the points you want to make in a letter or an essay, how do you structure your ideas so that your paragraphs are unified and flow naturally from one to the next? The following Transition Tips are designed to help you with the how-to essay you'll be assigned at the end of this chapter, as well as with any letter or essay you attempt.

How to Write Cohesive Paragraphs: Transition Tips

One of the most convenient aspects of the how-to essay is that it is the easiest type of essay to organize. Its structure is usually determined by the arrangement of the steps involved in the order of their occurrence. This chronological order is often signaled by words like *First . . . Second . . . Next . . . Finally.* Such *transitions* help to transform a list of directions into a how-to essay.

Transitions, from the Latin for "to go over or across," are words and phrases that provide bridges between sentences, ideas, and paragraphs. They are used to indicate relationships in time or space, to introduce illustrations or examples, and to show logical connections. When used appropriately, transitions enable your reader to follow the development of your essay more easily. The most common ways to make the transition between one sentence or paragraph and the next are the following:

Repeating Key Words or Phrases—Restating significant words is an especially useful way to carry a theme through a succession of sentences, and to keep your reader's mind on your topic. Observe, for example, how we got from the first paragraph of this section to the second:

> Such *transitions* help to transform a list of directions into a how-to essay. *Transitions*, from the Latin. . . .

Using Personal Pronouns or Demonstratives—Instead of repeating a key word, you can substitute a pronoun, which will refer your reader back to the word it replaces (the antecedent). Again, the introductory paragraphs of this section provide a few examples of this method:

> ANTECEDENT
> |
> *One* of the most convenient aspects of the how-to essay is that *it* is the easiest type of essay to organize. *Its* structure. . . .

> ANTECEDENT
> |
> *Transitions* . . . are words and phrases that provide bridges between sentences, ideas, and paragraphs. *They* are used. . . .

But please take note: Do not use a pronoun if its antecedent appears in another paragraph. Instead, repeat the word it stands for.

Demonstratives (*this, that, these, those*) are also used to refer back to a word or idea. On page 70, for instance, you'll find the following transition:

> . . . . So, if you want to know "How to Get Rich Quickly," think about writing a how-to book.
> One of our students, Marla Stern, has researched *this* modern-day sociological phenomenon.

Notice that in the above example, *this* is followed by a noun phrase. Writers sometimes omit the noun or noun phrase after the demonstrative. But this (this what? this noun? this demonstrative?) omission is liable to confuse the reader:

> UNCLEAR: One of our students, Marla Stern, has researched *this.*

Using Specific Transitional Words and Phrases—In addition to the previously-mentioned methods for achieving cohesive paragraphs and essays, you can employ a number of words that express precise relationships between ideas. Below are listed some of these transitions according to the different purposes they serve. In later chapters, we'll be discussing how these transitions are used in various kinds of essays. For now, however, you can use this list as a reference.

But we caution you not to rely too heavily on "ready-made" transitions. Don't just plug in one of these expressions when your sentences don't seem to mesh into a unified paragraph. The words on this list don't automatically produce a cohesive paper—they simply clarify the structure of a paper that has already been logically organized.

- *To Show Similarity*
  in the same way, likewise, similarly

- *To Show Difference*
  but, however, and yet, despite, even so, though, although, even though, on the other hand, in contrast, on the contrary, in spite of, still, regardless, though, notwithstanding

- *To Add*
  and, again, also, in addition, next, first, second, last, finally, moreover, in the first place, too, besides, furthermore, further, equally important, even more important, most important

- *To Give Examples or Emphasize*
  for example, for instance, in fact, to illustrate, indeed, truly, actually, after all, of course, specifically, that is

- *To Indicate Time*
  now, soon, next, then, after, afterward, earlier, before, later, in the meantime, at the same time, simultaneously, meanwhile, as soon as, as long as, since, shortly, lately, formerly, subsequently, thereafter, until, when, finally

- *To Indicate Place**
  above, around, adjacent to, below, under, underneath, here, there, near, nearby, to the north, to the right, elsewhere, on the other side, beyond, over there

- *To Indicate Cause or Effect*
  accordingly, as a result, therefore, thus, because, consequently, hence, since, then

- *To Summarize, Restate, or Conclude*
  in conclusion, all in all, overall, in other words, finally, on the whole, in short, to summarize, as we have noted, in summary

Without transitions, even a well-organized, adequately developed paragraph can sound choppy and disconnected. On the other hand, too many transitions or the wrong choice of transition can be equally damaging. This next exercise will show you what we mean.

EXERCISE 3.11

Here is a paragraph lifted from the first draft of a student's autobiographical essay. (The revised version appears on pages 201–202.) You'll notice that the paragraph is drowning in transitions. In your own revision of this excerpt, which ones will you omit? When you're finished, you may want to compare your rewrite with the author's.

> In addition to being the "tornado mouth" of the fifth grade, I talked constantly at home. In the first place, I loved to tell short stories to my little brother. Reciprocally, he delighted in following me around and listening to my tales. Moreover, I always told my parents what I had done in school during the day, and what I would do tomorrow. My mouth, in fact, always seemed to be open, except maybe when I went to sleep. Conclusively, talking was one of my hobbies. You can see that chatting all day long gave me great pleasure.

* For further discussion of these transitions of place, see the preposition review at the end of this chapter.

EXERCISE 3.12

In the following selection, taken from a student's paper on "How to Fail an Exam," we've eliminated crucial connecting words and phrases. For the sake of coherence, please fill in the blanks with appropriate transitions.

_____ I have never failed an exam, I can tell you how it is done. _____ I was a teacher, I saw many students in my school who failed their exams several times. Failing an exam may not seem so terrible at the time, _____ most students who do poorly don't realize that the school year is slipping through their fingers. _____, now that I've said all this, if you still want to fail a test, I will show you how. _____ _____ it's up to you.

_____ is to go to class as little as possible. _____, why sit in class during such beautiful weather, especially when you know that in a short time winter will come and you won't have warm, sunny days to enjoy anymore? If, _____, you do decide to attend class, daydream about being outdoors, or about going to a movie or disco.

—*Sohileh Aran*

JOURNAL EXERCISE 3.13

Now that you have the beginning of an essay on "How to Fail an Exam," you may want to try writing an outline of how you would complete this essay. How many steps can you think of? And what examples can you offer to make your directions clear to your reader?

We offer the following exercise for two reasons: to give you further practice in the use of transitions, and to provide pointers on how to succeed with the third step in getting a job, the job interview.

STEP 3: THE JOB INTERVIEW

If an employer judges from your cover letter and resume that you're a likely candidate for the job, he or she will undoubtedly call you in for an interview. Although you don't know the interviewer or the questions that will be asked, you can still prepare for this important meeting by following the advice offered in this next exercise.

EXERCISE 3.14

Here are fourteen sentences compiled from two student essays explaining how to have a successful job interview. Examine the steps, and then put them into a logical order. (There may be more than one way to do this.) Next, see if you can combine some of these sentences, using coordinators discussed in Chapter 2 (*and, but, or, for, nor, so, yet,* and the semicolon). Finally, with the help of "Transition Tips," write a list of steps—in sentence outline form—describing this process. Try to use introductory clauses and phrases such as "The night before" and "After the interview" to show chronological order, as well as other transitional expressions to emphasize and conclude.

- Don't shrug if you don't know the answer to a question.
- You don't want your employer to wait for you.
- Always bring a pen with you in case you have to write something or take a test.
- Being on time is very important.
- Avoid wearing too much makeup or jewelry.
- Make a list of possible questions and appropriate responses.
- Companies hire people who will be the best representatives for the firm, so being a well-dressed person is a real "plus."
- Be honest and assertive.
- Don't chew gum or smoke.
- Thank the employer for his or her time.
- Speak respectfully and try to be charming.

- Consider questions such as: Why do I need this job? What do I know about this company? What do I hope to be doing ten years from now?

- Nobody wants a human parrot whose only comment is "Yes, sir," or "You're right, Ms. Brown."

- A smile and a firm handshake will leave a good impression.

How to Use Your Journal for a How-to Essay

Once you've decided to write a how-to essay, how do you decide what to write *about*? One way to proceed is to glance through your journal to see what subjects and questions have been on your mind recently. Below are some excerpts from a few weeks' worth of a student's journal entries. Can you see a unifying theme here?

I don't know Italian, but I think it's a beautiful language. Maybe I'll take Italian some semester. I'm taking German now. I like it, but it's so hard— even worse than English. I'll have to stop writing for today, because I have to study for my German test on Monday.

I used to be afraid to speak English. I was always thinking that I might make a mistake, and I didn't want to be embarrassed. That was my problem with English. When I was among Americans I would seldom say anything. During classes I would just sit by myself, and I wouldn't start a conversation with anyone else. That's why I wasn't able to make friends for a while.

By the way, I like the way American people use their language. I like their accent, too. I seem to enjoy English more now. I'm hoping one day I'll speak the language the way Americans do.

For me, a successful person is someone who feels good about herself. It's someone who has self-confidence, tries her best, does well at school or at her job, and makes her family proud.

In rereading her journal, this student found that she had been preoccupied with the progress she was making in her language studies. Noticing that her entries offered a few suggestions for further progress in English, she wound up asking herself, "What can I do to learn more?" She then jotted down some possible answers that popped into her mind:

1. Become friends with some Americans in my classes.

2. Read more in English.

3. Pay more attention to English programs on radio and TV.

4. Have courage!

In reviewing this brief list, she tried to ask herself specific questions that would help her develop her ideas:

1. How can I become friends with Americans?
   How do I get used to their customs, which are very different from mine?

2. What reading material has helped me improve my English in the past year?
   - newspapers
   - magazines
   - books

3. What radio and TV programs have I learned from?
   - news programs
   - my favorite shows

4. Why do I think courage is so important in learning a language?
   - You shouldn't be afraid to speak, or to make a mistake.
   - You have to practice, and to solve your problems by facing up to them.

Through her journal, this writer discovered a topic she wanted to explore: How to Learn English. This idea provided her with a focus for an essay.

The central idea that controls an essay is called the *thesis.* Your thesis, either stated or implied in the introduction of your paper, tells the reader the main point you want to communicate—your reason for writing this particular essay. Finding the thesis for your how-to paper is a simpler task than for most other kinds of essays, since the controlling idea for this essay type is almost always, "If you want to know how to _____, follow these steps. . . ." Of course, this basic idea may be stated in any number of ways. What, for example, is Jerrold Simon's thesis statement in his article on "How to Write a Resume" (page 80)?

After this student had formulated her thesis, she made a brief outline of the major ideas she wanted to cover in her essay. Her outline is a rough list of the broad questions she wanted to discuss—along with the ideas she planned to develop in each paragraph—arranged in the order in which she wanted to discuss them. An outline can be an informal "sketch" of this kind, or a more formal ordering of related details grouped under major headings. Some writers choose to make lengthy sentence outlines, such as the one used to summarize the Malcolm Forbes article on pages 81–82; other writers simply jot down key words or phrases, and rearrange them later. An especially useful format is the topic sentence outline. A *topic sentence* introduces the main idea of a paragraph, just as the thesis statement introduces the main idea of an essay. By composing an outline of topic sentences, therefore, a writer is able to plan the sequence of the paragraphs in his or her essay. You can choose any pre-writing pattern that suits you: the point of an outline is to keep your thoughts on the right track and to ensure that none of your ideas gets lost along the way.

Our student's next step was to write the first draft of her essay, which you will find reprinted on pages 93–97. But the essay still wasn't finished. In the following section of this chapter, we will ask you to consider an important step in the process of drafting any essay: offering *support* for the points you want to make.

How to Support a Point

A how-to essay is more than a list of steps. A set of instructions often includes warnings, alternatives, descriptions, explanations, and reasons. Most of all, a process paper should include lively, concrete examples from the writer's own experience. On the following pages we have reprinted the first draft of our student's essay. As you will see, it is well-structured and clear, but lacks development. It is a skeleton that needs flesh and blood to become animated. We have left lines between the paragraphs of the writer's paper to indicate the natural places for examples to occur. The subject of this essay is one about which all ESL students are knowledgeable—learning English.

CLASSROOM ACTIVITY 3.15

Your task is to make each paragraph more specific by providing examples that add support to the *topic sentence*—the sentence that expresses the main idea of each paragraph. Work in groups to enliven this paper with your own concrete details.

It may help you to look at the final paragraph of the author's revision of her paper. The author has made the revised paragraph more informative and energetic by citing an *example* of when courage helped her learn English:

> Fourth, and most important of all, is self-confidence and not being embarrassed by making a mistake. The point is to talk and practice; therefore, you should not be shy or afraid of talking to Americans. When you make a mistake, you should try to correct yourself. You may encounter a lot of problems, but you have to be patient and face your problems and solve them courageously. Last semester, for example, I had to give a speech in English about marriage in Iran. At first it was very difficult for me to stand in front of everybody and talk. I thought if I made a mistake, they would

laugh at me. But I told myself, "If you want to learn English, you should speak out, and this class is the best place for proving yourself." I made a very good speech. I tried my best and overcame my self-consciousness.

And that is how to learn English.

See if you can develop this essay by providing equally helpful details from your own experiences in learning English.

How to Learn English

To learn English, you have to follow some steps, which are not very difficult if you know how to handle them.

_____

_____

_____

_____

_____

_____

_____

_____

_____

_____

First, becoming friends with Americans is very important. In order to become friends with them, you have to get used to their customs. Although accepting some of their customs, such as eating junk food, watching too much TV, and living together before marriage, is very difficult, little by little you'll get used to these foreign practices if you convince yourself that you need English-speaking friends.

_____

_____

_____

_____

_____

_____

_____

_____

_____

_____

Second, reading different newspapers and magazines in English will help you a lot. If you read every day, find new words and write them in your notebook, and try to use them when talking to your friends. You'll see how much your English progresses in just a few months.

_____

_____

_____

_____

_____

_____

_____

_____

Third, listening to the radio and watching TV are among the most important things you can do. I think watching TV at least an hour a day is necessary, because it is much easier to understand than radio. Fortunately, there are many different channels on TV, which gives you the chance to choose your favorite program. In my opinion, the best program on TV is the news.

Also, there are many different shows and movies to choose from; they will help you too.

_____

_____

_____

_____

_____

_____

_____

_____

_____

Fourth, and most important of all, is self-confidence: don't be embarrassed about making a mistake. The point is to talk and practice; therefore, you should not be shy and afraid of talking to Americans. When you make a mistake, you have to try to correct yourself. You may have a lot of problems, but you have to be patient and face your problems and solve them courageously.

_____

_____

_____

_____

_____

_____

_____

_____

_____

And that is how to learn English.

—Afsaneh Basnejad

_____

Verb Tense Review: How to Use the Present Perfect

Descriptions of processes, as you have probably discovered, rely heavily on the present and present perfect verb tenses. For example, we've taken a paragraph from an article in which a scientist discusses the *physics* behind the process of making ice cream at home. First, however, he includes his grandmother's recipe, which calls for 1 quart of light cream, 1 cup of sugar, and 2 teaspoons of pure vanilla extract. Notice the way he uses the present perfect tense in describing this procedure:

> To investigate the process, I *have chosen* one of my grandmother's recipes for a moderately rich vanilla ice cream. . . . Warm the cream, stirring in the sugar. Continue to heat and stir the mixture, but do not let it boil. Once it is hot and the sugar *has fully dissolved*, cool it to room temperature and then add the vanilla extract. Pour the mixture into the metal container and put it into the refrigerator for at least an hour. Then mount the container in the bucket and insert the dasher, which you *have also cooled* in the refrigerator. Pack the ice and salt around the container and begin cranking.
>
> *—Jearl Walker*

As you can see, the combination of the present and present perfect verb tenses is one way to combine two or more steps into one sentence. Dependent clauses that begin with words such as "Once" and "After" often employ the present perfect tense:

Dissolve the sugar. + Cool it to room temperature.
= *Once the sugar has dissolved*, cool it to room temperature.

Prepare your resume. + Write a cover letter.
= *After you've prepared your resume*, write a cover letter.

When the verb in the dependent clause is in the *present perfect tense—* HAVE/HAS + PAST PARTICIPLE—the verb in the main clause is generally in the *present tense.*

The present perfect indicates an action that began in the past, continues into the present, and may or may not extend into the future. Unlike the other present tenses, it always has an element of the past in it. Unlike the past tenses, it says something about the present:

In the past few years, the offensive game of football has changed radically.

You've spent a lifetime building your good name. Make certain you use it wisely.

Adverbials such as *since, so far, until now, up to now, up to the present, always,* and *never* often accompany this tense because they express past-to-present time.

Since the beginning of time, people have relied upon the virtues of wholesome foods for maintaining good health.

"I've never done a collection without a classic crew-neck cable sweater."
—Perry Ellis

PAST: I *met* him *in 1964.*

PRESENT PERFECT: I *have _always_ liked* him.

It is important to understand that the present perfect is commonly used to express an action that took place at an *unspecified* past time. Adverbials such as *already, finally, ever, never, always, just, recently,* and *yet* commonly accompany this use of the tense because they do not necessarily specify an exact time. (These adverbials come between the auxiliary and the past participle.) Thus, the present perfect is never accompanied by definite past time expressions such as *on May 4, 1963, in 1983, last month, yesterday.*

You've recently been promoted. Or should be.

LIFE HAS CHANGED!

CORRECT:　　My father *has finally retired.*

CORRECT:　　*I've lived* here *since 1980.*

INCORRECT:　She *has quit* her job *yesterday.*

Note that the present perfect can also express an action or state that occurred at an unspecified time in the past and may be repeated in the future:

PAST: My grandmother *swam* across the English Channel last year.

PRESENT PERFECT: My grandmother *has swum* across the English Channel five times.

EXERCISE 3.16

Compose sentences about three mistakes you've made—or three good deeds you've done in the past—that you'll probably repeat in the future.

EXERCISE 3.17

Combine each of these pairs of sentences by using an "After" or a "Once" clause in the present perfect tense. You may want to use the contracted form of have (*'ve*) as some of the preceding examples do.

1. Lose ten pounds. Stop dieting.

2. Boil the broth for five minutes. Add the meat and seasonings.

3. Load the camera. Advance the film.

4. Finish your essay. Proofread it carefully.

5. Read the directions. Begin to take the test.

A NOTE ON THE PRESENT PERFECT PROGRESSIVE

The present progressive is formed with HAVE/HAS + BEEN + -ING: "I'm glad you finally got here. I *have been waiting* for an hour." The progressive form of the present perfect is used *only* for an action or a state that began in the past and *continues into the present.* It never appears with repeated actions or events that began and ended in the past, and it is not accompanied by words such as *already, ever, never, finally, at last,* or *yet.* Its purpose is to stress the *duration* or *continuity* of an activity or a state:

> We've been worshiping the sun for over 2,000 years. Come join us.

CORRECT: I *have been studying* English *since 1981.*

INCORRECT: I *have finally been passing* English.

CLASSROOM ACTIVITY 3.18

Make a list of five questions you might ask of a friend you haven't seen in several weeks. Compare your questions with those of your classmates, and decide which of them can be expressed by the progressive form of the present perfect—for example, "Have you been working hard?" Choose five of these questions to answer in complete, present perfect progressive sentences.

JOURNALS: MORE PRACTICE WITH THE PRESENT PERFECT TENSE

From 1875 through 1887, an American girl named Clara Whitney kept a diary of her experiences while living in Japan. At age sixteen, she paused to reflect:

> Just two years ago today we were in San Francisco. How vividly at these anniversaries does the past present itself to me. In spite of all my failures and mistakes, I believe I have grown in experience during these two years. It is very certain that I have seen a great deal of this world, met a great number of persons of every station in life and have been wonderfully let into their lives too, although how much good I've done to them I know not—I dare not ask. Two years ago I was doing just what got me into so much trouble this year—flirting.

Notice how the present perfect tense is used to indicate that these experiences began in the past but continue in the present.

JOURNAL EXERCISE 3.19

Although Clara's diary is usually filled with charming and vivid details, this particular entry lacks the specific information that would have made it more interesting. Use Clara's idea as a jumping-off point for a more detailed entry in your own journal. In a paragraph, summarize the strangest and most varied experiences you *have had* in the time you *have been* in this country. What *have* you *seen*? Who are some of the people you *have met* who *have let* you into their lives? What good *have* you *done* for them? Clara mentions that flirting *has gotten* her into trouble both in the United States and in Japan: end your own paragraph with a sentence or two about something you *have done* here that also got you into trouble in your own country.

PASSIVE VOICE CONSTRUCTIONS IN THE PRESENT PERFECT TENSE

As you've seen in some of the previous examples, advertising headlines often use the present perfect tense:

In 16 years, our magazine has featured 2,439 cars.

Warning: The Surgeon General Has Determined That Cigarette Smoking Is Dangerous to Your Health.

We've collected perfectly charming ideas
for you to give to favored men

Not many people have seen a bottle of Cruzan Rum. Most of it disappears in the Virgin Islands.

All of these examples are in the *active voice*; that is, they have subjects that are *performing the action*. How would you rewrite them in the *passive voice*, so that the subjects are not acting, but *being acted upon*, receiving rather than creating the action? The construction of the present perfect verb phrase in the passive voice is simply HAS/HAVE + BEEN + PAST PARTICIPLE. For example:

NOTICE.
DUE TO THE WILD NATURE OF LAST YEAR'S PARTY, THE FOLLOWING PEOPLE HAVE BEEN ASKED NOT TO ATTEND THIS YEAR'S PARTY.

Observe the difference between active and passive in these examples:

ACTIVE: The college *has announced* a new grading policy.

PASSIVE: A new grading policy *has been announced* by the college.

EXERCISE 3.20

Rewrite the four headlines above in the passive voice.

EXERCISE 3.21

Below is an excerpt from one student's response to Journal Exercise 3.19. Fill in each of the blanks with the appropriate form of the verb given. Although the dominant tense is the present perfect, you'll find that the simple present, past, and future tenses are also required. Watch out for the passive voice.

I [to be] _____ born 21 years ago. Since then, my

family and I [to travel] _____ from country to

country and [to experience] _____ many differ-

ent customs and cultures. We [to be] _____ in

Argentina, Mexico, Colombia, Panama, Venezuela, Peru, Israel, and the

United States, where I [to live] _____ for the past

few years.

Wandering from one country to another [to teach] _____

_____ me many things about myself and others. I

[to discover] _____ that most people [to want]

_____ the same things: family, friends, and security.

I [to learn] _____ that beginning a new life [to be]

_____ hard everywhere, but I [to have] _____

_____ to overcome this problem many times. When

I first [to come] _____ to the United States, for

example, I [to feel] _____ lonely, frightened, and

depressed. But since then I [to make] _____ a lot

of friends. I [to be exposed to] _____ many new

ideas and opinions, and [to be forced] _____ to

take care of myself. Now I [to think] _____ I

[to find] _____ myself because I [to know] _____

_____ what I [to want] _____

to do with my life. I [to study] _____ to become an

accountant for two years and I [to enjoy] _____

every minute. I [to expect] _____ that I [to continue]

_____ to love this work for the rest of my life.

EXERCISE 3.22

Change the underlined verbs in the selection below from the past tense to the present perfect. You will also have to eliminate exact dates and times of events. How does the meaning of the paragraph change when it is rewritten in the present perfect?

The last five years <u>were</u> difficult ones for me. In January of 1980, I <u>sprained</u> my ankle several times, which <u>ended</u> my career as a ski instructor. That spring, I <u>began</u> to study the piano. I <u>practiced</u> for fourteen hours every day. I <u>ate</u>, <u>slept</u>, and <u>thought</u> nothing but music. I <u>stopped</u> seeing friends and <u>eliminated</u> books and movies from my life. In 1982, I <u>started</u> giving concert performances. In that year alone, I <u>traveled</u> to fifty cities and <u>lived</u> in cheap hotels. My manager repeatedly <u>told</u> me not to give up. He <u>sent</u> me encouraging letters with every bill. Last year I <u>attained</u> success: I <u>played</u> at the Albert Hall in London and <u>received</u> excellent reviews. My triumphs <u>brought</u> increases in both income and tension. I <u>took</u> weekend trips to the Italian Alps to relax. Last month, I <u>broke</u>* my right hand while skiing down a slope. Yesterday I <u>enrolled</u> in a training program for radio announcers.

Assignment: The How-to Essay

Choose a subject that interests you and begin working on your own process essay. You may wish to combine some practical advice with humorous observations, as in this paragraph which one student wrote in response to Afsaneh Basnejad's paper on "How to Learn English" (pp. 93–96). Here, the writer gives advice on how to meet Americans in order to practice your English:

---

* Can you use the present perfect here?

As a rule, it isn't easy to find anyone to talk to in a big city like New York. However, some tips will improve your chances. First, get (or borrow) a dog and walk him several times a day. Americans love pets, especially dogs, and usually stop to talk to anyone with a dog. Second, try to eat in cafeterias. People generally share tables and will sometimes complain about the weather, their boss, or the food to a stranger. (You may wonder what sort of food Americans do eat. The answer is simple: nothing but junk foods like hot dogs and pizza.) Next, bring your dirty clothes to a laundromat. It takes about an hour and a half to wash and dry them, and many people will be waiting with you. They often pass the time talking to the other customers, so you may get a chance to practice your English.

—Shahram Namanim

You may select a topic for your paper from one of three general categories:

1. *Practical*—How to Buy a Used Car, How to Succeed in a _____ Course, How to Plan a Party . . .

2. *Abstract or Emotional*—How to Recover from a Broken Heart, How to Overcome Shyness, How to Accept Defeat . . .

3. *Humorous*—How to Arrive on Time for an 8 A.M. Class, How to Make Intelligent Conversation in an Elevator . . .

The composing process we've reviewed in this chapter should help you with your essay. Now that you're ready to begin working on a how-to paper, you may want to proceed in the following way:

1. Look through your journal to see what topics you've been thinking, reading, and writing about.

2. Once you've decided on a subject, ask yourself specific questions about the process you intend to describe.

3. Make a list—or a brief, informal outline—that offers concrete answers to the questions you've raised. Write down all the specific details and examples you can think of to support your main points.

4. Perhaps do some "research" by reading about your topic or talking with friends who might know something about it.

5. Arrange your ideas in a logical order, and use transitions to make your paper sound smooth and coherent.

6. Read your first draft aloud—preferably to a friend or classmate—and listen carefully for missing transitions, choppy sentences, ideas that may need further support, and so on.

7. Put your paper away for a day or two before you attempt to revise it. You'll be able to analyze it more objectively when you haven't seen it for a while.

As an additional step after you've written the first draft of your paper, go through the preposition review on the following pages. Then exchange papers with a classmate to edit for possible errors in preposition use.

Function Word Review: Prepositions

Prepositions are among the most troublesome function words for ESL students. They are used in a good many of our expressions concerning time, space, direction, and manner, but to non-native speakers, the rules governing their usage may seem quite arbitrary. Edward T. Hall, an anthropologist, gives this example of how differences in the way various languages use prepositions really reflect different ways of thinking about space, time, and natural events:

> We [native English speakers] say, "I'll see you *in* an hour." The Arab says, "What do you mean, 'in an hour'? Is the hour like a room that you can go in and out of it?" To him his own system makes sense: "I'll see you before one hour," or "I'll see you after one week." We go out *in* the rain. The Arab goes *under* the rain.

Of course, prepositions of time, space, and manner are indispensable to writers of the how-to essay. Before you submit the final draft of your process paper, review the following summary of preposition rules and examples.

A preposition shows the relationship between a noun or pronoun and the other words in a sentence. The preposition may be one word (*for, since, above, by, with*) or a phrase (*in back of, on top of, by way of*).

Three of the most common prepositions are *in, on,* and *at*; they can be used as prepositions of time, place, or manner. It may help you to think of these three words in visual terms:

in = surrounded by; beneath the surface

on = in contact with a surface or time line

at = a point on a diagram, map, or clock

PREPOSITIONS OF TIME

A. One point in time: *in, at, on*

The first time I saw her was . . .

in   December
1948   (for months, years, seasons, parts of
the winter   the day)
the morning, the afternoon

at*
4:00
midnight
night
noon
(for a more specific point in time)

DINNER AT 8. A.M.OR P.M.?

on Monday
December 13, 1948
(before days of the week or day of the month)

B. Extended time: *for, during, since, from—to*:
For is frequently used with a specified number of minutes, weeks, years, etc., or in such expressions as *for a while, for a few hours,* and so on.

For 50 years, our customers have been enjoying the best.

During, used with the definite article, refers to a block of time. Whereas *for* usually implies continuous action, *during* suggests intermittent action:

It snowed for six hours. (continuously)

It snowed during the night. (on and off for six hours)

HAS NOTHING NEW HAPPENED IN THE SCIENCE OF KEEPING FIT DURING THE PAST 1,000,000 YEARS?

Since refers to a period of time extending from some point in the past to another point in the past or present:

---

* Compare *at* and *by*: Be there *before* 4:00
 at 4:00 (precisely 4:00)
 by 4:00 (not later than 4:00)
 after 4:00

Since 1970, when his first food column was published, **DeLuca has written over 500 recipes.**

Note: In the above examples, observe the use of the present perfect and present perfect progressive tenses.

From—to; *From—until*: Both expressions state the period of duration for an event.

Open Today, Sunday,
in New York and Springfield
from 12 to 5 p.m.;
in White Plains and Garden
City from 11 a.m. to 6 p.m.;
in Stamford from 12 to 6 p.m.

But only *from—to* can be used to refer to *place,* or to refer to an entire *range* of items:

Bargains range from panettone to potholders.

On the Road From Nazareth To Bethlehem

PREPOSITIONS OF PLACE

A. The point itself: *in, inside* (surrounded by); *on* (the surface); *at*

**ONE OF THE
WORLD'S GREAT SPAS
IS IN FLORIDA.**

That cheese on your pizza may not be cheese.

SUCCESS IS A MATTER OF BEING AT THE RIGHT PLACE, AT THE RIGHT TIME.

Note: In American English, *at* usually indicates a specified location; *in* refers to a location *within* a building, city, country, etc.

He lives *on* Pine Street *in* Philadelphia.

I'll meet you *at* the main desk *in* the library.

B. Higher than the point: *over, above*; farther than the point: *past, beyond*

C. Lower than the point: *under, underneath, beneath, below*

Days sunning off the Greek Isles.

Nights dancing under the stars in Venice.

D. Neighboring the point: *near, by, next to, off, among, between, against, behind, in back of, in front of, beside**

THE WORLD'S MOST LUXURIOUS AIRLINE INTRODUCES THE ONLY NON-STOP FLIGHTS BETWEEN NEW YORK AND LAS VEGAS.

And suddenly the nine-to-five world you left behind you seems very far behind you indeed.

E. In the direction of, or moving from point to point: *around, across, through, to, toward, out of, into*

---

* Don't confuse the preposition *beside* (on one side of) with the conjunctive adverb *besides* (in addition).

COME WITH US TO THE BAHAMAS, THROUGH THE CARIBBEAN, AROUND THE MEDITERRANEAN, UP TO ALASKA, AND ACROSS THE CANAL.

Note the difference between *in* and *into*: *in* usually refers to *place,* whereas *into* usually refers to *motion:*

The car was *in* the garage.

The car pulled *into* the garage.

EXERCISE 3.23

Below is a map from Betty Bao Lord's novel, *Spring Moon,* showing a nobleman's estate in China during the 1890s. Write a paragraph telling someone how to get from point A to point F, using as many prepositions of place as you can.

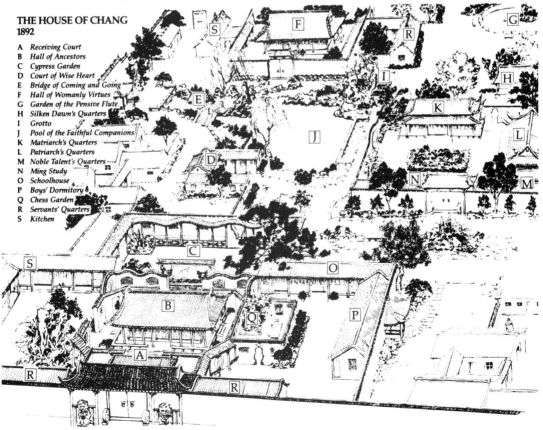

THE HOUSE OF CHANG
1892

A   Receiving Court
B   Hall of Ancestors
C   Cypress Garden
D   Court of Wise Heart
E   Bridge of Coming and Going
F   Hall of Womanly Virtues
G   Garden of the Pensive Flute
H   Silken Dawn's Quarters
I   Grotto
J   Pool of the Faithful Companions
K   Matriarch's Quarters
L   Patriarch's Quarters
M   Noble Talent's Quarters
N   Ming Study
O   Schoolhouse
P   Boys' Dormitory
Q   Chess Garden
R   Servants' Quarters
S   Kitchen

PREPOSITIONS OF MANNER

by, on, in, like, with:

> You can travel from San Francisco to Seattle *by train, by ship, by bus, by car,* or *by plane.*
>
> I even know someone who made the trip *on foot*—and *on purpose!*
>
> Of course, by the end of her journey she was walking *like* an ape, *with* her knuckles on the ground.
>
> So I think I'll go to Seattle *in a car, with* pleasure.

PREPOSITIONS OF AGENT AND PURPOSE

A. *By* and *with* are used to indicate the *agent* or *instrument* by which an action is performed:

> The play was performed *by* amateurs.
>
> She sliced the turkey *with* a carving knife.

B. *For* is used to mean *on behalf of* or *for the purpose of*:

> I'd like to make reservations *for* two people *for* dinner at 8:00.

TWO-WORD VERBS AND IDIOMS

Two-word verbs, and many idioms, consist of common verbs and prepositions:

Tonight...call off your curfew.

The brand-new album that starts where others left off

START OUT WITH 25¢ OFF. END UP WITH YOUR BEST CHECKUPS.

Cast off for new horizons—fairwinds, freshwater, sunshine, the smell of pine, and warm sandy shallows. Take off and take it easy—Ontario's resorts await you. Hike, boat, swim, sail, go riding, play golf or tennis. Come day's end, gather round for fish fries, old fashioned barbecues and new found friendship. Slip away for a while.

And many prepositional phrases, used idiomatically, give *visual* clues as to their meaning. For example:

> If you're *in the dark* about prepositions, you may feel as though you're *in hot water, up against the wall, up a tree,* and *at sea.* But with a little practice, these words will be *at your finger tips*—that is, *on the tip of your tongue.* Now you've been alerted: stay *on your toes.*

For a discussion of prepositions used in phrasal combinations, see Appendix 2.

EXERCISE 3.24

Fill in the blanks with appropriate prepositions:

I am supposed to meet my friend Eva _____ 1:00 today _____ the information desk _____ the train station _____ Market Street. I hope she is _____ time; my mother made reservations _____ the restaurant _____ five people _____ 7:30, and Eva and I have a lot to discuss _____ then.

I have not seen my friend _____ six months. _____ July, she has been traveling _____ a station wagon _____ the U.S., all the way _____ Maine _____ California. Unfortunately, her car broke down somewhere _____ San Diego and Los Angeles, so she had to return _____ train. She has been _____ the train _____ Tuesday. I'm sure she'll be relieved when the train pulls _____ the station.

EXERCISE 3.25

_____ Thursday, September 23, the musical *Cats* will come _____ the Winter Garden Theater. *Cats* will have preview performances _____ two weeks, and will officially open _____ October 7. The play—based

_____ a book _____ T. S. Eliot, and _____ music by Andrew Lloyd Webber—received enthusiastic reviews when it opened _____ London _____ 1981. _____ 1981, it has played _____ packed audiences, and will probably continue to run _____ some time _____ England.

Reservations _____ *Cats* can be made _____ mail or telephone. Tickets are now on sale _____ the box office _____ the Theater, which is located _____ 50th St. and Broadway _____ New York City. The box office opens today _____ 10 A.M. You can also purchase tickets _____ calling Telecharge, which is open _____ 8 A.M. _____ midnight, seven days a week; _____ group sales, call 239-6262.

unit 3 | Description

4 | Setting the Scene

The Descriptive Essay

Chances are that at some point in the process essays you wrote for Chapter 3, many of you included a description of what the finished product was supposed to look like. The next two chapters are designed to strengthen your powers of observation and your ability to describe a scene or a person in sufficient and accurate detail, so that your reader can say, "Yes, I can see that—I know what you mean."

Rarely does an essay consist entirely of description, but description is usually an essential element of the stories you tell, as well as the definitions, explanations, and arguments you write. For example, if you want to convince your reader that your city's health care services are inadequate, you might begin your essay by describing the run-down, understaffed health care center in your neighborhood. A specific and developed description encourages the reader to see something through your eyes, from your point of view. It helps *persuade* the reader to accept your thesis.

We have already seen how an essay is built around a thesis, or principal idea. The descriptive paragraph or essay is no exception. In a description, your thesis may be implied rather than stated outright, but having a central idea about your subject is crucial for organizing all the details you record. Obviously, you cannot write down every single detail about the appearance of a room or a person—nor would you want to. Instead, you select the important elements of your subject: like a photographer, you put a frame around the picture you wish to present to your reader.

The photograph on page 116, taken by Diane Arbus at the entrance to America's most famous amusement park, illustrates the importance of a dominant impression or focus in description. Study it for a few moments.

CLASSROOM ACTIVITY 4.1

After studying the Arbus photograph, write brief answers to the questions on page 116 in your notebook, and compare your observations with those of your classmates:

Diane Arbus, *A Castle in Disneyland, California, 1962.* Copyright © 1972 by the Estate of Diane Arbus. Print by Neil Selkirk.

A.) What mood or emotion does the photograph convey to you? If you had to pick one word to describe the feeling you get from this picture, what word would you choose?

B.) Now think about *why* you chose that word. What exactly do you see in the photo? List all the elements you observe. What objects did the photographer focus on to suggest a particular mood?

Abstract and Concrete

In the preceding activity, you were asked to make a general statement about the photograph and to support it with specific details. The generalization, or broad statement, is an *abstract* idea that you back up by pointing to specific details, or *concrete* evidence. Our minds, in fact, naturally operate along these lines. We tend to imagine an abstract concept like "sadness" or "innocence" in terms of its concrete illustrations, and, in turn, we have an inborn talent for grouping specific examples under broader categories of generalization.

In a recent experiment, researchers attempted to analyze this mental process. Subjects were asked to voice their thoughts while writing an essay. The experimenters then tried to diagram their subjects' thought patterns. The following diagram portrays—in concrete, observable form—one writer's stream of thought as it branches out in various directions and entertains new ideas from the unconscious.

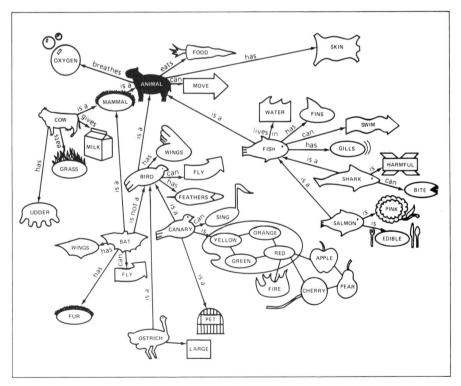

The semantic network: *Unlike a computer, which retrieves data according to a fixed program, the mind—as this diagram illustrates—can creatively summon up words, images or memories by proceeding along one or several interlacing networks of association.*

We can see that the human mind is arranged in far more complex ways than the computer's memory. As a result, when we write or speak, a single word or vague idea can set our minds racing through a vast map of creative routes.

As the chart shows, the general term "animal" led this writer to think of sub-categories such as *bird, pet,* and *canary.* Which of these three terms is the most specific? Which is the most general—that is, the most inclusive? Another group of associations on the chart includes *food, fish,* and *salmon:* which of these words is the most specific?

EXERCISE 4.2

Take five minutes now and try free-associating in your notebook on one word, suggested by your teacher, such as "swim," "danger," or "bread." Set down on paper whatever images or thoughts come into your head. Then re-read what you have written and pick out the most specific phrases and images.

Now exchange your freewriting with a classmate. As you will see, almost any piece of freewriting demonstrates this play between abstract and concrete. What different concrete details did your classmate associate with the abstract word?

When asked to freewrite for five minutes about the word "bread," for example, these students went in strikingly different directions:

> Bread is food for our body. Bread is also the food for our soul; it is the symbol of the body of Christ which we witness every time we go to church and in our daily meal. Man does not live by bread alone—he needs some sleep.
> Our body does not live by bread alone. We must have three kinds of food every day, food for our stomach, food for our spirit, and food for our heart.
> Stomach, spirit, and heart must be fed equally for us to survive in this crazy world.
> Bread is something to share while also sharing needs.
>
> *—Joselito del Fierro*

> Bread is a very important food, but it has changed with the times. It was wonderful when people made it at home and with natural ingredients. It's true that it took a lot of time to make bread that way, but it was worth it. When people bake bread at home, the whole house smells great and you get hungry. Christmas bread is the kind I like best, but I don't have any idea about how to prepare it. I would like to learn.
>
> *—Dulce Maria Morales*

> I don't know how to write about bread.
> They have two famous kinds of bread in America. One is Taystee and the other is Wonder Bread. These two bread companies are in competition with each other. I don't know which one is better—I don't even like bread. My

country's main meal is rice. When I came here, I started to eat bread, but I still don't know which bread tastes better. . . .

—*Ayoung Kim*

In a small country in South America, the death announcement of bread came over the radio. It read, "We are all here to pay our last respects to bread, sometimes known as dough, the son of flour, cousin of barley, brother of lard, butter, salt, and sugar. The uncle of biscuits, crackers, cookies, and pastries. Bread was the favorite friend of many at breakfast. It died because of a flour shortage, which led to the strangulation of bread and finally death."

—*Mary Harry*

Using Details in Descriptive Writing

We continually define our ideas and feelings with images that are highly specific. Cartoonist Charles Schulz made this point in his comic-strip collections, *Happiness Is a Warm Puppy* and *Security Is a Warm Blanket*—statements that became so popular they are now clichés to the American public. It is doubtful that these cartoons would have had such widespread appeal with titles like *Happiness Is a Warm Feeling* or *Security Is the Sense of Being Protected from Harm*. Instead, Schulz was able to make an abstract term like "happiness" meaningful and touching by equating it with a specific word picture—a concrete illustration that was fresh and original, yet at the same time immediately recognizable.

Today, books based on such humorous "definitions" continue to capture the public imagination. One such example can be found at the top of the best-seller list on the first page of Chapter 3. In *Real Men Don't Eat Quiche*, author Bruce Feirstein offers a satirical definition of the "Real Man of the 1980s"—an updated version of the "tough guy" John Wayne always played in the movies. To poke fun at this American stereotype, Feirstein begins with a series of general observations, and then proceeds to list specific examples of what today's "Mr. Macho" does or does not do. For instance:

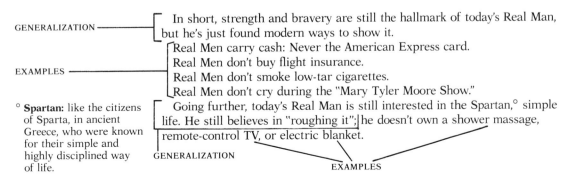

GENERALIZATION ⎡ In short, strength and bravery are still the hallmark of today's Real Man, ⎣ but he's just found modern ways to show it.

EXAMPLES ⎡ Real Men carry cash: Never the American Express card.
Real Men don't buy flight insurance.
Real Men don't smoke low-tar cigarettes.
⎣ Real Men don't cry during the "Mary Tyler Moore Show."

° **Spartan:** like the citizens of Sparta, in ancient Greece, who were known for their simple and highly disciplined way of life.

⎡ Going further, today's Real Man is still interested in the Spartan,° simple life. He still believes in "roughing it"; he doesn't own a shower massage, ⎣ remote-control TV, or electric blanket.

GENERALIZATION

EXAMPLES

° **floss:** to use dental floss, waxed thread used to clean between teeth.
° **Snoopy:** a comic-strip beagle created by Charles Schulz.

> Real Men don't floss.°
> Real Men don't use zip codes.
> Real Men don't have telephones in the shape of Snoopy.°

EXAMPLES

EXERCISE 4.3

Create a few humorous or serious definitions of your own (Security is _____; Real Students don't _____, etc.), equating an abstract word or concept with a specific image. What is success? anxiety? wisdom? Try to come up with your own satirical or sincere definition of a "real man" or a "real woman."

Our writing clearly derives vitality and expressive power from this movement back and forth between the abstract theme and its concrete demonstrations. Take a look at how Beatles John Lennon and Paul McCartney used rhetorical questions to state the *general idea* of lonely people in the chorus of their song, "Eleanor Rigby." Rhetorical questions do not require answers; they are used in speech and writing to introduce or emphasize a theme. In the three verses of the song, what specific details are used to illustrate that general theme?

Eleanor Rigby

Aah, look at the lonely people.
Aah, look at the lonely people.

Eleanor Rigby picks up the rice in the church
Where a wedding has been
Lives in a dream.
Waits at the window
Wearing the face that she keeps in a jar by the door.
Who is it for?

(Chorus)
All the lonely people,
Where do they all come from?
All the lonely people,
Where do they all belong?

Father McKenzie writing the words of a sermon
that no one will hear
No one comes near.
Look at him working
Darning his socks in the night when there's nobody there.
What does he care?

All the lonely people,
Where do they all come from?
All the lonely people,
Where do they all belong?

Aah, look at all the lonely people.
Aah, look at all the lonely people.

Eleanor Rigby died in the church
And was buried along with her name
Nobody came.
Father McKenzie wiping the dirt from his hands
As he walks from the grave
No one was saved.

All the lonely people,
Where do they all come from?
(Aah, look at all the lonely people.)
All the lonely people,
Where do they all belong?
(Aah, look at all the lonely people.)

—John Lennon
Paul McCartney

CLASSROOM ACTIVITY 4.4

A.) How do Lennon and McCartney's portraits of Eleanor Rigby and Father McKenzie clarify our understanding of the abstract feeling of loneliness?

B.) Feelings are abstract, but they are often expressed in physical, observable ways. For instance, students might infer that their new teacher is nervous when they see him biting his lips, running his fingers through his hair, dropping the chalk, and so on. (For additional clues, you can turn to Kuan Kuan Wei's description of her lab teacher on pages 164–165.) From your own experience and your observations of others, can you describe what people look or act like when they are (1) nervous, (2) embarrassed, (3) proud, (4) angry? How many illustrations can you supply for these words?

Point of View in Descriptive Writing

DESCRIBING MOODS AND FEELINGS

Let's look at the opposing emotions triggered in two students who responded to the general topic of "Saturday night" in their journals. What is the *main idea* in each of these entries? How does each writer help you to understand this idea?

It's Saturday night again and the journal topic is to describe a Saturday night. Our teacher played a joke on us. She drew a picture after the word "night" on the board and then wrote two more words after it, "Have fun." To a foreign student, Saturday night is just another night to watch lovers in doorways, people singing at bus stops, hearth fires in houses. Solitude is the word which he can taste. It is bitter and usually nibbles the heart of a lonely exile.

—Dickson Lam

To me, my time is like a bird who will fly away unless I cage him in a tight schedule. But when a bird becomes a pet, he is usually given some time for freedom and relaxation. People know that a pet bird does not misuse his liberty, but comes back to his cage as soon as his free-flying time is over.

After a long term of practice, my well-scheduled time is now like a pet bird. It stays in its schedule-cage all week, and then takes little flights on weekends, especially on Saturday night. On that day my time flies around without giving a care about cleaning, cooking, or homework. It pays no attention to the seriousness of my English language study. It only flies and flies, thinking about downtown in the city, nearby shopping malls, elegant restaurants, or a gorgeous evening party at a friend's house.

Sometimes I worry that he will fly away from me forever, and I chase him around, even on a pleasant Saturday. I try to get him back into his schedule-cage, but he plays a hide-and-seek game on that particular day. He takes me to my friend's house, to a dance, or to a magnificent restaurant.

At last I get tired, and I just let time go as he pleases. I sit down, turn on soft music, and relax with a drink. My time playfully flies, flies, and flies far . . . far beyond my vision. The weekend passes. On Monday morning I see my bright-faced time is back in his cage again.

—Bani Lahiri

Each of these selections effectively communicates the author's mood. It is not surprising that the same topic can evoke gaiety from one writer, gloom from another. What is interesting to note, however, is that both writers associate the same basic elements with Saturday night: the English homework assignment that the foreign student must complete over the weekend, people singing and dancing, the warmth of gatherings in the city or at home.

These observations are the factual, verifiable components in both selections. It is the writer's *point of view* that colors what he describes and accounts for the difference between the two reports. Whereas the first author writes (on this occasion, at least) as an outsider or "lonely exile," the second writer is a participant in the festivities she depicts. The writer's selection of detail according to a particular slant, or angle of vision, is called *slanting*. The following chart shows how each writer's *attitude* influences his or her choice of details, modifiers, and images:

	FIRST WRITER	SECOND WRITER
Saturday night is	just another night	that particular day a pleasant Saturday time for freedom and relaxation

Saturday night is
a time to
	watch:
	   lovers in doorways
	   people singing at bus
	     stops
	   hearth fires in houses
		think about:
		   downtown in the city
		   nearby shopping malls
		   elegant restaurants
		   a gorgeous evening
		     party at a friend's
		     house
		
		go to:
		   a friend's house
		   a dance
		   a magnificent restaurant
		
		sit down
		turn on soft music
		relax with a drink

Saturday night is
like
(central image)
	solitude: a word
	       he can taste
	       it is bitter
	       it nibbles at
	          the heart
		a pet bird:
		   he playfully flies
		   without giving a care
		   plays a hide-and-seek
		     game
		   bright-faced, comes
		     back to his cage

JOURNAL EXERCISE 4.5

This week, use your notebook to explore any especially intense mood or emotion—such as fear, joy, or anxiety—that you have experienced recently. What scene or incident do you associate with the feeling? What "word picture" can you summon up to help the reader understand what you felt?

DESCRIBING OBJECTS: FOOD FOR THOUGHT AND VICE-VERSA

It goes without saying that moods and feelings are subjective, or personal. But even in the case of the most neutral topic, it is difficult to imagine a purely objective description. Because any object can be viewed from a variety of perspectives, the writer must choose one point of view, comparable to a thesis or main idea, about the object to be described. Most descriptions are composed with a specific purpose in mind—to illustrate or clarify, instruct, entertain, persuade, and so on. The writer's purpose determines the focus and organization of the description.

EXERCISE 4.6

Compare, for example, how the following writers treat the subject of food from various points of view. As you read, keep these questions in mind:

A.) What is the writer's chief *purpose* in each selection? What is the *focus* of each paragraph?

B.) Does the writer seem to have a particular *attitude* toward the topic? If so, what words indicate this personal reaction? If the writer does not reveal a "slant," how is objectivity conveyed?

C.) Which *senses* does the writer appeal to? Try to underline the most vivid verbs and concrete nouns. How are adjectives and adverbs used to persuade?

° **aficionado:** (Spanish) an enthusiastic admirer; a "fan."

Bring a large pot of salted water to the boil (a tablespoon or two of oil in the water helps keep the pasta separate). Add the spaghetti, ravioli, talierini or whatever, a little at a time to keep the water boiling all the while. The different pasta shapes cook for varying amounts of time: fresh noodles cook in four to five minutes, no longer, whereas dried thick lasagne may take fifteen to twenty minutes. Some aficionados° have their own fool-proof methods of testing for doneness, such as flinging a strand of spaghetti against the wall (if it sticks to the wall, it's cooked), but we find that simply tasting is the best method. Run a strand of the pasta under cold water for a moment to cool it quickly. If it tastes done but is still firm, it's ready.

—*David and Marlena Spieler,* Naturally Good

In the morning they rose in a house pungent with breakfast cookery, and they sat at a smoking table loaded with brains and eggs, ham, hot biscuits, fried apples seething in their gummed syrups, honey, golden butter, fried steak, scalding coffee. Or there were stacked battercakes, rum-colored molasses, fragrant brown sausages, a bowl of wet cherries, plums, fat juicy bacon, jam. At the midday meal they ate heavily: a huge hot roast of beef, fat buttered lima beans, tender corn smoking on the cob, thick red slabs of sliced tomatoes, rough savory spinach, hot yellow corn bread, flaky biscuits, a deep-dish peach and apple cobbler spiced with cinnamon, deep glass dishes piled with preserved fruits—cherries, pears, peaches. At night they might eat fried steak, hot squares of grits fried in egg and butter, pork chops, fish, young fried chicken.

—*Thomas Wolfe,* Look Homeward, Angel

Technological innovation has done great damage not only to reading habits but also to eating habits. Food is now available in such unpleasant forms that one frequently finds smoking between courses to be an aid to digestion.

* * *

Civilized adults do not take apple juice with dinner.

* * *

Bread that must be sliced with an ax is bread that is too nourishing.
—*Fran Lebowitz,* Metropolitan Life

His heart astir he pushed in the door of the Burton restaurant. Stink gripped his trembling breath: pungent meatjuice, slop of greens. See the animals feed.

Men, men, men.

Perched on the high stools by the bar, hats shoved back, at the tables calling for more bread no charge, swilling, wolfing gobfuls of sloppy food, their eyes bulging, wiping wetted moustaches. A pallid sweetfaced young man polished his tumbler knife fork and spoon with his napkin. New set of microbes. A man with an infant's saucestained napkin tucked round him shovelled gurgling soup down his gullet. A man spitting back on his plate: halfmasticated gristle: no teeth to chewchewchew it.

—*James Joyce*, Ulysses

This last example might seem rather difficult at first glance. Begin by looking up the definitions of any unfamiliar words, paying special attention to all the *-ing* verbs and adjectives in the selection. Next, find the topic sentence of the excerpt. What *comparison* forms the basis of Joyce's description of the Burton restaurant? What words reinforce that comparison? Now read the selection aloud: what is the effect of the repeated sounds in a phrase like "gurgling soup down his gullet"? What is the purpose of a word combination like "chewchewchew"? Do you have an appetite after reading this description?

JOURNAL EXERCISE 4.7

Describe the scene of a family dinner or holiday feast that comes to memory—or describe any event involving food. Make the scene as inviting or repellent as you can.

EXERCISE 4.8

Invent your own product—a new chain of fast food restaurants, a beverage, a beauty cream, a mousetrap. . . . Then compose a magazine advertisement or a television commercial to sell it to your audience. Naturally, your description should make the product as attractive as possible. You may use visual aids such as drawings or photographs to help you sell the product. And don't forget to start off with an eye-catching headline or title.

DESCRIBING PLACES

You can see that effective writing employs precise words, phrases, and comparisons that leave a particular impression in the reader's mind. The clarity of the image you wish to create depends upon your attention to detail. Your job, like the painter's, is to make every stroke of your "brush" reveal some aspect of the person, place, or object you are painting.

Consider, for example, the way Edgar Allan Poe sets the scene for one of his best-known horror stories, "The Fall of the House of Usher." What is the dominant mood of Poe's opening paragraph? (You might want to read this aloud to get the full effect.) The narrator of the tale begins:

During the whole of a dull, dark, and soundless day in the autumn of the year, when the clouds hung oppressively low in the heavens, I had been passing alone, on horseback, through a singularly dreary° tract of country, and at length found myself, as the shades of evening drew on, within view of the melancholy° House of Usher. I know not how it was—but, with the first glimpse of the building, a sense of insufferable gloom pervaded my spirit. . . . I looked upon the scene before me—upon the mere house, and the simple landscape features of the domain—upon the bleak walls—upon the vacant eye-like windows—upon a few rank sedges°—and upon a few white trunks of decayed trees—with an utter depression of soul. . . .

° **dreary** and **melancholy** both mean gloomy or depressing. (Melancholy usually refers to human sadness, whereas dreary most often applies to a scene.)

° **sedges:** grass-like plants

CLASSROOM ACTIVITY 4.9

Poe's narrator gives us the essentials for a spooky scene: the ancient house with its vacant "eyes," the bleak landscape of rotting weeds and decaying trees. With the other members of your group, continue this haunting description of the house and its surroundings. Use Poe's paragraph as a starting point for your own more detailed vision of horror.

An alternative suggestion: You are still surveying the scene through the eyes of Poe's narrator. The great door slowly swings open, and you enter the darkened hallway of the House of Usher. Describe the room you see before you.

Now contrast the mood of Poe's paragraph with the tone of the following description. In this excerpt from Catherine Drinker Bowen's autobiography, *Family Portrait,* the author recalls the cottage on the New Jersey shore where she spent many summers of her childhood:

° **indigenous:** native to an area.

There was a special smell to the cottage at Beach Haven, indigenous,° I think, to the Jersey shore. The minute one opened the front door one met it—a combination of dampness, beach sand, old wicker furniture, oil from the guns that stood racked with the fishing rods in the little west room off the hall. Whatever the mixture, to my nostrils it was very sweet. This whiff, this musty breath meant running barefoot on the beach, bathing in the foam of the breakers.° It meant sailing on the bay, crabbing from the dock, riding one's bicycle on the wide yellow-pebbled streets, easy and free. . . .

° **breakers:** waves.

The memories of Beach Haven run all to smells and sounds and sights; they are physical, of the blood and appetite, as is natural to summertime. At the west end of Coral Street the marshes began, turning soft with color at sunset, pink and lilac and golden green. The ocean beach at low tide lay hard underfoot, wet sand dark below the water line. On the dunes—we called them sandhills—we played King of the Castle or slid down on our

° **bloomers:** old-fashioned underclothes for women.

bloomer° seats, yelling with triumph and pure joy. The floors of Curlew Cottage, the chairs, even the beds were sandy. Always a lone sneaker sat beneath the hall sofa; by August our city shoes were mildewed in the closets, and towels were forever damp.

EXERCISE 4.10

What is the prevailing mood of this passage? Underline the phrases in which Bowen conveys this feeling with "smells and sounds and sights."

Autobiographies often begin with a description of a special place recollected from the author's childhood. The writing assignment that follows asks you to consider this question: With what scene would you begin your autobiography?

Assignment: The Significant Scene

Think about a place that has particular meaning for you—the house you lived in as a child, a movie theater or a playground where you spent many hours—and try to capture its unique qualities in a detailed description. Choose the most precise words and phrases you can to re-create this place and your feeling for it. Can you use all five senses in your description? Make a list of everything you recall, and then group these items into sensory details of sight, sound, smell, taste, and touch, in addition to memories you associate with the scene. What is your chief impression of the place you have chosen to describe?

You might, instead, choose a familiar locale (your bedroom, the classroom, a student hangout) or an unfamiliar one (a laundromat, a luncheonette) and write down as many observations as you can. Then compose a description using these details to enable your reader to experience this place as you have.

It is important to remember that good writing is a cycle of drafting and revising. Here is how one student, Su-Chuan Tsai, proceeded with the assignment. The steps she followed may help you with your own essay.

Step one: Writers often begin with a journal entry or freewriting. Su-Chuan's in-class freewriting shows the writer starting out with a broad topic —"Grandmother's home"—and gradually narrowing it down to separate rooms and specific items of furniture:

When I was a child, my favourite place was my grandmother's home. It was full of beautiful memories.

Grandma's home was at the fourth floor of an apartment. I used to look out from the window observing people walking and cars running down on the street.

I remember that grandma had a huge fish tank which had hundreds of gold fish in it. I was so naughty to put my hand in the tank trying to catch them. It was fun to till fish started to die. I was scared to death that the fish would take revenge on me for what I had done to them.

Sometimes, my brothers and I pretened that we were pirates, and jumped from one piece of furniture to another one; those furnitures were supposed to be our battle ships. And our base camp was grandma's bed. It was a heavy wooden bed enclosed in three sides which made it an ideal castle.

After long period of wild fighting, we would stop fighting and had some ice cream and cookies. However, I loved to hang around in the kitchen where I could always find delicious food being cooked on the stove.

Step two: When she had finished, Su-Chuan decided that Grandmother's bed was the focal point of her memories of the house.

Step three: She then made a list of the general characteristics of the bed, organized according to the five senses. Under each heading, she grouped all the details she could recall about the bed. Notice how the task of summoning up these sensory impressions seems to have brought back many specific images, and, in turn, generated a second list of memories associated with the bed:

Physical details
  looks like a box { solid
                { strong

✗ fine details of carving: even though carvings are in such
             ~~forms that~~ fragile forms, the impression
              I have is that the bed is strong.

✗ color of the bed: color has darken over the years, so it
              reminds me of what life was like decades
        ago.

✗ the bed dominates the whole room (things around it did
not seem important.)

  there is an equivalent bed in Western culture — the canopy
bed.   Both are elegant but my grandma's bed is so
strong.   grandma's bed - ~~ying~~ yang
          canopy bed - ~~yang~~ ying

✗ smell of wood (sweet)
  smell of grandma's cream
  smell of cookies: we weren't supposed to, but ~~sometimes~~
             we ate snakes — candy, cookies — and
             got crumbs in the bed.

  durability of bed: made to be passed on through generations
             of the family. When my uncle get
             married, the bed was given to him.
             And my uncle is going to pass the bed
             to his eldest son, ~~but~~ I wish I could
             have ~~the~~ bed.

Memories
✗ wedding night → romantic ideas.
✗ games - a tent, we were camping
        a castle, imagine ~~base on~~ the pictures that I
          had seen of European castles and I
          pretended ~~that~~ I was a princess.

play house
jumping on the bed → shook and ~~creaked~~ creaked
we tried to make a rhythm
like a drum on the bed
low bench to step up on the bed: When I was small, I
couldn't reach the bed.
I had to climb on the
bench to get on the bed.
When I sat on the edge,
my legs dangled.
& carvings { I know some of the stories (ancient Chinese
made up some of my own.   legends & myths)

Step four: Su-Chuan re-read her list. She came to the conclusion that her *primary recollection* was of the bed as a "child's castle"—a place where she and the other children in the family played and acted out imaginary scenes. This was what she really wanted to talk about in her essay: the notion of an "imaginary world" became the *controlling idea* of her first draft:

```
            Grandmother's Bed

                                            stood
    In the center of my grandmother's bedroom ~~standed~~ a

wooden bed which always received praises from her visitors.

In their eyes, it was a piece of fine antique, but in a

child's eyes, it was more than that.

    The bed was about seven feet wide, seven feet long, and

ten feet high, which included the height of the posts and

the roof of the bed.  Aside from the body of the bed, three

sides were enclosed with wooden boards which extended from
         base
the ~~bast~~ of the bed half way up to the roof.  It was made of

timber of lichee, which is found only in southern China.
                                    darkened        the
The color of the material had ~~been darken~~ through ∧ages, and

made a strong contrast with the surrounding white walls.
```

Can I make my description clear here, and tighten some of these sentences?

This is a new idea - I should make it a new ¶.

Because this bed was one part of Grandmother's dowry, the base of the bed was decorated with the elaborate classical Chinese motif that symbolized good luck and fertility. I used to imagine ~~image~~ that on Grandmother's wedding night, Grandmother, a shy ~~and~~ young bride, sat ~~sit~~ quietly on the edge of her bed and waited patiently for her husband. [That was such a romantic scene!] *do I need this?*

Do the ideas in this ¶ belong together?

The board ~~body~~ of the bed was plain wood~~en~~ ~~board~~. One of my favorite games ~~game~~ was to dance and jump on the bed with my brothers and cousins. We were too ~~so~~ happy to worry ~~that the bed~~ about the sound that the bed made. Luckily, the bed did not crash.

Can I find a word to describe this sound?

In winter Grandmother placed a thick cotton mat *another new idea* on top of the bed to keep her warm, but in summer she slept directly on the wooden board, which remained cool even on ~~in~~ a hot day. [However, if one is not used to sleeping ~~sleep~~ on a hard surface, he might have serious backache in the next morning.]

Maybe this should be in the next ¶.

does this add anything?

After my grandfather died, I spent ~~spend~~ most of my childhood in Grandmother's home. I remember how cozy ~~comfortable~~ it was to sleep next to Grandmother; the familiar smell of her night cream mixing ~~mixed~~ with the sweet scent of the natural wood accompanied me to my dreams ~~?~~

As I have mentioned earlier, the bed was closed in three directions. All the sides were carved with folk stories. On the edges of the bed were some two-inches tall human figures in different positions ~~with different postures~~. They were so realistic that people could see the expressions of their faces. I even remember that there was a portion depicting a young sage who rescued his playmate from drowning. Sometimes I pretended that I was one of the characters in the board and made my own stories.

Is this clear?

Can I combine some of these sentences?

From the four corners of the base were four posts which supported the wooden ceiling of the bed. Also the roof was

Does this ¶ have a main idea?

carved into ~~hallow~~ *hollow* geometric patterns.   A mosquito net was

placed on the roof.   When the mosquito net was free and

draped, I ~~imaged~~ *imagined* that I was sleeping in a tent.

[margin note: My ending doesn't mention grandma!]

In a child's eyes, this huge and heavy bed was a

castle where she could have daydreams or ~~played~~ *play* with her

friends.   Moreover, it was a treasury of beautiful memories.

Su-Chuan Tsai

[handwritten note, left: Can I reorganize this to make it easier to follow? Maria said that I jump around a lot. Maybe I should describe the bed in the first half, and then show why it was such a special place in the second half.]

[handwritten note, right: Maria also noticed that I describe sights, sounds, and smells. I should mention that I loved to touch the carving on the bed, too.]

Step five: This first draft shows the author's sensitivity to objects, emotions, and recollections. It is brimming with beautifully realized details. The organization is a problem, however, chiefly because the writer is wrestling with two main ideas. Let's look more closely at the structure of the paragraphs. Observe how almost every paragraph shifts from physical details to memories:

#2. General description → memory (Grandmother's wedding night)

#3. Description (wooden board) → memory (children playing) → description (the bed in summer and winter)

#4. Memory (the smell of Grandmother's cream)

#5. Description (carvings of folk stories) → memory (making up stories)

#6. Description (posts and roof of bed) → memory (sleeping under the mosquito net)

Step six: Su-Chuan's next step was to get "objective" listeners for her essay. A few students remarked that they were somewhat confused by the organization of the paper. With their comments in mind, she re-read her composition and made notes for revision in the margin.

Step seven: Su-Chuan then returned to her list to pick up fresh ideas she hadn't used in the first draft. More important, she found the idea that helped her organize her revision: the *durability* of the bed and the family tradition that it represents. She was now ready to compose her second draft:

Grandmother's Bed

In the center of my grandmother's bedroom stood a wooden bed which always received praises from her visitors. In their eyes, it was a fine antique, but in a child's eyes, it was more than that.

When you walked into the bedroom, all you noticed was the bed itself. It stood ten feet high, and was about seven feet wide and seven feet long. From the four corners of the base rose four slender posts that supported the wooden ceiling of the bed, which was carved into hollow geometric patterns. Three wooden sides enclosed the bed, so that it looked like an enormous box. The bed was made of timber of lichee, which is found only in southern China, and is valued for its durability. The rich red wood had darkened with time, and made a strong contrast with the surrounding white walls.

Because this bed was one part of Grandmother's dowry, the base was decorated with the elaborate classical Chinese motif that symbolized good luck and fertility. I used to imagine that on her wedding night, Grandmother, a shy young bride, sat quietly on the edge of her bed and waited patiently for her husband. The bed was intended not just for Grandmother, though. It was made to last, for it would be passed on through generations of the family. When my uncle got married, the bed was given to him. And my uncle will pass the bed on to his eldest son some day.

Even though Grandmother's bed will never belong to me, I will always have my memories of it. One of my favorite games was to dance and jump on the bed with my brothers and cousins. We tried to make a rhythm like the beating of a drum, and we were too happy to worry about the creaking sound that the wood made. When we were tired of this, we would smuggle cookies and cake from the kitchen and have a small picnic in the middle of the bed.

I also enjoyed being alone on the bed. Its sides were carved with ancient Chinese legends and myths, and along the top of the edges were several two-inch human figures in various poses. They were so realistic that people could see the expressions on their faces. There was even a portion depicting a young sage who rescued his playmate from drowning. I loved to close my eyes and run my fingers across the cool, smooth wooden figures. Sometimes I pretended that I was one of the characters in the carvings and made up my own stories. Because the bed reminded me of the old European castles I had seen in pictures, I often imagined that I was a princess or a queen. Other times, when the mosquito net was down, I dreamed I was living in a tent.

After my grandfather died, I spent most of my childhood in Grandmother's home. In winter Grandmother placed a thick cotton mat on top of the bed to keep her warm, but in summer she slept directly on the wooden board, which remained cool even on a hot day. I remember how cozy it was to sleep next to Grandmother; the familiar smell of her night cream mixing with the sweet scent of the natural wood accompanied me to my dreams.

In a child's eyes, this huge and heavy bed was a castle where she could have daydreams or play with her friends. Best of all, here she always felt loved and secure with Grandmother.

—Su-Chuan Tsai

As you can see, in the revised version, Su-Chuan's thesis remains the same —the bed was a fine antique, but was also something more than that. Most of the details, too, are the same; what has changed in the second draft is the structure. This is how the details are now presented:

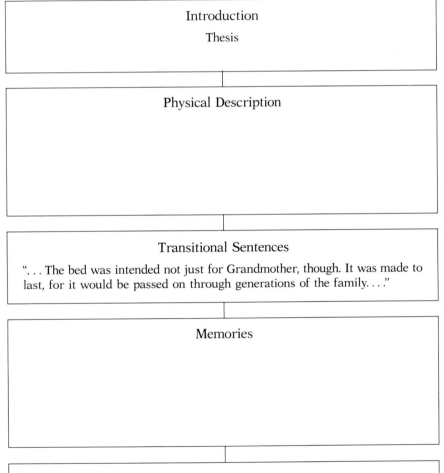

Introduction
Thesis

Physical Description

Transitional Sentences

". . . The bed was intended not just for Grandmother, though. It was made to last, for it would be passed on through generations of the family. . . ."

Memories

Conclusion

The last paragraph unites the three ideas of the essay: the durability of the bed, the bed as a child's castle, and the child's sense of security with her grandmother.

Before you begin revising your description, we'll pause to look at a few ways of building on simple sentence patterns to express more complex relationships between ideas and clauses. Brief, simple sentences are often effective, but a writer's options are limited when he or she relies upon only a few sentence patterns. As the writing samples in this chapter illustrate, effective prose depends in part on the variety of sentence patterns and combinations that skillful sentence combining can produce. The following section introduces a few of the ways in which sentences can be gracefully combined.

Sentence Combining with Coordinators and Subordinators

USING COORDINATORS

As we noted in our summary of basic sentence patterns in Chapter 2, any part of a sentence—subjects, verbs, completers, or modifiers—can be expanded by using coordinating conjunctions such as *and, or,* and sometimes *but*:

SUBJECTS: *Children, teenagers, and adults* will love the circus.

VERBS: The monkeys *walk tightropes and ride unicycles.*

OBJECTS: Vendors sell *popcorn, soda, ice cream, and hot dogs.*

MODIFIERS: The clowns are *sad but funny.*

These coordinating conjunctions can also be used to expand sentences by combining independent clauses. As you know, an independent clause is a group of words that contains a subject and a predicate and can stand alone as a complete sentence. One easy way to join simple sentences is to use a comma + a coordinating conjunction to form a *compound sentence:*

    The phone rang.
+   I didn't answer it.
=   The phone rang, but I didn't answer it.

Pick out the coordinator in each of the following headlines:

Watch For Lucky Numbers
And You Could Be Watching
A Free TV.

"Right! All the Hilton International hotels have Teleplan, so I'll call again after the Athens meeting."

AT $100 A SEAT IT COULD HAVE BEEN A BLEAK HOUSE ON BROADWAY BUT DICKENS PROVED A SMASH

You get remarkable print quality
or you get your money back.

Notice that advertising headlines often join independent clauses with only a coordinating conjunction. The comma is sometimes left out when the clauses in a compound sentence are very short. You'll never be incorrect, however, if you include the comma.

Because each of the coordinators signals a different relationship between the independent clauses it connects, it's important to choose the one that best expresses the relationship you intend. Here are the seven coordinators and their customary uses:

and (also, in addition)　　　　　*so* (as a result)
but and *yet* (in contrast)　　　　*for* (because)
or (indicates alternatives)
nor (used to set up a second negative that means *and not, or not, and neither*)

A NOTE ON *NOR*

Clauses that begin with *nor* reverse the usual order of the subject and X-word:

He never worked, nor *did he* ever want to work.

Notice that in the *nor* clause, *never* turns into *ever*:

　　I've never seen a flying cow.
+ I *never* want to see one.
= I've never seen a flying cow, nor do I *ever* want to see one.

Clauses that begin with *and so* or *and neither* also reverse the subject and X-word:

I love pizza, and so *does my dog.*
I don't like spinach, and neither *does my dog.*

EXERCISE 4.11

Make each of these groups of simple sentences into compound sentences by using commas and an appropriate coordinator. Use each coordinator at least once.

1. Speak softly. Carry a big stick.

2. The child was exhausted. He couldn't fall asleep.

3. The team struggled to win. They knew it was their last chance.

4. Money can't buy happiness. Many people sacrifice love for it.

5. I called him before. There was no answer. I'll try again later.

6. You must get some sleep. You'll be exhausted in the morning. You won't be able to concentrate.

7. My sister doesn't go to school. She doesn't have a job.

EXERCISE 4.12

Combine the pairs of sentences below by using *nor, and neither,* or *and so*:

1. My little brother is afraid of the dark.
   I am afraid of the dark.

2. My little brother isn't afraid of the dark.
   I'm not afraid of the dark.

3. The students didn't want to go to school.
   The teachers didn't want to go to school.

4. The cat never caught a mouse.
   She never tried to catch a mouse.

EXERCISE 4.13

Some writers fall into the "weak *and*" trap: they use *and* when another coordinator would be a far better choice. Edit the following paragraph, replacing *and* with a different coordinator wherever there is a more suitable choice:

I know of a park that is beautiful and tranquil, and very few people go

there. It has many trees, and the birds have a variety of places to build

their nests. In the park, I can admire the surroundings, and I can simply

sit and think. Sometimes I bring a book with me, and I often forget to

read it, and I daydream about wonderful things. I am never disturbed

here, and I never feel alone, and I have the company of nature.

USING SEMICOLONS AND COLONS

Another way to join two independent clauses is by placing a *semicolon* (;) between them:

"The computer does all the calculating for you; all you do is make the decision. **"**

Steady nerves and a quiet mind are not things we go out and find; they are things we create.
JOHN R. MILLER

In this sense, the semicolon is like a weak period. Use it to join two related sentences to which you want to give equal emphasis. But remember, the semicolon acts as a coordinator, or *balance*, so there must be an independent clause on either side of it:

_____ **;** _____.

The *colon* (:) is also used to join independent clauses that are closely related. The colon tells your reader to sit up and pay special attention to the clause ahead: it points to a significant detail, example, or explanation in the second clause.

Among a few katydid species, sex roles are reversed: aggressive females compete for choosy males. Why?

OTHER USES OF THE SEMICOLON AND THE COLON

There is only one other use of the semicolon. When you are listing a number of items, and the items themselves contain commas, use semicolons to set off the main items. For example, without the semicolons in the sentence below, the reader might think that the governor was accompanied by six people rather than three:

The governor was accompanied by her husband, a lawyer; her son, a banker; and her daughter, a medical student.

Other uses of the colon include:

1. To introduce a list of items or examples—

   On the menu were a variety of tempting dishes: mussels marinara, prime ribs of beef, roast duck, barbequed chicken, lasagne, and fresh Dover sole.

   There are three types of athletes: those who win, those who lose, and those who simply play the game.

2. To introduce a long or a formal quotation—

   We should remember the words of Franklin Delano Roosevelt: "The only thing we have to fear is fear itself."

EXERCISE 4.14

We've looked at three ways of forming compound sentences. Join each of the pairs of simple sentences below with the method you think best communicates the relationship between the clauses. Be prepared to explain your decision.

1. The boys had devoured hot dogs, hamburgers, potato salad, and french fries. They still complained of hunger.

2. Ask not what your country can do for you. Ask what you can do for your country.

3. My neighbor never asks for help. He never offers help.

4. That skinny girl eats all the time. She never gains weight.

5. He went to bed early. He'll feel rested tomorrow.

6. Be smart. Invest in art.

7. He refused to apologize. He believed he had done nothing wrong.

8. I can finish my homework now. I can do it later.

9. The class was dreadful. I learned nothing.

10. Thinking is the sport of the mind. It exercises the brain.

USING SUBORDINATORS

The following headlines illustrate another way to combine sentences. Can you explain how they are different from the compound sentences you've just formed?

MAKE $12,200 FOR COLLEGE WHILE YOU'RE GOING TO COLLEGE.

If you stick with the herd, you could end up as a lamb chop.

BEFORE MAN MADE FIRE, THE EARTH MADE PERRIER.

When a hotel is letter–perfect, guests keep coming back.

As warmer weather approaches, fragrances turn lighter and cooler.

"We sailed to a lovely little Bermuda cove where we were the only couple."

The leading typewriter corrects mistakes after they're made.

Each of these headlines is made up of two clauses. But only one of the clauses in each sentence is an independent clause. Use the yes-no question test to find the clause in each of these headlines that is able to stand alone as a sentence. This part of the sentence, of course, conveys its main idea. Can you now explain why the other clause is *not* independent?

When a sentence contains two or more clauses that are not of equal importance, one is *subordinate to,* or *dependent upon,* the other. Sentences composed of both dependent and independent clauses are called *complex sentences,* and the connecting words that make a clause dependent are called *subordinators.*

All of the subordinate clauses in the headlines above are *adverbial* clauses. That is, they are groups of words with a subject-verb unit that act as adverbs. Below is a list of subordinators that commonly introduce adverbial clauses:

TIME: *before, after, as, when, while, until, since*

PLACE: *where*

CONTRAST: *although, even though, though, while, whereas*

CAUSE OR RESULT: *because, since, as, inasmuch as, so that, in order that, that*

CONDITION: *if, unless, in case, provided that, in the event that*

EXERCISE 4.15

Underline the subordinators in the headlines on page 142.

EXERCISE 4.16

As you can see from the list, adverbial subordinate clauses can communicate time, place, cause, result, condition, or contrast. Underline each of the subordinate clauses in this selection. What general rule can you now form for the punctuation of subordinate clauses when they come *before* the main clause? When they come *after* the main clause?

Before I came to the United States to study, I lived in a small town where everyone knew one another. There was always someone around if you wanted company. When I first arrived here, I didn't know anyone. It was difficult for me to make friends until my English improved. Although I had studied English at home, my pronunciation was very hard to understand. After I had spent several months in English classes, I was able to talk to Americans comfortably. I now find it easy to make friends wherever I go because I can speak the language quite fluently.

CLASSROOM ACTIVITY 4.17

We've taken a paragraph from one student's response to the Edgar Allan Poe paragraph on page 127, but we've rewritten it in simple sentences, which destroys much of its effect. Form groups of four or five students, and work together on ways to combine these sentences so that the passage reads more fluidly. Try to vary your use of coordinators, subordinators, semicolons, and colons. (After each group has agreed on its revision, your teacher may ask you to write the different versions on the blackboard.) Discuss why you made the changes that you did and how those changes affect the meaning of the paragraph. Which revision does the class feel is most effective? Why?

I had been riding in the snow for more than two hours. Suddenly I found myself plunged in thick fog. I could see little around me. Trails of mist were moving through the air. I don't know how. I don't know when. I found myself standing in front of a dilapidated old mansion. The gloomy darkness glided silently over my head. A cloud of heavy mist descended slowly from the wild mountains. The mist shrouded the dead landscape. I walked toward the house. A wolf howled. It broke the mystic silence of the night. It sent chills through my body. The house looked threatening. I had nowhere else to go. I would soon die from the freezing air.

EXERCISE 4.18

Here's another paragraph from a student's descriptive essay. We've not only taken his sentences apart, but we've also added punctuation errors. Correct any run-ons, comma splices, or fragments, and combine choppy sentences:

I was 17 years old. When I spent 9 months living in a school dormitory. My life there with the other "dormies" was fascinating. I can remember the noisy nights. I can remember the dark halls. I can remember the smell of freshly washed clothes. The scrambling clatter of feet. The alarm clock pierced the air. In the early morning long lines of hungry students waited on the stairs of the cafeteria, I can see the girls, blonds and brunettes, I can hear the silly comments from the guys. They walked past. After we had eaten and were on our way to class. I can remember the happy times. We had finished our exams. We all gathered in one room we celebrated. There were frustrating times. When everything went wrong and homesickness knocked on our doors.

Function Word Review: Articles

One of our students vibrantly recaptures the summer afternoons she shared with a friend in the countryside of Greece. In the following excerpt from her essay, we have deleted many of the articles. To find out how much you already know about article usage, fill in each blank with *a, an,* or *the.* If no article is needed, place an <u>X</u> in the blank:

We explored the countryside together. We liked to call ourselves "the New Robinsons." We became excited when we discovered _____ new area of _____ countryside. In late afternoon, we loved to sit on _____ big rock with _____ two deep crevices, under _____ old olive tree, watching _____ sun changing colors in _____ sky. When _____ chameleon appeared in _____ grass, we liked to watch it, as it changed its colors according to _____ colors of the weeds and the earth. We discussed how people seem like chameleons in the way they try to please. As the night fell around us and changed _____ colors into gray, we were still sitting on _____ big rock, wondering and dreaming about _____ future. Perhaps it would be our last summer in _____ country.

During the summer noons we liked to wear _____ big straw hats and _____ very large glasses, and walk around _____ big yards of _____ house, or in _____ streets of the village. When at last we felt exhausted by _____ hot sun of the noon, we fell asleep until late afternoon.

Our great enjoyment was to steal fruits from the surrounding orchards. In our afternoon promenade in the fields, we climbed trees and found branches with _____ fresh ripe pears and plums. We cut the fruits down with _____ great pleasure and ate them very hurriedly because we didn't want _____ stranger's eye to see us, so the syrups dripped from our mouths and we always returned home with _____ dirty dresses.

—Koula Markantonatous

CLASSROOM ACTIVITY 4.19

Pair up with a classmate and compare your results. Can you explain the reason behind your choice of *a, an, the,* or <u>X</u>? The following review of articles should help to answer your questions about article usage.

WHEN TO USE INDEFINITE/DEFINITE/NO ARTICLES

The smallest English words are often the ones that create the greatest confusion for the non-native speaker. The most common function words in the English language are the definite and indefinite articles, *the, a,* and *an,* which modify nouns. An article is always used before a singular countable noun. Whether the article is definite or indefinite depends upon the context of the sentence. Here are the most important differences between definite and indefinite articles:

INDEFINITE ARTICLES (A, AN)

1. *A* is used before a word that begins with a consonant sound; *an* is used before a word that begins with a vowel sound.

2. The indefinite article is used before an unspecified noun, usually a singular countable noun.

3. Sometimes the indefinite article means *one* or *each.* This meaning often applies to expressions of time such as "*a* week ago," "*a* year before," "*a* month from now," "ten dollars *a* week."

4. The indefinite article is never used before a plural noun. (Don't be confused by nouns that have the same form for singular and plural, such as *series, scissors,* and *species.*)

DEFINITE ARTICLE (THE)

1. *The* can be used before both singular and plural nouns.

2. *The* specifies a *particular* noun; it serves to restrict the meaning of the noun that follows it.

3. Commonly *the* is used before nouns that are followed by identifying phrases, such as *that, of,* and *for* phrases.

4. *The* is used when a speaker or a writer is referring to a noun that has been identified in previous comments, or when referring to a noun that is familiar to the listener or reader.

5. *The* precedes the proper names of rivers, oceans, mountain ranges, and deserts.

In most cases, the article is not used with a plural countable noun—unless that noun is modified by an identifying phrase. In this instance, the definite article is used. For example:

> *Books* are often fun to read.
> *The history books I read* were fascinating.

> She collects *antiques.*
> *The antiques that she collects* are from colonial times.

One common exception to this rule occurs when a speaker or a writer is referring to a noun that has already been identified in the context of his comments, or when he has particular members of a noun class in mind. A statement such as "The boys were always fighting" or "The dogs barked all night" points to a specific group of boys or dogs.

No article is used for the proper names of countries, cities, or towns unless the name of the place is a plural noun or includes an identifying phrase. This identifying phrase is usually an "of" or a "that" phrase. For example:

New York
The New York *that* I love is full of life.

America
The United States *of* America

Roslyn
The Village *of* Old Roslyn

France
The Union *of* Soviet Socialist Republics

The Netherland*s*

The Philippine*s*

Determiners other than articles—words such as *your, one, another, this,* and *that*—can replace the definite article:

Your idea will solve *one* problem.

That woman never smiles.

Another class is held in *this* room.

Some of, none of, most of, one of, any of, and *each of* are *never* preceded by an article:

Some of the students complained about the test.

Most of them had studied hard.

One of my classmates didn't know any of the answers.

Each of the questions was worth ten points.

However, *the* follows *some of, none of, most of, one of, each of,* and *any of* unless a possessive pronoun, a possessive proper noun, or a plural demonstrative (*these, those*) follows the phrase instead. For example:

Some of *the* books are missing from my desk.

Some of *my* books are missing.

Some of *Paul's* books are lost.

Some of *these* books are helpful.

Most of *the* faculty agrees with the President.

None of *the* snow has melted.

Do you know any of *those* people?

EXERCISE 4.20

Fill in the blanks below with the correct article or determiner. If no article is required, put an <u>X</u> in the blank:

1. Buying _____ house is often _____ excellent invest-

   ment. _____ house that my parents own has doubled in value

   over _____ past ten years.

2. _____ year ago, he was earning $2,000 a month.

3. _____ cats don't usually like _____ dogs, but _____

   _____ cat loves them.

4. _____ California that my grandparents grew up in was largely
   undeveloped land.

5. _____ most of _____ students haven't had any of

   _____ exams yet.

6. When I was in _____ Philippines, I stayed in _____
   Manila.

Uncountable Nouns

Certain English nouns are called *uncountable* because they name some-thing that cannot readily be counted as a single object. As a rule, an article is not used with an *uncountable noun*. Uncountable nouns fall into the following categories:

- *Mass Nouns:* liquids such as water, coffee, tea, ink, and rain; gases such as air, oxygen, nitrogen, and smoke; solids made up of many tiny particles such as sugar, pepper, snow, ice, and sand.

- *Abstract Nouns:* whereas *concrete* nouns name physical objects that we can see or smell or touch, abstract nouns represent ideas or concepts

or qualities that cannot be perceived by our senses. Examples of abstract nouns are love, peace, beauty, greed, justice, life, freedom, wisdom, misery, sadness, loneliness, happiness, health, success, security, nature, and truth.

- *Names of Subject Areas and Recreational Activities:* music, economics, computer science, art, English; swimming, football, baseball, singing, dancing.

Below are examples of other common uncountable nouns:

advice	baggage	bread
darkness	discrimination	equipment
eternity	frailty	furniture
hair	happiness	grass
homework	honesty	hardware
information	intelligence	infinity
mankind	merchandise	luggage
money	patience	misery
nature	property	pollution
poverty	trouble	scenery
superiority	vocabulary	violence
wealth		

work (when it means a job or chores)

Uncountable nouns are treated as singular subjects and take singular verbs:

Milk contains calcium.

Coffee keeps me up at night.

Swimming is a favorite summer activity.

Math has always been difficult for me.

Honesty is the best policy.

No article is used before an uncountable noun *unless that noun is modified by an identifying phrase.* Then *the, a,* or *an* can be used depending upon the context of the sentence. For example:

Love is blind.

A love that is pure is rare.

The love that I have for you is great.

Indefinite adjectives (*some, more, many, any, much,* etc.) are often used with mass nouns to show indefinite quantities:

Food with *some* sugar in it can give you *more* energy.

Teaching requires *much* patience.

There hasn't been *any* rain in weeks.

Mass nouns may also be preceded by units of measure to indicate quantity:

Children should drink *three glasses* of milk every day.

She toasted *four slices* of bread.

To make this punch, you'll need *two quarts* of fruit juice, *three tablespoons* of sugar, and *three cups* of wine.

EXERCISE 4.21

Look at these model sentences. Can you write down the rule that explains each of the underlined articles (or lack of an article) in these examples?

1. I ate <u>an</u> apple with my lunch.

2. Everyone likes <u>a</u> good joke.

3. I have <u>a</u> football and <u>a</u> baseball in my garage, but <u>the</u> football isn't mine.

4. She hates _____ bananas.

5. _____ Students often neglect their homework.

6. <u>The</u> books from our attic are dusty.

7. <u>The</u> apples that I picked were not yet ripe.

8. _____ Experience is the best teacher.

9. He is a man who possesses _____ wisdom.

10. There are many ways to enjoy _____ life.

11. I love _____ football.

12. I enjoy _____ English.

13. I want <u>the</u> dress that is in <u>the</u> shop window.

14. <u>The</u> math that I studied this semester was very difficult.

15. <u>The</u> book is on <u>the</u> table.

16. I like _____ milk and _____ cookies.

17. Professional athletes practice for several hours <u>a</u> day.

18. _____ Many of _____ my friends live on <u>the</u> West Coast.

19. Most people put _____ sugar in their _____ tea.

20. <u>A</u> new comedy series starts on _____ Monday night.

EXERCISE 4.22

Now analyze the following sentences taken from student papers. Explain why the use of articles is or is not correct. Then rewrite all incorrect sentences.

1. Communication exists in all forms of life.

2. The person who is responsible for assigning computer should often go to see if there are empty machines.

3. I want to go to the beach today.
   I want to go to a beach today.

4. Since there were no witnesses, he really got into the trouble.

5. At registration you will see crowd of students waiting in long lines.

6. The most of the students are intelligent, but some are not.

7. One of my friends is in game room when he should be studying the English.

8. When I go to the library, I always forget my library card.

9. A bouquet of roses is a perfect gift on Valentine's Day.

10. When couple live together, they can divide the household chores.

11. Most of people have some education.

12. I live in the South Side of Chicago, but I used to live in South Jersey.

13. I can't believe beauty of that girl.

14. I am amazed at intelligence that my friend possesses.

15. Money can't buy the happiness.

16. Money can't buy the happiness that I want.

17. The accounting is fun.

18. I enjoy reading before I go to bed.

19. Science that I took when I was in tenth grade was biology.

20. I went to Spain month ago.

EXERCISE 4.23

Before you submit your revised description, exchange papers with a classmate and edit each other's work for possible article errors.

5 | Describing People

Portraiture

Examine each of the four portraits of women by well-known artists on the following pages.

CLASSROOM ACTIVITY 5.1

Begin your discussion of each painting by listing all of the specific details you observe. From these observations, what conclusions can you draw about each woman—that is, what *inferences* can you make on the basis of what you see? In each portrait, can you name one particular impression or mood conveyed by the artist? What insight do you have into the character of the woman? What details does the portraitist use to communicate this central idea?

Each of these pictures is the artist's interpretation of his subject: each highlights one clue to the character of the sitter. This organization of details around a central impression or focus is what we attempt to achieve in written description as well. The prose portrait, like the painting, tries to re-create its "real-life" subject for the reader.

Jean-Honoré Fragonard, *The Love Letter*.
The Metropolitan Museum of Art,
The Jules Bache Collection, 1949.

Pablo Picasso, *Gertrude Stein*, 1906.
The Metropolitan Museum of Art,
Bequest of Gertrude Stein, 1946.

Camille Pissarro, *Girl with a Switch*, 1881.
Musée du Louvre, Paris.

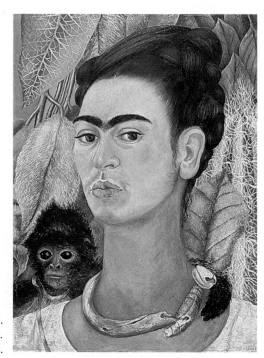

Frida Kahlo, *Self-Portrait with Monkey*, 1938.
Albright-Knox Art Gallery, Buffalo, New York.
Bequest of A. Congre Goodyear, 1964.

Observing Those Around Us

As we noted in the previous chapter, autobiographies often begin with a description of a special place recalled from childhood. Just as frequently, autobiographies open with a description of a parent, for who else has such a profound and lasting effect on our lives? To take one recent example, when the well-known newspaper columnist Russell Baker applied himself to the task of writing his memoirs, he began with a portrayal of his mother as he sees her now and contrasted this image with the vigorous young woman he remembers from his youth.

What follows is Chapter One of Baker's autobiography, *Growing Up*. As you read this selection, pay special attention to the wide variety of methods and devices the author employs to animate this touching description of his mother: imagined scenes and extended dialogue, personal memories and family anecdotes, photographs, letters, and close observation. How does Baker use these devices to illustrate his central idea, or thesis, about his mother's character?*

At the age of eighty my mother had her last bad fall, and after that her mind wandered free through time. Some days she went to weddings and funerals that had taken place half a century earlier. On others she presided over family dinners cooked on Sunday afternoons for children who were now gray with age. Through all this she lay in bed but moved across time, traveling among the dead decades with a speed and ease beyond the gift of physical science.

"Where's Russell?" she asked one day when I came to visit at the nursing home.

"I'm Russell," I said.

She gazed at this improbably overgrown figure out of an inconceivable° future and promptly dismissed it.

° **inconceivable:** incapable of being conceived; unbelievable.

"Russell's only this big," she said, holding her hand, palm down, two feet from the floor. That day she was a young country wife with chickens in the backyard and a view of hazy blue Virginia mountains behind the apple orchard, and I was a stranger old enough to be her father.

Early one morning she phoned me in New York. "Are you coming to my funeral today?" she asked.

It was an awkward question with which to be awakened. "What are you talking about, for God's sake?" was the best reply I could manage.

"I'm being buried today," she declared briskly, as though announcing an important social event.

---

* In addition to providing a glossary for some of the words in this selection, we have *italicized* certain words whose meaning can be guessed from the root of the word or from the context of the paragraph in which the word appears. When you come to an italicized word, try to figure out its meaning, and jot down a synonym or brief definition in your notebook. When you have finished reading, consult your dictionary and your teacher to see how close you came to the actual definition of the word.

"I'll phone you back," I said and hung up, and when I did phone back she was all right, although she wasn't all right, of course, and we all knew she wasn't.

She had always been a small woman—short, light-boned, delicately structured—but now, under the white hospital sheet, she was becoming tiny. I thought of a doll with huge, fierce eyes. There had always been a fierceness in her. It showed in that angry, challenging thrust of the chin when she issued an opinion, and a great one she had always been for issuing opinions.

"I tell people exactly what's on my mind," she had been fond of boasting. "I tell them what I think, whether they like it or not." Often they had not liked it. She could be sarcastic to people in whom she detected evidence of the *ignoramus* or the fool.

"It's not always good policy to tell people exactly what's on your mind," I used to caution her.

"If they don't like it, that's too bad," was her customary reply, "because that's the way I am."

° **formidable:** arousing fear and admiration.

And so she was. A formidable° woman. Determined to speak her mind, determined to have her way, determined to bend those who opposed her. In that time when I had known her best, my mother had hurled herself at life with chin thrust forward, eyes blazing, and an energy that made her seem always on the run.

She ran after squawking chickens, an axe in her hand, determined on a beheading that would put dinner in the pot. She ran when she made the beds, ran when she set the table. One Thanksgiving she burned herself badly when, running up from the cellar oven with the ceremonial turkey, she tripped on the stairs and tumbled back down, ending at the bottom in the debris of giblets, hot gravy, and battered turkey. Life was combat, and victory was not to the lazy, the timid, the *slugabed*, the *drugstore cowboy*,

° **libertine:** a person who acts without moral restraint.

the libertine,° the *mushmouth* afraid to tell people exactly what was on his mind whether people liked it or not. She ran.

° **inevitable:** incapable of being avoided or prevented.

But now the running was over. For a time I could not accept the inevitable.° As I sat by her bed, my impulse was to argue her back to reality. On my first visit to the hospital in Baltimore, she asked who I was.

"Russell," I said.

"Russell's way out west," she advised me.

"No, I'm right here."

"Guess where I came from today?" was her response.

"Where?"

"All the way from New Jersey."

"When?"

"Tonight."

"No. You've been in the hospital for three days," I insisted.

"I suggest the thing to do is calm down a little bit," she replied. "Go over to the house and shut the door."

Now she was years deep into the past, living in the neighborhood where she had settled forty years earlier, and she had just been talking with Mrs. Hoffman, a neighbor across the street.

"It's like Mrs. Hoffman said today: The children always wander back to where they come from," she remarked.

"Mrs. Hoffman has been dead for fifteen years."

"Russ got married today," she replied.

"I got married in 1950," I said, which was the fact.

"The house is unlocked," she said.

So it went until a doctor came by to give one of those oral quizzes that medical men apply in such cases. She failed catastrophically,° giving wrong answers or none at all to "What day is this?" "Do you know where you are?" "How old are you?" and so on. Then, a surprise.

° **catastrophically:** disastrously.

"When is your birthday?" he asked.

"November 5, 1897," she said. Correct. Absolutely correct.

"How do you remember that?" the doctor asked.

"Because I was born on Guy Fawkes Day," she said.

"Guy Fawkes?" asked the doctor. "Who is Guy Fawkes?"

She replied with a rhyme I had heard her recite time and again over the years when the subject of her birth date arose:

> "Please to remember the Fifth of November,
> Gunpowder treason and plot.
> I see no reason why gunpowder treason
> Should ever be forgot."

Then she *glared* at this young doctor so ill informed about Guy Fawkes' failed scheme to blow King James off his throne with barrels of gunpowder in 1605. She had been a schoolteacher, after all, and knew how to glare at a *dolt*. "You may know a lot about medicine, but you obviously don't know any history," she said. Having told him exactly what was on her mind, she left us again.

The doctors diagnosed a hopeless senility. Not unusual, they said. "Hardening of the arteries" was the explanation for laymen.° I thought it was more complicated than that. For ten years or more the ferocity with which she had once attacked life had been turning to a rage against the weakness, the boredom, and the absence of love that too much age had brought her. Now, after the last bad fall, she seemed to have broken chains that imprisoned her in a life she had come to hate and to return to a time inhabited by people who loved her, a time in which she was needed. Gradually I understood. It was the first time in years I had seen her happy.

° **layman:** one who does not have special or advanced training.

She had written a letter three years earlier which explained more than "hardening of the arteries." I had gone down from New York to Baltimore, where she lived, for one of my infrequent visits and, afterwards, had written her with some banal° advice to look for the silver lining, to count her blessings instead of burdening others with her miseries. I suppose what it really amounted to was a threat that if she was not more cheerful during my visits I would not come to see her very often. Sons are capable of such letters. This one was written out of a childish faith in the eternal strength of parents, a naive belief that age and wear could be overcome by an effort of will, that all she needed was a good pep talk to recharge a flagging° spirit. It was such a foolish, innocent idea, but one thinks of parents differently from other people. Other people can become frail and break, but not parents.

° **banal:** trite; predictable; *to look for the silver lining* (in a cloud) and *to count one's blessings* are worn-out expressions used for comforting someone.

° **flagging:** drooping; weakening.

She wrote back in an unusually cheery vein intended to demonstrate, I suppose, that she was mending her ways. She was never a woman to apologize, but for one moment with the pen in her hand she came very close. Referring to my visit, she wrote: "If I seemed unhappy to you at times—" Here she drew back, reconsidered, and said something quite different:

"If I seemed unhappy to you at times, I am, but there's really nothing anyone can do about it, because I'm just so very tired and lonely that I'll just go to sleep and forget it." She was then seventy-eight.

Now, three years later, after the last bad fall, she had managed to forget the fatigue and loneliness and, in these free-wheeling excursions back through time, to recapture happiness. I soon stopped trying to wrest° her back to what I considered the real world and tried to travel along with her on those fantastic swoops into the past. One day when I arrived at her bedside she was radiant.

"Feeling good today," I said.

"Why shouldn't I feel good?" she asked. "Papa's going to take me up to Baltimore on the boat today."

At that moment she was a young girl standing on a wharf at Merry Point, Virginia, waiting for the Chesapeake Bay steamer with her father, who had been dead sixty-one years. William Howard Taft was in the White House, Europe still drowsed° in the dusk of the great century of peace, America was a young country, and the future stretched before it in beams of crystal sunlight. "The greatest country on God's green earth," her father might have said, if I had been able to step into my mother's time machine and join him on the wharf with the satchels packed for Baltimore.

I could imagine her there quite clearly. She was wearing a blue dress with big puffy sleeves and long black stockings. There was a ribbon in her hair and a big bow tied on the side of her head. There had been a childhood photograph in her bedroom which showed all this, although the colors of course had been added years later by a restorer who tinted the picture.

About her father, my grandfather, I could only guess, and indeed, about the girl on the wharf with the bow in her hair, I was merely sentimentalizing. Of my mother's childhood and her people, of their time and place, I knew very little. A world had lived and died, and though it was part of my blood and bone I knew little more about it than I knew of the world of the pharaohs.° It was useless now to ask for help from my mother. The orbits of her mind rarely touched present interrogators for more than a moment.

Sitting at her bedside, forever out of touch with her, I wondered about my own children, and their children, and children in general, and about the disconnections between children and parents that prevent them from knowing each other. Children rarely want to know who their parents were before they were parents, and when age finally stirs their curiosity there is no parent left to tell them. If a parent does lift the curtain a bit, it is often only to stun the young with some exemplary tale of how much harder life was in the old days.

I had been guilty of this when my children were small in the early 1960s and living the affluent° life. It galled° me that their childhoods should be, as I thought, so easy when my own had been, as I thought, so hard. I had developed the habit, when they complained about the steak being

° **wrest:** to obtain as if by a violent, twisting, pulling motion.

° **drowse:** to be half-asleep; to doze.

° **pharaohs:** kings of ancient Egypt.

° **affluent:** rich.

° **galled:** irritated, "rubbed the wrong way."

overcooked or the television being cut off, of lecturing them on the harshness of life in my day.

"In my day all we got for dinner was macaroni and cheese, and we were glad to get it."

"In my day we didn't have any television."

"In my day . . ."

"In my day . . ."

At dinner one evening a son had offended me with an inadequate report card, and as I leaned back and cleared my throat to lecture, he gazed at me with an expression of *unutterable resignation* and said, "Tell me how it was in your days, Dad."

I was angry with him for that, but angrier with myself for having become one of those ancient bores whose highly selective memories of the past become transparently dishonest even to small children. I tried to break the habit, but must have failed. A few years later my son was referring to me when I was out of earshot as "the old-timer." Between us there was a dispute about time. He looked upon the time that had been my future in a disturbing way. My future was his past, and being young, he was indifferent to the past.

As I hovered over my mother's bed listening for muffled signals from her childhood, I realized that this same dispute had existed between her and me. When she was young, with life ahead of her, I had been her future and resented it. Instinctively, I wanted to break free, cease being a creature defined by her time, consign her future to the past, and create my own. Well, I had finally done that, and then with my own children I had seen my exciting future become their boring past.

These hopeless end-of-the-line visits with my mother made me wish I had not thrown off my own past so carelessly. We all come from the past, and children ought to know what it was that went into their making, to know that life is a braided cord of humanity stretching up from time long gone, and that it cannot be defined by the span of a single journey from diaper to shroud.

I thought that someday my own children would understand that. I thought that, when I am beyond explaining, they would want to know what the world was like when my mother was young and I was younger, and we two relics° passed together through strange times. I thought I should try to tell them how it was to be young in the time before jet planes, superhighways, H-bombs, and the global village of television. I realized I would have to start with my mother and her passion for improving the male of the species, which in my case took the form of forcing me to "make something of myself."

Lord, how I hated those words. . . .

° **relic:** an object or custom that has survived, wholly or partially, from the past.

CLASSROOM ACTIVITY 5.2

Use the following questions as a guide to a discussion of Baker's portrait of his mother:

- What incidents stand out for you in the story? Why? Pick out the details you find especially effective, and discuss how Baker uses them to convey his central impression of his mother.

- Locate at least three places where the narrative shifts from present to past or from past to present. What devices does the author use to signal a movement in time?

- Although the doctors diagnose his mother's illness as "hopeless senility" caused by hardening of the arteries, Baker believes her escape into the past is more complicated than that. What is his explanation for her behavior? Do you agree?

- Baker incorporates quite a bit of dialogue in this portrait. What can you tell about the speakers from their quoted speech?

- What does the author suggest was one reason for writing his autobiography? What other reasons might one have for writing an autobiography?

- What does this description of Baker's mother reveal about its author?

- Look at the last line in the selection. How might it act as a "bridge" into Baker's next chapter—what do you expect in Chapter Two of Baker's autobiography?

JOURNAL EXERCISE 5.3

A.) Baker includes family anecdotes to enrich his description. For example, he mentions the Thanksgiving when his mother fell down the stairs, burning herself badly with the hot turkey, giblets, and gravy. Spend ten minutes writing about a memorable or humorous incident that involved a member of your family—an anecdote you may someday want to tell your own children. What does the incident tell us about the person you are describing?

B.) Baker observes that "Children rarely want to know who their parents were before they were parents, and when age finally stirs their curiosity there is no parent left to tell them." Imagine you are writing your autobiography, and want to begin with a reminiscence about one of your parents, as Baker has done. In your journal, record a story you have heard about your mother or your father before they were parents. Perhaps, like Baker, you want to describe an old photograph that shows your parent at an early age. What does the story or photograph tell about your parent in the days before you were born? Does this "early portrait" explain anything about the way your parent appears today?

People-Watching

In this chapter, we will be working toward a full-length description of a person who interests you. You may wish to begin thinking about a person who has played a significant role in your life—a friend, a neighbor, a teacher, a relative.

On the other hand, you don't have to be intimately acquainted with your subject to write a great descriptive essay. These next three selections, in fact, were written by students who chose to describe people they didn't know—intriguing strangers who came into their lives for only an hour or so. Yet notice how much the authors were able to observe and to imagine about their subjects.

This first paragraph is a quick sketch that the author was prompted to jot down in her journal. Still, she seems to have captured her impression of the man on paper. Is there one comic image that catches your eye?

> This afternoon I went to watch a basketball game at my old high school. From where I was standing, I could see one of the coaches very well. He was a tall, fat guy with blond hair and a beard. He was wearing black pants and a white shirt. He never stopped walking up and down, and got very upset when his team was losing. He shouted at the players, blaming them. When a young girl said something against his school, he got so mad that he ran toward her and had her sent out of the gym. Then something else caused him to shout at the other team's coach. When at last his team won, he looked so happy—even his ears were laughing. It was such a funny thing to watch him kissing the players and running around like a pig.
>
> *—Vathoula Michaels*

JOURNAL EXERCISE 5.4

Carry your journal around with you for several days. Write down the details of ordinary—or extraordinary—situations: describe a stranger on a train, an old man walking his dog, a lover's quarrel on campus. Record an interesting conversation you happened to overhear. From your observations, what can you guess about the personalities of the speakers and their relationship with each other? It might be fun to make up a story using these real-life characters and that snatch of dialogue you overheard. Then, too, you may want to use your notes later on to develop descriptions of those people who most interest you, as the authors of the next two essays have done.

As you read the next two essays (p. 162; pp. 164–165), ask yourself: what aspect of the person does each writer focus on? What details does the author use to support this central impression? What specific words or memorable images in each essay stand out in your mind—why, for instance, does the author of "An Old Man with Dignity" tell us that the old man's wrists "*fought* out of short, frayed sleeves"? The author of "My Statistics Lab Teacher" uses several *similes*: these are comparisons that are introduced by *like* or *as*. Look for these similes and consider the effect each of them creates. Finally, what have you learned, not only about the subject but about the author of each essay?

An Old Man with Dignity

It was my second visit to Paris from London. I did not feel as bored during this long journey as I usually do. I was attracted by an old man who was sitting beside the window when I got on the train. In fact, nobody would pay attention to such a common person. However, exactly this, his commonplace appearance, provoked my interest.

Unlike the other passengers, this man had no luggage, not even a small suitcase or handbag. As soon as he got into the train, he sat quietly beside the window and started to look through it. The last rays of the afternoon penetrated the window and outlined his strong features in golden color. His wrists fought out of short, frayed sleeves; his skin was old, brown, and wrinkled, showing that he often exposed himself to the sun. He had a low forehead, and the narrow slits of his eyes lacked energy and spirit. Secretly I gazed at his weather-beaten face, which seemed to tell me of all the hard times in his life.

Long journey: it was very easy to make friends. Instead of chattering with others, he leaned towards the window and let the strong wind attack his face. What a lonely picture it was: sitting alone in a corner of a cabin, looking through the window with no purpose, an old man was waiting for the end of his life. Perhaps I should not permit such silly ideas to come into my head. But somehow, when I looked at him, this feeling was buried deeper in my mind. Only in that brief moment, while the train ran through birchwoods full of summer villas where many children were playing, yelling and running, I caught a brilliant glare in his eyes, but this dream disappeared at once, as if nothing had gone before. I wished he would speak, even a few words, for he looked so attractive to me that I was sure his voice would be very pleasant.

The train, gathering speed, was approaching Paris. I suddenly had a strange feeling that I should pay respect to this old man as he might be one of those who contributed their lives to build our society.

—Chung Mun Yuen

Moving from Journal to Essay

Let's pause for a moment to look at the evolution of the next essay. This is how the author's idea first appeared in her journal:

Our statistics lab teacher was sick last week, so we had a substitute instructor for two class periods. I believe our class was the first he had ever taught, and he was so nervous! The second time wasn't any better. He was very shy. His hands trembled, and whenever he talked, he faced the blackboard. Our real teacher had assigned some homework problems, so the substitute spent most of the class solving these problems. He didn't ask any of the students for the answers; he just turned to the board and sort of talked to himself. Everyone was bored, I think.

The nervous teacher stayed in the author's mind through the following week, prompting two more related journal entries:

The teacher was kind of handsome—I think some of the girls in the class liked him, because they started giggling when he turned around to face the board. He was very serious; he didn't make jokes. Yet he had the strangest smile on his face. It looked to me as if he were trying to calm down, and smiled to seem casual, but he couldn't smile properly. His face just froze. I wanted to laugh, but didn't.

I know how this teacher felt. My mother was an elementary school teacher in Taiwan. One day when she was sick I substituted for her and taught her class of second-graders. I'll remember that day forever. You know, they lied to me! All these little kids said, "Teacher, this is the last period, can we go home now?" They packed up their books noisily and started shuffling out. The teacher in the room next door said, "But there's one period left—don't let them leave!"

These kids didn't mean to be bad, but they sure were energetic. When I turned my back to write at the board, they passed notes, threw things at each other, giggled. So I understand how my substitute instructor felt in lab class, and I have sympathy for him.

These thoughts provided the writer with a *subject* she wanted to explore in an extended description: a young teacher's first classroom experience. The writer also discovered the *focus* of her description: he was shy, nervous. The journal notes reveal her *attitude* toward her subject, and indicate her reason for wanting to write about this man: I know how this teacher felt, because I had once had a similar experience. Thus the *thesis* of her paper emerged from a blending of these ideas: I can understand how shy and nervous this substitute teacher must have been.

As we have mentioned, a description doesn't always come out and state the thesis explicitly. But the implied thesis should be perfectly clear to the reader—otherwise, the description is an aimless jumble of details. As you read Kuan-Kuan's paper, take note of the ways in which she illustrates her implied thesis.

CLASSROOM ACTIVITY 5.5

Kuan-Kuan's original paper is composed of six logically ordered and connected paragraphs, all of which relate back to her theme. But we have reprinted the essay as one long paragraph, which makes it considerably more difficult to read and to follow.

Read the essay through. Then form groups of three or four students, and work on dividing the essay into paragraphs. You will find that there are a variety of ways to do this. When you have finished, discuss why you separated the paragraphs where you did. How did you know when to start a new paragraph? What makes the paragraph complete or incomplete? What made you decide to include a sentence in one paragraph rather than the other?

My Statistics Lab Teacher

It was near two p.m.; everybody was waiting with curiosity in the statistics lab classroom. Whenever a person came in, everyone turned his head to observe, suspecting that that was the teacher. Since he was the assistant of our black statistics teacher, it was very possible that he was not a white and it greatly increased the curiosity about what the assistant would look like. At one minute to two, a chubby young man about 5'7" with short, curly brown hair and profound, big blue eyes, walked into the classroom, holding a few books and pieces of chalk. "He is quite punctual," I thought. I glanced at his eyes, and I was puzzled by them. His eyes were charming and full of warmth, so that when they were looking at you, it seemed as if they were talking to you and telling you of his strong love. As soon as he saw so many students sitting there and waiting for him, he hesitated for a while; then he bowed his head, walking quickly toward a table in the classroom. It was regrettable that I couldn't see the beautiful, shining eyes anymore, but it was also fortunate because otherwise I was going to "view" him instead of listening to him. Putting his books on the table, he paused for a long time, his head still bowed. I saw his hand trembling and his face muscles stiffening. Some students started giggling and I saw him blush all of a sudden. Eventually, after a deep breath, he raised his head bravely and mumbled, "Hi. My name is. . . ." I believe that nobody actually knew what his name was because a lot of students frowned and leaned forward to "catch" the words he had just spoken. Realizing the reaction and expression we had, he smiled as shyly as a child caught stealing candies hidden in a kitchen cabinet by his mother. I guessed that he was from Europe because of his accent. While he explained problems, his voice trembled, babbled and stuttered; he went up and down the platform, opened, closed, piled, and separated his books, turning his papers frequently. He changed his position a great deal unconsciously, sometimes with his right foot in front and sometimes his left. He kept his face toward the blackboard and it seemed as if he were talking to the blackboard. After solving all the homework problems, he sighed and relaxed like a loosened balloon. Slowly piling his materials together, he walked out of the classroom as weakly as a beaten boxer. I picked up the chalk he was using and then I laughed. It was wet and sticky with sweat. I left the classroom and watched him disappear around a corner. "May God bless him and help him. Let him do better next time," I prayed sincerely.

—Kuan-Kuan Wei

Guidelines for Paragraphing

A paragraph is a group of sentences that are all related to a single subject. Visually, the beginning of a new paragraph is signaled by indenting the first line. Unfortunately, as you probably discovered in the preceding classroom activity, there are no sure-fire rules for dividing an essay into paragraphs. The only definite rule is common sense.

In general, people do not like to read long, uninterrupted blocks of writing. A page consisting of one 250-word paragraph often seems like a wall of words: forbidding and impossible to penetrate. Our eyes, as well as our thoughts, desire form, so writers separate their ideas into distinct units. In each unit, the reader expects that a different aspect of the thesis of the essay will be developed. For writers and readers alike, paragraphing is a way to break up a general idea into smaller and more manageable parts.

Each paragraph should be unified—the sentences should all work toward the development of one idea. In many paragraphs, this main idea is stated in a *topic sentence*, which can occur anywhere in the paragraph but most often comes at the beginning. The purpose of the rest of the sentences in the paragraph is then to support, explain, or illustrate the main idea stated in the topic sentence.

For example, turn back to Russell Baker's description of his mother and re-examine the first paragraph. Underline the topic sentence. How does Baker illustrate the main point of the paragraph? Underline the transitions he uses to lead from one sentence to the next. How do these devices unify the paragraph?

Most paragraphs in an expository essay—an essay that explains or analyzes—have a topic sentence. But in descriptive and narrative essays, as you might expect, many paragraphs have implied rather than stated topic sentences. Even so, each paragraph you write should have a clear *topic*, and should explore that topic by providing sufficient details.

In general, then, a paragraph should consist of more than one or two sentences—except in the case of a brief *transitional paragraph*, which is occasionally used to signify a major shift in topic. It is up to you as a writer to present your ideas in fully developed paragraph units; don't depend on the reader to guess what you're thinking.

THE USES OF PARAGRAPHING

As we have indicated, paragraphing is used to show the reader how the ideas in an essay are related to one another. For example, when giving instructions in the how-to essay, you might have used this kind of format to order your steps:

First

Second

Next

After . . . then

Finally

Similarly, the narrative essay is usually structured *chronologically*—according to the way events are ordered in time:

The first time we met, I disliked her immediately _____

_____

Our second meeting was a surprise to both of us _____

At Ahmed's party, three weeks later, we became close friends _____

Paragraphs can also be arranged to show *shifts in location*. This is often true of paragraphs in a descriptive essay:

My favorite room in Grandmother's house was her bedroom _____

Two flights up the stairs was a dark and dusty attic, where all sorts of playthings were stored _____

From the attic window I used to gaze down at the sunlit garden _____

An expository essay is frequently organized to present a sequence of *supporting ideas or examples*:

The greatest benefit of jogging is good health _____

Another benefit is weight loss _____

One example of a democratic society is the U.S. _____

The government of India is also based on democratic ideals _____

Some little-known benefits of jogging are an improved self-image and increased energy _____

Japan is a third example of a working democracy _____

Or the essay may present a sequence of *contrasting ideas*:

There are many advantages to owning your own home _____

But homeowners must also face certain disadvantages _____

JOURNAL EXERCISE 5.6

Naturally, essays don't have to stay within the boundaries outlined in the preceding section. Writers usually use various kinds of transitions within one essay. For example, examine an essay you have written and try to explain how you led from one paragraph to the next.

Then, experiment by writing a journal entry based on one of the patterns illustrated on pages 166–167. Try to make use of transitional words and phrases, examples of which are listed in Chapter 3. Remember, these words and phrases are used to show the connections between your ideas; they help your reader to move easily from one paragraph to another.

When you have written the descriptive essay assigned at the end of this chapter, you will be asked to edit your own paragraphs using the preceding guidelines.

Vocabulary Building: Using What You Know

A journal entry is, of course, a "snapshot" rather than a finished portrait. In contrast, in the two completed student essays you have read so far in this chapter, the writers had time to reflect, to develop, to revise, to pay greater attention to word choice. Whereas the journal writer uses the verb "shout," for example, the first essay writer selects "chattering" and "yelling," and the second essay writer chooses "mumbled," "trembled," "babbled," and "stuttered." The purpose of the next three exercises is not to introduce new vocabulary words, but to encourage you to make better use of the vocabulary you already possess.

EXERCISE 5.7

List as many variants as you can think of for the verbs *to speak* (ranging from *whisper* to *shout*) and *to walk* (ranging from *stroll* to *run*). After you have compiled your list, go back to Vathoula's journal entry (page 161) and replace any vague verbs with more explicit ones.

EXERCISE 5.8

Although writers usually work to vary their verbs and make them more precise, occasionally an author will purposely repeat a word for emphasis. An extraordinary example of this device appears in the Baker selection at the beginning of this chapter when Baker repeats a verb throughout a paragraph to make a point about his mother's character. Can you locate this paragraph, and explain the effect of the repetition?

EXERCISE 5.9

Test your memory by replacing the blanks in this summary of the Russell Baker story with words from the following list. (Not all of the words will be used, and some will require a change in form.)

relic	glare	formidable	dolt
hurl	flagging	laymen	gall
gaze	inevitable	banal	wrest
libertine	ignoramus	resignation	affluent

In his autobiography, Russell Baker depicts his mother as a deter-

mined, _____ woman who _____

herself at life. She _____ at _____

and has contempt for _____, slugabeds, and mush-

mouths.

When his mother first becomes senile—the doctors call it "hardening

of the arteries," in _____'s terms—Baker cannot

accept what is _____ . Instead, he tries to _____

_____ her back to the "real world." In an effort to

lift her _____ spirits, he writes her a letter full of

_____ advice.

Later on, sitting at his mother's bedside, Baker wonders about his rela-

tionship with his own children. He remembers how he used to resent the

fact that his own children's lives had been easier than his. It _____

_____ him that they had lived a comparatively

_____ life, and that they used to _____

_____ at him with _____

whenever he started to lecture them about "the old days." He begins to

feel that he and his mother are two _____ from the

distant past.

Using Comparisons in Descriptive Writing

We have pointed out that the student essay entitled "My Statistics Lab Teacher" contains several similes, or comparisons introduced by *like* or *as*. Can you locate them? How do they help you to "see" the lab instructor more clearly?

You might recall that Russell Baker uses a similar device in his portrait of his mother. For example, he refers to his mother's mental wanderings as her "time machine," and writes that for his mother, "Life was combat." This kind of comparison is called a *metaphor*. A metaphor acts like an equal sign: it *implies* a comparison by omitting the *like* or *as*:

> SIMILE: Life was like combat.
>
> METAPHOR: Life was combat.
>
> SIMILE: My mother's senility was like a time machine.
>
> METAPHOR: "If I had been able to step into my mother's time machine. . . ."

Speakers and writers use these kinds of comparisons—known as *figures of speech*—all the time. Unfortunately, too often we rely on old, stale similes and metaphors—He was as fat as a house; She was as skinny as a toothpick —that don't help our audience to imagine what we're trying to describe. If you're going to use a comparison in your own writing, reach for a fresh, inventive, unexpected image. For instance, with what noun phrase would you complete this sentence: She was as skinny as _____.

COMPLETING A SIMILE: NOUNS AND NOUN PHRASES VS. CLAUSES
Remember to use a noun or noun phrase for comparisons introduced by the preposition *like*.

As, as if, and *as though* are subordinating *conjunctions*. They come before a *clause*. Compare:

NOUN
He acts *like* a clown.

CLAUSE
He acts *as* a clown does.

The *as . . . as* construction also precedes a noun or noun phrase. However, you must use the *as . . . as if* construction before a clause. Compare:

NOUN PHRASE
His smile was *as* stiff *as* a starched shirt.

CLAUSE
His smile was *as* stiff *as if* he had starched it.

The following exercise is meant to get you thinking about the kinds of comparisons that you can use to enliven your essays. But be careful to apply this technique sparingly, like salt to a well-prepared dish. Otherwise, you run the risk of spoiling your creation with a tasteless mixture of metaphors.

EXERCISE 5.10

These sentences are adapted from a detective novel entitled *Farewell, My Lovely,* by Raymond Chandler, an author known for his startling similes and metaphors. Complete the sentences with your own comparisons (you'll notice that some of them are intended to be humorous exaggerations). Then compare your efforts with Chandler's, reprinted on pages 184–185.

1. He was a big man but not more than six feet five inches tall and not

   wider than _____.

2. He wore a shaggy hat, a rough gray sports coat with white golf balls on it for buttons, a brown shirt, a yellow tie, pleated gray flannel slacks and alligator shoes with white explosions on the toes. There were a couple of colored feathers tucked into the band of his hat, but he didn't really need them. Even on Central Avenue, not the quietest dressed street in the world, he looked about as inconspicuous

   (= unnoticeable) as a _____.

3. She was an ugly, middle-aged alcoholic with a face like _____

   _____.

4. She began to laugh—a high-pitched old woman's laugh. The sound

   was like _____.

5. The fog had cleared off outside and the stars were as bright as_____

   _____against a sky

   as dark as _____.

6. His smile was like an executioner's smile; it was as stiff as _____

   _____.

EXERCISE 5.11

Now go back and change the similes in sentences 3–6 into metaphors. Do you prefer one version over another? Why?

Paragraph Practice: Supporting a Topic Sentence

We've cautioned you against salting an essay with too many comparisons, and against mixing different kinds of metaphors within one paragraph. But writers often find it effective to develop a descriptive paragraph by *extending* one or several related metaphors. Below is a famous example of a description based on comparison. We borrowed this paragraph from Washington Irving's comic description of the schoolmaster, Ichabod Crane, in his story of "The Legend of Sleepy Hollow." Naturally, we left out the best parts. Your job is to fill in the blanks with the most vivid words, phrases, and comparisons you can think of.

EXERCISE 5.12

Let the topic sentence (in this example, the opening sentence) guide you as you flesh out the description. As you know, the *topic sentence* of a paragraph, like the *thesis statement* of an essay, announces the main point of the selection. Washington Irving begins his description by telling us that Crane's name is appropriate—in other words, the schoolmaster resembles the type of bird we have pictured in the margin. All the details you add to the rest of the paragraph must support the image presented in this topic sentence. (The original version of the paragraph appears on page 185.)

The cognomen [= name] of Crane was not inapplicable to his person. He was tall, but _____, with narrow

shoulders, _____ arms and legs, hands that

_____ feet that _____,

and his whole frame most loosely hung together. His head was small,

and _____ at the top, with _____ ears,

_____ eyes, and a _____ nose, so that it looked like

_____. To see him striding along the profile of a hill

on a windy day, with his clothes bagging and fluttering about him, one

might have mistaken him for the genius of famine [= severe hunger]

descending upon the earth, or _____

It should be clear by now that you have a wide range of tools for describing the person you choose. You can learn a great deal about people—even about strangers—by paying close attention to their appearance, speech, gestures, clothing, and possessions. Obviously, you have additional resources to draw on when describing a person you know well. In your portrait of a friend or relative, you can quote your subject's typical speech patterns or expressions, narrate an experience you shared, or analyze the nature of your relationship with that person, as the following author has done in the first draft of her descriptive essay.

This writer introduces her subject in the first paragraph by emphasizing her friend's dominant physical characteristic—her height. Then, in paragraphs 5 and 6, she goes on to *contrast* her own appearance and personality with her friend's—thus providing a wonderfully concrete demonstration of the old saying that "opposites attract."

My Friend Kumba

① I saw her and liked her because she is not beautiful but she is very friendly. Her feet are not just right and something is wrong about her ears. Her ears lap over. When she stands up, there is much to say about her tallness, for the length from her hips to her feet is equal to the length from her hips to her shoulders. She is a tall girl and that's all about her.

② She is very simple and frank. She likes to enjoy herself. She goes to discos, and dances. Although she is aware of the fact that she is not beautiful, she likes making friends. She does not like anything to bother her.

Can you recall one evening you spent together at a disco or party?

How do you know she doesn't like anything to bother her?

③ This girl likes to help people who need it. She sometimes visits the sick in the hospital, or goes to the home for the blind. She is always in sympathy with people.

what one incident can you narrate that would dramatize Kumba's behavior with hospital patients?

④ Maybe I liked her the first time I talked to her because I found that she has ideas. She is very clever in her talking.

Perhaps quote a conversation you had with Kumba. This might lead naturally into the contrast you set up in the next ¶.

⑤ I am not tall. I am built almost too close to the ground. Perhaps that is why she told me that I have old-fashioned ideas about everything, ideas that are simple but pure. My eyes see more on the ground because I am closer to it. I am what you might call compact. My ideas are squeezed together.

⑥ We are a funny pair, the tall girl and I, funny because we are different in everything. I am a slow walker and she has to hold back. She talks in long lines and I use short ones.

⑦ We became friends, why I do not know. We do crazy things. We play basketball, and do many other things together. These things make us agree. She is a real friend and we will always remain friends. I love her because she is nice.

—Ma-Zia Kamara

Using the comparison/contrast technique, this author has created several energetic and purposeful paragraphs. Yet she seems to have had some trouble with paragraphs 2, 3, and 4, which are brief and underdeveloped. In this middle portion of her paper, the author lists some general statements about her friend: *Kumba is simple, frank, friendly, sympathetic, and clever.* But the writer need not limit herself to this list of present-tense observations. We have written a few questions in the margin to suggest ways she can revise her essay. She might dip into the past and recollect a single incident or conversation that would illustrate her friend's simplicity, honesty, or intelligence. Instead of *telling* the "facts" about a person with a series of statements, it is usually more convincing to *show* these characteristics by dramatizing them with a story, an example, or a quotation.

The following essay should clarify the difference between *telling* and *showing*. As you will see, the man described in this piece shares a number of character traits with Kumba. But how does the author *demonstrate* that his friend Joe "likes to help people who need it" and "is always in sympathy with people"?

A Good Neighbor Is Better Than a Distant Relative

Two days ago, he came over to our house with a basketful of apples. He said that his daughter had gone to pick apples. His name is Joe; his house is right next to ours.

He is about 5 feet 7 inches in height, his shoulders somewhat narrow and a little stooped, his weight about 140 pounds. He is fifty years old and the color of his hair is changing into gray. Perhaps because he is short and skinny, he looks younger than he actually is.

It is a habit with him to say "you know" when he talks, as many people in this country do. But unlike most Americans, he doesn't use gestures very much. He speaks rather quickly; however, his voice sounds very soft despite his rapid speech. He gazes at me when I talk to him. He never opens his mouth until I finish what I am saying, even though I often have to take time to think about what I want to say. He knows how to be patient with a poor speaker of English.

He is a welder, and he teaches welding twice a week at an institute in Brooklyn. I wonder if the students in his class understand him, for as I have told you, he speaks very gently. He usually wears a polo shirt or T-shirt and jeans when he goes to work. He dresses like a college student. In fact, I have never seen him wearing a suit except on his daughter's wedding day.

Joe had wanted to buy a new car before his younger daughter's wedding. We went to a car dealer to take a look at some of the cars he had in mind. But since his daughter's marriage, he has never talked about getting a new car. He must have spent the money he had saved for a car on the wedding.

His other daughter lives with her husband, and recently had a baby. Whenever she visits Joe with her baby, he comes over to our home with his granddaughter in his arms. We say, "She resembles you very much and is very cute!" Imagine what kind of a face he makes; he has fallen in love with his granddaughter.

Sometimes he comes to our home with his wife to spend spare time. They chat for a while and leave. I could say he is nothing but an average man; you will see a person like him no matter where you may be. Still, he is something special to us.

—Hiroyuki Araseki

Assignment: The Prose Portrait

Your assignment in this chapter is to paint a word portrait of someone. Begin by thinking about someone—stranger, relative, friend, or enemy—

you've had the opportunity to observe closely. Write down as many observations about this person as you can. Then review your list carefully, and try to decide what your central impression of your subject will be. This central impression, like the thesis statement of any other essay, should be supported and developed in every aspect of your portrait. The details you mention in each paragraph should in some way relate back to the main point of your description. Remember, your goal is to enable your reader to "see" this person as you do.

REVISION EXERCISE 5.13

After you have finished the first draft of your essay, exchange papers with a classmate. Read each other's papers with these questions in mind:

- What is the main idea the writer wants to convey?

- Does the essay provide sufficient details to *illustrate* this point—that is, does it *show* rather than tell?

- Are the paragraphs arranged logically? Do transitions connect paragraphs and ideas?

- Finally, are there groups of short sentences that would sound better if they were combined? Before you revise your essay, go on to the next section for a review of additional ways to combine sentences effectively.

Sentence Combining with Adjective Clauses

In Chapter 4 we discussed subordinate clauses that perform adverbial functions. In this section, we'll return to our discussion of ways to combine sentences and look at another type of subordinate clause that is equally valuable to writers of the descriptive essay.

Adjective clauses, like adjectives, can describe or identify a noun or a pronoun. Unlike adjectives, however, they immediately follow the noun they modify. Sometimes called *relative clauses*, adjective clauses most often begin with *who, whose, whom, that,* or *which*. These are the *relative pronouns* that join a clause to the noun it describes or identifies. As we will see, a relative pronoun can act as the subject or the object of an adjective clause.

RESTRICTIVE ADJECTIVE CLAUSES

Several good examples of adjective clauses appear in Russell Baker's portrait of his mother at the beginning of this chapter. Let's take two sentences from his opening paragraph to see one way in which adjective clauses function:

> Some days she went to weddings and funerals *that had taken place a half century earlier.*

> On others she presided over family dinners cooked on Sunday afternoons for children *who were now gray with age.*

If we were to "uncombine" these sentences, they would lose much of their effect:

> Some days she went to weddings and funerals. The weddings and funerals had taken place a half century earlier.

> On others she presided over family dinners cooked on Sunday afternoons for children. The children were now gray with age.

Both of these sentences contain adjective clauses that are essential to the meaning of a sentence: they *identify* the nouns they modify. In the first sentence, the adjective clause tells *what* weddings and funerals she had gone to. Similarly, the second example identifies the children for whom the family dinners were cooked. This kind of adjective clause *restricts* or *limits* the meaning of the words it modifies. Because *restrictive* adjective clauses are necessary to the meaning of a sentence, they are *never* set off by commas:

For those of you who don't love tennis, here's a sunset.

THE JEANS THAT WON THE WEST ARE STILL MAKING HISTORY.

Notice that the restrictive clause in the second example—*that won the West* —tells exactly which jeans are still making history. Without the restrictive clause, the sentence would read: *The jeans are still making history.* But, as you learned in Chapter 4, the use of the definite article points to a specified noun, so we are left wondering *what* jeans? Now try removing the restrictive clause in the first example. Does the sentence still make sense?

We use *who, whom,* or *whose* when referring to people. *Who* functions as the subject of the verb in a relative clause; *whom* acts as the object of a verb or a preposition; and *whose* introduces a clause that shows possession.

> The girl *who delivers our newspaper* is only ten years old. (*Who* is the subject of *delivers.*)

The man *whom I introduced you to* is a mystery writer. (*Whom* is the object of the preposition *to*.)

The woman *whose house we bought* is now living in a tent. (*Whose* functions as a possessive pronoun.)

That always signals a restrictive clause:

The dress *that I wore* was most uncomfortable.

He recommended a restaurant *that had singing waiters*.

That is occasionally used to refer to people: *The man* that *I told you about is my new boss*. But as a rule, use *who* for people.

NON-RESTRICTIVE ADJECTIVE CLAUSES

Adjective clauses that simply give additional information about a noun —information that is not essential to the meaning of the sentence—are called *non-restrictive* clauses. Non-restrictive clauses are *always* set off by commas:

My teacher, *who raises chickens*, is a computer expert.

His computer, *which is several years old*, doesn't work.

His wife, *whom I met recently*, doesn't like chickens or computers.

They have two children, *whose names I have forgotten*.

As you can see from these examples, the non-restrictive clause does not limit or restrict the noun it modifies. In other words, the adjective clause can be removed from the sentence without changing the basic meaning of the sentence.

Use *which* in adjective clauses that simply give more information about places or things. Never use *which* to refer to people.

CORRECT: They spent the summer on Nantucket, *which is an island off Cape Cod*.

CORRECT: Orchids, *which are delicate flowers*, die quickly.

INCORRECT: My brother, *which is a genius*, often forgets to eat.

EXERCISE 5.14

Expand each of these sentences by adding non-restrictive adjective clauses. Pay attention to punctuation:

1. My new car doesn't have an engine.

2. Her husband collects cats.

3. Her winter coat needs cleaning.

4. My boss was recently promoted.

5. The roast beef was dreadful.

EXERCISE 5.15

Now combine the following pairs of sentences by using non-restrictive adjective clauses.

1. My best friend comes from an unusual family.
   My best friend is a circus clown.

2. Her mother is a writer.
   Her mother sleeps all day and works all night.

3. Her father runs a small zoo in their house.
   He works all day and sleeps all night.

4. The house has three levels.
   The house is perfect for them.

5. My friend practices her clown act in a large tent.
   The tent is set up in the basement.

6. Her father's collection of animals includes birds, fish, reptiles, and mammals.
Her father lives on the first floor and takes care of his collection of animals.

7. Her mother composes her books on a word processor.
Her mother resides in the attic.

Whether a clause is restrictive or non-restrictive depends on the meaning you wish to convey. Consider these examples:

My husband who has only one tooth is a dentist.

My husband, who has only one tooth, is a dentist.

The first sentence suggests that I am a bigamist: I have more than one husband. The restrictive clause in this example serves to *identify* which of my husbands is a dentist—the husband with only one tooth. When the same clause is set off by commas in the second sentence, it indicates that I have only one husband. The fact that this husband has only one tooth is, in this case, an added bit of information, and is not essential to the meaning of the sentence.

EXERCISE 5.16

Combine the following pairs of sentences by using restrictive or non-restrictive adjective clauses:

1. The man won the lottery.
He immediately quit his job.

2. He kissed his wife.
He had married her thirty years ago.

3. He had bought his ticket from a man.
He cheered the man.

4. The winner is a grocer.
   His shop was robbed last month.

5. The lottery winner purchased something first.
   It was a Mercedes Benz.

6. He had always dreamed of owning a luxurious cabin cruiser.
   A luxurious cabin cruiser was next on his shopping list.

7. He won five million dollars.
   Five million dollars will buy many dreams.

8. The lottery winner lives near me.
   He has become famous.

9. The money is now in the bank.
   The money earns interest daily.

EXERCISE 5.17

Fill in each blank in the sentences below with a suitable relative pronoun. Then use commas to set off any clauses that you feel are non-restrictive:

1. My father _____ grew up during the Depression used to tell us
   _____ life was much harder when he was a teenager.

2. He had only one pair of trousers _____ he ironed every night.

3. The man _____ house they rented was always threatening to throw them out.

4. Every day, even in driving rain and sub-freezing temperatures, my father had to walk to school _____ was seven miles away.

5. To save money, my father's mother made a soup _____ consisted of boiling water, a carrot, an onion, and a potato.

6. My father _____ I sometimes suspected of exaggerating told us these stories over and over again.

So far we have been discussing adjective clauses that are introduced by relative pronouns. But adjective clauses can also be introduced by other subordinators such as *where, when, why, before, as* (when it follows *the same*), and *after*:

My father often recalls the day *when he met my mother. (*modifies *day*)

The weeks *before we moved to San Francisco* were hectic. (modifies *weeks*)

Give me one reason *why I should listen to you.* (modifies *reason*)

The weary movie star wanted to relax in a place *where no one would recognize her.* (modifies *place*)

I made the same mistake *as you made.* (modifies *mistake*)

EXERCISE 5.18

Complete each of the following sentences with your own adjective clause:

1. I started college the year before _____

   _____.

2. I go to a school where _____

   _____.

3. There are several reasons why _____

   _____.

4. I look forward to next semester when _____

   _____.

5. I hope to have a good job a month after _____

   _____.

6. I would like the same life as _____

_____

The following exercises ask you to make use of all the techniques you've learned for sentence combining so far. Try to apply what you now know about coordination, subordination, and restrictive and non-restrictive clauses in this next set of tasks.

CLASSROOM ACTIVITY 5.19

Here is a paragraph from a description written by one of our students. The author characteristically writes in short, simple sentences. The passage is precise and concrete, but it would sound smoother and more musical if some of the sentences were rearranged and some combined. Work with a partner to revise the paragraph through sentence combining. Then compare your version with those of your classmates.

> Her name is Mina. She is my aunt. She is one of the most wonderful women that I have ever known. Her height is 5'6" and her weight is about 120 pounds. She has a bright face. Sometimes she has a spiritual face and other times she has a smiling face. Her face is round and a little fleshy. She has large brown eyes. Her nose is small and upturned. Her eyelashes are long and exuberant. Her eyebrows are a little thick. Her lips are like a bud. When she smiles, everybody can see her regular teeth and two pug cheeks. Her hair is long and brown. Her age is about forty-five, but she only looks about thirty-five. She cares about her skin and looks after it carefully. Her skin is very soft and pink.

EXERCISE 5.20

Reprinted here are a number of very moving excerpts from one student's journal. As you will see, the sentences are correct and often effective, but we'll ask you to combine some of the sentences in each paragraph so that each passage reads more fluently. Investigate the *variety* of ways to say things in English. Then select one paragraph as the starting point of a longer freewriting exercise in your own journal.

Sept. 26
> I kept a diary for the first time in my life. I don't like to leave my finger-prints on the paper. But I know it is good for me to improve my English composition. So I keep going on.

Sept. 27

There are many things to do, so I can't waste any time. I recognize that there is an obstacle in front of me. This is a language problem. I can't express myself in English very well. It is a kind of great torture to me. I wonder how much time it will take to learn.

Oct. 1

I played tennis with my friends today. I had known it was not so easy to play. When I saw on TV that someone like Jimmy Connors played tennis easily, I supposed there was no problem for someone like me to play. But I made a wrong estimate. I could see there was nothing to be done without great effort.

Oct. 2

I made a chemical experiment today. I found there was a big difference between fact and theory. That made me fall into a difficult situation. For all that, I couldn't change the results. Anyway, I had a time of it.

Oct. 6

I have been here for two years already. I really agree that time flies. It seems as if I am getting much better. But it is not enough to feel satisfaction. There is a long way to go.

Oct. 7

Today was a great day. I was elected to be President of the _____ Student Association. I felt dazed for a moment. This was the first time that I had a responsible post. So I was anxious about what I should do. I don't have any experience in these matters. I feared that I was going to make a mistake. The die is cast. So I'm going to do my best. That's the only way I can act.

Oct. 14

Winter is just around the corner. Today was very cold. I suppose that fall is very short here in America. Sometimes I remember the landscape of fall in my country. It was very beautiful. Now I think it is a kind of homesickness. I'm wearying for home.

SOURCES FOR EXERCISES 5.10 AND 5.12

Sentences from Raymond Chandler's *Farewell, My Lovely*

1. He was a big man but not more than six feet five inches tall and not wider than a beer truck.

2. He wore a shaggy borsalino hat, a rough gray sports coat with white golf balls on it for buttons, a brown shirt, a yellow tie, pleated gray

flannel slacks, and alligator shoes with white explosions on the toes. From his outer breast pocket cascaded a show handkerchief of the same brilliant yellow as his tie. There were a couple of colored feathers tucked into the band of his hat, but he didn't really need them. Even on Central Avenue, not the quietest dressed street in the world, he looked about as inconspicuous as a tarantula[1] on a slice of angel food.[2]

3. She's a charming middle-aged lady with a face like a bucket of mud and if she has washed her hair since [President] Coolidge's second term, I'll eat my spare tire, rim and all.

4. The eyes gleamed at me. She began to laugh—a high-pitched old woman's laugh. . . . I left her laughing. The sound was like a hen having hiccups.

5. The fog had cleared off outside and the stars were as bright as artificial stars of chromium[3] on a sky of black velvet.

6. "Please give it to me at once," he said with a smile you would get to love. It was like the executioner's smile when he comes to your cell to measure you for the drop. . . . His smile was as stiff as a frozen fish. His long fingers made movements like dying butterflies.

Ichabod Crane

. . . The cognomen of Crane was not inapplicable to his person. He was tall, but exceedingly lank, with narrow shoulders, long arms and legs, hands that dangled a mile out of his sleeves, feet that might have served for shovels, and his whole frame most loosely hung together. His head was small, and flat at top, with huge ears, large green glassy eyes, and a long snipe[4] nose, so that it looked like a weathercock[5] perched upon his spindle[6] neck, to tell which way the wind blew. To see him striding along the profile of a hill on a windy day, with his clothes bagging and fluttering about him, one might have mistaken him for the genius of famine descending upon the earth, or some scarecrow[7] eloped from a cornfield.

— *Washington Irving,* "The Legend of Sleepy Hollow"

---

[1] **tarantula:** a large, hairy, chiefly tropical spider.

[2] **angel food:** a white, spongy cake.

[3] **chromium:** a metallic chemical element, highly resistant to rust.

[4] **snipe:** a bird with a long bill, or beak.

[5] **weathercock:** a weathervane (especially in the shape of a bird)—an instrument that tells which way the wind is blowing.

[6] **spindle:** a thin rod.

[7] **scarecrow:** a crude figure of a man set up in a field to scare birds away from growing crops.

unit 4 Narration

6 | Writing and Revising the Narrative Essay

WRITING THE NARRATIVE ESSAY

Stories and Storytellers

Narrating—telling the story of a sequence of real or fictional events—seems to be a more natural activity for most people than, say, giving directions or describing a scene. To illustrate this point, we gave a group of students the first line of Franz Kafka's most famous tale, "The Metamorphosis," and asked them to continue the story in their journals. These excerpted paragraphs indicate the variety of responses produced in a brief freewriting session:

> *As Gregor Samsa awoke one morning from uneasy dreams, he found himself in his bed transformed into a giant insect.* The thought dawned on him that he might still be in a dream. The figure who had once been Gregor Samsa slid off the bed and moved toward the mirror.
> The image reflected was not the sight of an unshaven man but of a terrifying creature. Gregor spun around the room wildly like a blind man. His cry came out as a terrible buzzing. Then he calmed himself. He realized that the humanity of Gregor Samsa was still intact but trapped in this nightmare.

> *As Gregor Samsa awoke one morning from uneasy dreams, he found himself in his bed transformed into a giant insect.* He glanced down at his body and noticed he had six legs with three toes and a claw on each. His arms had spikes protruding from them and he had only two fingers and a thumb on each of his hands. Gregor's body was covered with a gluey, stinky substance. His eyes glowed red in the dark. He could see two tiny bugs crawling on the floor even though the room was pitch black.
> Gregor licked his stinger and plucked one of the bugs off the floor. But before he could drop the little bug into his big mouth, the baby insect said,

"Daddy." Gregor flipped out. His whole family had turned into insects. His wife walked in and saw Gregor holding his kid above his open mouth. She flew at Gregor, beating her large wings and stinging him in the face. She screamed, "What do you think you're doing?" Gregor said, "How come you have wings and I don't?" His wife answered, "Because I'm a girl."

As Gregor Samsa awoke one morning from uneasy dreams, he found himself transformed into a giant insect. He found his appendages difficult to move and his entire body stiff. Because he was lying on his back, he was quite helpless, and it wasn't until he rocked his bed that he was able to get out of it.

Gregor looked around the room for another insect, but he was alone. Even if there were another insect with him, he thought, he wouldn't be able to communicate with it anyway. He didn't know that in addition to English, he could speak the insect's language, too.

CLASSROOM ACTIVITY 6.1

Flex your storytelling ability with a similar warm-up exercise in your notebook. You may want to freewrite using one of these opening lines from three contemporary stories:

"A pine forest in the midafternoon. Two children follow an old man, dropping breadcrumbs, singing nursery tunes."

—Robert Coover

"The year was 2158 A.D., and Lou and Emerald Schwartz were whispering on the balcony outside Lou's family's apartment on the seventy-sixth floor of Building 257 in Alden Village, a New York housing development that covered what had once been known as Southern Connecticut."

—Kurt Vonnegut

"The ghost that got into our house on the night of 17 November, 1915, raised such a hullabaloo of misunderstandings that I am sorry I didn't just let it keep on walking, and go to bed."

—James Thurber

No one knows for how many thousands of years people have been telling and listening to narratives, but we do know that every culture has a storytelling tradition, even if it does not have a writing system. Well before *Homo sapiens* learned to read and write, they had evidently framed much of their wisdom in story form. Fiction has always been a natural vehicle for people to communicate their experiences, fantasies, and fears.

Similarly, children delight in stories long before they are able to read or write. Almost as soon as a child has learned to talk, she can enjoy not only listening to stories, but making up her own as well. She may pretend, for example, that her stuffed animal is alive and wants a cookie, or she may scold a doll for some imaginary misbehavior. These baby stories become more elaborate as the child acquires more experiences to weave into her fiction, and she will often develop her own version of a story she has heard.

We adults gossip, share jokes, complain about what happened to us this morning, speculate about the future. And in telling even these informal tales, we are likely to pay careful attention to the sequence of the events we are speaking about. Because stories create an order that life lacks, we naturally draw upon narrative. To make sense of our lives, we need to think of beginnings, middles, and endings, and we use these fictions to try to organize the past, the present, and the future.

The Structure of Narrative

William Labov, a noted sociolinguist who has studied the way people tell stories, has observed that most narratives answer this series of underlying questions:

1. What was this about?

2. Who, When, What, Where?

3. Then what happened?

4. So what?

5. What finally happened?

In this chapter, we'll be using these questions to examine the process of storytelling. Whether a story appears as a news report, a narrative poem, or a narrative essay, the structure it follows is essentially the same. To take one illustration of this structure, we have reprinted one of the most famous narrative poems in American literature. Actually, this narrative is the product of two cultures, since it is an English version of a work written in the 8th century A.D. by Li T'ai Po, one of China's greatest poets. The 20th-century American poet Ezra Pound discovered a rough translation of the poem, and, though he knew no Chinese, was moved to attempt his own translation.

EXERCISE 6.2

The poem is in the form of a letter written by a woman to her husband, who has gone away on a business trip. In the letter, the wife narrates the story of their courtship and marriage. As you read, jot down in your notebook your observations about the poem, using this list of questions as a guide: How do the poets make the characters, setting, and action vivid and real for us ("Who, When, What, Where")? How does the relationship between husband and wife change over the years ("Then what happened")? What is the underlying point ("So what?") of the letter—what leads the wife to write something more than a simple account of how she has spent her time since her husband departed?

The River-Merchant's Wife: A Letter

While my hair was still cut straight across my forehead
I played about the front gate, pulling flowers.
You came by on bamboo stilts, playing horse,
You walked about my seat, playing with blue plums.
And we went on living in the village of Chōkan:
Two small people, without dislike or suspicion.

At fourteen I married My Lord you.
I never laughed, being bashful.
Lowering my head, I looked at the wall.
Called to, a thousand times, I never looked back.

At fifteen I stopped scowling,
I desired my dust to be mingled with yours
Forever and forever and forever.
Why should I climb the look out?

At sixteen you departed,
You went into far Ku-tō-en, by the river of swirling eddies,
And you have been gone five months.
The monkeys make sorrowful noise overhead.

You dragged your feet when you went out.
By the gate now, the moss is grown, the different mosses,
Too deep to clear them away!
The leaves fall early this autumn, in wind.
The paired butterflies are already yellow with August
Over the grass in the West garden;
They hurt me. I grow older.
If you are coming down through the narrows of the river Kiang,
Please let me know beforehand,
And I will come out to meet you
         As far as Chō-fū-Sa.

Notice how the narrative takes us from the past to the future: the verb tenses shift from *past* to *present perfect* ("you have been gone five months") to *present* ("now, the moss is grown") to *future* in the final lines. How does the letter conclude ("What finally happened")?

JOURNAL EXERCISE 6.3

Write a letter to someone close to you in which you narrate three brief memories that show three different stages in the development of your relationship. For example:

- When we were six years old and living in Athens . . .

- At 15 we had an argument about politics . . .

- At 18 you went away to college . . .

You can narrate entirely in the simple past tense, or you can use a variety of tenses as Pound does. (For a review of the past tenses, see pages 202–209.)

The Narrative Essay

A writer of fiction is primarily a storyteller, an enchanter. But the writer of a narrative *essay* must also be something of a teacher. A good story is hard to forget, which is why narratives are especially useful when we try to communicate an idea or explain a principle. In this chapter, we'll be working toward the narrative essay—a composition that uses a story to illustrate a general lesson.

The similarities between storytelling and essay writing are often greater than we realize. Think back for a minute to your how-to assignment in Chapter 3. How did you organize the steps involved in the process you were describing? Like a story, a how-to essay usually follows a logical "First . . . Next . . . Finally" pattern. Your descriptions of people and places in Chapters 4 and 5 probably dip into narrative as well. In addition to providing details about the person or the place, you may have included an account of your own experiences with your subject.

Similarly, histories are frequently written as if they were stories, and newspaper or magazine articles sometimes use a narrative pattern, too. What, for example, would you expect from a piece in *Popular Science* with the following title?

Take a look at the first three paragraphs:

Computerized tomography has worked wonders in hospitals. Now it could transform quality testing in the factory

By DAVID LAMPE

It was a contrast between the very old and the very new. In a basement laboratory at the Smithsonian Institution in Washington, D.C., the tube of a special kind of X-ray machine was pointed at an ancient pottery vessel. Inside, an unnamed 20th-century object had been sealed.

Dr. Lon Morgan turned on the machine, and the tube slowly rotated 360 degrees around the pot. Seconds later, a shadowy, conical image appeared on the video monitor connected to the machine. Morgan adjusted a knob to vary the contrast and confidently announced that the object inside was a Kentucky Fried Chicken leg. He then pointed out where its crispy batter coating was the thickest and where it was thinnest.

Making such an identification is child's play for Morgan and his computerized industrial tomography (CIT) scanner. The newly patented version of the CAT-scan imager used for medical diagnostics is capable of much more precise —and much more significant—measurements than the chicken-leg demonstration at the Smithsonian indicated. By mating the power of the computer to traditional radiology techniques, the CIT scanner provides a potent tool for testing the quality of industrial components without having to disassemble them.

Although the purpose of this article is to give rather technical information about a new kind of computerized X-ray machine, it begins with narrative. Why do you think the author chose to present his topic in this way?

The same blend of story and essay appears in many autobiographies. For example, Richard Rodriguez's autobiography, *Hunger of Memory*, is designed as a long narrative essay. Rodriguez, the son of Mexican immigrants, uses childhood memories to support his views on the widely-debated issue of bilingual education. He begins with a story about his difficult first day at an English-speaking school, and then states his thesis. Can you locate it?

I remember to start with that day in Sacramento—a California now nearly thirty years past—when I first entered a classroom, able to understand some fifty stray English words.

The third of four children, I had been preceded to a neighborhood Roman Catholic school by an older brother and sister. But neither of them had revealed very much about their classroom experiences. Each afternoon they returned, as they left in the morning, always together, speaking in Spanish as they climbed the five steps of the porch. And their mysterious books, wrapped in shopping-bag paper, remained on the table next to the door, closed firmly behind them.

An accident of geography sent me to a school where all my classmates were white, many the children of doctors and lawyers and business executives. All my classmates certainly must have been uneasy on that first day of school—as most children are uneasy—to find themselves apart from their families in the first institution of their lives. But I was astonished.

The nun said, in a friendly but oddly impersonal voice, "Boys and girls, this is Richard Rodriguez." (I heard her sound out: *Rich-heard Road-ree-guess*.) It was the first time I had heard anyone name me in English. "Richard," the nun repeated more slowly, writing my name down in her black leather book. Quickly I turned to see my mother's face dissolve in a watery blur behind the pebbled glass door.

Many years later there is something called bilingual education—a scheme proposed in the late 1960s by Hispanic-American social activists, later endorsed by a congressional vote. It is a program that seeks to permit non-English-speaking children, many from lower-class homes, to use their family language as the language of school. (Such is the goal its supporters announce.) I hear them and am forced to say no: It is not possible for a child—any child—ever to use his family's language in school. Not to understand this is to misunderstand the public uses of schooling and to trivialize the nature of intimate life—a family's "language."

Rodriguez continues, "Memory teaches me what I know of these matters; the boy reminds the adult." This is the purpose of the essay based on childhood recollection: memory teaches.

"What Was This About?": Choosing a Topic

Most brief personal narratives center on a single experience that changed the writer's outlook. Any incident, however minor, can drastically alter the way we look at things. A seemingly ordinary day was somehow special, meaningful to you; you discovered something about yourself or others, and you want to pass that insight on to your reader.

Your assignment for this chapter is to write a narrative essay. The topic is up to you. You'll find that your journal is an especially rich mine of ideas. Perhaps the following excerpts from student journals will remind you of similar experiences you want to record in your own journal or eventually develop into a full-fledged essay—memories of leaving your country, of a first love, of a friend who helped you or disappointed you:

It is said that friends are the most important things in anybody's life, but I had thought of this as just an abstract idea until my own experience proved that I was wrong.

Something that happened to me once was that I fell in love. It was beautiful. It happened like this . . .

What can be worse than emigration? I think just war. This is impossible to imagine for the person who has never felt it. But it is so, because it is really hard to leave everything at once—your country, your home, your friends. To leave and know you will probably never see them again, that sometimes, waking up during the night, you will discover that this is not your home.

I used to believe that I had to think as my parents thought, but now I believe that we can have different opinions.

Once I was a wild teenager; now I am much more serious and well-behaved. There was a time in my life when I was "messed up." I was what people call a "hopeless case."

You can focus on an event that occurred as recently as yesterday, or in the distant past. In an essay that appears further on in this chapter, a student concludes, "I never confessed the truth to anybody. Just now, I dare to reveal it, to write about it." The meaning of the experience has emerged in the process of remembering and recording it—just as the significance of Richard Rodriguez's first day in school has become clear to him in retrospect.

A particularly fertile source of personal discovery is the relationship between a writer and his or her parents. We mentioned in the previous chapter that professional writers often begin by writing their autobiographies, and these autobiographies frequently open with a recollection of one of the author's parents. As you recall from Chapter 5, Russell Baker begins his autobiography by talking about how his mother has changed with the passage of time and the effect this change has had on his own life. In the same vein, you might base your own essay on a specific event that has altered your relationship with a parent.

Another useful structure for a narrative essay is suggested by the last two journal excerpts we've quoted. This is the "contrasting" structure: "I used to believe . . . / but now I believe . . ." or "Once I was . . . / now I am . . ." In this kind of narrative essay, you record an incident that shows how you used to act or think, and contrast that event with illustrations of how you have changed. A good example of this essay type is S. P. Chan's narrative, which appears on pages 201–202.

It's important to remember that *all* narrative essays really have two parts: the story of what happened, and the point behind it—what you *make* of your experience. This is the thesis that gives shape to your story. No matter what topic you decide on, you should strive to leave the reader with a thought he or she didn't have before.

"So What?": The Point of the Story

A friend of ours reports that whenever she sits down to write, she keeps in mind her two-year-old son's favorite phrase—"Who cares?"—and this keeps her on the right track. Narratives must have a point, which we may liken to a thesis—a reason for telling the tale. If you've ever been the victim of a bore at a party, you know that nothing is more exasperating than a pointless story. The storyteller should have a direction in mind. And a narrative that is both detailed and focused makes it impossible for your audience to think, "So what?" or "Who cares?"

Usually the direction of a story is made clear from the beginning. A writer lets us know where she's going to take us. Unfortunately, we have removed the first paragraph of this next student's narrative. What's left is a terrific story in which there are a few hints of a thesis.

EXERCISE 6.4

When you've finished reading this story, try writing down what you think the opening sentence or two might be. What do you think the author learned from her experience? What have you learned from it?

I was, then, happy like all children, and I was very fanciful. My parents had a pretty house in Melo, near the Brazilian frontier. I liked that place very much because it had a beautiful forest. One of my childhood adventures was to escape to the forest alone during the warm months of summer vacation. The forest was thick, full of rough brambly ground and high arches of flexible branches.

In the center of the forest, there was a narrow brook, dark and mysterious, with its transparent water full of reflections. A double row of quince trees ran alongside it. During the spring and summer, this quince orchard was covered with flowers, and later with heavy fruits.

I used to escape into the forests at siesta time, and I felt a very sweet fear to know myself alone there. My mother and my aunts used to tell me tales about brigands and monsters hiding there, and I very much wanted to meet them—to discover the novelty of fear.

One afternoon, I heard an alarming noise of broken branches and the loud shriek of a bird. Maybe it was just a cat hunting, but I felt myself prisoner in an invincible fear. I wanted to run to my house, but the surprise and the dread paralyzed me. However much I wanted to flee, I could not take a single step. My mouth was dry, my body covered by a frozen perspiration, and I could hardly breathe. When I could finally move, I had the frightful sensation that somebody was following me.

As I ran home, I saw my mother coming to search for me, angry and alarmed. "You are very pale," she said. Stuttering with fear, I told her, "A man . . . wearing gray pants . . . told me . . . to come to the house . . . and to bring him . . . rapidly . . . bread, sugar. If not, he would kill me. He, he was carrying a big wild beast . . . tied with a rope . . . A big wild beast full of big spots . . . who was throwing fire from his eyes."

They told me later that I fainted. Now I know that I was the victim of my own fable.

Nobody doubted my story. My mother cried, and put vinegar and cold water on my face. Everybody woke up, and my father and grandfather went in search of the "wild beast" that they thought was some dangerous animal.

I was seated on my mother's knees, receiving like a sovereign the care of my aunts, who were always very severe with the restless little girl that I used to be. Of course, nobody found anything. My "ferocious man with his fabulous beast" had disappeared.

For many days, I continued feeling weak, obedient, scared, and petted. The fiction became reality to me, and I never went alone into the forest again. I never confessed the truth to anybody. Just now, I dare to reveal it, to write about it.

—*Laura Sabani*

If you compare notes with your classmates, you'll no doubt find that they have come up with a number of possible theses for this narrative. For instance, you might have speculated, "There is nothing more vivid than a child's imagination," or "Fear may cause us to invent horrors that don't exist," or "We all have a natural tendency to make up stories that somehow explain things we cannot understand."

These are all reasonable guesses, substantiated by Laura's story. The author's actual introduction, however, takes us along a different path:

One day, when I was about eight years old, I was struck by the power of my own imagination. Perhaps it was then that I decided I wanted to be a writer.

So you can see, the way you introduce your story is as important as the story itself.

INTRODUCING YOUR ESSAY

You know, of course, that the *title* of a story or article is meant to grab the audience's attention and let them know what the piece is about. After all, which book would you rather read:

My Father

or one of these recent biographies:

Best Father Ever Invented

Photographs of My Father

Forgive the Father

The *introduction* of any essay you write has the same two-fold mission as the title. The opening paragraph acts as a hook that pulls readers into your paper, and leads them toward the point you want to make. It usually provides some background information, and then states the thesis of the paper.

Here is how four students began when we asked them to record stories that have been passed down through their own families. Naturally enough, the students had some difficulty getting started, until they figured out what the point of the family story really was. Like this first student, you may begin with a few lines to "get you going" and discard these sentences in your final paper:

> Traditionally, my family has been a boring family from generation to generation so there aren't any dramatic family stories to tell. However, I do have one story to tell which I heard from my grandmother several times. It is about my father. My father was seven or eight years old when this happened, so it was way before I arrived in this world.

This next student discovered the "moral" of her story in the process of writing her paper, so the first two sentences she wrote are no longer valid. We usually can't write the beginning until we've come to the end of the essay:

> ~~Sometimes it is difficult to know what the moral behind a family story is. There are times when a story has no moral behind it. Anyway, the~~ one story that I have heard many times over is about how people can frighten someone to death. It's a story my father always brings up when I decide to play a practical joke on my sister.

The following student's paragraph is typical of many introductions. It's too general—so broad, in fact, it could serve as the introduction for *any* family story:

> For generations, families have been telling and retelling many stories, which, after many years, have become legends. These tales, which relate events that have occurred in the past to some member of the family, provide enjoyment for everyone, and at the same time carry a moral. That is, they serve as lessons for family members of all ages. My family has been especially active in the propagation of these anecdotes, including several that have been passed down for many generations. However, among these ancient fables, one story, although only about 15 years old, stands out as interesting.

Most of the sentences in the above paragraph don't say anything new. Keep in mind: this is *your* paper. It's unique. Jump right into your topic and let the reader know what's special about the story you're going to tell.

In contrast, the rewritten paragraph is brief, simple, direct:

> Most families pass down stories from generation to generation to serve as parables for the children. One story that has always been told at family gatherings when my parents reminisce is about my brother Amir, who used to be a very mischievous boy. They remind Amir of that awful incident in kindergarten fifteen years ago, and the memory of it seems to keep him manageable.

CLASSROOM ACTIVITY 6.5

Here's another common problem: the scrambled introduction. The author has all the pieces of an opening paragraph, but has assembled them in a confusing way. For one thing, the sentences move back and forth in time, making it very difficult for the reader to follow. How would you help her to rearrange the paragraph? In piecing together this puzzle, decide whether you want to place the sentences in the order in which the events actually occurred, or according to some other arrangement. You may also wish to clarify the meaning of certain sentences by combining them. Then choose the sentence that you think expresses the main point of the paragraph: do you want to begin with that general statement or to lead up to it by placing the more specific sentences before it? When you have finished, compare your solution to those of your classmates.

> (1) A few years ago I was told that my father was a very naughty boy. (2) My grandma told me so after listening to what my father had just told us about not causing any trouble on the farm. (3) My grandparents live on a farm and they used to plant a lot of vegetables every year. (4) They also have a lot of chickens. (5) We used to run after the chickens and startle them. (6) Grandma, trying to save her chickens, told us a story about her youngest son—my father.

STRUCTURING YOUR ESSAY: TOPIC SENTENCES

So far we have been talking about introductions and thesis statements. Within the body of the essay, *topic sentences* show how an author has subdivided the thesis statement into a group of supporting ideas that are developed in individual paragraphs. As we discussed in Chapter 5, a topic sentence is to the paragraph what the thesis statement is to the whole essay. And like the thesis statement, which usually appears near the beginning of the essay, the topic sentence often—though not always—comes at the beginning of a paragraph. If we were to lift the topic sentences out of an essay and string them together, they would give us the rough outline of the composition, and show us how the author moves from one general point to another. And if the author has done her job, we should be able to guess the topic sentence of a paragraph simply by looking at the kinds of specific details she has included in the rest of that paragraph.

EXERCISE 6.6

We have reprinted a student's essay, although, as you can see, we've done her a disservice by eliminating all the topic sentences. We have, however, left the author's transitions from one paragraph to the next. Read the essay carefully, and then go back and try to supply the missing sentences.

Once I Was Talkative: Now I'm Silent

Eight years ago _____

_____. No matter where I was, or with whom I was, I always opened my mouth and talked. For instance, I was called the "tornado mouth" of my class in fifth grade. I used to sit all the way in the back of the classroom and shout out answers to the teacher. While the teacher was giving a lesson to the class, I would sit back and talk to a friend next to me. When the lessons were interesting or when I knew them well, I loved to raise my hand and try to answer all the questions. Of course, there were times when the teacher didn't call on me to reply, but still I would yell out the answers.

In addition _____

_____. I loved to tell short stories to my little brother. Reciprocally, he delighted in following me around and listening to my tales. I always told my parents what I had done in school during the day and what I would do tomorrow. My mouth always seemed to be open, except maybe when I went to sleep. Conclusively, talking was one of my hobbies. Chatting all day long gave me great pleasure.

Now _____.
There are a few reasons for this change in my behavior. First, when I arrived here in the United States eight years ago, I didn't understand any English at all. Therefore, I was unable to communicate with anyone. One day, for example, I went to McDonald's for lunch. When it was my turn to place my order, I stood there not knowing how to say what I wanted. I told the lady at the counter, in Chinese, that I wanted a hamburger, but she didn't understand me. So I had to go over to the corner of the counter and point at a huge colorful poster of a hamburger. . . . This was a period

of exclusion, confusion, and frustration. Due to my inability to express myself to the English-speaking foreigners, I was forced to be silent.

Second, _____

_____. This was the worst period of my life. It wasn't because the job was difficult or strenuous; it wasn't because of the low salary; it wasn't because of the long working hours—it was because of the atmosphere of the factory. Every day from 9:00 A.M. until 5:00 P.M., I would sit next to my mother and do simple handiwork. At first, picking out loose threads and puncturing button holes in blouses was fun. But after days and days of performing exactly the same operation, I found it tedious and horrible. In addition to my weariness with the job, I was lonely. Unlike the other workers, I had no friends of my own age to talk with. Because all the other workers were much older than I, I had very little in common with them. Therefore, I seldom spoke with them. Gradually, I became silent and somewhat solemn.

Even though I no longer work in that terrible factory, and I've managed to learn and to speak English, I'm still much quieter than I once was.

—*S. P. Chan*

Topic sentences serve to unify your essay. Another unifying element of any essay is the predominant verb tense. Narratives are usually governed by some form of the past tense. The following section will help you to understand the subtle time differences indicated by the various past tenses in English.

"Then What Happened?": The Past Tenses

Verbs are the wheels that set in motion any piece of writing. But narrative, in particular, is *about* time: it allows us to relive past experiences by relating a series of events, usually told in the order in which they happened and kept in order through a sequence of tenses so that the reader can easily follow the action. English has a number of ways to express past time.

THE SIMPLE PAST

The simple past tense for *regular verbs* is formed by adding -*ed* or -*d* (if the verb already ends in -*e*) to the base form of the verb. The past verb form does not change for singular and plural.

The best way to learn *irregular verb* forms is to memorize them. They are listed in Appendix 1.

We use the simple past tense for events that happened at a specific time in the past, or that took place over a period of time that is now finished:

> We went to school early yesterday.

> He went to school in France for five years.

EXERCISE 6.7

In Exercise 6.1, we quoted the first line of Robert Coover's modern fairy tale, "The Gingerbread House." What makes this particular tale so interesting—and unsettling—is that it is narrated in brief, numbered paragraphs, all of which are in the present tense. Given here is paragraph 21. Change the verbs to the past tense, where all conventional fairy tales take place. Don't be fooled by the -ed and -ing phrases used as adjectives and adverbs. Remember, only the main verbs change to the past tense:

> The forest is dense and deep. Branches reach forth like arms. Brown animals scurry. The boy makes no furtive [= secret] gestures. The girl, carrying her flowerbasket, does not skip or sing. They walk, arms linked, eyes wide open and staring ahead into the forest. The old man plods on, leading the way, his heavy old leather-thonged shoes shuffling in the damp dust and undergrowth.

DID + BASE FORM

Did + the base form of the verb is a past tense form that is occasionally used for emphasis:

> I did say that, but I didn't mean it.

USED TO/WOULD + BASE FORM

Used to and *would* + the base form of the verb are sometimes employed for an action that was repeated over a period of time in the past. For instance, in the essay "Once I Was Talkative: Now I'm Silent," S. P. Chan writes:

I *used to* sit all the way in the back of the classroom and shout out answers to the teacher. While the teacher was giving a lesson to the class, I *would sit* back and talk to a friend next to me.

Notice that this past form emphasizes habitual past action.

JOURNAL EXERCISE 6.8

Compose a paragraph that summarizes typical or habitual activities from some period in your past. You might, for example, want to write about what you *used to* do during summer vacations when you were a child. Try to use both *would* + base form and *used to* + base form in your paragraph. (You can also use *did* + base form for emphasis: I *did* love those long summer days.)

THE PAST PERFECT TENSE

The past perfect is formed with *had* + the past participle of the main verb. Like the simple past, the past perfect does not change for singular or plural.

This tense is used if you are writing about two events that occurred at different times in the past and you want to show which came first. Although native English speakers often neglect this form in informal speech, the past perfect tense is essential to written narrative. Sometimes called the "before past," it shows a state or activity that preceded another state or activity in the past.

Here are two examples from the opening pages of this chapter:

PAST   PAST PERFECT
Gregor *flipped* out. His whole family *had turned* into insects.

        PAST PERFECT   PAST   PAST
The figure who *had* once *been* Gregor Samsa *slid* off the bed and *moved* toward the mirror.

EXERCISE 6.9

A.) Supply the past and past perfect forms for each of the following verbs:

BASE FORM	PAST	PAST PERFECT
throw		
spin		
awake		
beat		

BASE FORM	PAST	PAST PERFECT
think		
speak		
lie (to recline)		
lie (to tell an untruth)		
lay (to set down)		
tear (to rip)		
hustle		
drink		

B.) Now make up 12 sentences that use the past *and* the past perfect forms of the verbs in this list. (For example: He *had thrown* several snowballs at me before I *threw* one at him.)

FORMING QUESTIONS IN THE PAST PERFECT TENSE

As you know, questions are formed by moving the first X-word in a sentence to the front of the sentence:

Had you ever *studied* English before you came to this country?
No, I *had* never *studied* English before.

Remember that adverbs of frequency or relative time such as *never, ever, often, seldom, rarely, usually, already, hardly, still,* and *just* come between the X-word and the main verb.

EXERCISE 6.10

Answer these questions by using the past perfect tense:

1. Had you and your sister ever flown in a plane before last summer?

2. Had you already studied for the exam before you went on vacation?

3. Had Janet just left for work when the snow started?

As you can see from the preceding exercise, the past perfect tense can be used when you join two related sentences by subordination, to show more clearly the relationship between two past events:

> The students entered the room.
> + The bell rang.
>
> = The students had entered the room before the bell rang.

> They arrived at the station.
> + The train pulled away.
>
> = They arrived at the station after the train had pulled away.

EXERCISE 6.11

Combine these pairs of sentences using a subordinator plus the past perfect tense. Try to vary the subordinators you use.

1. We brought 500 hamburgers to the picnic.
   The rain started coming down in buckets.

2. I thought I was funny.
   He said I was merely silly.

3. The police arrived.
   The thieves fled.

4. She graduated from college.
   She went to work for a consulting firm.

5. I started singing.
   Everybody left the room.

6. My little brother always believed what I said.
   I told him I could fly.

7. I admired him for years.
   I met him last summer.

THE PAST PROGRESSIVE TENSE

This tense is formed with *was* or *were* + the present participle (*-ing*) of the main verb. The past progressive expresses a continuous past action, and is usually used for an action that *was going on* at a time when another event *occurred.*

> We were just biting into our hamburgers when the thunder started.
>
> They say Nero was fiddling while Rome burned.

Note that *while* and *when* are often used to show the relationship between the past and the past progressive tenses.

The past progressive is also used for an uncompleted action in the past:

> We were cleaning the house all morning. (But the kitchen is still a mess.)
>
> I was trying to reach you all week. (But you never picked up the telephone.)

THE PAST PERFECT PROGRESSIVE

This tense is formed with *had been* + the present participle of the verb. The past perfect progressive is used to show an action that continued over a period of time in the past. It is often used to emphasize the duration of an action that was going on *when* or *before* something else happened:

> Vladimir Nabokov had been writing in Russian for several decades before he wrote his first novel in English.
>
> He had been living in Berlin for 20 years when he decided to move to the U.S.

Caution: As we mentioned in Chapter 1, ESL students tend to overuse the progressive tenses. Keep in mind that they are chiefly used to express an action that was taking place when another event occurred.

EXERCISE 6.12

Use subordinators and the past progressive or the past perfect progressive tense to combine these pairs of sentences:

1. My brother tried to fix his car for weeks.
   He gave up and took it to a mechanic.

2. I struggled all night with my math homework.
   The rest of the family slept peacefully.

3. The President flew back to Washington.
The astronauts landed on the moon.

4. The burglar alarm rang for hours.
The police finally came.

5. My neighbor worked in a bank for 45 years.
Poor health forced him to retire.

EXERCISE 6.13

Here is a paragraph from a student essay you'll encounter later on in this chapter. Fill in the blanks with these forms of the past tense: past perfect progressive, past progressive, would + base form (each of these used only once), past perfect and simple past (used more than once).

Another time, Uncle Tony [play] _____ soc-

cer with his friends and [lose] _____ track of

the time. While he [hurry] _____ home late

that night, my great grandmother [meet] _____

him halfway up the hill to the house and [take] _____

_____ a swing at him with her fist. Uncle Tony

[duck] _____ and my great grandmother [fall]

_____ down and [break] _____

_____ her arm. The next day she [tell] _____

_____ all her friends that her grandson [push]

_____ her down and [break] _____

_____ her arm. Whenever anyone [ask] _____

_____ Uncle Tony why he [break] _____

_____ his grandmother's arm, he [try] _____

_____ unsuccessfully to prove himself innocent.

REVISING YOUR ESSAY

Let's say you've written your story. You've stated your thesis, supplied lots of details, paid attention to verb tense changes. Even so, you feel the essay needs work. Perhaps it's not developed sufficiently, or a particular paragraph seems out of place, or the paper just trails off at the end. . . . How to proceed? The following notes on revision will help you to make your paper as good as it can be.

"What Finally Happened?": Rewriting

When the Russian author Vladimir Nabokov taught literature at Cornell University in New York, he began by lecturing about the relationship between "Good Readers and Good Writers." He explained that creative readers are really re-readers, experiencing a story first to get the whole picture and then going back to take note of all the details. In much the same way, most authors will tell you, good writers are _re-writers._

Here is the conclusion of Nabokov's introductory lecture, in which he argues that a wise reader delights in the "magic" of a piece of writing not only because it makes sense but also because it is clear and pleasing to the eye and ear:

> In order to bask in that magic a wise reader reads the book of genius not with his heart, not so much with his brain, but with his spine. It is there that occurs the telltale tingle even though we must keep a little aloof, a little detached when reading. Then with a pleasure which is both sensual and intellectual we shall watch the artist build his castle of cards and watch the castle of cards become a castle of beautiful steel and glass.

Nabokov's observation applies not only to a great novel but also to a great poem, short story, or essay. Naturally, as a reader and a writer, Nabokov followed his own counsel. Below you'll find his rough draft of the three sentences we've quoted. Note that even though the lecture was to be spoken to his class rather than published in written form, the author rewrote extensively. His revisions range from adding a missing article (a natural error for a native Russian speaker) to deleting sentences and changing images:

In order to ~~experience that~~ bask in that magic, ~~and to magnify many times the image~~

a wise reader reads the book of genius not with his heart, not ~~even~~ so much with his brain — but with his spine. It is there that occurs the tell-tale tingle — ~~while the brain attends with a smile and the heart tiptoes in the wings~~ ~~In a later lecture I shall discuss this business of the spine.~~ ~~So to conclude this talk do not knowingly tears, do so~~ Let us keep a little aloof, a little detached when reading, ~~let us hold~~ and then with a pleasure which is both sensual and intellectual ~~and not unquizzical~~ we shall watch the artist build his castle of cards and watch the castle of cards become a castle of ~~marble~~ beautiful steel and glass

Consider, for a moment, how through rewriting the author pared the selection down to three elegant sentences. What is the difference between "*experience* that magic" and "*bask in* that magic"? Why do you think Nabokov crossed out the sentences in the middle of the paragraph—those referring to the smiling brain and the tip-toeing heart, as well as to a later lecture? Most important, can you give reasons for the change from "castle of marble" to "castle of beautiful steel and glass"?

Artists continually re-work to improve what they have created. Turn back to the beginning of Chapter 5 and re-examine Picasso's portrait of Gertrude Stein. The face, you might have already remarked, seems more like a mask than a human face: the features have been smoothed over. Yet Stein reported that Picasso asked her to pose eighty or ninety times for this painting. He kept revising various aspects of the portrait, including its composition—X-rays show, for example, that the head was originally framed higher and to the right. Then, after this exhaustive series of sittings, Picasso painted out his subject's face and arrived at an interpretation that satisfied him.

Most good writers, similarly, regard their work as a series of drafts. It is not unusual for some writers to go through eight or nine drafts to achieve the results they want. Don't panic. We're not asking you for an endless sequence of revisions. But you have learned by now that rewriting means more than just correcting spelling and grammar. As writers, you are constantly faced with more important choices. In the narrative essay, as in previous essays you've written, don't be surprised if your material leads you in an unexpected direction: during the process of writing, you may recall memories you didn't know you possessed. This process of addition and selection will probably require several drafts.

In the preceding chapters, we've illustrated the steps that various student writers have found helpful when revising their papers. The following revision and editing checklists offer a more detailed series of questions that should guide you in the composing process. You will probably want to refer to these lists when working on drafts of essays assigned in subsequent chapters of this text. The first checklist asks you to look at the whole essay and reassess the major structures and controlling ideas. The second, an editing checklist, deals with grammar and mechanics.

QUESTIONS FOR REVISING THE WHOLE ESSAY

Introduction: Do you think the opening of your essay will stimulate your reader's interest? Does it effectively introduce the theme of your paper?

Thesis: Is there a clear statement of the main idea of the essay in the first paragraph or two of the paper? And is there some sort of restatement of the thesis in the last paragraph of the paper?

Paragraphs: Have you divided your essay into paragraphs, and is each paragraph indented? Is there a logical reason for the way you've made these divisions—is the structure of the paper clear? Do transitions create a flow between sentences and paragraphs?

Support: In the body of the paper, do you cite illustrations or proof for the main idea of the essay? Have you clarified all generalizations with specific details? Is there any point you want to see expanded? What can be eliminated (or shortened)?

EDITING CHECKLIST

1. *Fragments:* Does every sentence turn into a yes-no question?

2. *Run-ons and Comma Splices:* Does every sentence that will turn into *two* yes-no questions have either a coordinating conjunction (*and, but, or, so, yet*) or a semicolon between the two independent clauses?

3. *Verb Tenses:* Have you checked irregular verb forms? Is there one governing tense that unifies the essay?

4. *Verb Endings:* Is there an *-ing* or a past participle ending on any verb that follows a form of *be, have, feel, get, seem,* or *become*?

5. *Subject-Verb Agreement:* Do subjects and verbs agree in number? Have you remembered the *-s* endings on third-person singular verbs?

6. *Subject-Pronoun Reference:* Does every *he, she, it* refer back to a specific singular noun, and does every *they* refer back to a plural noun?

7. *Plurals:* Is there an *-s* ending on every plural noun except for irregular ones like *men, women, advice,* or *homework*? Have you paid attention to plural noun signals like *these, those,* and *one of the . . .* ?

8. *Possessives:* Have you remembered possessive *'s* and *s'* endings? (See Appendix 4 for rules on forming plurals and possessives.)

9. *Modifiers:* Do *adjectives* modify nouns or pronouns? Do *adverbs* modify verbs, adjectives, other adverbs, phrases, clauses, or sentences?

10. *Articles:* Is there an article before every singular, countable noun? Is *the* used only to mean something specific and not used with general or mass nouns like *beauty, life,* or *air*?

11. *Vocabulary and Idioms:* Have you consulted your dictionary for spelling and definitions, and checked idiom usage with your teacher or a friend?

12. *Proofreading:* Have you proofread to correct word order, punctuation, capitalization, and other careless errors?

CLASSROOM ACTIVITY 6.14

Here is the *body* of an essay by one of our students, Michael Vryonides. (You'll see his introduction and conclusion later on.) In this part of the story, Michael tells what happened one day to one of his bosses, a young man named Nick, who is "a real dictator." The essay you'll be reading, however, is *not* exactly the essay Michael wrote, for we've changed his paper to make sure that every type of error mentioned on the editing checklist appears in it. Read the story through; then work together in groups to correct all the mistakes we've added.

One day a beautiful girl walks into the dinner and sitted down at the counter. Nick got all excite it was time to strike again. As usual, he start to give orders. After each order, he turned and looked at the girl, he had the look of ten Robert Redfords and five Marlon Brandos. Surprisingly, the girl was smilling at nick and her behavior encouraged him more. His next step was to scream at Carlos, the cook. Nick complained that the food was over-cooked or undercooked. He shouted that the toasts were burned or they hadn't enough butter. All this time the girl was smiling and Nick was hoping. But when Nick told Carlos he couldn't do anything correct, Carlos said, "Do it yourself, Mr. Perfect, I am leaving and here take my apron you'll need it."

Nick stood their like a statue for some moment and then said, "Lets go boys we have a lot of work to do." He worn the apron and began to cook.

He was the clumsiest person I ever seen. His hamburgers looked like tennis balls and his eggs had a mysterious black color. He cut his finger making a salad and he burn his hand trying to turn a western omlette over.

Naturally, he delayed all the orders and the customers complained everybody was hungry except the girl she was still smiling. Nick quarrel with the customers, everybody started yelling, one of the customer who seem to be very hungry threw his empty plate at Nick. That was the beginning of a war, a war different from other wars. Instead of using weapons, the customers used plates and glasses and Nick used hamburgers and eggs. It lasted only five minutes because the lunch break was over and the customers had to returned to work. Everybody left except the girl, Nicks last hope after such a bad day.

We did our best to clean the shop. When we were ready to leave, the girl stood up opened her handbag and took out a nice little gun. Nobody ex-pected this. With a smile on her lips, the girl said, "Hey, Cassanova, fill my handbag with your moneys and dont try anything foolish." After she had the money, she walked out like an aristocrat. We couldn't go after her because Nick had fainted and we were pouring water on his head.

The next student used classmates' comments and the revision guide and editing checklist for three revisions of his essay. The essay is an expanded version of the "family story" exercise referred to on page 208. In every family, members of the older generation love to talk about the ten-mile hike to school and the five-cent-a-week allowance to illustrate how tough life was in "the old days." The author's Uncle Tony is no exception. As you can see, in the course of rewriting, the author decided that his real subject was not just how hard times were for his Uncle Tony in the old days, but also how much Uncle Tony exaggerated those hardships to teach his nephews and nieces a lesson.

EXERCISE 6.15

Use the editing checklist to correct some of the technical errors in the author's first draft. Then compare the original and final drafts of the paper to see what major changes the author made.

DRAFT #1:

Is this a plural signal? (7)

I'm shifting tenses here. (3)

can I phrase this more gracefully?

What Life Was Like for Uncle Tony in the Old Days

Uncle Tony loves to talk and remind me what life was like

in the old days. He is also (one) of the world's greatest (liar.)

He would tell me that I did not know what hard work was like

and yet he is so lazy and can fall asleep in any position and

anywhere.

In the past my Uncle Tony had to spend some time living

with my great-grandmother. My great-grandmother was said to be

a miserable, loud-mouthed woman and my uncle said life with

her was torture. In one episode that occurred between my uncle

Punctuation? (11)

and my great-grandmother; Uncle Tony wanted to go to the

movies with his friends. Great-Grandmother Mary always seemed

This is really 2 sentences (2)

to know what her grandson was thinking, during the showing of

the film my great-grandmother entered and began to shout for

my uncle as she went along the rows of chairs filled with peo-

ple. Uncle Tony said that his friends had to sneak him out of

"embarrass" is used as an adjective here — use -ed ending (4)

the place and home; he had never <u>been more embarrass</u> in his whole <u>life</u> he said. —Punctuation missing.

clarify for the reader: Why was she so angry?

At another time, he had left home to play some soccer with his friends. When he was returning my great-grandmother met him halfway up the hill to his home and took a swing at him with her fist. Uncle Tony ducked and my great-grandmother fell down and broke her arm. The next day she went and told all her friends that her grandson had pushed her down and broken her

word order for past questions? (11) spelling!

arm. Whenever anyone asked uncle Tony why did he brake his grandmother arm he would try unsuccessfully to prove himself innocent.

these details probably belong in #2, with the general description of great-grandmother

My great-grandmother had a great throwing arm too and old pairs of shoes and other missiles would follow close behind Uncle Tony. She had this great ability to embarrass anyone. Anyone around could know if my great-grandmother Mary wanted my uncle because whenever she called his name out loud it would echo among the hills and my uncle would never answer.

Uncle Tony would tell me these stories with tears stream-ing down his face brought on by too much laughter.

How do I get from this # to this one? This sentence, too, seems out of place.

One could not escape a spanking since Great-Grandmother would wait until he wanted to sleep and then she had him.

this is a brand-new idea. If I introduce it here I've got to tie it somehow to my thesis. What does this sentence say about Great-grandmother and about Uncle Tony? Use this idea to expand the conclusion.

Whenever the younger generation of the family complain about small inconveniences, we were reminded what life was like with great grandmother. But now she is older now and when I saw her for the first time she was wonderful.

DRAFT #3: Growing Up with Uncle Tony

Uncle Tony loves to talk and remind me of what life was like in the old days when he was a boy. He is also one of the world's greatest liars. He will tell me over and over that I don't know what hard work is like, and yet he is so lazy that he can fall asleep anywhere and in any position.

When Uncle Tony was growing up, he spent his vacations living with my great-grandmother Mary. My great-grandmother, Uncle Tony said, was a miserable, loud-mouthed woman, and he called life with her "torture." She had a strong throwing arm, too, and old pairs of shoes and other missiles would follow close behind Uncle Tony. Everyone knew when she wanted him because whenever she called his name, it echoed loudly among the hills. Even if he didn't answer, he could never escape a spanking. According to Uncle Tony, Great-Grandmother would wait until he came home to sleep, and then she had him.

One episode that Uncle Tony loved to recall took place on a hot afternoon on our tropical island. He wanted to go to the movies with his friends but he knew Great-Grandmother would disapprove, so he quietly sneaked out of the house. Great-Grandmother, however, always seemed to know what her grandson was thinking. While Uncle Tony was watching the film, Great-Grandmother walked into the theater and began to shout for my uncle as she searched the rows of people. Somehow Uncle Tony managed to crawl out of the movie house and race home. His heart was pounding and his face was burning; he had never been more embarrassed in his whole life. For months afterwards, his friends teased him with tales of that day.

Another time, Uncle Tony had been playing soccer with his friends and lost track of the time. As he was hurrying home late that night, my great-grandmother met him halfway up the hill to the house and took a swing at him with her fist. Uncle Tony ducked and Great-Grandmother fell down and broke her arm. The next day she told all her friends that her grandson had pushed her down and had broken her arm. Whenever anyone asked Uncle Tony why he had broken his grandmother's arm, he would try unsuccessfully to prove himself innocent.

With tears of laughter streaming down his face, Uncle Tony would tell these and other stories to convince us that Great-Grandmother was a tyrant. And whenever my cousins or I complained about small inconveniences, we were asked if we wanted to spend our vacation with Great-Grandmother.

It was finally time for me to meet Great-Grandmother, and, after hearing all these stories, I expected a strong-willed, stern-faced woman. Instead, she greeted me with a big smile and warmth in her eyes. She embraced me and kissed me on the cheek. Was this gentle, fragile, gray-haired woman the tyrant that my uncle had described? Uncle Tony later claimed that Great-Grandmother had mellowed with age. I had always known that my uncle was a great storyteller, and it was then that I began to suspect he was one of the world's greatest liars as well. He had surely been lazy and disobedient, and had given Great-Grandmother good cause to discipline him. Uncle Tony just didn't want us to make the same mistakes he had.

—Donville Jones

Writing Conclusions

Observe how this student has expanded and clarified his conclusion in the final version of his essay. You probably felt confused or were "left hanging" by the original ending, for Donville simply *stopped* his essay without *concluding* it. The revised conclusion is far more effective because Donville has tied together the loose ends of his essay and has made sure we understand the implications and significance of his subject.

As you can see from Donville's rewritten version, a good conclusion underscores the thesis and brings the main points of an essay into sharper focus. It is not simply a dry summary or an exact repetition of the introduction, but rather a fresh and imaginative rephrasing of the theme.

The conclusion of your essay is not the place to introduce a completely new idea or to reverse a point you've made earlier. Instead, you use it to re-examine the controlling idea of your essay in terms of the illustrations and examples you have given in the body of the paper. In Donville's first draft, the last paragraph ends with a surprise: Grandmother is not fierce but lovable. In effect, the last line refutes all the stories that have gone before it.

In the conclusion to his third draft, however, Donville *begins* with the surprise information, and then goes on to *explain* it in terms of his thesis. Was this gentle woman really the tyrant Tony had described? What was the *real* point of Tony's stories? The conclusion suggests several answers to these questions:

- We know Tony was a great storyteller; he might have exaggerated for the sake of a good story.

- Tony had been a lazy and disobedient boy, and had probably given Great-Grandmother good reason to be a tyrant.

- Perhaps, then, Great-Grandmother had been somewhat "tougher" in the old days, but had mellowed with age.

- So Tony really told these stories because he wanted us to see how much easier life was for our generation—and because he didn't want us to be lazy and disobedient, as he had been.

Your conclusion should thus "wrap up" the points you introduce in your first few paragraphs. It should satisfy the expectations you have set up in your introduction, and remind the reader that you have delivered the information you promised. For an excellent demonstration of this point, consider the first and last paragraphs of an essay you've already seen part of, Michael Vryonides' "A Lesson About Bosses." In his revised version of the essay, here's how Michael introduced his story:

THESIS:

> Any person who has employees is a boss, and every boss is a kind of dictator. But there are really two kinds of bosses: one is a benevolent dictator, and the other pretends to know everything and to do everything without a

HINT OF STORY
THAT FOLLOWS:

BACKGROUND:

ILLUSTRATION OF THESIS:

single mistake. This type of employer uses his position to show off and cover his weaknesses. But when it comes time to prove how good he is, he often turns out to be a clumsy clown.

    Several months ago I was working in the kitchen of a diner called "Jimmy's Place." I had two bosses: Jimmy, who was an old man, and his son Nick, a young man about 28 years old. The old man often worked the counter, and helped all of us when the shop was busy. He didn't mind doing the hard jobs that bosses don't usually do. But his son didn't take after him: he was a real dictator. He lived to show off, especially when he wanted to impress a beautiful woman.

The body of the narrative, as you have seen, illustrates how Nick turns out to be "a clumsy clown." Now observe how, in his conclusion, Michael gives the reader a fresh restatement of his thesis, taking into consideration the comic details of the story you read about in Exercise 6.14:

>   The next day when I walked into the shop I found Nick cleaning the floor with the mop. This was quite a change from the boss I knew—the dictator who was full of advice and orders. I offered to help him. But the old man told me, "Mike, leave him alone. It is time for him to learn that no one is born to be a boss; you have to work really hard to be one." Nick wasn't the only one who learned something that day. The old man had taught me a lesson about being a responsible worker, whether you're a boss or an employee.

With this generalization, Mike shows that the "lesson" he learned has universal meaning. In the conclusion, as in the introduction, a writer tries to show the reader how the lesson, or point, or thesis, of an essay has meaning for the reader as well as the author. Ideally, the reader should be able to say, "Yes, I recognize that situation; this story (or explanation, or argument) means something to me." Your ending may include a quotation, a question, an illustrative anecdote, another example, or an evaluation of the points you've raised in the body of your paper: in any case, remember that in your last paragraph or two, you are giving your readers a final thought or image to take away with them.

Sentence Combining: Using Verbals

After you've re-thought and revised the organization and development of your essay, you may want to start revising and combining sentences, too. Sentence combining not only adds variety and sophistication to your prose style, but is also particularly useful when you are narrating a sequence of events.

EXERCISE 6.16

° **deranged:** mentally unbalanced.

For example, on pages 220–221 we've reprinted twelve illustrations from Edward Gorey's strange little tale, "The Deranged° Cousins." Since we have removed the captions from these pictures, the series becomes a kind of murder mystery. Your job is, first, to list the events you think are taking place in the pictures, using the clues we have provided below. Add whatever descriptive details you think are important. Then see if you can narrate the story in the past tense, in six sentences. Can you do it in four? After you've consulted the following verbal review, try this exercise again.

CLUES:

There are three cousins.

At night they are merry.

By day they look for objects washed ashore by the sea.

One day two cousins argue: about what, and how does it end?

One cousin becomes religious; one drinks too much.

What happens to them?

In earlier chapters, we talked about sentence combining using semicolons, colons, coordinators, and subordinators. Still another method involves using *verbals*. A verbal is a verb form that can be used as another part of speech. Because they are derived from verbs, verbals look like verbs, but they are used as *nouns* or *modifiers*. Let's look at the three kinds of verbals and the ways they can be used to combine sentences.

GERUNDS

A gerund is a verbal that ends in -*ing* and acts like a noun. Observe how gerunds work in each of the following noun positions:

> *Thinking* is the sport of the mind. (Subject)
>
> The sport of the mind is *thinking*. (Completer)
>
> Great books influence our *thinking*. (Object of a verb)
>
> The goal of *writing* is clarity. (Object of a preposition)

Because verbals are closely related to verbs, they can take objects or modifiers as verbs do. Note the ways in which sentences can be combined

1

4

2

5

3

6

7

10

8

11

9

12

by first reducing one sentence into a *gerund phrase* and then combining it with another sentence:

> Many people eat a lot of fast food.
> + This can be unhealthy.
> SUBJECT
> = *Eating a lot of fast food* can be unhealthy.

> They visited Paris last summer.
> + They enjoyed it.
> OBJECT OF A VERB
> = They enjoyed *visiting Paris* last summer.

> I ripped my shirt.
> + My mother yelled at me.
> OBJECT OF A PREPOSITION
> = My mother yelled at me *for ripping my shirt.*

EXERCISE 6.17

Use gerund phrases to combine the following pairs of sentences:

1. He traveled through Europe and Asia for two years.
   This taught him a great deal.

2. My brother went to college in England.
   He loved it.

3. The students left their books at home.
   The teacher scolded them.

4. I thanked my friend Carlos.
   He gave me a birthday present.

5. My mother doesn't have a college education.*
   She regrets it.

---

* All verbal constructions are made negative by placing *not* before the verbal.

6. Leora reads the newspaper from the first page to the last. It is her daily routine.

INFINITIVES

The present infinitive is a verbal made up of *to* + the base form of the verb: *to think, to read, to write.* The perfect infinitive consists of *to have* + the past participle: *to have thought, to have read.* Infinitives can act as nouns, adjectives, or adverbs:

SUBJECT AND COMPLETER: *To read* is *to think.*

OBJECT OF A VERB: Nabokov loved *to write.*

ADJECTIVE: He is a writer *to challenge* the best readers.

Infinitives have six different forms:

	PRESENT FORMS	PERFECT FORMS
PRESENT:	to give	to have given
PROGRESSIVE:	to be giving	to have been giving
PASSIVE:	to be given	to have been given

The present forms of infinitives express time that is the same as, or future to, that of the main verb:

To graduate soon is his goal.

The crowd seems *to be leaving* now.

To be given this award is a great honor.

The perfect forms express time that precedes the time of the main verb:

I seem *to have caught* a cold.

To have been nominated for President as a young man was his most cherished memory.

Notice how infinitive phrases can be used to combine sentences:

They hope something.
+ They will return to Paris soon.

= They hope *to return to Paris soon.*

He was commended for his bravery by the President.
+ This was the finest moment of his life.

= *To have been commended for his bravery by the President* was the finest moment of his life.

EXERCISE 6.18

Fill in the blanks with infinitive phrases. Try to use the various present and perfect forms.

1. I'll begin _____ today.

2. _____ is a rare experience.

3. The fortune-teller advised me _____.

4. _____ was my mother's lifelong dream.

5. He seems _____.

6. The librarian asked me not _____.

7. It was her goal _____ for three hours a day.

PARTICIPLES

Participles and participial phrases are verbals and verbal phrases that are always used as adjectives. Like verbs, they express an action or a state of being, but they modify nouns. Look at the ways in which these participle forms enable us to combine sentences.

Active Voice

The *present participle* is simply the-*ing* form of the verb *when it is used as an adjective.* (Remember that a gerund is also the -*ing* form of a verb, but it is used as a *noun.*)

The students work.
+ They carry a double burden.

= *Working* students carry a double burden.

The man is speaking to the faculty.
+ I have met him.

= I have met the man *speaking to the faculty.*

The *perfect participle* shows that the time expressed by the participle *precedes* the time expressed in the main verb. The perfect participle in the active voice is formed by *having* + the *past participle*:

We worked hard all day.
+ We decided to go out for dinner.

= *Having worked hard all day,* we decided to go out for dinner.

The *perfect progressive participle* is formed by *having* + *been* + *the -ing form of the verb*:

I had been studying since early morning.
+ I was exhausted that evening.

= *Having been studying since early morning,* I was exhausted that evening.

EXERCISE 6.19

Combine the following pairs of sentences using the participles you've just studied:

1. Jaime walked quietly up the stairs.
   The stairs creaked.

2. The sun shines brightly.
   It hurts my eyes.

3. The pianist memorized the concerto.
   She was ready for the performance.

4. Nina relaxed all week.
   She failed the exam on Friday.

Passive Voice

In the active voice, the *present participle* is used as an adjective. In the passive voice, the *past participle* is used as an adjective. The past participle is the *-ed* form of a regular verb. (Past participles of certain irregular verbs may also be used as adjectives.)

>   The army was tired.
> +   The army was defeated.
> +   The army surrendered.
>
> =   The *tired, defeated* army surrendered.

The *progressive participle* is *being* + the *past participle*:

>   I was starved.
> +   All I could think about was food.
>
> =   *Being starved,* all I could think about was food.

The *perfect progressive participle* is *having* + *been* + the *past participle*:

>   She was insulted at the meeting.
> +   She left immediately.
>
> =   *Having been insulted at the meeting,* she left immediately.

EXERCISE 6.20

Combine these pairs of sentences by using participial phrases in the passive voice:

1. My bicycle broke.
   It needed repair.

2. I was left with no means of transportation.
   I walked to work.

3. I had just been given a Walkman radio.
   I listened to rock music as I strolled to the office.

4. I was distracted by the music.
I stepped in a pothole on Chestnut Street.

5. I broke my foot.
I had to stay home from work.

EXERCISE 6.21

Now use what you've learned about participial phrases to combine these groups of sentences:

1. The children laughed.
The clown sang.
The children followed the clown.

2. The woman is singing the National Anthem.
I know her.

3. We were victorious.
We were excited.
We celebrated until dawn.

4. Uri was offered a new job.
He was very pleased.

5. He had been disappointed many times before.
He was not optimistic.

6. The baby had been crying for an hour.
She finally fell asleep.

7. That physician is respected by all her patients.
   She is admired by all her colleagues.
   She enjoys her career.

CLASSROOM ACTIVITY 6.22

Earlier in this chapter, we looked at Ezra Pound's version of a famous poem by Li T'ai Po. Here, we've taken the first four sentences of another translation of this work and broken them down into simple sentence units. Work together in groups to arrange these simple sentences in meaningful and interesting combinations. Be sure to use what you've learned about verbals, as well as coordinators and subordinators:

1. My hair had hardly covered my forehead.

2. I was picking flowers.

3. I was playing by my door.

4. You, my lover, came on a bamboo horse.

5. You were trotting in circles.

6. You were throwing green plums.

7. We lived near each other.

8. We lived on a lane in Ch'ang-Kan.

9. Both of us were young.

10. Both of us were happy-hearted.

11. At 14 I became your wife.

12. I was so bashful.

13. I dared not smile.

14. I lowered my head toward a dark corner.

15. I would not turn to your thousand calls.

16. But at age 15 I straightened my brows.

17. I laughed.

18. I learned something.

19. No dust could ever seal our love.

20. Even unto death I would await you by my post.

21. And I would never lose heart in the tower of silent watching.

Idiom Review: Verb Chains

As you've seen, both gerunds and infinitives can act as objects of verbs. Some verbs, however, are followed only by a gerund, while others take only an infinitive. There is also a group of verbs that can be followed by either a gerund or an infinitive. The following lists should help you to remember which common verbs are followed by gerunds, which are followed by infinitives, and which can be followed by either a gerund or an infinitive.

VERBS FOLLOWED BY GERUNDS

advise	enjoy	postpone
avoid	escape	practice
cease	fear	put off
confess	finish	recall
consider	imagine	recommend
delay	include	regret
deny	insist on	resent
detest	keep	risk
dislike	mention	stop
dread	mind	suggest
	miss	

VERBS FOLLOWED BY INFINITIVES

ask	have	promise
beg	hope	refuse
cure	intend	resolve
dare	learn	strive
decide	need	swear
endeavor	offer	threaten
expect	plan	want
fail	prepare	wish
get	pretend	

VERBS FOLLOWED BY EITHER GERUNDS OR INFINITIVES

begin	like	start
continue	love	try
hate	prefer	

EXERCISE 6.23

Complete the following sentences with the correct kind of verbal phrase:

1. Everybody needs _____.

2. Students should avoid_____.

3. I really hate _____.

4. I would prefer _____.

5. Do you think I should continue_____?

6. Would you dare_____?

7. Teachers often pretend _____.

8. I'd never ask my teacher _____.

9. I promised my girlfriend/boyfriend _____.

10. I really love _____.

11. We should always keep _____.

12. Students can't escape _____.

13. I deeply regret _____.

14. My father wouldn't consider _____.

15. The class denied _____.

16. Don't mention_____.

17. Let's start _____.

18. Stop _____!

19. I begged my dentist_____.

20. More than anything else, I want _____.

7 | Writing Fables

Proverbs

In the previous chapter we concentrated on one type of story—the personal narrative, based on the writer's own experience. In this chapter, we'll be talking about a second form of narrative, the fable. Fables are teaching stories that make their point with a concrete tale drawn not from the writer's life, but from his or her imagination.

As we shall see, the way a fable operates is by *analogy*, that is, by an *extended comparison*. When a writer wants to teach a particular lesson, he or she often finds it useful to make the point with a fictional story that is comparable, or analogous, to a real-life situation. In Chapter 8—part of the unit on exposition—we'll be working with different kinds of analogies. So our present discussion, like the earlier units on process, description, and narrative, is designed to give you another important tool for developing analytical and persuasive essays later on.

At the beginning of this book we looked at proverbs—those brief, wise sayings which are part of every culture's heritage. Many of the proverbs we remember today, in fact, very likely began as fables; the story has disappeared, but the *lesson* or *moral* of the story remains. For example, examine the painting on page 232, entitled *Proverbs*, by the 16th-century Flemish painter Pieter Brueghel the Younger.

CLASSROOM ACTIVITY 7.1

The painting consists of nine panels, each of which illustrates a different Flemish proverb. As we mentioned in Chapter 1, proverbs are often difficult to translate from one culture to another, so we'll give you three of these colorful sayings in literal translation, plus their English equivalents. Then we'll ask you to try making up a story to fit one of these proverbs.

- In the bottom row of the painting, the roundel on the left depicts the proverb, "What is the use of blocking up the well after the calf has drowned?" In English, we would say, "Why lock the stable door after

Peter Brueghel the Younger, "Proverbs." Bildarchiv Foto Marburg, Marburg, West Germany.

the horse has been stolen?" (Can you think of an equivalent for this proverb in your own language?)

- The middle roundel in the bottom row shows a man drinking and not paying attention to the objects falling out of his basket, thus illustrating the proverb, "Continual drunkenness leads to poverty and dishonor."

• The roundel on the right in the bottom row is a representation of the saying, "If anyone wants to labor in vain, let him throw roses before swine." The English equivalent is "to cast pearls before swine"—to give something to someone who cannot appreciate it.*

Take five or ten minutes in class to make up a brief story that illustrates one of these three proverbs. At the end of your story, write "The moral of this fable is . . ." and state the proverb you have chosen. When you have finished, read some of these fables aloud to compare your response with those of your classmates.

Parables and Fables

Because proverbs, fables, fairy tales, parables, and myths provide entertaining lessons to "grow on," they act as a sort of school, teaching children—and reminding adults—about what they need to become accepted members of their society. Indeed, there is no race or nation that does not include the parable and the fable as part of its educational and religious heritage. Both of these ancient types of "teaching tales" use a narrative to illustrate a moral point or lesson.

Parables usually have human characters, and their stories are simple, short, and straightforward. One of the best-loved parables in the Bible, for example, is the story Jesus tells of the Good Samaritan (Luke 10: 25–38). Like many biblical parables, it is presented as the answer to a question asked of Jesus:

> On one occasion a lawyer stood up to pose him this problem: "Teacher, what must I do to inherit eternal life?" Jesus answered him, "What is written in the law? How do you read it?" He replied: "You shall love the Lord your God with all your heart, with all your soul, with all your strength, and with all your mind; and your neighbor as yourself."

---

* Here are the other six proverbs depicted in the painting:

Top row, left to right: (1) An opportunist turns his coat in the direction that the wind is blowing. (2) An indecisive person winds up sitting on ashes between two stools. (3) An unfaithful wife puts a blue cloak on her husband: he becomes notorious, however much he may try to hide.

Middle row, left to right: (1) He can't bear to see the sun reflected in the water (he's envious of someone else's property or success). (2) A fool fishes outside of other people's nets. (3) Attempting an impossible task is like trying to urinate on the moon (!).

(For Exercise 7.1, you may instead wish to make up a story that fits one of these six proverbs.)

Jesus said, "You have answered correctly. Do this, and you shall live."

But because he wished to justify himself, he said to Jesus, "And who is my neighbor?" Jesus replied: "There was a man going down from Jerusalem to Jericho who fell prey to robbers. They stripped him, beat him, and then went off leaving him half-dead. A priest happened to be going down the same road; he saw him but continued on. Likewise there was a Levite who came the same way; he saw him and went on. But a Samaritan who was journeying along came on him and was moved to pity at the sight.

"He approached him and dressed his wounds, pouring in oil and wine. He then hoisted him on his own beast and brought him to an inn, where he cared for him.

"The next day he took out two silver pieces and gave them to the innkeeper with the request: 'Look after him, and if there is any further expense I will repay you on my way back.'"

Jesus asked, "Which of these three, in your opinion, was neighbor to the man who fell in with the robbers?" The answer came, "The one who treated him with compassion." Jesus said to him, "Then go and do the same."

The world's greatest teachers, among them Lao Tzu, Buddha, Jesus, and Mohammed, recognized that "teaching stories" are often most successful when the listener is allowed to infer the *moral*—the abstract lesson, or thesis, that the story teaches. How would you state the moral or principle point of Jesus' parable?

JOURNAL EXERCISE 7.2

Part of growing up is learning from the mistakes we have made. Think about a time in your life when you ignored the advice of someone more experienced than you—a parent, teacher, older brother or sister. What happened? Write down everything you remember about this incident and the consequences you suffered as a result. Include specific details and dialogue to make your tale a convincing one. When you have finished, make this teaching story less personal and more universally meaningful by changing all the personal and possessive pronouns (*I, me, my, mine*) to the third person (*he/she, him/her, his/hers*).

CLASSROOM ACTIVITY 7.3

Break up into groups of four or five and read your stories aloud. After each story has been read, take a minute or two to infer the moral of the tale. Write a short statement that summarizes the lesson its writer learned. Then compare the morals you've come up with and discuss the ways in which the story illustrates them.

Different stories, of course, can be used to illustrate the same lesson or generalization. For further practice in class or at home, you may wish to trade morals with someone else in your group and write your own brief tale to support the moral of your partner's story.

The stories you have just written and talked about are fables. Like parables, fables point to a clear moral, although the moral may not be stated. Indeed, many morals are *implied* rather than stated, so that the reader or listener can supply different—though related—morals to suit the same tale. Through the words, actions, and experiences of the characters, fables tell us how we should behave. The first example we have chosen is a fable from China. Its moral will quickly become apparent—and, in fact, you can apply the same moral to the extended fable by D. H. Lawrence found on pages 243–254 of this chapter.

> In ancient times there was an old woodcutter who went to the mountain almost every day to cut wood.
> It was said that this old man was a miser who hoarded his silver until it changed to gold, and that he cared more for gold than anything else in all the world.
> One day a wilderness tiger sprang at him and though he ran he could not escape, and the tiger carried him off in its mouth.
> The woodcutter's son saw his father's danger, and ran to save him if possible. He carried a long knife, and as he could run faster than the tiger, who had a man to carry, he soon overtook them.
> His father was not much hurt, for the tiger held him by his clothes. When the old woodcutter saw his son about to stab the tiger, he called out in great alarm:
> "Do not spoil the tiger's skin! Do not spoil the tiger's skin! If you can kill him without cutting holes in his skin, we can get many pieces of silver for it. Kill him, but do not cut his body."
> While the son was listening to his father's instructions, the tiger suddenly dashed off into the forest, carrying the old man where the son could not reach him, and the old man was soon killed.

Very often the characters in fables are animals who talk and behave like people. You may have heard the stories of the grasshopper who played while the industrious ants stored up food for winter, the mouse who pulled the thorn out of the lion's paw, the overconfident rabbit who lost the race to the slow but steady tortoise. Many of you may also know the fable of the town mouse and the country mouse, which we have reprinted below. Actually, no creature is too small to provide an analogy to human beings. The American author Mark Twain went so far as to begin one of his fables, "Little Johnny Microbe begged and begged his mother to let him go to the picnic. . . ."

CLASSROOM ACTIVITY 7.4

Spend some time in class trading those fables from your childhood that immediately come to mind. See how many of your classmates have heard the same fables. What variations do you notice among the different versions of these stories?

Among the most famous fables in the West are those attributed to Aesop, a Greek slave who lived around 600 B.C. These tales have been retold in a variety of ways and languages ever since. The following selection is an 18th-century French version of one of Aesop's fables. As you read, look for particular details that suggest this is a French interpretation. How was this version modernized to fit 18th-century France?

The Town Mouse and the Country Mouse

A contented country mouse once had the honor to receive a visit from an old acquaintance belonging to the Royal court. The country mouse, extremely glad to see her guest, set before her the best cheese and bacon which her cottage afforded; and as to their beverage, it was the purest water from the spring. The repast was homely indeed, but the welcome hearty: they sat and chatted away the evening together very agreeably, and then retired in peace and quietness each to her little cell. The next morning when the guest was to take her leave, she kindly pressed her country friend to accompany her, setting forth in very pompous terms the great elegance and plenty in which she lived at court. The country mouse was easily prevailed upon, and they set out together. It was late in the evening when they arrived at the palace; however, in one of the rooms they found the remains of a sumptuous entertainment. There were creams and jellies, and sweetmeats; and everything, in short, of the most delicate kind: the cheese was Parmesan, and they wetted their whiskers in exquisite champagne. But before they had half finished their repast, they were alarmed with the barking and scratching of a lap dog; and the mewing of a cat frightened them almost to death; by and by, a whole train of servants burst into the room, and everything was swept away in an instant. "Ah! my dear friend," said the country mouse, as soon as she had recovered courage enough to speak, "if your fine living is thus interrupted with fears and dangers, let me return to my plain food, and my peaceful cottage; for what is elegance without ease; or plenty, with an aching heart?"

How do both the Chinese fable and the French translation of Aesop's tale treat the theme of riches? Can you state a moral that would fit each equally well?

JOURNAL EXERCISE 7.5

How would you update "The Town Mouse and the Country Mouse" to fit a 20th-century setting? In your journal, list the details you would change to make this fable contemporary.

How to Quote Dialogue

Like most stories, fables often include conversations between characters. One character may speak directly to another, as we can see in the last lines of "The Town Mouse and the Country Mouse," or the author may paraphrase (rephrase in his own words) what the characters have said. Quoting what your characters have to say can make any story more realistic and dramatic. But incorrect or missing punctuation may distort the meaning of your fable and leave your reader confused. Punctuating direct quotations is simple if you follow these four rules:

1. Place quotation marks (" ") at the beginning and the end of the speaker's exact words. The direct quotation is sometimes separated from the rest of the sentence with a colon—especially if it is a long quotation—but usually with a comma. Always begin a direct quote with a capital letter:

   Woody Allen said, "When the lion lies down with the lamb, the lamb isn't going to get much sleep."

   "We want more ice cream," the children chanted.

   When a quotation ends with a question mark or an exclamation point followed by words that identify the speaker, no comma is used:

   "Wolf!" cried the boy.

   "What did you say?" the shepherds asked angrily.

2. Use a comma before and after identifying words that interrupt a quotation:

   "Genius," Thomas Edison observed, "is one percent inspiration and ninety-nine percent perspiration."

3. Notice that commas and periods are placed *inside* quotation marks. Question marks and exclamation points are placed inside the quotation marks only if they are part of the quotation. But when a question

mark or exclamation point does not belong to the quotation, place it *outside* the quotation marks:

Who said "Genius is one percent inspiration and ninety-nine percent perspiration"?

4. When you are writing a conversation between two or more people, start a new paragraph each time the speaker changes so that your reader knows that someone else is now talking.

To demonstrate these rules, we'll quote "The Story-Teller" by H. H. Munro, a particularly interesting story because it is so humorously *ironic*— that is, it turns out contrary to our expectations. In this brief tale, a bachelor finds himself seated in a train compartment with a woman and her unruly nieces and nephew. The aunt tries unsuccessfully to quiet the three noisy children with a story. Notice that this section includes both *direct speech* and *reported speech* (a report of what someone else has said without quoting directly):

> In a low, confidential voice, interrupted at frequent intervals by loud, petulant questions from her listeners, she [the aunt] began an unenterprising and deplorably uninteresting story about a little girl who was good, and made friends with every one on account of her goodness, and was finally saved from a mad bull by a number of rescuers who admired her moral character.
> "Wouldn't they have saved her if she hadn't been good?" demanded the bigger of the small girls. . . .
> "Well, yes," admitted the aunt lamely, "but I don't think they would have run quite so fast to help her if they had not liked her so much."
> "It's the stupidest story I've ever heard," said the bigger of the small girls, with immense conviction.
> "I didn't listen after the first bit, it was so stupid," said Cyril.

Which part of this selection uses *reported speech*? Look at these two examples:

"I want to hear a story," said the child.

The child said that he wanted to hear a story.

What changes do you make to turn direct quotation into reported speech?

CLASSROOM ACTIVITY 7.6

Let's continue with H. H. Munro's story:

After listening to the aunt's unsuccessful tale, the bachelor tells the children one they truly relish. Like the aunt's fable, it too is about an extraordinarily good little girl. But contrary to our expectations, the little girl is not rewarded for her virtue. After winning several medals for goodness, which she always wears pinned to her dress, she is invited to walk in the Prince's park. Along comes a hungry wolf who immediately sees her spotless white dress and chases her. She hides in some bushes, trembling with fear, and the medal for obedience clinks against the medals for good conduct and punctuality. The wolf hears the clinking, drags her out of the bushes, and gobbles her up.

The children, of course, delight in the *irony* of the tale: if the girl had not been so good, she would not have been devoured.

Now use what you've learned about punctuating direct speech to supply the necessary commas, question marks, quotation marks, and capitals for the conclusion of "The Story-Teller." Remember to indicate a new paragraph each time the speaker changes:

The story began badly said the smaller of the small girls but it had a beautiful ending. It is the most beautiful story that I ever heard said the bigger of the small girls with immense decision. It is the *only* beautiful story I have ever heard said Cyril. A dissenting opinion came from the aunt. A most improper story to tell to young children! You have undermined the effect of years of careful teaching. At any rate said the bachelor, collecting his belongings preparatory to leaving the carriage, I kept them quiet for ten minutes, which was more than you were able to do. Unhappy woman! he observed to himself as he walked down the platform of Templecombe station; for the next six months or so those children will assail her in public with demands for an improper story!

The Updated Fable

The irony of H. H. Munro's fable gives it a very modern flavor. Your major assignment later on in this chapter will be to write your own modern fable. As a preliminary exercise for this final assignment, you can practice by updating an old fable in several ways.

One way to bring a fable up to date was suggested to us by two 19th-century books of fables: *A Collection of Fables Illustrated by Facts* by William Bourne, and *Fables Illustrated by Stories from Real Life* by Anne Jane Cupples. Each collection was designed, as Mrs. Cupples put it, "to present one or more anecdotes of a fitting character, as real-life witnesses to the truth of the moral contained in the text." Look at how one student incorporated a "real-life story" into his fable. Here is an excerpt from his journal —along with a sketch he drew in the margin—relating the incident that prompted his fable:

I jumped on the front seat of my friend's delivery van and we went to Brooklyn to deliver some 80 boxes of meat to a distributor. We passed by the old apartment where we used to live for a while.

I was very excited by the new graffiti on the walls and the funky music from the alley. But it broke my heart to see one little boy — he was so skinny and small for his age, you could

almost see the structure of his ribcage. He was the unwanted one, dependent upon marijuana . . . and bad company.

And here is his fictionalized version of the same event:

Little Boy Blue

Little Blue is a very skinny, very small fourteen-year-old. His eyes are gray, flashing to blue when he laughs, and his face shows a bittersweet smile. He is dressed in a mugger's uniform—Ralph Lauren T-shirt, designer jeans, and a pair of $45 Pumas with laces untied.

Little Blue is sitting on the steps of a typical Brooklyn apartment, rolling the fattest joint in the world. He keeps the other stuff hidden under his velvet hat. His entire crew is there too, their bodies and limbs carelessly stretched all over an elegant black limousine with tinted glass windows and six shiny doors. On the plate of the car is the name "Baby Devil."

Little Blue and his company enjoy listening and dancing in an energetic, funny way to the loud beating music from their heavy silver tape recorders. They pass around a long bottle covered with a brown paper bag; it seems to be a very special magic potion that they hide whenever they see a blue car with a red light on top.

The street is their school. They are very young, but they are mastering a degree in "How to Ruin Yourself." Kids like Little Blue soon learn the skills of gambling and stealing.

Do Little Blue's parents realize what is happening to their child? Little Blue runs so wild that redemption may come too late; help is what he needs. School is not a bad place to learn dignity and self-respect.

Little Blue's life is like a wild grapevine with its branches scattered, going in different directions. Now, there is a way to prevent Little Blue's destruction and straighten his direction. His parents must give him a sense of importance, discipline, and love—just like a grapevine he needs special care and time to produce sweet fruits.

MORAL: Do not let our children grow like wild plants.

—*Joselito del Fierro*

An 18th-century author named Edward Moore points to another way to adapt a fable to modern times in a book entitled *Fables for the Female Sex*. Writers of the 20th century have similarly concerned themselves with "fables for the female sex." But naturally they get beyond old-fashioned sexual stereotypes; their tales reflect centuries of change in women's roles. For instance, we know of two modern fables based on the fairy-tale character of Little Red Riding Hood. In the early version popularized by the Brothers Grimm, a hunter saves the little girl from the wolf. In James Thurber's "revised edition" from the 1930s, the young lady in question shoots the wolf with her automatic weapon ("Moral: It is not so easy to fool little girls nowadays as it used to be"). Angela Carter's 1979 rendition of the story, "The Company of Wolves," ends with the heroine seducing the wolf.

Consider, then, the fate of a contemporary "fairy princess" in another student's fable:

A Modern Fable

Somewhere in this world lived a small family: a husband and a wife. They loved each other all the time just as they had on their first date. They had a lovely house and good jobs. Everything was fine, but . . . they didn't have children.

And, as you know, people are such strange creatures: they always want what they can't have. So, the only wish of that family was to have a child.

One day, as it happens in fairy tales, an incredible thing took place—God took pity on them, and in nine months the woman gave birth to a child. The happy parents couldn't believe that their dream had come true. And from that moment the child became the center of the family. Now all love, all attention, all care was concentrated on the child.

Time passed and the child turned into a young lady. She was, like a million other girls, pretty enough, smart enough, but to her parents she was the prettiest and smartest girl in the world. Because she was raised in such an atmosphere, the girl believed that she was much, much better than all her girlfriends, that she was a special girl, and that an unusual life was waiting for her.

Looking for a better life, the family moved to America. "Now you will see a real life," her mother told her. "You are so beautiful, so smart that every man will be happy to make you his wife. But you have to choose the best one; you know your value."

Of course she knew her own value and she remembered it all the time, refusing one by one all offers to be somebody's wife. She was waiting for a modern prince—a millionaire.

In time all her girlfriends had their families, their children. They were living, they were enjoying life, and she was just watching.

Soon, her eyes lost their brilliance, her skin turned dry and wrinkled—she became old. She lived a long, empty, and colorless life. All her life she waited for the right time to start.

She didn't leave anything in this world after her. When she was dying, she tried to reproduce her life in her memory. But she couldn't remember anything but grey, identical days of waiting.

MORAL: Don't wait for fate to reward you.

—*Marina Isakova*

JOURNAL EXERCISE 7.7

With these student papers as examples, we have tried to suggest two possibilities for creating a contemporary fable:

- Take the moral from one of the stories in this chapter—or from any fable you can recall—and illustrate it with a "real-life story" you have heard or read about, perhaps in a newspaper or magazine.

- One author recently subtitled her collection of stories "Tales from the

Sisters Grimmer." Sketch your own modern version of a fable in which the heroine behaves in a distinctly 20th-century fashion.

On the other hand, traditional male roles in many cultures have also undergone considerable changes in the 20th century. So, if you prefer, write a fable in which the hero behaves in a decidedly contemporary manner.

A Modern Fabulist

Although people often think of the fable as a rather simple literary form, it can provide the structure for sophisticated fiction as well. This kind of literary work may have several themes or morals; different readers may have slightly varying interpretations of the story, see different "points." The richer and more complex a piece of fiction is, the wider and more varied the responses to it will be. Indeed, the best fiction invites us to re-read it many times, for each reading uncovers new themes, new connections, new questions.

CLASSROOM ACTIVITY 7.8

The story that follows was written by D. H. Lawrence, a coal miner's son from England who became a major 20th-century novelist. To begin the story, read the first four paragraphs of "The Rocking-Horse Winner," and then spend ten minutes freewriting about what you imagine will happen in this story. Afterwards, compare your expectations with those of your classmates.

EXERCISE 7.9

Before you read "The Rocking-Horse Winner," use your dictionary to look up any unfamiliar words on this list:

thrust	discreet	assert	knack
stealth	glare	flushed	serene
overwrought	divulge	anguish	obscure

The Rocking-Horse Winner

° **bonny** (Scottish or English dialect): handsome or pretty.

There was a woman who was beautiful, who started with all the advantages, yet she had no luck. She married for love, and the love turned to dust. She had bonny° children, yet she felt they had been thrust upon her,

° Here and throughout the story, we have preserved British spellings such as *centre, neighbourhood,* and *honour.*

° **racked her brains:** searched her mind; thought very hard.

° **smirking:** smiling in a superior and knowing way.

° **pram:** a baby carriage.

and she could not love them. They looked at her coldly, as if they were finding fault with her. And hurriedly she felt she must cover up some fault in herself. Yet what it was that she must cover up she never knew. Nevertheless, when her children were present, she always felt the centre° of her heart go hard. This troubled her, and in her manner she was all the more gentle and anxious for her children, as if she loved them very much. Only she herself knew that at the centre of her heart was a hard little place that could not feel love, no, not for anybody. Everybody else said of her: "She is such a good mother. She adores her children." Only she herself, and her children themselves, knew it was not so. They read it in each other's eyes.

There were a boy and two little girls. They lived in a pleasant house, with a garden, and they had discreet servants, and felt themselves superior to anyone in the neighbourhood.

Although they lived in style, they felt always an anxiety in the house. There was never enough money. The mother had a small income, and the father had a small income, but not nearly enough for the social position which they had to keep up. The father went in to town to some office. But though he had good prospects, these prospects never materialized. There was always the grinding sense of the shortage of money, though the style was always kept up.

At last the mother said: "I will see if *I* can't make something." But she did not know where to begin. She racked her brains,° and tried this thing and the other, but could not find anything successful. The failure made deep lines come into her face. Her children were growing up, they would have to go to school. There must be more money, there must be more money. The father, who was always very handsome and expensive in his tastes, seemed as if he never *would* be able to do anything worth doing. And the mother, who had a great belief in herself, did not succeed any better, and her tastes were just as expensive.

And so the house came to be haunted by the unspoken phrase: *There must be more money! There must be more money!* The children could hear it all the time, though nobody said it aloud. They heard it at Christmas, when the expensive and splendid toys filled the nursery. Behind the shining modern rocking-horse, behind the smart doll's-house, a voice would start whispering: "There *must* be more money! There *must* be more money!" And the children would stop playing, to listen for a moment. They would look into each other's eyes, to see if they had all heard. And each one saw in the eyes of the other two that they too had heard. "There *must* be more money! There *must* be more money!"

It came whispering from the springs of the still-swaying rocking-horse, and even the horse, bending his wooden, champing head, heard it. The big doll, sitting so pink and smirking° in her new pram,° could hear it quite plainly, and seemed to be smirking all the more self-consciously because of it. The foolish puppy, too, that took the place of the teddy-bear, he was looking so extraordinarily foolish for no other reason but that he heard the secret whisper all over the house: "There *must* be more money!"

Yet nobody ever said it aloud. The whisper was everywhere, and therefore no one spoke it. Just as no one ever says: "We are breathing!" in spite of the fact that breath is coming and going all the time.

"Mother," said the boy Paul one day, "why don't we keep a car of our own? Why do we always use uncle's, or else a taxi?"

"Because we're the poor members of the family," said the mother.

"But why *are* we, mother?"

"Well—I suppose," she said slowly and bitterly, "it's because your father has no luck."

The boy was silent for some time.

"Is luck money, mother?" he asked rather timidly.

"No, Paul. Not quite. It's what causes you to have money."

"Oh!" said Paul vaguely. "I thought when Uncle Oscar said *filthy lucker,* it meant money."

"*Filthy* lucre does mean money," said the mother. "But it's lucre, not luck."

"Oh!" said the boy. "Then what *is* luck, mother?"

"It's what causes you to have money. If you're lucky you have money. That's why it's better to be born lucky than rich. If you're rich, you may lose your money. But if you're lucky, you will always get more money."

"Oh! Will you? And is father not lucky?"

"Very unlucky, I should say," she said bitterly.

The boy watched her with unsure eyes.

"Why?" he asked.

"I don't know. Nobody ever knows why one person is lucky and another unlucky."

"Don't they? Nobody at all? Does *nobody* know?"

"Perhaps God. But He never tells."

"He ought to, then. And aren't you lucky either, mother?"

"I can't be, if I married an unlucky husband."

"But by yourself, aren't you?"

"I used to think I was, before I married. Now I think I am very unlucky indeed."

"Why?"

"Well—never mind! Perhaps I'm not really," she said.

The child looked at her, to see if she meant it. But he saw, by the lines of her mouth, that she was only trying to hide something from him.

"Well, anyhow," he said stoutly, "I'm a lucky person."

"Why?" said his mother, with a sudden laugh.

He stared at her. He didn't even know why he had said it.

° **brazening it out:** facing with bold or brash self-assurance.

"God told me," he asserted, brazening it out.°

"I hope He did, dear!" she said, again with a laugh, but rather bitter.

"He did, mother!"

"Excellent!" said the mother, using one of her husband's exclamations.

The boy saw she did not believe him; or, rather, that she paid no attention to his assertion. This angered him somewhat, and made him want to compel her attention.

He went off by himself, vaguely, in a childish way, seeking for the clue to "luck." Absorbed, taking no heed of other people, he went about with a sort of stealth, seeking inwardly for luck. He wanted luck, he wanted it, he wanted it. When the two girls were playing dolls in the nursery, he would sit on his big rocking-horse, charging madly into space, with a frenzy that

° **careered:** went at full speed; rushed wildly.

made the little girls peer at him uneasily. Wildly the horse careered,° the waving dark hair of the boy tossed, his eyes had a strange glare in them. The little girls dared not speak to him.

When he had ridden to the end of his mad little journey, he climbed down and stood in front of his rocking-horse, staring fixedly into its lowered face. Its red mouth was slightly open, its big eye was wide and glassy-bright.

"Now!" he would silently command the snorting steed. "Now, take me to where there is luck! Now take me!"

And he would slash the horse on the neck with the little whip he had asked Uncle Oscar for. He *knew* the horse could take him to where there was luck, if only he forced it. So he would mount again, and start on his furious ride, hoping at last to get there. He knew he could get there.

"You'll break your horse, Paul!" said the nurse.

° **leave off:** stop.

"He's always riding like that! I wish he'd leave off!"° said his elder sister Joan.

But he only glared down on them in silence. Nurse gave him up. She could make nothing of him. Anyhow he was growing beyond her.

One day his mother and his Uncle Oscar came in when he was on one of his furious rides. He did not speak to them.

"Hallo, you young jockey! Riding a winner?" said his uncle.

"Aren't you growing too big for a rocking-horse? You're not a very little boy any longer, you know," said his mother.

° **full tilt:** full speed.

But Paul only gave a blue glare from his big, rather close-set eyes. He would speak to nobody when he was in full tilt.° His mother watched him with an anxious expression on her face.

At last he suddenly stopped forcing his horse into the mechanical gallop, and slid down.

"Well, I got there!" he announced fiercely, his blue eyes still flaring, and his sturdy long legs straddling apart.

"Where did you get to?" asked his mother.

"Where I wanted to go," he flared back at her.

"That's right, son!" said Uncle Oscar. "Don't you stop till you get there. What's the horse's name?"

"He doesn't have a name," said the boy.

"Gets on without all right?" asked the uncle.

"Well, he has different names. He was called Sansovino last week."

° **Ascot, Lincolnshire, Leger, Grand National, Derby:** popular British horse races.

"Sansovino, eh? Won the Ascot.° How did you know his name?"

"He always talks about horse-races with Bassett," said Joan.

The uncle was delighted to find that his small nephew was posted with all the racing news. Bassett, the young gardener, who had been wounded in the left foot in the war and had got his present job through Oscar Cresswell, whose batman° he had been, was a perfect blade of the "turf."° He lived in the racing events, and the small boy lived with him.

° **batman:** the soldier servant of a British army officer.

° **blade of the "turf":** a gallant, good, free-and-easy fellow of the racetrack.

Oscar Cresswell got it all from Bassett.

"Master Paul comes and asks me, so I can't do more than tell him, sir," said Bassett, his face terribly serious, as if he were speaking of religious matters.

"And does he ever put anything on a horse he fancies?"

"Well—I don't want to give him away—he's a young sport, a fine sport, sir. Would you mind asking him himself? He sort of takes a pleasure in it, and perhaps he'd feel I was giving him away, sir, if you don't mind."

Bassett was serious as a church.

The uncle went back to his nephew and took him off for a ride in the car.

"Say, Paul, old man, do you ever put anything on a horse?" the uncle asked.

The boy watched the handsome man closely.

"Why, do you think I oughtn't to?" he parried.

"Not a bit of it! I thought perhaps you might give me a tip° for the Lincoln."

The car sped on into the country, going down to Uncle Oscar's place in Hampshire.

"Honour bright?" said the nephew.

"Honour bright, son!" said the uncle.

"Well, then, Daffodil."

"Daffodil! I doubt it, sonny. What about Mirza?"

"I only know the winner," said the boy. "That's Daffodil."

"Daffodil, eh?"

There was a pause. Daffodil was an obscure horse comparatively.

"Uncle!"

"Yes, son?"

"You won't let it go any further, will you? I promised Bassett."

"Bassett be damned, old man! What's he got to do with it?"

"We're partners. We've been partners from the first. Uncle, he lent me my first five shillings, which I lost. I promised him, honour bright, it was only between me and him; only you gave me that ten-shilling note I started winning with, so I thought you were lucky. You won't let it go any further, will you?"

The boy gazed at his uncle from those big, hot, blue eyes, set rather close together. The uncle stirred and laughed uneasily.

"Right you are, son! I'll keep your tip private. Daffodil, eh? How much are you putting on him?"

"All except twenty pounds," said the boy. "I keep that in reserve."

The uncle thought it a good joke.

"You keep twenty pounds in reserve, do you, you young romancer? What are you betting, then?"

"I'm betting three hundred," said the boy gravely. "But it's between you and me, Uncle Oscar! Honour bright?"

The uncle burst into a roar of laughter.

"It's between you and me all right, you young Nat Gould,"° he said, laughing. "But where's your three hundred?"

"Bassett keeps it for me. We're partners."

"You are, are you! And what is Bassett putting on° Daffodil?"

"He won't go quite as high as I do, I expect. Perhaps he'll go a hundred and fifty."

"What, pennies?" laughed the uncle.

"Pounds," said the child, with a surprised look at his uncle. "Bassett keeps a bigger reserve than I do."

° **give a tip:** give advance or "inside" information for betting on the outcome of an event.

° **Nat Gould:** a popular British writer of the late 19th century who wrote many newspaper articles, short stories, and novels about horse racing.

° **putting on:** betting on.

Between wonder and amusement Uncle Oscar was silent. He pursued the matter no further, but he determined to take his nephew with him to the Lincoln races.

"Now, son," he said, "I'm putting twenty on Mirza, and I'll put five for you on any horse you fancy. What's your pick?"

"Daffodil, uncle."

"No, not the fiver on Daffodil!"

"I should if it was my own fiver," said the child.

"Good! Good! Right you are! A fiver for me and a fiver for you on Daffodil."

The child had never been to a race-meeting before, and his eyes were blue fire. He pursed his mouth tight, and watched. A Frenchman just in front had put his money on Lancelot. Wild with excitement, he flayed his arms up and down, yelling *"Lancelot! Lancelot!"* in his French accent.

Daffodil came in first, Lancelot second, Mirza third. The child, flushed and with eyes blazing, was curiously serene. His uncle brought him four five-pound notes, four to one.

"What am I to do with these?" he cried, waving them before the boy's eyes.

"I suppose we'll talk to Bassett," said the boy. "I expect I have fifteen hundred now; and twenty in reserve; and this twenty."

His uncle studied him for some moments.

"Look here, son!" he said. "You're not serious about Bassett and that fifteen hundred, are you?"

"Yes, I am. But it's between you and me, uncle. Honour bright!"

"Honour bright all right, son! But I must talk to Bassett."

"If you'd like to be a partner, uncle, with Bassett and me, we could all be partners. Only, you'd have to promise, honour bright, uncle, not to let it go beyond us three. Bassett and I are lucky, and you must be lucky, because it was your ten shillings I started winning with. . . ."

Uncle Oscar took both Bassett and Paul into Richmond Park for an afternoon, and there they talked.

"It's like this, you see, sir," Bassett said. "Master Paul would get me talking about racing events, spinning yarns,° you know, sir. And he was always keen on knowing if I'd made or if I'd lost. It's about a year since, now, that I put five shilling on Blush of Dawn for him—and we lost. Then the luck turned, with that ten shillings he had from you, that we put on Singhalese. And since that time, it's been pretty steady, all things considering. What do you say, Master Paul?"

"We're all right when we're sure," said Paul. "It's when we're not quite sure that we go down."

"Oh, but we're careful then," said Bassett.

"But when are you *sure*?" smiled Uncle Oscar.

"It's Master Paul, sir," said Bassett, in a secret, religious voice. "It's as if he had it from heaven. Like Daffodil, now, for the Lincoln. That was as sure as eggs."

"Did you put anything on Daffodil?" asked Oscar Cresswell.

"Yes, sir. I made my bit."

"And my nephew?"

° **spinning yarns:** telling stories.

Bassett was obstinately silent, looking at Paul.

"I made twelve hundred, didn't I, Bassett? I told uncle I was putting three hundred on Daffodil."

"That's right," said Bassett, nodding.

"But where's the money?" asked the uncle.

"I keep it safe locked up, sir. Master Paul he can have it any minute he likes to ask for it."

"What, fifteen hundred pounds?"

"And twenty! And *forty*, that is, with the twenty he made on the course."

"It's amazing!" said the uncle.

"If Master Paul offers you to be partners, sir, I would, if I were you; if you'll excuse me," said Bassett.

Oscar Cresswell thought about it.

"I'll see the money," he said.

They drove home again, and sure enough, Bassett came round to the garden-house with fifteen hundred pounds in notes. The twenty pounds reserve was left with Joe Glee, in the Turf Commission deposit.

"You see, it's all right, uncle, when I'm *sure*! Then we go strong, for all we're worth. Don't we, Bassett?"

"We do that, Master Paul."

"And when are you sure?" said the uncle, laughing.

"Oh, well, sometimes I'm *absolutely* sure, like about Daffodil," said the boy, "and sometimes I have an idea; and sometimes I haven't even an idea, have I, Bassett? Then we're careful, because we mostly go down."

"You do, do you! And when you're sure, like about Daffodil, what makes you sure, sonny?"

"Oh, well, I don't know," said the boy uneasily. "I'm sure, you know, uncle; that's all."

"It's as if he had it from heaven, sir," Bassett reiterated.

"I should say so!" said the uncle.

But he became a partner. And when the Leger was coming on, Paul was "sure" about Lively Spark, which was a quite inconsiderable horse. The boy insisted on putting a thousand on the horse, Bassett went for five hundred, and Oscar Cresswell two hundred. Lively Spark came in first, and the betting had been ten to one against him. Paul had made ten thousand.

"You see," he said, "I was absolutely sure of him."

Even Oscar Cresswell had cleared two thousand.

"Look here, son," he said, "this sort of thing makes me nervous."

"It needn't, uncle! Perhaps I shan't be sure again for a long time."

"But what are you going to do with your money?" asked the uncle.

"Of course," said the boy, "I started it for mother. She said she had no luck, because father is unlucky, so I thought if *I* was lucky, it might stop whispering."

"What might stop whispering?"

"Our house. I *hate* our house for whispering."

"What does it whisper?"

"Why—why"—the boy fidgeted—"why, I don't know. But it's always short of money, you know, uncle."

"I know it, son, I know it."

° **writs:** written orders, issued by courts, that command a person to do something. Paul's mother is probably being ordered to pay her debts.

° **uncanny:** strange; inspiring wonder; not to be explained in a logical way.

"You know people send mother writs,° don't you uncle?"

"I'm afraid I do," said the uncle.

"And then the house whispers, like people laughing at you behind your back. It's awful, that is! I thought if I was lucky . . ."

"You might stop it," added the uncle.

The boy watched him with big blue eyes, that had an uncanny° cold fire in them, and he said never a word.

"Well, then!" said the uncle. "What are we doing?"

"I shouldn't like mother to know I was lucky," said the boy.

"Why not, son?"

"She'd stop me."

"I don't think she would."

"Oh!"—and the boy writhed in an odd way—"I *don't* want her to know, uncle."

"All right, son! We'll manage it without her knowing."

They managed it very easily. Paul, at the other's suggestion, handed over five thousand pounds to his uncle, who deposited it with the family lawyer, who was then to inform Paul's mother that a relative had put five thousand pounds into his hands, which sum was to be paid out a thousand pounds at a time, on the mother's birthday, for the next five years.

"So she'll have a birthday present of a thousand pounds for five successive years," said Uncle Oscar. "I hope it won't make it all the harder for her later."

Paul's mother had her birthday in November. The house had been "whispering" worse than ever lately, and, even in spite of his luck, Paul could not bear up° against it. He was very anxious to see the effect of the birthday letter, telling his mother about the thousand pounds.

° **bear up:** to resist; to fight against stress or difficulty.

When there were no visitors, Paul now took his meal with his parents, as he was beyond the nursery control. His mother went into town nearly every day. She had discovered that she had an odd knack of sketching furs and dress materials, so she worked secretly in the studio of a friend who was the chief "artist" for the leading drapers. She drew the figures of ladies in furs and ladies in silk and sequins for the newspaper advertisements. This young woman artist earned several thousand pounds a year, but Paul's mother only made several hundreds, and she was again dissatisfied. She so wanted to be first in something, and she did not succeed, even in making sketches for drapery advertisements.

She was down to breakfast on the morning of her birthday. Paul watched her face as she read her letters. He knew the lawyer's letter. As his mother read it, her face hardened and became more expressionless. Then a cold, determined look came on her mouth. She hid the letter under the pile of others, and said not a word about it.

"Didn't you have anything nice in the post for your birthday, mother?" said Paul.

"Quite moderately nice," she said, her voice cold and absent.

She went away to town without saying more.

But in the afternoon Uncle Oscar appeared. He said Paul's mother had had a long interview with the lawyer, asking if the whole five thousand could not be advanced at once, as she was in debt.

"What do you think, uncle?" said the boy.

"I leave it to you, son."

"Oh, let her have it, then! We can get some more with the other," said the boy.

"A bird in the hand is worth two in the bush, laddie!" said Uncle Oscar.

"But I'm sure to *know* for the Grand National; or the Lincolnshire; or else the Derby. I'm sure to know for *one* of them," said Paul.

So Uncle Oscar signed the agreement, and Paul's mother touched the whole five thousand. Then something very curious happened. The voices in the house suddenly went mad, like a chorus of frogs on a spring evening. There were certain new furnishings, and Paul had a tutor. He was *really* going to Eton, his father's school, in the following autumn. There were flowers in the winter, and a blossoming of the luxury Paul's mother had been used to. And yet the voices in the house, behind the sprays of mimosa and almond blossom, and from under the piles of iridescent cushions, simply trilled and screamed in a sort of ecstasy: "There *must* be more money! Oh-h-h; there *must* be more money. Oh, now, now-w! Now-w-w— there *must* be more money!—more than ever! More than ever!"

It frightened Paul terribly. He studied away at his Latin and Greek with his tutors. But his intense hours were spent with Bassett. The Grand National had gone by: he had not "known," and had lost a hundred pounds. Summer was at hand. He was in agony for the Lincoln. But even for the Lincoln he didn't "know," and he lost fifty pounds. He became wild-eyed and strange, as if something were going to explode in him.

"Let it alone, son! Don't you bother about it!" urged Uncle Oscar. But it was as if the boy couldn't really hear what his uncle was saying.

"I've got to know for the Derby! I've got to know for the Derby!" the child reiterated, his big blue eyes blazing with a sort of madness.

His mother noticed how overwrought he was.

"You'd better go to the seaside. Wouldn't you like to go now to the seaside, instead of waiting? I think you'd better," she said, looking down at him anxiously, her heart curiously heavy because of him.

But the child lifted his uncanny blue eyes.

"I couldn't possibly go before the Derby, mother!" he said. "I couldn't possibly!"

"Why not?" she said, her voice becoming heavy when she was opposed. "Why not? You can still go from the seaside to see the Derby with your Uncle Oscar, if that's what you wish. No need for you to wait here. Besides, I think you care too much about these races. It's a bad sign. My family has been a gambling family, and you won't know till you grow up how much damage it has done. But it has done damage. I shall have to send Bassett away, and ask Uncle Oscar not to talk racing to you, unless you promise to be reasonable about it; go away to the seaside and forget it. You're all nerves!"

"I'll do what you like, mother, so long as you don't send me away till after the Derby," the boy said.

"Send you away from where? Just from this house?"

"Yes," he said, gazing at her.

"Why, you curious child, what makes you care about this house so much, suddenly? I never knew you loved it."

He gazed at her without speaking. He had a secret within a secret, something he had not divulged, even to Bassett or to his Uncle Oscar.

But his mother, after standing undecided and a little bit sullen for some moments, said:

"Very well, then! Don't go to the seaside till after the Derby, if you don't wish it. But promise me you won't let your nerves go to pieces. Promise you won't think so much about horse-racing and *events*, as you call them!"

"Oh, no," said the boy casually. "I won't think much about them, mother. You needn't worry. I wouldn't worry, mother, if I were you."

"If you were me and I were you," said his mother, "I wonder what we *should* do!"

"But you know you needn't worry, mother, don't you?" the boy repeated.

"I should be awfully glad to know it," she said wearily.

"Oh, well, you *can*, you know. I mean you *ought* to know you needn't worry," he insisted.

"Ought I? Then I'll see about it," she said.

Paul's secret of secrets was his wooden horse, that which had no name. Since he was emancipated from a nurse and a nursery-governess, he had had his rocking-horse removed to his own bedroom at the top of the house.

"Surely, you're too big for a rocking-horse!" his mother had remonstrated.

"Well, you see, mother, till I can have a *real* horse, I like to have *some* sort of animal about," had been his quaint answer.

"Do you feel he keeps you company?" she laughed.

"Oh, yes! He's very good, he always keeps me company, when I'm there," said Paul.

So the horse, rather shabby, stood in an arrested prance in the boy's bedroom.

The Derby was drawing near, and the boy grew more and more tense. He hardly heard what was spoken to him, he was very frail, and his eyes were really uncanny. His mother had sudden strange seizures of uneasiness about him. Sometimes, for half-an-hour, she would feel a sudden anxiety about him that was almost anguish. She wanted to rush to him at once, and know he was safe.

Two nights before the Derby, she was at a big party in town, when one of her rushes of anxiety about her boy, her first-born, gripped her heart till she could hardly speak. She fought with the feeling, might and main,° for she believed in common-sense. But it was too strong. She had to leave the dance and go downstairs to telephone to the country. The children's nursery-governess was terribly surprised and startled at being rung up in the night.

"Are the children all right, Miss Wilmot?"

"Oh, yes, they are quite all right."

"Master Paul? Is he all right?"

"He went to bed as right as a trivet.° Shall I run up and look at him?"

"No," said Paul's mother reluctantly. "No! Don't trouble. It's all right. Don't sit up. We shall be home fairly soon." She did not want her son's privacy intruded upon.

"Very good," said the governess.

It was about one o'clock when Paul's mother and father drove up to their

° **might and main:** all one's strength.

° **as right as a trivet:** perfectly all right; steady.

house. All was still. Paul's mother went to her room and slipped off her white fur cloak. She had told her maid not to wait up for her. She heard her husband downstairs, mixing a whisky-and-soda.

And then, because of the strange anxiety at her heart, she stole upstairs to her son's room. Noiselessly she went along the upper corridor. Was there a faint noise? What was it?

She stood, with arrested muscles, outside his door, listening. There was a strange, heavy, and yet not loud noise. Her heart stood still. It was a soundless noise, yet rushing and powerful. Something huge, in violent, hushed motion. What was it? What in God's name was it? She ought to know. She felt that she knew the noise. She knew what it was.

Yet she could not place it. She couldn't say what it was. And on and on it went, like a madness.

Softly, frozen with anxiety and fear, she turned the door-handle.

The room was dark. Yet in the space near the window, she heard and saw something plunging to and fro.° She gazed in fear and amazement.

Then suddenly she switched on the light, and saw her son, in his green pyjamas, madly surging on the rocking-horse. The blaze of light suddenly lit him up, as he urged the wooden horse, and lit her up, as she stood, blonde, in her dress of pale green and crystal, in the doorway.

"Paul!" she cried. "Whatever are you doing?"

"It's Malabar!" he screamed, in a powerful, strange voice. "It's Malabar!"

His eyes blazed at her for one strange and senseless second, as he ceased urging his wooden horse. Then he fell with a crash to the ground, and she, all her tormented motherhood flooding upon her, rushed to gather him up.

But he was unconscious, and unconscious he remained, with some brain-fever. He talked and tossed, and his mother sat stonily by his side.

"Malabar! It's Malabar! Bassett, Bassett, I *know*! It's Malabar!"

So the child cried, trying to get up and urge the rocking-horse that gave him his inspiration.

"What does he mean by Malabar?" asked the heart-frozen mother.

"I don't know," said the father stonily.

"What does he mean by Malabar?" she asked her brother Oscar.

"It's one of the horses running for the Derby," was the answer.

And, in spite of himself, Oscar Cresswell spoke to Bassett, and himself put a thousand on Malabar: at fourteen to one.

The third day of the illness was critical: they were waiting for a change. The boy, with his rather long, curly hair, was tossing ceaselessly on the pillow. He neither slept nor regained consciousness, and his eyes were like blue stones. His mother sat, feeling her heart had gone, turned actually into a stone.

In the evening, Oscar Cresswell did not come, but Bassett sent a message, saying could he come up for one moment, just one moment? Paul's mother was very angry at the intrusion, but on second thought she agreed. The boy was the same. Perhaps Bassett might bring him to consciousness.

The gardener, a shortish fellow with a little brown moustache, and sharp little brown eyes, tip-toed into the room, touched his imaginary cap to Paul's mother, and stole to the bedside, staring with glittering, smallish eyes, at the tossing, dying child.

° **to and fro:** forward and backward.

"Master Paul!" he whispered. "Master Paul! Malabar came in first all right, a clean win. I did as you told me. You've made over seventy thousand pounds, you have; you've got over eighty thousand. Malabar came in all right, Master Paul."

"Malabar! Malabar! Did I say Malabar, mother? Did I say Malabar? Do you think I'm lucky, mother? I knew Malabar, didn't I? Over eighty thousand pounds. I call that lucky, don't you, mother? Over eighty thousand pounds! I knew, didn't I know I knew? Malabar came in all right. If I ride my horse till I'm sure, then I tell you, Bassett, you can go as high as you like. Did you go for all you were worth, Bassett?"

"I went a thousand on it, Master Paul."

"I never told you, mother, that if I can ride my horse, and *get there*, then I'm absolutely sure—oh, absolutely! Mother, did I ever tell you? I *am* lucky!"

"No, you never did," said the mother.

But the boy died in the night.

And even as he lay dead, his mother heard her brother's voice saying to her: "My God, Hester, you're eighty-odd thousand to the good, and a poor devil of a son to the bad.° But, poor devil, poor devil, he's best gone out of a life where he rides his rocking-horse to find a winner."

° **to the good:** signifies profit or gain, and **to the bad** means loss.

JOURNAL EXERCISE 7.10

Writing in response to something—a problem, an experience, a story—often helps us to discover what we actually *think* about it. Use your journal to reflect upon your reactions to "The Rocking-Horse Winner." Spend ten minutes of focused freewriting on each of the following topics: Paul; Paul's mother; your thoughts on the "fairy tale" or supernatural qualities of the story; any experiences the story calls to mind. Then make a list of any questions you have about this fable.

Hearing your classmates' journal entries may help you with your own interpretation of the story. As you listen to each other's responses to the story, you may wish to write down those ideas and observations that particularly interest you.

EXERCISE 7.11

When we read a story for the first time, we often read primarily to find out *what happens.* Once we know what happens, we can re-read the story more reflectively, and notice numerous details that we probably overlooked in our first reading. As a result, our opinion of the story and what we think it means may change. You may wish to re-read "The Rocking-Horse Winner" at a leisurely pace for the next class, and record any new thoughts, questions, and feelings you have about this story in your journal.

CLASSROOM ACTIVITY 7.12

Like any good story, "The Rocking-Horse Winner" provokes a number of questions that don't have single or simple answers. In talking about the story in class, you'll find that no two readers have responded in exactly the same way, noticed exactly the same things, shared exactly the same interpretation. Discuss with your classmates the questions listed here. As you talk about your ideas, try to point to details in the text that lead you to think the way you do.

- Why can't Paul's mother love her children?

- What does Paul think luck means? What causes him to think this? What does luck mean in your culture? What does it mean to you?

- What does the rocking horse symbolize to Paul? to you?

- Why won't Paul divulge his "secret within a secret" to Bassett or his Uncle Oscar?

- Why does Paul die?

- What moral or morals might fit this tale?

- If you were to continue this story where Lawrence left off, how would you portray the family's life? Is the house finally quiet? Why or why not?

EXERCISE 7.13

Fill in each blank with the most appropriate word from the vocabulary list on page 243. You may have to change the word form to suit the sentence:

1. When Paul rode his rocking horse to find a winner, his eyes took on

   a strange _____.

2. Frenzied, he would _____ his rocking horse forward at full tilt.

3. Paul became more and more _____ as the Derby approached.

4. The family's servants behaved _____: they were always reserved and respectful.

5. Paul _____ that he was lucky but refused to

_____ the secret of his success.

6. Paul went around with a sort of _____, secretly searching for luck.

7. Paul bet on an _____ horse named Daffodil to win the Lincoln.

8. Until he was certain he knew the winner of a race, Paul's face was

_____ with _____.

9. Then, when he was sure he knew the winner, his blue eyes became

_____.

10. Paul's father had no _____ for making money.

Assignment: A Fable/Parable for the End of the Century

At the end of the 19th century, Mark Twain wrote *Fables of Man*. Some fifty years later, James Thurber created *Fables for Our Time*. In the 1950s, another author came up with *Fables and Parables for the Mid-Century*. Your assignment is to write an extended "Fable (or Parable) for the End of the Century." You may want to use your journal entries from this chapter for the rough draft of your essay.

Because fables are stories that are used to illustrate what *may happen if* we behave in a certain way, they often make use of the conditional and sub-junctive tenses. Consult the following modal and verb tense reviews to help you in composing your fable.

Function Word Review: The Modal Auxiliaries

"The Rocking-Horse Winner" is the story of an unusually sensitive boy who believes that it is his responsibility to bring luck to his family. This sense of obligation dominates the tale: the house seems to whisper continually, "There must be more money! There must be more money!" *Must* is an example of a *modal auxiliary* that expresses absolute necessity.

Modals make up a group of auxiliary verbs that add a particular meaning to the verb phrase. Modals help express the mood or attitude of the speaker toward what he or she is saying. Review the following explanations of common modals before you study the conditional tenses, which are formed with modals. The first three categories we list are modals of necessity or obligation; the other modals are used to express ability, permission, preference, and habitual action.

1. *Must* and *have to* both point to actions we cannot avoid, either because life gives us no choice or because we have a strong sense of duty:

   All living things *must* have oxygen to survive.

   I *have to* work, and he *has to* go to school.

   Paul felt he *had to* find luck.

   Notice that *must* has only one form. For the past meaning of *must* we use *had to*.
   Must is also used to express an *inference* — a conclusion or deduction based on evidence:

   Paul *must be* an unhappy child. (present time)

   Paul *must have been* an unhappy child. (past time)

   Paul feels that because he rides his rocking horse so furiously he *must* soon find luck. (future time)

   Note that *must* can be used for the past tense when it expresses an inference.

2. *Need,* or the phrase *need to,* is another way of saying *have to.* Like *have, need* functions like a regular verb. It changes according to tense and subject-verb agreement.

   Paul's mother *needed to* raise money.

   Paul *needs* his mother's love.

3. *Should, ought to,* and *had better* are not as strong as *must, have to,* and *need to* in meaning; they indicate what is wise or advisable:

   Paul's mother says, "I wonder what we *should* do?"

   Paul answers, "I mean you *ought to* know you needn't worry."

   When Paul's mother notices how overwrought he is, she says, "You'd *better* go to the seaside."

Should and *ought to* can also show expectation:

They *should* (or *ought to*) arrive shortly.

JOURNAL EXERCISE 7.14

Write a letter telling a high school student what he or she should do to prepare for college. Use each of the modals of obligation at least once.

Or, make a list of your responsibilities in the coming week. Use each of the modals of obligation in a complete sentence that states what you must accomplish.

---

4. *Can* (*could*) and *be able to** express ability:

Paul *can* ride his rocking horse to find a winner.

Paul *could* ride his rocking horse to find a winner.

It seemed Paul's father would never *be able to* do anything worth doing.

5. As you will see in the Verb Tense Review, *may, might, can,* and *could* are used to indicate possibilities in conditional sentences. *May, might, can,* and *could* are also used to express permission:

Can (or *could*) I call you tonight?

Yes, you *may.*

Carla asked if she *might* borrow the book.

May/might is usually considered to be a more formal way to express permission than *can/could.*

6. *Would rather* indicates preference:

Paul's mother *would rather have* money than love.
(present or "timeless" time)

Paul's mother *would rather have had* money than love.
(past time)

---

* *Be able to* and *be used to* follow the usual conjugation of the verb *to be. Be used to* is followed by a gerund (*-ing* noun), not an infinitive:

CORRECT: He is used to *having* his own way.

INCORRECT: He is used to *have* his own way.

7. *Would* and *used to* express repeated or customary past action:

Paul *would* ride his rocking horse to find the winner before each race.
Paul's mother *used to* think she was lucky before she married.

8. The phrase *be used to** means "accustomed to":

I *am used to* getting up early.

EXERCISE 7.15

Answer each of the following questions with a complete sentence.

1. May I buy you dinner this evening?

2. What can you do best?

3. When you were five years old, could you read?

4. What made you realize that you might want to learn English?

5. What should you be doing right now?

6. Where would you rather be at this moment?

7. Can you describe a place where you used to go on vacations when you were a child?

8. What are you used to eating for breakfast?

---

* See note on page 258.

EXERCISE 7.16

Below are some examples of the modals discussed on the previous pages. Try to come up with your own statements, aphorisms, or advertising headlines, using each of these modals.

> "Life can only be understood backwards; but it must be lived forwards." Kierkegaard

You only need to read half of this ad.

Only Toshiba could make a document filing system this advanced.

We think everyone in the picture, should really be in the picture.

It may not please you to learn that the world's best address is now Ten Five Sixty.

'I don't think we ought to raise any tax for the sake of raising taxes. My starting point is the spending side.'

It doesn't have to be English gin to be exceptional. It has to be Fleischmann's.
AMERICA'S EXCEPTIONAL GIN SINCE 1870

You'd Better Hurry!

Across the fields of yesterday he sometimes comes to me a little child just back from play the child I used to be.

America's Favorite Crossword Game

SCRABBLE® is the registered trademark of Selchow & Righter Co. Bay Shore, NY for its line of word games and entertainment services.

Verb Tense Review: The Conditional and Subjunctive

In English grammar, what is called the *mood* of a sentence refers to the speaker's position or attitude in the communication. From either the word order or the verb form, we can tell if the speaker or writer is making a statement (indicative mood), asking a question (interrogative mood), issuing a command (imperative mood), or showing the uncertainty or unreality of the statement being made (subjunctive mood).

In the subjunctive mood, which is used to express wishes or "if" statements, the verb form signals the mode of discourse. The *conditional* or "if" tenses are used to speculate about something in the past or future, or to talk about situations contrary to fact. These tenses express possibilities, not certainties. There are a number of types of "if" sentences; the three most common types are listed here.

TYPE I

Meaning: The proposition is possible or is likely to happen.

VERB IN IF-CLAUSE	AUXILIARY + VERB IN MAIN CLAUSE	
present tense	*can, may, will, should, must, have to, had better, ought to* (sometimes *could* and *might*)	+ base form

If John *comes* to the party, he*'ll bring* the wine.

If she*'s* sick tomorrow, she *may* not *go* to school.

If you *ask* me that question one more time, I*'ll scream.*

They *have to wake* up early if they *have* a class at 8:00 A.M.

EXERCISE 7.17

Rewrite these morals to famous fables using the "if" construction. For example, the moral "Those who violate friendship do not escape punishment" might be rewritten, "If you treat your friends like enemies, you will end up alone."

1. "Before you criticize others, make sure you are without fault."

2. "He who desires another man's food often loses his own."

3. "Liberty should not be sold for all the world's silver and gold."

4. "Evil comes to those who wish evil upon others."

5. "People can get so puffed up with pride that they explode."

6. "What we cannot accomplish by force we can accomplish by invention and industry."

7. "In serving the wicked, hope for no gains,
And be glad if you come out alive for your pains."

8. "Ah Love, whoever bows to you
Should bid his sanity adieu."

TYPE II

Meaning: The proposition is imagined or untrue; it is impossible or unlikely to be realized in the near future.

VERB IN IF-CLAUSE	AUXILIARY + VERB IN MAIN CLAUSE
simple past tense (for the verb *to be*, always use *were*)	could would might } + base form

If I *spoke* ten languages, I'*d work* at the U.N.

If he *didn't have* so many problems, he *might relax* more.

Ms. Reese *would be* a better boss if she *were* more understanding.

Ringo Starr sang, "What *would* you *do* if I *sang* out of tune, / *Would* you *stand* up and *walk* out on me?"

A Note on the Subjunctive Mood

Were should be used for all forms of the past subjunctive *to be*, although this usage is quickly dying out in American English. In fact, writer William Safire was so dismayed by one politician's faulty grammar that he offered this tough defense of the subjunctive *were*:

> "If I was to make a political decision," said Senator Edward Kennedy, withdrawing from the 1984 Presidential race, "it would be a different announcement today."
>
> Wrong. (Not the decision, the mood.) When you are posing a hypothesis contrary to fact, you must use the subjunctive. That's the rule, and no horsing around is allowed. Senator Kennedy was saying that he was not making a "political decision," but one based on family concerns; therefore (to take him at his word) making a "political decision" was a situation contrary to fact. He ought then to have said, "If I *were* to make a political decision," followed with the parallel construction, "I would be making a different announcement today."
>
> Got that? If you have *would* in the main clause, you must use *were* (the subjunctive) in the "if" clause. If I were to let this one go by, I would be derelict in my duty as self-appointed guardian of good grammar. . . .
>
> Can you ever use "If I was"? Of course, when you are examining a real possibility, or even a likelihood: "If I *was* speeding, Your Honor, I didn't realize it." . . . Or, in the Senator's case, "If I was thinking about stimulating a draft at the 1984 Democratic convention, I am not about to tell you that today."

The subjunctive *were* is also used to express another imagined or untrue proposition—when we make *wishes*.

1. In English, one cannot say, "I wish I can (present tense) swim." For wishes in the present, use *were* or the *simple past tense*:

   Mother wishes she *could* swim.

   Sophia wishes she *were* taller.

2. If the wish refers to a past condition, use *had* + the past participle:

   Mother wishes she *had learned* to swim.

   After Juan got sick, he wished he *hadn't eaten* the whole cake.

3. If the wish can still come true in the present or future, use *would* or *could* + the base form of the verb:

   I wish you *could hear* yourself.

   And I wish you *would sing* somewhere else.

EXERCISE 7.18

Now make three wishes, of the past, present, and future.

EXERCISE 7.19

Because the past conditional tense is used to state a hypothesis contrary to fact, it, too, is often used to express wishes and dreams. Nowhere is this usage more evident than in popular songs. Here is a well-known example:

If I Had a Hammer (The Hammer Song)

If I had a hammer, I'd hammer in the morning,
I'd hammer in the evening all over this land,
I'd hammer out danger, I'd hammer out warning,
I'd hammer out love between all of my brothers,
All over this land. ©

—Lee Hays and Pete Seeger

Use your imagination to complete the following song titles:

"If I Were a Rich Man"

"If I Ruled the World"

"If I Loved You"

"If Love Were All"

"If I Were King of the Forest"

"If Ever I Would Leave You"

EXERCISE 7.20

In complete conditional sentences, explain what you would do if you were a rock star; an architect; a professional writer; a cowardly lion.

TYPE III

Meaning: The proposition is impossible, because the action has been completed and you can't change it. You are simply wondering what *would have happened* if things *had been* different.

VERB IN IF-CLAUSE	AUXILIARY + VERB IN MAIN CLAUSE
past perfect tense	could have would have } + past might have participle

If we *had known* John was sick, we *would have visited* him at the hospital.

If you *had done* the assignment, your grade *might have been* better.

The thief *couldn't have entered* the house if you *had locked* the door.

EXERCISE 7.21

If you had been born (a) in the United States, (b) in the time of Aesop, (c) in 1900, (d) on another planet, how would your childhood have been different? Again, respond with *complete* conditional sentences.

EXERCISE 7.22

Put the verb in parentheses in the correct tense:

1. If I [to feel] _____ tired, I may take a few days off and rest.

2. She [to become] _____ an artist if she had more talent.

3. You [not to understand] _____ the world if you never read the newspapers.*

4. If I [to live] _____ on a farm, I'd get up at dawn every day.

5. If she forgets my birthday again, I [to be] _____ very upset.

6. I'd tell the truth if I [to be] _____ you.

7. If you had called me, I [to be] _____ glad to meet you.

---

* There are two possible answers here: please give both.

8. If you (not to brush) _____ your teeth, you can get cavities.

EXERCISE 7.23

Finish these conditional sentences:

1. If today were a holiday, _____.

2. If I were the teacher in this class today, _____.

3. If people had three sets of shoulders, _____.

4. She might not have caught a cold if _____.

5. I would have bought a car if _____.

6. I could have been a movie star if _____.

7. Columbus might not have discovered America if_____.

unit 5 | Exposition

8

Defining, Classifying, Comparing, Contrasting
or
Four Ways of Looking at a Computer

Points of View

We have been exploring different kinds of writing—keeping a journal, giving directions, describing people and places, telling stories. In the next three chapters, we'll be looking at various methods of *exposition*. The purpose of expository writing is, as its name implies, to *expose* or reveal a subject: that is, to explain, analyze, or argue by examining the components of a subject to find out what makes it work. News articles, book reviews, lab reports, essay exams, and political commentaries are all common forms of exposition.

As we've seen in previous chapters, writing an essay is always a process of choosing a group of details from the mass of raw data available to any observer. We seek out the details that will "prove" our hunch, our hypothesis. As the scientist Karl Popper once remarked, "Observation is always selective. It needs a chosen object, a definite task, an interest, a point of view, a problem." (Popper illustrated this idea in a famous fable, which is quoted later on in this chapter.)

So there are many ways to shape material for an essay, depending upon the particular problem you're trying to solve. In this chapter—really four "mini-chapters"—we'll be looking at four common expository patterns:

Definition	Analogy
Classification	Comparison/Contrast

Our present concern, then, is with the variety of viewpoints from which a writer can examine the same subject. Before we discuss each of these four modes of perceiving and explaining, it might be useful to look more closely at the process of perception itself.

In an earlier chapter, we noted that a word or a concept is only part of an extensive network of associations in a writer's mind. The characteristic way each individual organizes perceptions and ideas depends on a number of factors. The simple act of "seeing" is often a matter of interpretation. For example, a person's psychological makeup can influence the way he looks at the world. A well-known illustration of this phenomenon is the Thematic Apperception Test, widely used by psychologists, in which patients are asked to respond to a series of pictures. To see how varied people's perceptions of the same picture can be, try the following task in your notebook.

CLASSROOM ACTIVITY 8.1

Take about ten minutes to make up a story about the following painting by the American artist Edward Hopper. Briefly explain the situation it represents, discuss the events that led up to the situation, indicate the feelings and thoughts of the characters in the picture, and describe the outcome of the situation. Comparing responses with your classmates will no doubt reveal considerable differences in the way people "read" the same material.

Edward Hopper, "Room in New York," 1932. F. M. Hall Collection, Sheldon Memorial Art Gallery, University of Nebraska—Lincoln.

An individual's cultural background, as well, influences the way he or she thinks—as this cartoon implies:

"I think in English and dream in English. However, I still conceptualize in Russian."

Drawing by Ed Arno; © 1982 The New Yorker Magazine, Inc.

Cross-cultural studies have repeatedly shown how perceptions and inferences vary from nationality to nationality. For example, compare the following two advertisements: on the left is an advertising poster for Matsuya Department Store in Japan; on the right is a magazine advertisement for Marshall Field's in the U.S.:

(In English, the headline would read "Cast a Lover's Spell.")

A new slant on stripes. Simply by slicing the shoulders, splicing the sides, tilting the stripes Cee Gee creates a whole new angle of appeal. Gray and white cotton wedge in sizes 4 to 12, $128. Dress Room, Sixth Floor, State Street; Water Tower Place, Oakbrook, Old Orchard, Woodfield, and River Oaks, Chicago; Mayfair in Milwaukee; The Galleria and Town and Country in Houston; Galleria in Dallas.

Marshall Field's

CLASSROOM ACTIVITY 8.2

What similarities and differences do you and your classmates observe in the two ads on the previous page?

In an article on Japanese design, authors Ko Nada and Mill Roseman discuss some of the differences between Japanese and American advertising techniques. They point out that in Japan "there is a single system of education for all, and far less diversity than in the United States in terms of ethnic, cultural, and educational background. As a result, communication does not focus on logical conviction or argument; the important aspects are sensitivity and feeling." Japanese advertising practices reflect a consistent cultural preference for indirect and subtle ways of communicating. Indeed, the Japanese distrust the direct, concrete, "hard-sell" promotion that is common in American advertisements, which often tell us exactly why we should buy a product.

To most Americans, the Japanese advertisement would be perplexing because it does not offer specific information about Matsuya Department Store. They might wonder what a Western model dressed in traditional Indian garb has to do with selling the kinds of goods associated with department stores. In fact, fifty percent of the models used in Japanese advertising are Western, and their purpose is to identify the product as Western and therefore somewhat exotic. Further, in Japan, things Indian are thought to be mysterious, involved with spells and sorcery. The Japanese consumer would understand these implied meanings in the poster.

Then, too, what an individual has been trained to see affects his or her perceptions. Below is an image that has been deliberately altered by a computer.

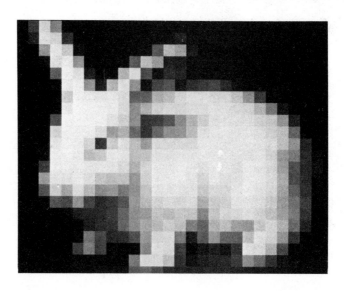

At first glance, the subject of this picture may not be recognizable. But once you have read the headline and first sentence of the ad—

Kill this rabbit.

Scientists will soon be able to sacrifice *electronic* rabbits instead of living, breathing lab animals.

you should be able to "see" the picture in a different way, and to identify the subject. Oftentimes, discovery depends on knowing what to look for.

Thus, this next illustration can be viewed in two different ways—you just have to be flexible enough to change your point of view:

The same kind of flexibility is required to solve verbal problems in logic. Just as flexibility of viewpoint helps you to see a picture in a variety of ways, so mental flexibility helps you to "see" various solutions to an intellectual puzzle. You may want to test your powers of logic with this example:

Many years ago when a person who owed money could be thrown into jail, a merchant in London had the misfortune to owe a huge sum to a money-lender. The old money-lender proposed a bargain: He said he would cancel the merchant's debt if he could marry the merchant's beautiful young daughter.

Both the merchant and his daughter were horrified at the proposal. So the cunning money-lender proposed that they let Providence decide the matter. He told them that he would put a black pebble and a white pebble into an empty money-bag and then the girl would have to pick out one of the pebbles. If she chose the black pebble she would become his wife and her father's debt would be cancelled. If she chose the white pebble she would stay with her father and the debt would still be cancelled. But if she refused to pick out a pebble her father would be thrown into jail and she would starve.

Reluctantly the merchant agreed. They were standing on a pebble-strewn path in the merchant's garden as they talked and the money-lender stooped to pick up the two pebbles. The girl, sharp-eyed with fright, noticed that he picked up two black pebbles and put them into the money-bag. He then asked the girl to pick out the pebble that was to decide her fate and that of her father.

Adapted from NEW THINK: *The Use of Lateral Thinking in the Generation of New Ideas* by Edward de Bono. © 1967, 1968 by Edward de Bono. Reprinted by permission of Basic Books, Inc., Publishers.

EXERCISE 8.3

Imagine that you are standing on that path in the merchant's garden. What would you have done if you had been the unfortunate girl? (You'll find her solution at the end of this chapter.)

Clearly, the ability to respond flexibly to situations (or to think "laterally" in De Bono's term) is one essential attribute of intelligence. Douglas Hofstadter, a computer expert interested in the creation of so-called "artificial intelligence" systems, lists the following additional characteristics of intelligence. Hofstadter's chief concern is with the extent to which these distinctly human characteristics can be "programmed" into computers: the ability to

take advantage of fortuitous [= happening by accident or chance] circumstances

make sense out of ambiguous [= having two or more possible meanings] or contradictory messages;

recognize the relative importance of different elements of a situation;

find similarities between situations despite differences which may separate them;

draw distinctions between situations despite similarities which may link them;

synthesize new concepts by taking old concepts and putting them together in new ways;

come up with ideas which are novel.

In other words, intelligence consists of the ability to reason, to judge, to classify, to compare, to contrast, to define, and to create new ideas out of old concepts. These are the tools we wish to sharpen in this chapter.

To demonstrate these skills, we'll show how they can be used to clarify a current and very complex issue: the much-debated question of whether the next generation of computers (often called the "Fifth Generation") can be programmed to think as humans do. On one side of the debate are the researchers in artificial intelligence (AI); they generally believe that all human experience and intelligence can ultimately be analyzed as a set of principles, and that in time it will be possible to create a machine with the same mental abilities as humans. Their opponents, however, argue that to give a computer real reasoning power and understanding, we would need to give it a human's complex knowledge of the world—knowledge that is impossible to attain without a body, senses, and emotions.

We'll show how a writer can approach this problem of artificial intelligence from four different directions—which is why we've subtitled this chapter "Four Ways of Looking at a Computer." In each section, we'll begin with a different view of the subject of "intelligent" machines, and then see how those lessons in definition, classification, analogy, and comparison/contrast can be applied to other subjects as well.

View 1: "The Computer Is the Main Artifact of the Age of Information": Definition

Let's start with *definition*. What do we mean by the seemingly contradictory term *artificial intelligence*? Here is a brief definition of the term:

> **artificial intelligence:** Computer programs that can approximate some of the capacities of human intelligence, such as reasoning and pattern recognition. In principle, a perfect AI program could reproduce other human traits, such as learning from experience and initiating plans.

Now look at how two authors, Pamela McCorduck and Edward Feigenbaum, use an extended definition to make this phrase clear to the readers of their book on the "fifth generation" computers of the future. As you read, consider: What is the purpose of this piece? What is the thesis? How do the authors use definition to develop their thesis?

> The word *intelligence* derives originally from the Latin *leger*, meaning literally to gather (especially fruit), to collect, to assemble, and hence to choose and form an impression. *Intellegere* means to choose among, hence to understand, perceive, and know. If we can imagine an artifact that can collect, assemble, choose among, understand, perceive, and know, then we have an artificial intelligence. . . .

The difficulty most of us have in thinking about intelligent machines is that our concept of "machine" is conditioned by the machines that have surrounded us all our lives. Almost without exception their function is to process energy—that is, to amplify, to distribute, to transform, or otherwise to modify energy. Thus the automobile transforms fossil-fuel energy (itself already transformed by refining) into kinetic° energy, and that transformation amplifies human kinetic energy and serves human purposes. We can drive farther than we walk. Furthermore, all such energy transformations can be clearly described by the classical scientific disciplines.

° **kinetic:** relating to or produced by motion.

The computer, however, is a different kind of machine. It processes not energy, but information. Of course, there is some energy involved, just as information transformation is involved in telephones and broadcast media, but except to certain kinds of engineers, the energy transformations of the computer are its least interesting features.

To understand the essential function of computers—as machines—we have to shake the old metaphors from our heads and begin thinking in a new way. The computer is the main artifact of the age of information. Its purpose is certainly to process information—to transform, amplify, distribute, and otherwise modify it. But more important, the computer *produces* information. The essence of the computer revolution is that the burden of producing the future knowledge of the world will be transferred from human heads to machine artifacts. . . .

The artifacts have been misnamed, however, and that is misleading us. The word *computer,* with its overtones of counting and calculation, tells us only what the machine's historical uses have been, not its potential.

—The Fifth Generation

Recent scientific developments have resulted in many new terms and phrases that, like *artificial intelligence,* are really redefinitions or combinations of familiar words. Consequently, we are now expected to be acquainted with concepts such as *future shock, jet lag,* and *earth station,* as well as computer terms such as *expert systems, bubble memory, computer language, bit, disk,* and *menu.* Indeed, not long ago one fashion magazine even printed a "Dictionary of Information-Age Terms" for its readers, arguing that "Whether you're a hacker or just a computer layman, technical words are becoming a necessary part of your everyday vocabulary." What other terms could you add to this glossary? And how would you go about defining one of them?

JOURNAL EXERCISE 8.4

Pick one of these "Information-Age" terms—drawn from electronics, computers, or biotechnology—and write (1) a one- or two-sentence definition of the term, and (2) an extended definition of it. For example, here is a one-sentence definition of *computer language:* "Any of a number of special instructional codes that tell the computer what to do." Most likely, an extended definition would provide examples of different computer languages, and might also include a comparison/contrast of these languages.

You may, instead, wish to choose a technical term from your major field —for instance, *petri dish, projective test, balance sheet, nuclear family*—and write both a brief and an extended definition of it. Your teacher may ask you to read your definitions to the class, so try to make your definition clear and comprehensible to those members of the group who are not familiar with the term you're defining.

At the conclusion of this section on definition, return to this exercise to see if you can further expand your definition of the term you've selected.

Whether a definition is a dictionary entry, a paragraph, or an entire essay, it must accomplish two things. First, it must place an item into a class of items like it. Second, it must specify the distinguishing characteristics of the item: how is it different from other members of the same class? There are a number of ways of going about these tasks, and the techniques you choose will depend on your purpose and audience. In an *extended* definition like the one just quoted, several—if not all—of the following methods may be employed:

1. Assign the word to a class and clearly describe its essential characteristics.

2. Isolate a distinguishing characteristic.

3. Cite familiar examples.

4. Use comparison/contrast to point out its similarities to or differences from other things of this nature.

5. Draw an analogy to define the word by relating it to more easily understood concepts.

6. Include the *connotations*, or associations and emotional overtones, of the word.

7. Give both common and rare meanings of the word.

8. Summarize the *etymology* of the word; that is, give its origin and historical development.

EXERCISE 8.5

How many of these characteristics can you locate in the definition of artificial intelligence on pages 275–276? Return to the passage and label these elements as you come upon them. When you have finished, underline the transitional words or phrases (including demonstratives, pronouns, and repeated words) that the authors use to connect the various elements of their definition.

EXERCISE 8.6

As languages evolve, the meanings of many individual words undergo changes. *Deer,* for example, used to mean any kind of animal. *Silly* was once a synonym for happy or blessed. And *liquor,* now an alcoholic beverage, started out as any kind of fluid. Investigate the etymology of the following words: *brat, shrew, villain, mistress, hysterical.* You will have to consult an unabridged English dictionary that includes the historical development of words. (The *Oxford English Dictionary* in your college library is probably the most comprehensive source.) You'll encounter some of these words in an exercise later on.

Definition helps us not only to describe what we actually observe around us, but also to explain the things that we imagine. Every culture, for example, has magical, fantastic beings that populate its folklore. In *The Book of Imaginary Beings,* Argentinian author Jorge Luis Borges defines such mythical creatures as the Celestial Horse of China, the Minotaur of Crete, the Sphinx of Egypt, and the Trolls of England. In the following excerpt, Borges draws upon history, description, and etymology to define the fabled creatures called Gnomes:

° **alchemist:** a practitioner of alchemy, which was an early form of chemistry with magical associations. Its chief aims were to change baser metals into gold and to discover the elixir of perpetual youth.

The Gnomes are older than their name, which is Greek but which was unknown to the ancients, since it dates from the sixteenth century. Etymologists attribute it to the Swiss alchemist° Paracelsus in whose writings it appears for the first time.

They are sprites of the earth and hills. Popular imagination pictures them as bearded dwarfs of rough and grotesque features; they wear tight-fitting brown clothes with monastic hoods. Like the griffons of Greece and of the East and the dragons of Germanic lore, the Gnomes watch over hidden treasure.

Gnosis, in Greek, means knowledge, and Paracelsus may have called them Gnomes because they know the exact places where precious metals are to be found.

JOURNAL EXERCISE 8.7

Define an imaginary being from the folklore of your own culture—or make up a creature of your own. Either way, define the creature in precise enough terms that we'd instantly recognize it if it trotted (or flew, or slithered) into the room. Remember, a definition is more than a description. Use as many of the elements of definition (listed on page 277) as you can.

Denotation and Connotation

Another aspect of many definitions is the cluster of *associations* attached to a particular word. Look, for example, at the ways in which four different writers define *marriage*:

marriage (mar'ij) n. 1.a. The state of being husband and wife; wedlock. b. The legal union of a man and woman as husband and wife. 2. The act of marrying or the ceremony of being married; a wedding.

—The American Heritage Dictionary

Marriage, n. The state or condition of a community consisting of a master, a mistress and two slaves, making in all, two.

—*Ambrose Bierce,* The Devil's Dictionary

Marriage *is* a funny institution. A man loves a woman so much, he asks her to marry—to change her name, quit her job, have and raise his babies, be home when he gets there, move where his job is.
You can hardly imagine what he might ask if he didn't love her.

—*Gabrielle Burton,* Pulling Our Own Strings

There is no more lovely, friendly and charming relationship, communion or company than a good marriage.

—*Martin Luther,* "On Marriage"

The first example is, of course, a standard, objective dictionary definition —the *denotation* of the word. The other three examples reflect the writers' attitudes toward marriage, something that dictionary definitions avoid. "Slanted" definitions, which are often humorous, reveal the author's bias. In Chapter 4 we looked at the way in which an author's point of view colors his description: for one student, the topic "Saturday night" evoked loneliness; for another, festive images. So, too, the feelings we associate with a word, the images that come to mind when we hear that word, are likely to influence the way we define the word. It is wise for an author to be aware of his or her personal feelings and attitudes and to try to avoid them in definitions that are supposed to be objective.

In contrast to individual reactions, however, many words have developed over the years *general* emotional associations—*connotations*—that the writer can be reasonably sure his readers share with him. The denotation, or literal meaning of a word, may be neutral, neither good nor bad, but its connotation may charge it with strong feeling. One interesting example is *machismo*, a Spanish word that has recently become part of the English language:

> It is so new to English that dictionaries published before the seventies did not include it: the qualities it describes were unacknowledged. In its native Mexico (the word comes from the Spanish *macho*, meaning "male"), machismo is used to compliment men for virility and a sense of pride in themselves as males. It has overtones, however, of excessive concern with "masculinity," and it is this connotation especially that has carried over into English. The definition in the 1973 edition of the American Heritage Dictionary is explicit in this regard: machismo, it says, is "an exaggerated sense of masculinity stressing such attributes as physical courage, virility, domination of women, and aggressiveness or violence."
>
> —*Casey Miller and Kate Swift*, Words and Women

JOURNAL EXERCISE 8.8

Can you think of a word (or words) that English has borrowed from your native language? Has the meaning of that word—either its denotation or connotation—changed in the translation from one language to another? If so, in what way?

Simply knowing the literal meaning of a word or a few synonyms for it is often not enough. Ignorance of the connotation of a word may color your writing in a shade you don't intend. If you were to look up synonyms for the adjective *thin*, for example, you'd probably find "skinny," "scrawny," "slender," and "slim" among them. Both *skinny* and *scrawny*, however, suggest an undesirable or unpleasant quality, whereas *slender* and *slim* are generally used in an admiring or complimentary sense. Similarly, both *house* and *home* can be used to denote the same residence, but as the old song goes, "A house is not a home"—*house* is a neutral word for a residence, whereas *home* implies a place of warmth, security, and love.

CLASSROOM ACTIVITY 8.9

A.) If you had to be described with one of the adjectives from each of the following groups of words, which word would you choose? Which would you least like to be called? Explain why. (Again, you may wish to consult your dictionary.)

1. assertive   aggressive   pushy

2. fat   plump   overweight

3. shrewd   crafty   clever

4. self-satisfied   confident   smug

B.) Below are three words that figure prominently in this chapter. What feelings and images do they call to mind? Try to determine which connotations are personal, and which are shared by your classmates:

housewife   computer   gorilla

CLASSROOM ACTIVITY 8.10

The following paragraph is a slanted description. Your job is to find the words with negative denotations and connotations and to replace these words with other words or phrases that have more positive overtones. Refer to your dictionary for help.

> Although my neighbor has a college degree, she is a full-time housewife whose days are filled with menial tasks. She's gotten scrawny from chasing her two children around all the time, but she is always babbling about how cute the little brats are. She stubbornly insists that she's happy with this tedious existence. She becomes hysterical if one of the children is ill, and she never fails to giggle at their silly antics. But when they misbehave, she turns into a shrew. With her husband, she's submissive and servile; she slavishly cooks, cleans, and shops. Like most drudges, she pretends her job is important.

A Note on Choosing the Appropriate Tone

We often talk about a speaker's tone of voice in conversation: for example, we can say that a speaker sounded sarcastic, or indignant, or angry. But how is this tone of voice communicated in a piece of writing? Because the words you choose help to determine the *tone* of your writing, it's important to select words that are appropriate for your topic and your readers. Both sentence structure and word choice show your reader the attitude you have toward your material and your audience. A letter to an old friend would probably be informal in tone, and might well be peppered with slang and casual diction. As we demonstrated in Chapter 3, however, the language of everyday speech is unsuitable for a business letter or a formal essay on a serious subject.

In Chapter 10, we will see how tone plays a crucial role in the argumentative essay. For now, we offer the following exercise to remind you of the importance of adopting a suitable tone for a particular writing task.

EXERCISE 8.11

You've probably been in this situation at least once in your school career: you haven't done your homework and you wish to apologize to your teacher. Naturally, you want your apology to sound sincere and serious. What follows is our favorite example—a note received from a student who found himself falling behind in his work. He tried to make his apology convincing by striking a formal tone, but he unintentionally chose certain words and phrases that have a decidedly casual ring to them. See if you can rewrite his note in the manner he surely intended:

Dear Professor:

Hi! Sorry that I haven't handed in my assignments on numerous occasions.

Though my assignments are done, I feel terribly sorry about my lousy handwriting and untidiness. I hope that my poor offerings do not bring you too much trouble, and that you don't go blind reading them.

And again, I beg your pardon for my "French leave,"° but I have "burned the midnight oil" to finish this. I am so pooped now that I can hardly maintain the vitality to attend your class.

Thanks for your patience in reading this note.

Your student,
Alfred

° **"French leave"**: an expression used by British servicemen for taking an unexcused absence from duty.

CLASSROOM ACTIVITY 8.12

This exercise in description asks you to draw upon what you've learned about slanting, connotation, and tone. Begin by considering the facts in the following paragraph, a neutral description of a hypothetical car called the Gnome:

The Gnome is a compact car that seats four passengers. Its fuel-injected engine accelerates from 0 to 50 m.p.h. in 7.2 seconds, and the car gets approximately 35 miles to a gallon of gas in highway driving. The Gnome is equipped with an automatic transmission, power steering, power brakes, and front wheel drive, as well as electric tinted-glass windows, air conditioning, and a quartz digital clock. The manufacturer's suggested retail price is $9,195. The car comes with a limited 5 year/50,000 mile warranty (whichever comes first).

In a group with two or three of your classmates, rewrite this description from two points of view:

1. You are an advertising executive whose job it is to promote this car: compose a description that is sure to attract buyers.

2. You happen to be the unhappy owner of a Gnome, and a friend of yours is thinking about buying one. Write a slanted description of the automobile to convince your friend that purchasing a Gnome would be a serious mistake.

View 2: "The Computer . . . Is a Different Kind of Machine": Classification

Classification is the filing system of the mind. As we've pointed out, classification is an important element of any definition. Definition and analysis both depend on our ability to recognize patterns and to group items in classes according to their shared characteristics. The definition of artificial intelligence quoted earlier, for instance, is based on the distinction between two classes of machines:

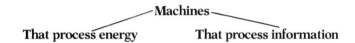

Machines

That process energy   That process information

This ability to divide and classify a group of items is essential for organizing a large body of material and making it manageable. Here's an example of division and classification taken from one research institute's outline of research and development plans for fifth-generation computer systems. The example is rather technical; *skim* it (= read it quickly) to get a sense of how a classification may be structured. The authors divide the *functions* required of an artificial intelligence system into four broad categories, and then explain what is included in each classification group:

Research and Development Themes

The Fifth-Generation Computer Systems aim at knowledge information processing based on innovative inference functions and technologies that meet the needs anticipated in the 1990s, including intelligent interaction between man and machine and inference using knowledge bases.

The functions required of such a system can be broadly divided into four types:

(1) Problem solving and inference function

This function is intended to enable the system to find solutions to problems by carrying on logical reasoning using data and knowledge stored in the system as well as information given to it from outside. This capability covers deductive inference, inductive inference including guessing based on incomplete knowledge, and cooperative problem solving by mutual complementation of several bodies of knowledge.

(2) Knowledge base function

This function is aimed at providing systematic storage and retrieval of not only so-called data but also reasonable judgments and test results organized into a knowledge. Besides knowledge accumulation, it includes knowledge representation tailored to problem solving, knowledge acquisition and updating, and simultaneous utilization of distributed knowledge sources.

(3) Intelligent interface function

This function is intended to enable computers to handle speech, graphics, and images so that the computers can interact with humans flexibly and smoothly. It might be regarded as giving computers the equivalents of human eyes, mouth, and ears, but its primary objective is to provide computers with a linguistic ability close to that of man.

(4) Intelligent programming function

This function is intended to enhance the intelligence of computers so that they can take over the burden of programming from humans. While its ultimate goal is to achieve an ability to automatically convert problems into efficient computer programs, it is aimed preliminarily at achieving a modular programming system and a program verification system and at establishing a specification description language.

—The Institute of New Generation Computer Technology

The same topic can often be divided and classified in a number of ways. The principle of division you choose depends on the purpose of your analysis: in your choice of categories, you are eliminating elements that are not important. For example, if you're in the market for a personal computer, and you need to assess the relative merits of the various computers currently available to the consumer, the color of the machine will probably not be a significant characteristic. You might, however, classify the computers you're assessing according to the *functions* they can perform using available software:

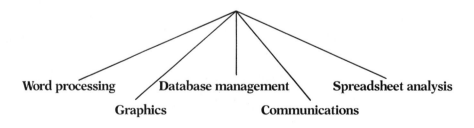

or *size* (in terms used by the computer industry):

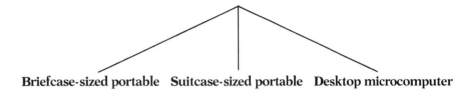

Briefcase-sized portable   Suitcase-sized portable   Desktop microcomputer

or *cost*:

Under $1,000 $1,000–$4,000   Over $4,000

Whatever classification system you're using, two rules are important to observe:

1. Your principle of division should include all the main varieties of the class you're discussing. For example, to divide all computers into "briefcase-sized" models and "desktop microcomputers" would be to ignore the important intermediate category.

2. Your principle of division must be sharp and consistent; categories should not overlap. For example, you wouldn't divide personal computers into "briefcase-sized," "suitcase-sized," and "over-$4,000." To begin with, the principle of division is inconsistent: the first two categories concern size, whereas the third category concerns cost. In addition, the subsets overlap—a suitcase-sized computer can cost well over $4,000.

To take a few more examples of faulty classification, which item in each of these categories does not belong? Why?

PAINTINGS: watercolors, oil, tempera, landscapes

CARS: foreign-made, compact, American-made

MUSIC: classical, rock-'n'-roll, jazz, symphonic

Before we ask you to practice these skills in an exercise in classification, we'd like to give you an example of the way classification can be used as the basis of a much longer essay. The excerpt under consideration comes from *Gorillas in the Mist,* Dian Fossey's book-length study of a species of great ape. As you may know, the basis of biological science is a system of classification that divides all living things into two general kingdoms, Plant or Animal. This organization, known as the Linnaean system, further divides these categories into smaller and more specific groups:

Phylum

Subphylum

Class

Subclass

Order

Superfamily

Family

Genus

Species

Dian Fossey thus begins her book by defining *Primate,* an order which includes orangutans, chimpanzees, gorillas, and humans. She then goes on to classify the various subspecies of gorilla, each according to its habitat and distinguishing characteristics:

In 1758 Carl Linnaeus, the first serious student of classification, officially recognized the close relationship between humans, monkeys, and apes. He devised the order name Primates to encompass them all and to denote their high ranking in the animal kingdom. Man and the three great apes— orangutan, chimpanzee, and gorilla—are the only primates without tails and, like most primates, have five digits on each hand and foot, the first of which is opposable. Anatomical features shared by all primates are two mammae (nipples), orbits [eyes] directed forward to permit binocular vision, and, usually, a total of thirty-two teeth.

Because of the scanty record of ape fossils, there is no universal agreement on the origin of the two families, Pongidae (the apes) and Hominidae (mankind), which have been separated for millions of years. None of the three great apes is considered ancestral to modern man, *Homo sapiens,* but they remain the only other type of extant primate with which human beings share such close physical characteristics. From them we may learn much concerning the behavior of our earliest primate prototypes, because behavior, unlike bones, teeth, or tools, does not fossilize.

Several million years ago the chimpanzee and gorilla lines had already separated from one another, and the orangutan line even earlier than that.

Throughout the eighteenth century there remained a considerable amount of confusion in distinguishing between orangutans, chimpanzees, and gorillas. The orangutan was the first to be recognized as a distinct genus— only because of its remote habitat in Asia. It was not until 1847, on the basis of a single skull from Gabon, that the gorilla was confirmed as a separate genus from the chimpanzee.

° **morphological:** having to do with form and structure.

Just as there are separate subspecies among orangutan and chimpanzee, there are separate subspecies of gorilla, also with morphological° variations related primarily to habitat. In western Africa there remain some 9000 to 10,000 lowland gorilla (*Gorilla gorilla gorilla*) in the wild. It is this subspecies most frequently seen in captivity and mounted in museum collections. Some 1000 miles to the east within the Virunga Volcanoes of Zaire, Uganda, and Rwanda live the last surviving mountain gorillas (*Gorilla gorilla beringei*), the subjects of my field study. Only about 240 mountain gorillas remain in the world. None are found in captivity. The third subspecies is known as the eastern lowland gorilla (*Gorilla gorilla graueri*). Only about 4000 *graueri* remain in the wild, mainly in eastern Zaire, and less than two dozen live in captivity.

° **terrestrial:** living on land rather than in water, in air, or in trees.

There are some twenty-nine morphological differences between the lowland and the mountain gorilla, adaptations related to altitudinal variations. The mountain gorilla, the more terrestrial° of the two and living at the highest altitude in the gorillas' range, has longer body hair, more expanded nostrils, a broader chest girth, a more pronounced sagittal crest, shorter arm limbs, a longer palate, and shorter, broader hands and feet.

EXERCISE 8.13

Gorillas belong to the *phylum* of Chordata (= animals with a notochord or vertebrae), the *subphylum* of Vertebrata (= animals with vertebrae, or backbones), the *class* of Mammalia, the *subclass* of Eutheria (= placental mammals), the *order* of Primates, and the *superfamily* of Hominoidea (apes and men).* On page 288 we've begun a classification chart for the species of gorilla. Using the above information and the Fossey excerpt, fill in the rest of the chart. Then list (1) the distinguishing characteristics of primates, and (2) some of the differences between lowland and mountain gorillas.

---

* Primate classification is not static, and in recent years has been the subject of much dispute. Textbooks show a number of alternative schemes for classifying primates: for example, it has been suggested that chimpanzees and gorillas should be placed in the same genus; there is also the question of whether the African apes should be placed with man in the family Hominidae, while retaining the orangutan in the Pongidae. But according to A. F. Dixson, an expert in the field, "*Homo sapiens* has always been placed in his own family and many anthropologists argue that, despite his kinship with gorillas or chimpanzees, man is sufficiently unique to merit such a classification."

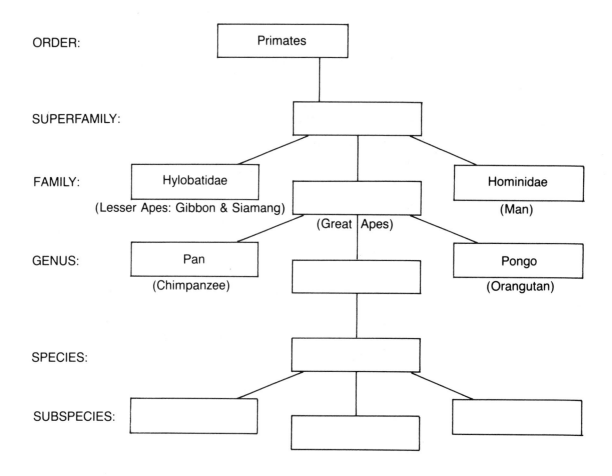

ORDER:	Primates	
SUPERFAMILY:		
FAMILY:	Hylobatidae (Lesser Apes: Gibbon & Siamang)	(Great Apes)	Hominidae (Man)
GENUS:	Pan (Chimpanzee)		Pongo (Orangutan)
SPECIES:		
SUBSPECIES:		

Fossey's classification of her subject prepares her readers for an intensive study, the result of the thirteen years Fossey spent living with mountain gorillas in Africa. One of the most striking features of the book is how the Linnaean system gives *shape* to all of Fossey's research and observations. Her findings show how closely related gorillas are to their fellow primates, human beings. Here she states the conclusion she reached as a result of her research:

> My research studies of this majestic and dignified great ape—a gentle yet maligned nonhuman primate—have provided insight to the essentially harmonious means by which gorillas organize and maintain their familial groups and also have provided understanding of some of the intricacies of various behavioral patterns never previously suspected to exist.

Fossey's observations and narratives repeatedly underscore the "kinship" between gorillas and humans. For example, contrary to the stereotype of the savage, chest-pounding ape, these enormous creatures proved to be loving and indulgent parents. Witness the behavior of a huge silverback (= mature male) that Fossey called "Beethoven":

> Slowly Beethoven shifted his great bulk, rolled over onto his back, gave a contented sigh, and speculatively regarded his latest offspring, six-month-old Puck. The infant was playfully tadpoling across the stomach of its mother, Effie, wearing a lopsided grin of enjoyment. Gently, Beethoven lifted Puck up by the scruff of the neck to dangle the exuberant baby over his body before casually grooming it. Puck was nearly obscured from sight by the massive hand, which eventually placed the wide-eyed infant back onto Effie's stomach.
>
> That observation of a silverback sire with his offspring was typical of similar scenes throughout the years to be spent with the gorillas. The extraordinary gentleness of the adult male with his young dispels all the King Kong mythology.

Fossey's discoveries about these amazingly "human" beasts emphasize how cruelly they have been treated by their human captors. In one instance, Fossey rescued a baby gorilla who had been confined in a wire cage by hunters hoping to sell it to a zoo. A few minutes after being brought to Fossey's cabin, the baby (which she named "Coco") crawled onto Fossey's lap:

> Coco sat on my lap calmly for a few minutes before walking to a long bench below the windows that overlooked nearby slopes of Visoke. With great difficulty she climbed onto the bench and gazed out at the mountain. Suddenly she began to sob and shed actual tears, something I have never seen a gorilla do before or since. When it finally grew dark she curled up in a nest of vegetation I had made for her and softly whimpered herself to sleep.

You can see that in the process of studying these primates, the scientist found behavioral patterns that linked this animal family back to the human members of the primate order. She was then able to use this evidence to support her argument against the inhumane treatment of these animals in captivity. Fossey thus demonstrates the number of ways in which a writer can put the skill of classification to good use.

JOURNAL EXERCISE 8.14

Of course, classification can also be put to frivolous use. For example, two Dutch authors, Wil Huygen and Rien Poortvliet, took Borges's definition of *gnomes* one step further by writing a book-length "scientific study" of gnomes and their habits. The book, which became a best seller here and abroad, describes and classifies—according to habitat—the following types of gnomes: woodland gnomes, dune gnomes, garden gnomes, house gnomes, farm gnomes, and Siberian gnomes. (This may be more than you ever cared to know about the subject.)

Before you go on to the next assignment, you may wish to practice your powers of classification with a similar exercise. In a paragraph or two, extend your definition of an imaginary being (Journal Exercise 8.7) by dividing that "class" of creatures into subspecies or types. Be sure to include the characteristics (e.g., habitat, eating habits, physical traits) that typify each subspecies you list.

EXERCISE 8.15

For a more developed essay in classification, discuss a group you belong to by dividing it into categories. You are, of course, a member of any number of groups, in school, at home, at work. For example:

son or daughter

student

computer science major

employee at McDonald's

customer at McDonald's

To take another example, a recent newspaper article used the following principle of division. Here is the opening paragraph of the article. To which group do you belong?

> All the world is divided into three parts—finger-feeders, fork-feeders, and chopstick-feeders. Why people fall into these categories, however, is a mystery. "There is no comprehensive account of the ways of putting solid food into the mouth," according to Dr. Lynn White Jr., an emeritus history professor at the University of California at Los Angeles and an expert on medieval technology.
>
> —*Bryce Nelson*

For your classification essay, divide one of the categories you belong to and analyze the characteristics of its subsets. As a brief pre-writing activity to help you with your essay, sketch a diagram of your classification of this category. (You may wish to refer to the diagrams and rules on pages 284–285 at this point.)

Then, in the introductory paragraph of your essay, state your principle of classification and list the groups you are going to discuss. For example, you might begin, "From my experience, I have observed that there are three kinds of college students: those who are chiefly interested in their major field, those who enjoy taking a sampling of courses, and those who complain about *all* their courses." You should then go on to give examples and distinguishing features of each category.

The principle of classification in the above example is attitude toward course work, though it could be dress, degree of preparation, participation in extra-curricular activities, and so on. Whatever principle of division you choose, be sure to name your categories in *parallel* form, using the same part of speech for each of them. For example:

> There are three kinds of college students:
> diligent, lazy, and inconsistent (adjectives)
> or
> hard workers, goof-offs, and sporadic workers (nouns)

Sentence Combining: Using Appositives

If you look back at the first sentence of Dian Fossey's classification of Primates on page 286, you'll notice that it tells both who Carl Linnaeus was and what he did. Fossey uses an *appositive* to include valuable identifying information about Linnaeus. Appositives are used to define, describe, or classify a noun within the context of a sentence. They are nouns, pronouns, noun clauses, or adjective phrases that precede or follow a noun and can replace the noun they refer to. Thus, appositives define a noun by re-naming it and provide at the same time a convenient way to combine two sentences.

Appositives are often used to tell the reader about the source of a piece of information. For example, why should we listen to the man cited in this ad?

Placido Domingo, the complete musician, discusses his favorite instrument.

Expository essays commonly include information from outside sources—especially from experts on the subject being discussed—and an appositive is a concise way to establish the authority of a source of information. Later on in this chapter, for example, you'll find these appositives:

> According to Jonathan Miller, *a writer and physician,* medical scientists through the ages have often learned about how the body works by observing how various machines operate.

Here is Marsha Norman, *Pulitzer-prize-winning playwright*, being interviewed about the ways she uses a home computer in her work.

In the preceding examples, the appositives follow the nouns they refer to. But an appositive can also precede the noun it identifies:

One of the first women to sign on as a secret agent during WWII, Louise Bushnell faced risk—and romance—for her country.

Notice that most appositives are non-restrictive; that is, they give added information about the word (or words) they refer to, but they do not limit or restrict that word. Non-restrictive appositives are always set off from the rest of the sentence by commas. Sometimes, however, an appositive limits or defines the word it modifies: in the following example, the appositive is restrictive because it is a proper noun, and the absence of commas indicates that Jacob Bronowski is not the world's only noted scientist. The appositive *Jacob Bronowski* identifies *which* noted scientist is being discussed:

The noted scientist Jacob Bronowski has written that "all science is the search for unity in hidden likeness."

Appositives can be used to reduce an adjective clause (discussed in Chapter 4) that contains a form of the verb *to be*. Simply drop the "who" or "which" and the verb:

Terry McEwen, ~~who is~~ a voice connoisseur, left the record business to run the San Francisco Opera.

Terry McEwen, a voice connoisseur, left the record business to run the San Francisco Opera.

The Orient Express, ~~which is~~ a glorious time machine, takes lucky passengers on a tour through a century of spies, murderers and courtesans.

The Orient Express, a glorious time machine,

takes lucky passengers on a tour through

a century of spies, murderers and courtesans.

Appositives can also follow a colon. This method of setting up categories is commonly used in classification:

> The order Primate includes four species: *orangutans, chimpanzees, gorillas, and humans.*

EXERCISE 8.16

Use appositives to combine the following pairs of sentences:

1. Dian Fossey is the author of *Gorillas in the Mist.*
   She spent 13 years living in Africa.

2. Fossey begins her book by defining *Primate.*
   Primate is an order that includes orangutans, chimpanzees, gorillas, and humans.

3. Mountain gorillas are gentle yet maligned nonhuman primates.
   Fossey's studies of mountain gorillas have provided insights into the ways these great apes organize and maintain their family groups.

4. Beethoven was a huge silverback gorilla.
   Beethoven gently lifted his six-month-old son and began to groom him.

5. The infant was playfully tadpoling across the stomach of its mother.
   Its mother's name was Effie.

6. Coco was a baby gorilla who had been captured by hunters.
   Coco crawled onto the bench and started to sob.

EXERCISE 8.17

Using appositives, introduce yourself and other members of your family. For example: "My sister Joyce, celebrated mechanic and rock-music expert, has something to say on every subject."

View 3: "We Have to Shake the Old Metaphors from Our Heads": Analogy

Analogy is another tool for making exposition convincing and colorful. This device brings together two essentially different items for purposes of illustration. When you are trying to explain an idea that is difficult to understand, it is often helpful to compare it to something familiar to the reader. To create an analogy, you use a concrete image or simple process to clarify an abstract or unfamiliar concept or process.

We use analogies again and again in informal speech. Our minds naturally seek connections or interrelationships in the world around us. For example, here is Marsha Norman, Pulitzer-prize-winning playwright, being interviewed about the ways she uses a home computer in her work. She is speaking about a highly technical piece of equipment, yet her thought patterns show that she instinctively "humanizes" the machine through the use of analogy. And, in turn, she thinks of the human mind in terms of the machine:

INTERVIEWER: So you don't subscribe to the old complaint that the computer will take over your work by forcing you to work its way?

MARSHA NORMAN: No. I find that the computer is the best working company in the world. I mean, it's an ideal collaborator because it shows me immediately what it is that I have done. I realize that this is kind of anthropomorphic,° but I think of it as a fellow worker. I think of the computer as "That's the brain that is writing it all down." And I do know that I have a very personal relationship to it. I think of it as the editor, and ascribe to it all kinds of human qualities. . . .

I definitely think of the spatial organization of the computer's brain, almost like a neighborhood, almost like an enormous office. Today we were talking about putting WordStar° onto a disk emulator in RAM,° and suddenly I realized as I was talking about it that I had created this other disk drive, this sort of invisible disk drive, that was located back deep in the heart of the machine.

But then I think about my own brain that way. I mean, I do think about it as an enormous office. You know, there are people who sit in the tiny room in the back, and there are some folks who are up in front taking care of press relations. There's R&D [Research and Development], and there's a basement with cleaning people, and all that. That's just what I do for entertainment.

° **anthropomorphic:** attributing human shape or characteristics to a god, animal, or inanimate object.

° **WordStar:** a word-processing program.

° **RAM:** Random Access Memory—a computer memory in which information can be retrieved in any order without disturbing the rest of the memory.

Most likely, in your descriptive essays, you've already used the comparisons called *similes* and *metaphors*. A simile, as you'll recall, is a comparison of two essentially different items, introduced by *like* or *as* ("My brain is *like* an enormous office"); in a metaphor, the *like* or *as* is eliminated ("My brain *is* an enormous office"). In a descriptive essay quoted in Chapter 5, a student writes that her nervous new instructor "sighed like a loosened balloon," and walked out of the classroom "as weakly as a beaten boxer." Through these similes, the author gives us two images that help us to visualize the teacher's relief and exhaustion after teaching his first class.

A developed analogy goes one step further by offering an *extended* comparison. It goes beyond a single image, concentrating instead on the common principle or relationship that links two different ideas or processes. So as we've pointed out, the fables you wrote in Chapter 7 are really analogies. These fanciful stories about imaginary characters provide parallels to our own lives. Through concrete example, they illuminate some generalization about human behavior.

Recognition of the connections between seemingly unlike things is crucial to all understanding and discovery. The noted scientist Jacob Bronowski has written that "all science is the search for unity in hidden likeness." Through analogy, scientists find order in the chaotic appearances of nature. Watch how Bronowski supports this generalization, in an essay on the importance of analogic thinking in science, with a fable and a true story:

° **trenchantly:** in a clear-cut or forceful manner.

This point has been put trenchantly° in a fable by Professor Karl Popper. Suppose that someone wished to give his whole life to science. Suppose that he therefore sat down, pencil in hand, and for the next twenty, thirty, forty years recorded in notebook after notebook everything he could observe. He may be supposed to leave out nothing: today's humidity, the racing results, the level of cosmic radiation and the stock market prices and the look of Mars, all would be there. He would have compiled the most careful record of nature that has ever been made; and, dying in the calm certainty of a life well spent, he would of course leave his notebooks to the Royal Society. Would the Royal Society thank him for the treasure of a lifetime of observation? It would not. It would refuse to open his notebooks at all, because it would know without looking that they contain only a jumble of disorderly and meaningless items.

Science finds order and meaning in our experience, and sets about this in quite a different way. It sets about it as Newton did in the story which he himself told in his old age, and of which the schoolbooks give only a caricature.° In the year 1665, when Newton was twenty-two, the plague broke out in southern England, and the University of Cambridge was closed. Newton therefore spent the next eighteen months at home, removed from traditional learning, at a time when he was impatient for knowledge and, in his own phrase: "I was in the prime of my age for invention." In this eager, boyish mood, sitting one day in the garden of his widowed mother, he saw an apple fall. So far the books have the story right; we think we even know the kind of apple; tradition has it that it was a Flower of Kent. But now they miss the crux of the story. For what struck the young Newton at the sight was not the thought that the apple must be drawn to the earth by gravity; that conception was older than Newton. What struck him was the conjecture that the same force of gravity, which reaches to the top of the tree, might go on reaching out beyond the earth and its air, endlessly into space. Gravity might reach the moon: this was Newton's new thought; and

° **caricature:** a representation in which the subject's features are exaggerated or distorted.

it might be gravity which holds the moon in her orbit. There and then he calculated what force from the earth would hold the moon, and compared it with the known force of gravity at tree height. The forces agreed; Newton says laconically°: "I found they answer pretty nearly." Yet they agreed only nearly: the likeness and approximation go together, for no likeness is exact. In Newton's sentence modern science is full grown.

It grows from a comparison. It has seized a likeness between two unlike appearances; for the apple in the summer garden and the grave moon overhead are surely as unlike in their movements as two things can be. Newton traced in them two expressions of a single concept, gravitation: and the concept (and unity) are in that sense his free creation. The progress of science is the discovery at each step of a new order which gives unity to what had long seemed unlike. Faraday did this when he closed the link between electricity and magnetism. Clerk Maxwell did it when he linked both with light. Einstein linked time and space, mass with energy, and the path of light past the sun with the flight of a bullet; and spent his dying years in trying to add to these likenesses another, which would find a single imaginative order between the equations of Clerk Maxwell and his own geometry of gravitation.

—"The Creative Mind in Science and Art"

CLASSROOM ACTIVITY 8.18

Discuss the Bronowski piece with these questions in mind:

- What is the point of the fable told by Popper?

- Why does Bronowski include the fable in his discussion? How is it related to the story of Isaac Newton?

- What is Bronowski's thesis? What further examples does he cite to support his thesis?

JOURNAL EXERCISE 8.19

At the end of this excerpt, Bronowski mentions other examples of scientists who have made discoveries with the aid of analogic reasoning. Can you cite an example from your own experience (or from a course you've taken in school) of how an analogy, a recognition of "a likeness between two unlike appearances," led to your discovery or understanding of something? Try looking through your journal to see if you've used any analogies—or if there's any place you *could* have used an analogy.

You may, instead, for the purposes of this exercise, expand the definition you wrote for Exercise 8.4 by using an analogy to clarify the term you have defined.

Analogies have been essential to the progress not only of physics and chemistry, but of biology as well. According to Jonathan Miller, a writer and physician, medical scientists through the ages have often learned about how the body works by observing how various machines operate: mechanical devices have provided analogic models for explaining the functions of the human body.

In their efforts to manage and master the physical world, human beings have shown a remarkable capacity for inventing devices which lift, dig, hoist, wind, pump, press, filter and extract. With the use of furnaces, crucibles,° ovens, hearths,° retorts° and stills,° they have learned to transform the substances of the physical world into useful commodities. They have mechanised warfare and extended their powers of communication. The practical benefits of such ingenuity have been so impressive that it is easy to forget how much we have learned from the image of such mechanisms. While they have helped us to master the world, they have been just as helpful in giving us a way of thinking about it and about ourselves. It is impossible to imagine how anyone could have made sense of the heart before we knew what a pump was. Before the invention of automatic gun-turrets, there was no model to explain the finesse of voluntary muscular movement.

—The Body in Question

° **crucible:** a container made of a heat resistant substance, used for melting.

° **hearth:** the floor of a fireplace.

° **retort:** a vessel in which substances are distilled, as in a laboratory.

° **still:** an apparatus used for distilling liquids, especially liquor.

JOURNAL EXERCISE 8.20

Marsha Norman (quoted on page 294) compares both the computer and the human brain to an enormous office. A more common analogy, found in biology texts as well as in computer handbooks, is the comparison of brain and computer. And, as we've pointed out, much of the AI controversy centers on whether human intelligence and machine intelligence are really all that similar. So, before we resume our discussion of AI, take a few moments now to list any points of comparison you note between brain and computer, and then organize these thoughts into a brief paragraph.

In your own expository or persuasive essays, an analogy can be a quick and imaginative way to get your point across. Analogies can serve as the basis for an entire essay, but more often are limited to a paragraph or two. Let's look first at a brief analogy, and then at a fully-developed example to examine how it was put together. For purposes of illustration, we'll return to the subject of the computer. Hubert Dreyfus, a philosopher interested in artificial intelligence, believes that despite some initial progress, AI efforts to simulate human intelligence are ultimately doomed to failure. To illustrate his point, he draws this analogy:

The AI endeavor is like a man climbing a tree to get to the moon: excellent progress is made at the beginning, but the project quickly gets harder and harder and soon peters out completely in the topmost branches.

On the other side of the AI controversy, authors Pamela McCorduck and Edward Feigenbaum want to convince their readers that the mass-production by the Japanese of "intelligent" machines is not only possible but inevitable. And so they search for a comparison to show us that this prediction is not as far-fetched as it seems:

The Intelligent Machine as Automobile

To fashion machines that behave intelligently—that act in ways such that, were a human to act so, we would say, "Ah, that's intelligent behavior"—has been the explicit goal of a scientific field called artificial intelligence, which started more than twenty-five years ago with the introduction of the digital computer. Despite evergreen° controversy and skepticism, the field has begun to create machines that, in some limited sense, reason. Often the reasoning power of these machines matches or exceeds the reasoning power of the humans who instructed them and, in some cases, the reasoning power of any human performing such tasks.

There's a fair parallel between intelligent machines and automobiles. In the world of artificial intelligence, it is, so to speak, 1890; the first automobiles have already appeared. They're handcrafted horseless carriages, to be sure, but they're distinctly different autos, different from wagons, carriages, and sleighs in good ways and bad.

The Japanese have studied this primitive horseless-carriage machine intelligence. They conclude that with certain major developments it can be a mass-market item. With the same kind of foresight Random Olds or Henry Ford° once had as he examined the custom-built machines of Benz and Daimler, the Japanese have decided to improve upon greatly and mass-produce the intelligent machine. That means all the vigorous hand cranking, throttling, and wrenching° a pioneer now accepts as the inevitable price of using the machine—the difficult programming languages, the struggles to make different programs compatible, the problems of putting human knowledge into machine form—are to disappear, eliminated in the new Japanese Fifth Generation of computers. This in itself would be remarkable enough, but the Japanese also intend to supply gas stations and roadways for the new machines, necessities for the users and sources of income for the supplier. Thus we recapitulate° the story of personal transportation from the first hand-built Benz Patent Motor Wagon to the Honda Civic, for these new machines will also be "autos": self-propelled vehicles of the intellect.

This change from the speed of walking—about four miles an hour—to the speed of automobiles—about forty miles an hour—was an order-of-magnitude change that, while it didn't represent so very much in numbers, has transformed our lives utterly. (The next great order-of-magnitude change, from automobiles to jet planes that travel at 400 miles an hour, has

° **evergreen:** persisting; remaining fresh.

° **Random Olds and Henry Ford:** pioneers in the American automobile industry.

° **hand cranking, throttling, and wrenching:** these are motions associated with the operating of horseless carriages. A hand crank was used to start early-model automobiles. A throttle is a valve that regulates fuel in an engine. A wrench is a sudden, sharp twist.

° **recapitulate:** to repeat in concise form.

made equivalent transformations in our lives.) This is central to what the Japanese plan for their new generation of computers: quantitative changes in computing speed, power, and reasoning must make qualitative changes in our lives that we can barely foresee. As for the computers that most of us are familiar with right now, they aren't horseless carriages. They're no more than bicycles.

—The Fifth Generation

How, then, do you go about writing an analogy? Read these guidelines, and use the above analogy to answer the accompanying questions:

1. Decide on a specific comparison—"A is like B"—that will help your reader to understand your point ("The Intelligent Machine as Automobile").

2. Let that comparison serve as the thesis statement of your paragraph or composition. What is the thesis statement of the McCorduck/Feigenbaum analogy?

3. Point out all the significant similarities between A and B by explaining A *in terms of* B. Remember to focus on A; B is used only to explain A. For example:

The present stage in
the development of   = (is like)   the 1890s
artificial intelligence

Intelligent machines   = (are like)   horseless carriages

4. Restate the point or controlling idea of the analogy in your conclusion. How do McCorduck and Feigenbaum conclude their essay?

EXERCISE 8.21

Using the previous reading selection, how many more items of comparison can you add to the list in #3, above?

What do you avoid when writing an analogy?

1. An analogy should be fresh and unexpected, but don't *strain* too much for a comparison. Comparing computers and cars makes sense. But a comparison of computers and ice cream cones—even if you could work it out somehow—would merely be silly.

2. In general, don't dwell on differences between A and B—this is not a comparison/contrast. Stick to similarities.

3. Avoid comparisons that are too broad to have any meaning. To say "My brother is like an animal" is hopelessly vague. What kind of animal? "My brother is like a gorilla" offers a far more specific basis of comparison.

4. Beware of the mistake in logic called *false analogy*. This is a comparison based on insufficient or superficial similarities. The headline given here is an acceptable attention-grabber in an advertisement, but it wouldn't hold up in an expository essay. Why not?

You Wouldn't Go to Work Without Your Pants
Why Buy an IBM-PC Without FAST FACTS

5. Finally, don't concentrate so much on B that you forget about A. Make sure your reader understands all the parallels between A and B.

The next exercise should help you solve this common problem.

CLASSROOM ACTIVITY 8.22

The author of the following selection came up with a useful observation: constructing a composition (A) is like building a house (B). She begins promisingly, comparing the frame of a house and the outline of a composition. But what are the "columns" she mentions in paragraph 2, and how do they support the "structure"? Similarly, the writer omits distinct parallels for other "B" terms such as "components," "built up," "floors," and so on. How would you rewrite her analogy to make it more specific and helpful? And how would you rework the conclusion of the analogy? (Your teacher may want you to start this activity by having you develop on the blackboard a chart such as the one on page 299, showing the relationship between the A and B terms in this analogy.)

Constructing a Composition

When I sit down to write a composition, I feel like a carpenter who is about to build a house. First I have to clear my head to make room for the ideas that will construct my composition. I must decide whether to structure it simply or elaborately, and I must prepare myself for all the time and labor that the construction will involve. As the wheels and machinery start rolling, I can begin to create.

The rules for writing a composition and building a house are the same. A strong foundation should be the first consideration, since it has to support the structure. Next comes the frame or outline, which is the skeleton around which the rest of the structure is built. Columns form the skeleton and support the body of the structure, and these columns must be of the sturdiest material in order to give the best support to the final work. The components are put together and built up until the work is complete. It can consist of one or more stories or floors, and should be inspected during and after construction in case repairs are needed.

The final product may be long or short, strong or weak, but whatever the case, there will be some people who like it and some who don't.

EXERCISE 8.23

Write a detailed analogy of at least one page. Here are some student-generated topics you might wish to work on: "A blind date is like a trial"; "High school is like a prison"; "A football game is like a war"; "Keeping a journal is like talking to a best friend."

To take another example, here's a brief excerpt from a magazine article on computers:

> "Getting involved with computers
> . . . is a little like visiting a foreign
> country for the first time. You'll
> have a more rewarding trip if you
> learn something about the land
> and its customs beforehand."

How would you develop this analogy?

Some other possibilities:

My friend X is like a _____.

Learning grammar is like _____.

Teenagers are like _____.

Buying a car is like _____.

You can describe a game, a sport, the latest dance—any object, process, or event.

View 4: The Computer "Processes Not Energy, but Information": Comparison/Contrast

Another common expository technique—suitable for analyzing machines, marriages, movies, and anything else you can think of—is the comparison/contrast:

"*For Willard, life is a ball. For me, it isn't.*"

Drawing by H. Martin; © 1983 The New Yorker
Magazine Inc.

Unlike analogy, comparison/contrast treats differences as well as similarities between subjects that are *essentially alike. Comparison* explores the significant similarities shared by subjects belonging to the same general class or category. And, because no two subjects are ever identical, *contrast,* or the noting of dissimilarities, goes hand-in-hand with comparison.

Let's return once more to our original topic, artificial intelligence, to see how a writer uses the comparison/contrast method to speculate about whether a machine can simulate the human mind in all its richness. Computer science professor Joseph Weizenbaum has his doubts. He begins by comparing the similar ways computers and humans acquire knowledge and then moves on to dissimilarities, including this contrast between machine language and human language:

> . . . even the kinds of knowledge that appear superficially to be communicable from one human being to another in language alone are in fact not altogether so communicable. [Computer scientist] Claude Shannon showed that, even in abstract information theory, the "information content" of a message is not a function of the message alone but depends crucially on the state of knowledge, on the expectations, of the receiver. The message

"Am arriving on 7 o'clock plane, love, Bill" has a different information content for Bill's wife, who knew he was coming home, but not on precisely what airplane, than for a girl who wasn't expecting Bill at all and who is surprised by his declaration of love.

Human language in actual use is infinitely more problematical than those aspects of it that are amenable° to treatment by information theory, of course. But even the example I have cited illustrates that language involves the histories of those using it, hence the history of society, indeed, of all humanity generally. And language in human use is not merely functional in the way that computer languages are functional. It does not identify things and words only with immediate goals to be achieved or with objects to be transformed. The human use of language manifests human memory. And that is quite a different thing than the store of the computer, which has been anthropomorphized° into "memory." The former gives rise to hopes and fears, for example. It is hard to see what it could mean to say that a computer hopes.

These considerations touch not only on certain technical limitations of computers, but also on the central question of what it means to be a human being and what it means to be a computer.

—Computer Power and Human Reason

° **amenable:** willing to follow advice or suggestion.

° **anthropomorphized:** What does this word mean? (You have seen a form of this word in an earlier selection.)

JOURNAL EXERCISE 8.24

Professor Weizenbaum gives one example of why it will be difficult to develop intelligent machines. If you were to continue his argument, what other *differences* would you cite between human and machine intelligence?

In addition, we often use the comparison/contrast method of exposition to judge the good points and the bad points of two comparable items, or to explain why we prefer or recommend one item over another. Consequently, comparison/contrast forms the basis of many advertisements:

WordStar® is used by more people, more often, to do more things than any other word processing software.

And you'll find it'll do more for you.

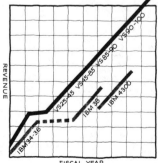

In an essay, of course, a comparison/contrast usually consists of more than one point of comparison. There are two ways of developing and structuring a comparison/contrast essay:

1. The *block* method, in which you discuss all the qualities of A, and then discuss—in the same order—all the qualities of B.

2. The *alternating* method, in which each paragraph contains a point-by-point comparison/contrast of A and B.

Toshio Sakai

Japanese school kids: Quadratic equations, biology and Pascal before high school

How the Japanese Do It

While American schools groaned under the burden of the post-World War II baby boom, Japan developed a public-education system that routinely produces graduates who've been judged, by many experts using many yardsticks, as the most knowledgeable in the world. A typical Japanese ninth grader, for example, has learned factorization and quadratic equations as well as the notions of deviation and probability in math. Also well versed in the laws of Pascal and Newton, he or she enters senior high school with a basic knowledge of biology and geology—and a transcript that boasts the equivalent of Chem 101.

There is nothing inscrutable about Japan's philosophy of education. The academic year runs 240 days, as compared with about 180 days in the United States, and even first graders are expected to spend one to two hours on homework each night. Moreover, the standards are so stringent that most Japanese students feel obliged to attend an afterhours "cram school" known as a *juku* in order to survive the dreaded "examination hells" that precede entrance into a higher division. The central government also encourages academic excellence by allocating the equivalent of $21 billion annually for education and the promotion of science and technology—roughly twice the national defense budget. Much of the money goes for teachers' salaries, standardized textbooks and teaching equipment, ensuring that the children in Japan's remote island fishing villages receive the same treatment as their counterparts in Tokyo's tonier suburbs.

At the heart of Japan's effective education system, however, is the national attitude toward teachers. When he taught school for a while in Wisconsin, Yukiji Kato, now a research fellow at Japan's National Educational Research Institute, was shocked to discover that American teachers were "making less than nurses, or even truck drivers. How can you expect to attract good teachers with that kind of social status?" he wonders. Japanese college seniors with credentials good enough to land the highly coveted job of public-school teacher started this academic year earning 2.2 million yen ($9,300), roughly the same as an engineer's starting salary at a big computer company. Equally important, they are more likely to be accorded great respect: the Japanese word for teacher, *sensei*, connotes a person of surpassing wisdom on matters both private and professional. Only recently have some youths, "left-outs" as they are called, rebelled against the regimentation of the schools and society in general, making discipline a problem.

Ability: Oddly enough, the Japanese now believe they can improve on the world's most successful school system by making it a bit more American. "There are pluses and minuses in the fact that the central government assumes so much responsibility in education," says Akio Nakajima, director for upper secondary schools at Tokyo's Ministry of Education. "The American system is superior in that it treats each child as an individual and offers an opportunity to develop his or her special ability." Feeling that they have overemphasized the concept of equal treatment for all students, some schools have begun the revolutionary (for Japan) practice of "tracking"—grouping children by their ability to learn. Before the Americanization process goes too far, however, it might be wise to have some Japanese seventh grader translate "A Nation at Risk."*

CHARLES LEERHSEN with AYAKO DOI in Tokyo

---

* "A Nation at Risk" is the report of the National Commission on Excellence in Education. (This report is discussed in Chapter 10.)

The article on page 305, taken from a *Newsweek* magazine article on the education system in the U.S., is a clear example of the alternating method. In this segment of the article, the American system is compared with that of the Japanese.

On the following pages are excerpted journal entries in which students responded to a question raised by the *Newsweek* article.* We simply asked the students, "What is considered proper classroom behavior in your native country?" What is fascinating to note is how many of them approached the assignment by comparing and contrasting their own school system with the American school system. Some students, as in the case of the first author, are critical of their own country's schools; others are critical of the American system; still others make no value judgments, confining themselves instead to a more objective record of similarities and differences between the two approaches to education.

In any case, these are not fully-developed essays. As you read, notice that the comparison/contrasts are often indirect, and that the writers generally take it for granted that the reader has some knowledge of American schools. Remember, a fully-developed comparison/contrast usually gives equal weight to all the elements under consideration.

Let's examine how this first student employs the *alternating* approach to talk about high schools in North America versus those in Iran (observe, by the way, the student's use of analogy):

I. Introduction

I went to school for ten years in my country, Iran. I changed schools every two years, and I studied at different high schools in different parts of the city. I also studied at several Canadian high schools, which are the same as American high schools. So from my experiences, let me tell you how American schools are different from Iranian schools.

II. School principal
A. In Iran
B. In Canada and America

First, in Iranian high schools, a principal is like the king of a country. All students respect him and most of them fear him because he is despotic and strong. Once when I was in third grade, I didn't do my homework, and I knew the principal would scold me. I was so worried that I got sick and couldn't go to school. But in Canadian and American schools, principals are like employees, and they are not despotic persons. During high school in Canada, I wasn't afraid of the principal at all. I only saw him once, and nobody in the school knew who he was. I remember in ninth grade in Iran when I once saw my principal and didn't say hello to him, he called me and hit me with a ruler. After that day I always said hello to him first thing in the morning, like a soldier marching in front of the king.

Second, in Iranian high schools we had to study 14 subjects for nine months, six days a week. Each day we had four classes, and each class for

---

* The samples quoted on these pages come from the journals of the following students: Afshin Mahabadi, Shahram Hagnazari, Frances Skevofilakis, Ketty Joseph, A. R. Fernando, Marta Lopez, Svetlana Danilova, Roman Khodosh, Lumi Kim, Ji Y. Chang, Alkis Petrides, Ioanna Achodakis, Terry Malliakas.

III. *Length of school*
week & class period

A. *In Iran*

B. *In Canada*
and America

two hours. School began at 8 A.M., and we had two classes in the morning and two in the afternoon. Sitting in classes was very boring, especially in history class. But who was brave enough to sleep? If you were lucky, your teacher just woke you up by smacking you on the head. If you were unlucky like me, you were soon standing in front of the principal's desk, waiting to be punished. But in Canadian and American schools, the fifty-minute class hours were too short for you to sleep. Having only five classes in a day and two days for weekends was so comfortable and enjoyable for me.

Third, most Iranian teachers were despotic, just like the principals. Iranian teachers acted like governors of their high school. They gave very hard exams and most of them were experts in their subjects, especially math and physics. In the tenth grade, my math teacher, who was an expert mathematician, tried to teach us some college math problems. In one of his exams, nobody in the class got more than 40%. In contrast, most Canadian and American teachers are friendly and patient. Their exams are fair and if you study you can get a good mark. Of course, if you don't study, no matter where you don't study, you'll get low grades.

IV. *Teachers & exams*

A. *In Iran*

B. *In Canada*
and America

Most Iranian students learned respect because they studied by force. In both American/Canadian and Iranian educational systems, there are some good things and some bad things, but the students are the same.

V. *Conclusion*

Had this writer developed his journal entry into an essay, he might have made the conclusion stronger and more thoughtful. Here, for example, is a more developed conclusion from another Iranian student's paper. This student's assessment is very different from that of his compatriot:

> In my country, one of the most important rules in school is to be polite. What I mean by polite is that everyone should respect one another, be on time for classes, and defer to the teacher. American students, however, are very informal, not only toward their teachers but toward people in general. They have little respect for their elders; perhaps they should change if they want the next generation to improve.

EXERCISE 8.25

Now re-examine the *Newsweek* article, and briefly outline its argument in your notebook by listing the topic sentences of the paragraphs, as well as the examples used to illustrate these main ideas.

The next example uses the *block* method to compare and contrast student behavior in the U.S. and in Greece. After stating her thesis, the writer describes a typical American classroom first, and then moves on to a Greek classroom:

The way students behave in my country is very different from the way they behave in the United States. Greek students are expected to work much harder and to behave much better.

In the U.S., students have too much freedom. For example, I was very surprised the first day I walked into an American classroom. I saw students chewing gum while they were talking to the teacher. Others were sitting on the chairs with their feet on the desks. But what struck me the most was that everyone was dressed differently. All of this gave me the impression that I was in the wrong place and not in a classroom.

However, if you go into a Greek classroom, you'll see all the boys sitting on one side of the room and all the girls on the other. You'll also notice that everyone is dressed in a blue and white uniform. When the teacher walks into the classroom, the students stand up and say, "Good morning." They are not allowed to chew gum, and they have to raise their hands for permission to talk. They respect, fear, and obey their teachers because teachers have the right to hit them. If you don't do your work, you get punished. You have a choice: either you do the work, or the teacher will hit you and embarrass you in front of your classmates.

(margin annotations: "All about the U.S." and "All about Greece")

If this student were to use her journal entry as the basis for an essay, she would undoubtedly try to balance its two parts, giving an equal number of details for each of the subjects she is treating. And for the sake of clarity, she would probably want to discuss the points of comparison/contrast in the same order in each paragraph.

The following paragraphs also come out of the journal exercise based on the *Newsweek* article. Despite a variety of approaches and many different observations, certain themes recur in many of these entries. For example, students from various countries talk about the importance of respecting teachers and the particular ways in which students show this respect. Take note of conflicting statements in these excerpts, and jot down certain generalizations (observations that are *generally* true) in your notebook.

An "Informal Research" Project

Read the following student samples with this two-part "informal research" exercise in mind:

First, compare and contrast your own country's education system with that of the U.S. (This should take a page or two.)

Second, using your own observations and data collected from other students as evidence, generalize about education in other countries versus this country. Read and think about your sources; perhaps interview some of your classmates for additional material. Then generate your *own thesis* about this subject—a sample thesis might read, "In general, American

students are given more freedom than students from other countries."
Remember to refer to your sources to support your thesis.

(Further suggestions for comparison/contrast essays appear at the end of
this section.)

Haiti

Haiti and the United States are different in many ways. In Haiti, people
don't have as much freedom, and they aren't as liberated as people are in
the United States. Haitian children are raised to respect older people, and
they never talk back to adults. But children here speak to their parents and
teachers in any way they like, and they even curse in front of older people.
In Haiti, both parents and teachers are strict with children, and there's a
big difference in the ways students behave in the two countries.

One of the most important things in Haitian schools is discipline. Classes
run from 8 A.M. to 4 P.M., and students are not allowed into the school if
they are not wearing their uniforms. In class, students must sit straight—
no slouching—with both feet on the floor. They do as the teachers tell them,
and there is no talking back to the teacher. On the other hand, American
students dress any way they want. They don't respect their teachers, so
they say anything they please. They sit with one foot on the floor and the
other on the chair in front of them.

In Haiti, students can't choose their own courses, and certain subjects,
like government and sex education, are not taught in high school. Moreover,
Haitian schools are much harder than American schools, and more subjects
are covered in a year. The teachers are stricter, and more homework is
given. There's no such thing as "I didn't do my homework" or "I forgot it,"
as students say here in the States. If you don't do it, you'll be punished. The
education system in the U.S. is easier and asks less of the students. American students have less discipline and more freedom to express themselves.

Sri Lanka (formerly Ceylon)

In Ceylon, early morning classes start with religious worship. Students
are more polite and pay more respect to their teachers than they do in the
U.S. When a teacher enters the classroom, students get up from their seats.
If someone wants to leave the classroom, he or she has to get permission.
There is no group discussion in any class, as no one is allowed to talk.
Students don't call out answers to questions, whereas American students
often just interrupt each other or answer without giving anyone else a
chance. And students in my country do not express their humor the way
American students do.

Spain

We have to enter and leave the classrooms in line and in silence, but here
only children in kindergarten do this. When the teacher speaks to us, we
must look down, whereas we have to look a teacher straight in the eyes in

this country. In Spain, we cannot talk back to the teacher, while here I have seen students insult their teachers. In Spanish schools, the teacher can hit a student, and the student is expected not to cry or to scream, but just to take it and to have no hard feelings about it. But here I've seen teachers yelling at students and students answering back. In my country, students cannot speak at all in class. They must sit straight with their legs together, and they cannot put their hands in their pockets because that is rude behavior.

USSR

When I first came to high school in this country, I found many differences between Russian and American schools. After each class period was up, the students jumped out of their seats and ran into the halls even if the teacher had not had a chance to finish his sentence. When the bell rings at the end of a class in my country, the students do not move until the teacher has finished his lecture, even if it takes the whole break for him to end. I don't think it's polite for students to finish the class by themselves.

There are also differences in the way teachers and students dress. Women teachers can't wear pants, a lot of make-up, or jewelry (except for a wedding ring). Students aren't allowed to wear any make-up, nail polish, or jewelry. The boys can't have long hair, and girls with long hair have to tie it up. In addition, students all over the country have to wear the same uniforms. Because the uniforms are expensive and you can't buy them at many stores, you have to be very careful with them and wear them all year long. Similarly, some American private schools have uniforms, but I'm sure the students have more than one uniform to wear during the year.

* * *

Soviet students spend only ten years in school instead of twelve as the Americans do. However, after finishing high school, Russian graduates have received a much wider education than the young people who go through American schools. But, living in a totalitarian country, they do not have many opportunities or much freedom in school. They cannot choose the subjects they wish to take. Maybe this is the reason for their well-rounded education. Yet even though knowledge is beneficial to everyone, it should be voluntary. That is why I prefer the American system of education. Here I can be as educated as I want to be.

Korea

In Korea, students cannot talk back to teachers, even when they are wrong. When a student is giving a paper to the teacher, he or she must use both hands. In my culture, it would be very impolite to use only one hand to give something to a teacher. Students have to obey their teachers at all times, and teachers have the right to hit students.

In America, however, school is almost like heaven compared to my country. Teachers are too nice to students, and sometimes they can't control certain students. Students don't respect teachers as much as they're supposed to. I think that's because students don't realize how lucky they are in America.

*   *   *

When I first started high school in the U.S., I was very confused. The noisy American classroom made me feel like a stranger. There was so much freedom and liberalism. Teachers in Korea won't begin their lectures until the students' desks are in straight lines. I couldn't talk to my friends during class. We had to sit and quietly listen. Teachers wanted us to respect them like gods. And we had to respect them as much as they wanted because they had the right punishments for students who didn't.

Once I asked my friend a question in class, and my teacher was very upset because I had disturbed his lecture. Another time, one of my friends asked to be excused so she could go to the bathroom. The teacher was very angry because my friend was not ready for class.

Unlike American students, Korean students often care too much about their grades. Some parents and teachers punish students who don't get good grades. Many students just study to make their parents and teachers happy. And many students cry when they think they didn't do well on a test and they can't stop worrying about it.

Cyprus

There are not many differences between classroom behavior here in the U.S. and in Cyprus. One of the things American and Cypriot students have in common is the freedom to speak freely and state their opinions without any fear. Like American students, Cypriot students can decide if they want to participate in a class discussion.

The next student outlines various rules that *should* operate in the Greek classroom (similar to the excerpt on page 308), but concludes:

Greece

Of course, Greek students don't follow these rules in most of their classes. There have been days when students didn't come into the class-rooms because they wanted to go for a walk, and the teachers had to go running after them. There are students who take exams with notes and books hidden on their bodies. Some teachers have sat on pins, and others have left the classroom completely white from the chalk dust that students had put all over their chairs.

Another Greek student develops this view of "the other side of the coin" —the way the students in his country often behave—by using a comic narrative:

By making a comparison between Greek and American teachers, I have come to the conclusion that Greek teachers are the most unlucky in the world. They have to deal with the strangest and wildest students, who only disobey and interrupt them in their classes. I believe that the story of one school day will help me to develop this point.

The time is 8:30 a.m. and all the students are sitting on their desks, trying to bother their classmates. One of them is pinching his friend in front of him, so his friend punches him in the face. Another one throws his lunch back into someone else's ear, while two more students are running around the room and making messes all over the place.

Suddenly the teacher arrives, and all the students try to get in their seats and act as calm and normal as they can. They stand up and greet the teacher, who always ignores what has been going on. He begins the lecture by asking the students to take out their homework. But, as usual, most of them haven't done it and start giving excuses that are made up instantly. Nick says, "I was sick." George says, "My grandmother died." And so forth. I think you can understand why teachers go home exhausted.

EXERCISE 8.26

Here are a few more suggestions for comparison/contrast essays:

1. Taking your cue from the last two selections, compare how students in your country are *supposed* to act with how they *really* behave.

2. From your own experience, compare high school and college.

3. Compare two cities (home versus where you live now), two books or films on the same general subject, two types of computers, two methods of studying, two species of teachers . . . or two types of anything!

4. Here are two "before and after" comparisons you can try:
   a. Compare what you thought America would be like before you came here with your first-hand observations of this country.
   b. Compare what you thought college would be like versus what you now know it to be.

When writing any essay or paragraph of this type, follow these three guideposts:

1. Always compare items that have a common base. There is an old saying, "Don't compare apples and oranges."

2. In your own mind and for your reader, establish the *point* or *thesis* of this particular comparison/contrast: is your goal to emphasize similarities or to stress differences? Or do you want to show why you like one item more? Or do you want to show how one item is gradually taking on the characteristics of the other? Or to demonstrate the advantages of one system over another?

3. Stay away from obvious or unimportant points of comparison/contrast. Concentrate on meaningful, specific details.

"Set Up" Words

Before you begin to write your comparison/contrast essay, you may want to review the comparative and superlative forms of adjectives and adverbs in Appendix 3. You may also find the following comparative transitions (listed in Chapter 3) useful:

To show difference: *in contrast, unlike, on the other hand, whereas, however, on the contrary, conversely.*

To show similarity or to add additional information: *similarly, like, in addition, moreover, in the same way, furthermore, also, first, next, then, besides.*

EXERCISE 8.27

We've deleted the comparative transitions in the following excerpts from the comparison/contrast papers in this chapter. Fill in each blank with an appropriate transition:

1. Most Iranian teachers were despotic, just like the principals. _____

   _____, most Canadian and American teachers are friendly and patient.

2. In Haiti, students are not allowed into the school if they are not wearing their uniforms. U.S. students, _____, dress any way they want.

3. In the U.S., most students don't spend all of their time worrying about their grades. _____ American students, Korean students often care too much about their grades.

4. In Ceylon, there is no group discussion in any class, as no one is allowed to talk. Students don't call out answers to questions, _____

   _____ American students often just interrupt each other or answer without giving anyone else a chance.

5. Korean students have to obey their teachers at all times, and teachers

   have the right to hit students. In America, _____, school is almost like a heaven compared to my country.

6. In Russian schools, girls aren't allowed to wear any make-up, nail polish, or jewelry. The boys can't have long hair, and girls with long

   hair have to tie it up. _____, students all over the country have to wear the same uniform. Because the uniforms are very expensive, you have to be very careful with them and wear them all year

   long. _____, some American private schools have uniforms, but I'm sure the students have more than one uniform to wear during the year.

7. In Haiti, students can't choose their own subjects. _____, Haitian schools are much harder than American schools, and more subjects are covered in a year.

8. One of the things American and Cypriot students have in common is

   the freedom to speak freely and state their opinions. _____ American students, Cypriot students can decide if they want to participate in a classroom discussion.

In addition to the comparative transitions, the following constructions are commonly used to set up comparisons:

1. *As . . . as* signals equality or strong similarity. It can be used to compare two different things:

   Your hair is as individual as you are.

   As . . . as can also show equality between two characteristics of the same thing:

   ## Our pastry tastes as good as it looks.

2. *More . . . than, less . . . than, different from,* and *the difference between* indicate dissimilarities:

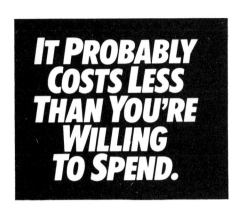

IT PROBABLY COSTS LESS THAN YOU'RE WILLING TO SPEND.

You need to spend more than a half hour a day at aerobics to make an exercise "diet" work.

What's the difference between a petard and a poniard?

3. *Whether ... or* points to different possibilities:

Whether you are typing your essay or figuring out your budget, a computer can save you time.

Correlative Conjunctions

Another group of words that help to set up the relationship between two ideas in a sentence are the *correlative conjunctions*. Like the other conjunctions that we looked at in Chapter 2, correlative conjunctions can also be used to combine sentences. Common correlative conjunctions are *both ... and, either ... or, neither ... nor,* and *not only ... but.* Look at the following examples:

All of the instruments read both quickly and clearly.

EITHER WE HAVE IT, OR WE'LL GET IT FOR YOU!

The fruit of timidity is neither gain nor loss.
ARAB PROVERB

Superior investment results demand not only creative portfolio management but a whole team of specialists to bring added dimensions to your account.

Notice that the correlative conjunction comes immediately before the word to be compared. Notice, too, that the items being compared should have the same grammatical form—both should be nouns, verbs, adjectives, and so on:

Both *humans* and the great *apes* are primates. (nouns)

Computers can neither *love* nor *hate*. (verbs)

Some people believe that computers are not only *efficient*, but also *intelligent*. (adjectives)

EXERCISE 8.28

A.) Complete the following sentences. Make sure that the words you supply for each correlative construction are the same part of speech.

1. I like neither _____.

2. My best friend is not only _____.

3. Both _____ are signs of intelligence.

4. Students must either _____.

B.) Now make up your own set of sentences using these correlative constructions.

EXERCISE 8.29

A.) Like other conjunctions, the correlative conjunctions can be used to combine sentences:

   Maria is going to the party.
+ I'm going to the party.

= Both Maria and I are going to the party.

Use correlative conjunctions to combine these pairs of sentences:

1. Greek students cannot chew gum in school.
Greek students cannot smoke in school.

2. I walk to school.
   I take a bus to school.

3. Israeli men must serve in the army.
   Israeli women must serve in the army.

4. My cat is stupid.
   My cat is lazy.

B.) Now see if you can identify and correct the errors in the following sentences:

1. If you hope to succeed, you must either work hard or maybe you'll get

   lucky.

2. My landlord is neither understanding nor a hard-working man.

3. Since the beginning of civilization, humans have been both builders

   and destructive.

4. Richard not only cheats at cards, but also is a liar.

EDITING EXERCISE 8.30

After you have completed your comparison/contrast essay, review it to see if some of your sentences might be combined or clarified with the help of set-up words, correlative conjunctions, and appositives.

Major Assignment

You have written several short papers in this chapter, each focusing on a particular expository pattern. But as you have realized by now, most essays employ more than one rhetorical mode; each mode is dictated by the particular problem you want to solve and how you want to communicate your solution to your reader.

For your final assignment, therefore, you are asked to draw on what you have learned by writing a longer paper that incorporates at least three of the methods of exposition you have practiced in this chapter. There are several ways to approach this task:

1. If several of the short papers you have written for this chapter are on the same general topic, you might try combining them in some way.

2. Pick the short paper you liked best and expand it by using two or three of the other rhetorical patterns.

3. Return to the extended definition you wrote for Exercise 8.4 and expand it further.

Obviously, you need more than transitions and set-up words to connect the rhetorical modes you're employing for this assignment. First decide on the purpose, audience, thesis, and general organization of your essay; then let these elements guide you in your use of a particular expository pattern.

Solution to the "Pebble Problem":

The girl put her hand into the money-bag and drew out a pebble. Without looking at it, she let it fall to the path where it was immediately lost among the others.

"Oh, how clumsy of me," she said, "but never mind—just look into the bag and you will be able to tell which pebble I picked by the color of the one that is left."

Since the remaining pebble is, of course, black, it must be assumed that she has taken the white pebble, since the money-lender would not want to reveal his dishonesty.

To many of us, there would seem to be only three logical possibilities: to refuse to choose a pebble; to reveal that there are two black pebbles in the bag; or to take a black pebble and accept defeat. None of these choices would help our heroine; it is the girl's flexibility of thought that enables her to triumph.

---

9 | Analyzing Causes and Effects

THE LOGIC OF CAUSES AND EFFECTS

In the previous chapter, we looked at four patterns of exposition: definition, classification, comparison, and contrast. Another common expository pattern is *cause-and-effect analysis*. Students are frequently asked in assignments and essay exams to discuss "The causes of World War II" or "The effects of factory waste on our city's air quality." This kind of essay aims to show the reader the connections between events or situations. The cause-and-effect essay may be purely informative or may be used to persuade. But this kind of essay generally differs from the argumentative paper—discussed in the next chapter—in that the writer does not confront an "opponent," but instead tries to make the reader see *why* and *how* events are related.

All of us look for the *reasons behind* the events of our daily lives. "Why do I have to pay $13.00 just to fill the gas tank of my car?" we ask ourselves, and "Why did I perform so poorly on the last chemistry exam?" By the same token, we all try to guess what the *results* of a particular action or situation will be: "If gasoline prices continue to rise, what will happen (to me, to my friends, to the people in this country, to OPEC)?" we speculate, and "What if I don't pass my chemistry midterm?"

Two different mental operations are at work here. When we look for *causes,* we observe a situation or event and try to figure out what forces produced it. In other words, we start with the observable data, and work our way back in time to the motivating circumstances:

This effect $\longleftarrow$ (has resulted from) this (these) cause(s)

When we look for *effects,* we start with an event or situation, and try to look ahead to what will happen as a result of it:

This (these) cause(s) $\longrightarrow$ (will lead to) this effect

This first exercise should help you see the two different directions a cause/effect analysis can take.

EXERCISE 9.1

A.) Think of these three items as *causes*. What do you think are the events that will result from each item? Try to list several probable effects for each:

1. Your best friend smokes two packs of cigarettes a day.
2. Public transportation fares have just been doubled in your town.
3. According to recent tests, the pollution level is rising in the river that runs through your county.

B.) Now reverse your thinking: Imagine that these three items are *effects*. What do you think were the causes for each of these effects—what made each occur?

Stop a moment. In your response to the above exercise, did you state that smoking two packs of cigarettes a day will lead to lung cancer or heart disease? Is this a fact; that is, can it be proved—if not by you, then by experts such as scientists and medical researchers? When you are deciding whether a statement might be disproved or disputed, ask yourself: Does this cause *always* lead to this effect? If not, the statement is most likely a judgment rather than a fact. If, on the other hand, you said that cigarette smoking *may* lead to such serious diseases, your statement would come within the realm of fact.

Qualifying Generalizations

One of the most common fallacies committed by writers of the expository essay is to state generalizations as though they were absolutes, or universal laws. What if you were to run across this generalization in your reading: "Exercise is good for your health"? Is this statement always true? What exceptions can you think of to this generalization? In your own writing, take care not to present your observations in such broad terms. Avoid absolutes like "definitely," "never," and "always," for these words are bound to provoke some of your readers to object: "Wait a minute—my own experience and research tell me something different. So that statement isn't *always* true." By the same token, judgmental superlatives like "Hockey is the most exciting game in the world" or "Swimming is the best form of exercise" don't persuade anyone; they merely advertise a writer's prejudices.

Instead, make an effort to *qualify* the statements you make with words that express *possibility* or *probability* rather than certainty. For instance, if we were to qualify the above statement concerning exercise, we would end up with a more accurate observation: "exercise is good for most (or many) people." Don't make the mistake of leaping from "once" or "in some cases" or "in my experience" to "*always*." In a cause/effect paper or an argument, a writer is usually dealing with speculations and expectations based on limited information. Modals such as *can, may, might,* and *should* let your reader know that you are making a logical assumption based on the evidence, rather than stating absolute fact. Words of probability such as *appears, seems,* and *apparently* indicate something stronger than possibility, but still allow for reasonable doubt.

Facts, Judgments, and Inferences

In discussing causes and effects, we rely on facts, judgments, and inferences. Effective exposition depends on the writer's ability to distinguish among these three kinds of statements. Let's compare facts and judgments before moving on to our discussion of inferences.

A *fact* is a statement which can be proved or verified; it is an external, objective report. A *judgment* or *opinion* is a subjective statement based on evidence that can be questioned; it is an interpretation or evaluation of a fact. A judgment shows the writer's attitude toward his subject.

> FACT: It's 30° outside.
> JUDGMENT: It's cold outside.
>
> FACT: Meat contains protein.
> JUDGMENT: Meat is an essential part of a healthy diet.

EXERCISE 9.2

Which of the following statements is a fact, and which is a judgment?

1. Children become more violent as a result of watching violent TV shows.

2. A strong military defense is necessary to a country's survival.

3. Because of the computer revolution, businesses today are more efficient than they've ever been.

4. The divorce rate is high because people are no longer willing to work at their marriages.

5. The telephone was invented by Alexander Graham Bell.

6. The telephone has enriched modern life.

CLASSROOM ACTIVITY 9.3

Each of the following sentences is composed of both facts and judgments. Label each clause in the sentence as either a fact or a judgment, and explain why.

1. The Baltimore Orioles, who won the World Series in 1983, were the best team in baseball that year.

2. You can lose a lot of money playing the stock market; you have to be a gambler or an idiot to invest in it.

3. The man driving that car next to us must be drunk because his car is weaving all over the road.

Read the following article to discuss sentences #4 and #5.

It Seems Clear: Less Cholesterol, Less Heart Risk

The results of a 10-year study of 3,806 middle-aged men were in last week, and for the first time scientists called it conclusive: Lowering blood cholesterol levels can prevent heart attacks. The $150 million study, sponsored by the Federal Government, showed that for each 1 percent fall in cholesterol levels participants were able to reduce the rate of coronary heart disease by 2 percent; the men who lowered their blood cholesterol by 25 percent cut their risk of heart attack by 50 percent.

Other factors, including smoking, heredity and stress, contribute to heart disease. But the new findings should increase confidence that diet and, when necessary, prescription drugs can cut the risk of dying prematurely from heart attack, said Dr. Basil M. Rifkind of the National Heart, Lung and Blood Institute, who was project director. George Lundberg, editor of The Journal of the American Medical Association, which will publish two papers drawn from the study, predicted: "They will be looked at 25 years from now as the definitive articles that secured the cholesterol theory of coronary heart disease."

4. After a 10-year study, a completely impartial team of researchers has proven conclusively that lowering blood cholesterol levels will prevent heart attacks.

5. The study on cholesterol, which involved 3,806 men, showed that diet and prescription drugs eliminate the risk of dying prematurely from heart attack.

JOURNAL EXERCISE 9.4

Select one of the statements from Exercises 9.2 or 9.3, and freewrite about that topic for 10 minutes. Then read what you have written, and pick out and label any facts or judgments you find. You may wish to exchange papers with a partner to check your labeling of facts and judgments.

Unlike facts, which are statements about what is known, *inferences* are "educated guesses." Inferences are statements about the *unknown*, made on the basis of what *is* known; they are conclusions based on what can be observed. We rely on inferences every day of our lives. You look out the window, see people carrying umbrellas, and assume that rain has been forecasted. Your nephew's eyes are red and puffy, so you infer he has been crying. Your boss walks past you on the street without saying hello, and you wonder, "What have I done to make her angry?" Without such unconscious and automatic inferences, you would probably find it difficult to get through the day.

Moreover, the ability to draw inferences from observable data is a skill that is crucial to reading comprehension and writing. The news article on page 324 reports the decline in students' scores on reading tests. According to the article, what is the cause of this decline?

Many of the sciences—paleontology (= the study of prehistoric life forms), geology, and physics are notable examples—depend on inference, since they are concerned with what cannot directly be seen. Of course, inferences may be wisely or carelessly made, by laymen and scientists alike. People often misinterpret data or attribute an effect to the wrong cause. For example, your red-eyed nephew may be suffering from allergies; your boss might not have seen you on the street because she was deep in thought or forgot to wear her contact lenses. In the same way, scientific hoaxes

---

Reading Data Indicate Decline in Reasoning Ability

---

by GENE I. MAEROFF

New evidence of lower achievement in schools throughout the country was provided yesterday by the National Assessment of Educational Progress, which found that the inferential reasoning of 13-year-olds and 17-year-olds declined on reading tests in the 1970's. . . .

The overall scores . . . are made up of three subtests—literal comprehension, reference skills and inferential comprehension—and the 13-year-olds as well as the 17-year-olds declined in the inferential category, which is crucial to reading for deeper meaning. This is the skill that enables students to draw conclusions, to form judgments and to create new ideas.

Thirteen-year-olds improved in the two other categories, but 17-year-olds did better only in reference skills, the least important of the three subtests.

Fears Voiced on Trends

"I am concerned that the downward trends in the reading of 13- and 17-year-olds, particularly in the area of inferential comprehension, are signaling deteriorating resources and instruction for those higher-order intellectual abilities that go beyond the basic skills," said Anthony Petrosky, a professor at the University of Pittsburgh who is a member of a panel of 14 reading experts asked by the National Assessment to interpret the results of the study.

"If these trends continue into the 1980's," Professor Petrosky added, "then it seems plausible that we are failing to give these students anything but basic skills."

For students who were 17 years old when they were tested in 1979–80 and therefore would have entered the first grade in 1968, education in the decade of the 1970's apparently did not do as much to develop reasoning skills in reading as in the 1960's.

---

sometimes succeed because observers are too willing to accept one explanation of a phenomenon without considering other possible causes behind the effect they have witnessed. Science writer Martin Gardner frequently exposes such errors in reasoning, especially those involving phenomena of parapsychology such as ESP (extrasensory perception), mental telepathy (mind-reading), and the like. Here are two cases discussed in his book *Science: Good, Bad, and Bogus*:

Lady Wonder was a horse that lived with her owner near Richmond, Virginia. It was said that this horse had the ability to read minds; she communicated her messages by spelling out words with large letters of the alphabet which she raised with her nose. A parapsychologist named Dr. Joseph B. Rhine was completely convinced of Lady's psychic ability to guess numbers written by visitors on a pad of paper provided by the horse's owner. Milbourne Christopher, who is a magician schooled in the art of deception, had his own session with Lady, and came to a very different conclusion. He proved that the horse's owner was "pencil reading"—the ancient art of determining what a person writes by the wigglings of a pencil—and then signaling the horse, by traditional animal-trainer's methods, to push up the appropriate letters of the alphabet.

Jule Eisenbud, a psychoanalyst at the University of Colorado, wrote a book called *The World of Ted Serios* (1967). It seems that Serios, a Chicago bellhop, had an extraordinary talent. He would glance at, say, a photograph in *National Geographic*. Years later, after he had forgotten about the picture, someone could aim a Polaroid camera at him, snap a picture, and ten seconds later, there on the print would be the *National Geographic* photograph! When *Life* magazine wrote up Ted Serios for its September 22, 1967, issue, the article's author withheld one crucial bit of information. Nowhere did he disclose that, before a picture was taken, Ted always held a small one-inch-wide paper tube (which he called his "gismo") in front of the camera lens, presumably to focus "psychic radiation" from his skull. Photographers David B. Eisendrath and Charles Reynolds, both also amateur magicians, had no difficulty constructing a simple optical device which, secretly loaded into a gismo and later secretly removed, could produce all the photographs in Eisenbud's book. The device is nothing more than a tiny cylinder with a positive transparency of a photograph at one end and a lens at the other. Light bouncing off the shirt and face of whoever holds the loaded gismo in front of the Polaroid camera is strong enough to produce excellent images on the film. After the photographers' sensational exposé in *Popular Photography,* October 1967, Ted quietly vanished from the public eye.

EXERCISE 9.5

In 1975, John G. Taylor, a mathematics professor at the University of London, published a book called *Superminds,* about children who had the power of psychokinesis (the ability to move objects by thought processes). The children he tested could bend metal objects such as spoons and forks; they would put paper clips in their pockets and later take them out twisted. Metal rods were put inside sealed plastic tubes and the children were allowed to take them home. The children came back with the tubes still sealed and the rods bent. Curiously, Taylor never actually *saw* anything bend. One minute a spoon would be straight; later it would be found twisted. Taylor named this phenomenon the "shyness effect."

Years later, Taylor repudiated the claims he had made for the children's psychokinetic powers. Can you think of normal explanations for these extraordinary phenomena? Write a paragraph in which you explain your theory about the causes behind these effects. (You'll find an explanation at the end of this chapter.)

The previous examples show how inferences can be carelessly made, even by trained scientists. By way of contrast, let's examine the way scientists concerned with what is called "the new physics" have used logical inferences to predict phenomena—such as "black holes"—which until recently would have seemed bizarre or even impossible. In the following reading selections, three science writers analyze the causes and effects of the death of a star, taking us from known facts about "red giants," "white dwarfs," and "neutron stars," to speculations about black holes based on inferences and evidence from x-ray satellites and radio telescopes. The first reporter is Isaac Asimov, who describes what happens when a star the size of our Sun begins to die:

Fortunately there is such an enormous quantity of hydrogen in the Sun that even at this rate of conversion we need not fear anything drastic happening in the near future. The Sun has been consuming hydrogen in its nuclear furnace for some 5 billion years, and even so there is enough left for at least 5 to 8 billion additional years.

But even 5 to 8 billion years is not eternity. What happens when the hydrogen is gone?

As nearly as astronomers can tell now from their studies of nuclear reactions and of the nature of the various stars they can see, it seems that the dwindling of the hydrogen is the prelude to stark changes in a star's structure.

° **core:** the central or inner-most part.

° **nuclei:** plural of nucleus, the central part of an atom. The fundamental particles of the nucleus are protons and neutrons —except for hydrogen, which is composed of one proton only.

As the Sun, for instance, uses up hydrogen and accumulates helium at the center, the core° will contract further as heavier nuclei° concentrate the inner portion of the gravitational field still further. The core will become denser and hotter. Eventually the heat of the core will begin to rise rather sharply, and the additional heat will force the outer regions of the Sun to expand enormously.

Although the total heat of the Sun's outer regions will then be considerably greater than it is now, it will be spread out over a vastly larger surface. Each bit of surface will have less heat than it now does, and the new surface will be cooler than the present surface is. Where the Sun has a surface temperature of 6,000°C right now, the surface of the expanded Sun will be no more than 2,500°C. At that lower temperature it will gleam only red hot. This combination of vast size and ruddy glow gives this stage of a star's life history the name of *red giant*. There are stars that have reached this stage right now, notably Betelgeuse and Antares.

Harvard astrophysicist Eric Chaisson outlines the final stages in the death of a star the size of our Sun:

° **mass:** size or magnitude.

All theoretical models suggest that the final stages of stellar evolution depend critically on the mass° of the star. As a rule of thumb, we can say that low-mass stars die gently, whereas high-mass stars die catastrophically. Our Sun and all smaller stars are members of the low-mass category, while stars much larger than our Sun are grouped in the high-mass category.

° **demise:** death.

The demise° of our Sun is destined to be rather straightforward and unspectacular. The Sun's core will become extraordinarily compact and hot. A single cubic centimeter of stellar core material will eventually weigh a ton. That's a thousand kilograms of matter compressed into a volume the size of a thimble. Yet, even at such high densities, collisions among nuclei are insufficiently frequent and violent to raise the temperature to the phenomenally high six hundred million degrees required to fuse carbon into any of the heavier elements. There's simply not enough matter in the overlying layers of the smaller stars to bear down any harder. Consequently, oxygen, iron, gold, uranium, and many other elements are not synthesized° in low-mass stars.

° **synthesize:** to bring separate parts or elements together into a whole. In chemistry, to form a complex compound by combining simpler compounds or elements.

Small stars like our Sun manage to work themselves into quite a pickle in their old age. Their carbon core is, for all intents and purposes, dead. Helium just above the core of carbon ash continues to transform into more carbon, while hydrogen in the intermediate layers converts into more

STARS

helium. This onslaught of heating slowly pushes away the outermost layers to ever greater distances. The theoretically expected upshot° is an object of weird posture having two distinct parts. Called a planetary nebula, it is predicted to have a halo of warm, tenuous° matter completely veiling a hot, dense core.

Nebula is Latin for "mist" or "cloud" of great extension and extreme tenuity. The adjective "planetary" is plainly misleading, for these astronomical objects are not related to planets in any way. The designation dates back to the eighteenth century, when optical astronomers could barely distinguish among the myriad° faint, fuzzy patches of light in the nighttime sky. Some researchers mistook all of them for planets. But subsequent observations clearly demonstrated that the nebula's fuzziness results from a shell of warm gas surrounding a small central star. Modern telescopes fully resolve these planetary nebulae, enabling astronomers to recognize their true nature.

Weird or not, nearly a thousand examples of planetary nebulae have been discovered in our Galaxy alone. Direct observations confirm the theoretical predictions that the shell consists of an envelope in the act of being gently expelled from the core of an aged red-giant star.

Further discussion of the evolution of the expanding envelope is not very interesting. It simply continues to spread out as time passes, becoming more diffuse° and cool, and eventually merging imperceptibly° with the interstellar medium. This is one way, then, that the interstellar medium becomes enriched with additional helium atoms and possibly some carbon atoms as well.

Continued evolution of a core, or stellar remnant, at the center of a planetary nebula, is not much more exciting. Formerly concealed by the atmosphere of the red-giant star, cores make their first appearance once the flimsy envelope has receded. These cores are small, hot objects, highly abundant with carbon, but no longer experiencing nuclear burning. They shine only by stored energy, though their small size guarantees a white-hot

° **upshot:** the conclusion or outcome.

° **tenuous:** not substantial or dense; rare, as air at high altitudes.

° **myriad:** any indefinitely large number.

° **diffuse:** spread out or dispersed.

° **imperceptibly:** gradually, subtly, as not to be easily perceived.

appearance. Not much bigger than planet Earth, they are called white-dwarf stars.

Analysis of the radiation emitted by white-dwarf stars shows their properties to agree pretty well with the computer model predictions. Many are found at the very center of planetary nebulae. Several hundred additional ones have been discovered naked in our Galaxy, their envelopes blown to invisibility long ago.

So astronomers are able to identify red-giant stars, planetary nebulae, and white-dwarf stars in the nearby cosmos. At different stages in their old age, each of these objects seems to match the overall disposition predicted by the theoretical calculations for elderly low-mass stars. Once again, though, we should not expect to witness the act of envelope expulsion during the course of a human lifetime. It takes several tens of thousands of years for a red giant's atmosphere to recede sufficiently for a white-dwarf star to appear.

Nothing exciting happens to dwarf stars after this. For all practical purposes, these "stars" are dead. They continue to cool, becoming dimmer with time, slowly transforming from white dwarfs to yellow dwarfs and then red dwarfs. The final state is that of a black dwarf—a cold, dense, burned-out ember in space. Such stellar corpses have reached the graveyard of stars.

Finally, British writer Nigel Calder discusses the death of a star more massive than the Sun. He begins with neutron stars—the "pulsars" which actually exist, according to radio and x-ray observers—and proceeds to black holes, which so far exist only in theory:

> The demise of a star more massive than the Sun could compress the central remains of the star violently enough to defeat the electric force. The remaining line of resistance to gravity was then the strong nuclear force. Theorists envisaged a star like one enormous atomic nucleus, and called it a neutron star. Electrons were in a sense squeezed into the protons to make neutrons, the uncharged relatives of the protons. The pulsars that turned up in 1968, flashing rhythmically many times a second, were very small stars associated with the remnants of the explosions of massive stars. They packed a mass greater than the Sun's into a ball only 20 or 30 kilometres in diameter. If you thought of standing on a neutron star you would weigh more than a million million tons and would be at once flattened into a pancake of atoms.
>
> How did nuclear matter behave under pressure, in a neutron star? A theoretical picture emerged of a solid crust subject to 'starquakes' which altered the rate of spinning of the neutron star. (Such 'glitches' were detected by the radio astronomers.) The crust enclosed a dense liquid of neutrons, under extremely high pressures. The core of a heavy neutron star might be a solid mass of neutrons, or perhaps a completely new state of matter. The pressures that nuclear matter might withstand depended on precisely what form it took, but it seemed unlikely that a neutron star would survive if it were more than about twice as massive as the Sun.
>
> Even before the discovery of the pulsars, theorists of gravity had taken

the argument a step further. If a star more massive than those which made the neutron stars were to collapse, gravity could overwhelm the nuclear forces too. Then the star would not stop shrinking at the size of the neutron star but would go on collapsing. Its gravity would grow more and more intense, until it could prevent all light escaping and made a black hole. The star effectively disappeared from the universe, except for the intense gravity that surrounded the place where it disappeared. The rubber sheet of space-time was distended in a narrow, very deep well. But the analogy was misleading, because you could circle as freely around a black hole as around any other object in space.

You might have reason for doing so, if you wanted to travel through time. The strong gravity churning space and time near a black hole would slow down clocks and life processes so greatly that the lapse of ten thousand years on Earth could seem like only a few weeks to the voyager orbiting

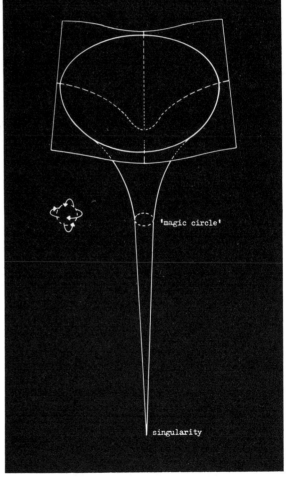

Black hole in curved space. Here the distortion of space-time becomes very great. But the flattened-space picture should not be taken too seriously. In practice, a black hole would be a small, spherical object, which one might pass around in any direction.

° **singularity:** at the center of a black hole, an infinitely small point where existence and even time would seem to cease.

the black hole. But there would be no going back in time, to return to your natural time-frame. And if you were careless enough to fall into the black hole, you could not return to Earth through space, either.

There would be a 'magic circle', actually a sphere around the vanished star, but a dire° perimeter not marked by any boundary posts. Anything falling through it would never come out again, because nothing could travel faster than light. For a black hole twice as massive as the Sun, the 'magic circle' would be about 12 kilometres in diameter.

° **dire:** dreadful or terrible.

Here indeed was an 'undiscovered country from whose bourn° no traveller returns'. And the fate of the imagined space-traveller who stumbled upon a black hole became a commonplace way of describing the extraordinary work of gravity, in and around a black hole. Before being trapped and crushed, the unwary astronaut would first be stretched into spaghetti.

° **bourn** (archaic): limit or boundary. (Calder is quoting from Shakespeare's *Hamlet*.)

The first hint of trouble might be his hair standing on end, his feet and hands feeling heavy, his head light. The astronaut's blood would drain into his limbs, bringing merciful unconsciousness before gravity rendered his body into meat, into molecules, into atoms, and eventually into a long beam of particles hurtling into the black hole.

Spaghettification was due to gravity intensifying, metre by metre, in the approach to a black hole. It was a tidal effect, an extreme version of the process by which the Moon would pull more strongly on sea-water immediately beneath it than on the oceans to the far side of the Earth. In the more severe conditions around a black hole, the force of gravity increased so rapidly towards the centre that it could easily be a million times stronger at the spaceman's feet than at his head. So he would be torn apart by the tide.

EXERCISE 9.6

A.) The authors of the three cause/effect analyses you have just read make use of a number of rhetorical patterns discussed in this book. Re-examine the passages: can you locate at least one example of comparison/contrast, definition, and classification? What analogies do the authors of the selections use, and how do these comparisons make abstract concepts easier to understand?

B.) Based on the readings, try to come up with brief definitions of red giant, white dwarf, and black hole.

EXERCISE 9.7

Earlier in this chapter, we discussed the need for writers to qualify their generalizations, and to differentiate between facts and assumptions. Return to the reading selections for a moment and underline the words the authors use to qualify their assertions—words like "seems" and "suggest," as well as modals such as "could" and "might." What would be the effect of these sentences and paragraphs *without* such qualifiers?

EXERCISE 9.8

The chart given here is a graphic depiction of the evolutionary process of stars discussed in the three selections you have just read. Using this cause-and-effect chart, write several paragraphs in which you summarize what you've learned about the death of low- and high-mass stars, beginning with the red-giant stage and ending with speculations about black holes. (To express these cause/effect relationships, you may want to make use of linking words and phrases such as *because, so, since, consequently, as a result, therefore,* and so on.)

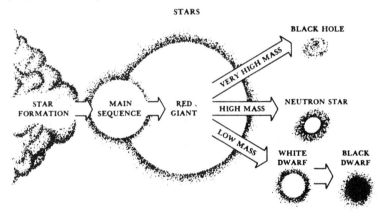

Making Inferences: Induction Versus Deduction

The purpose of a cause-and-effect analysis is to explain, to investigate, to draw conclusions, or to convince. This kind of analysis depends heavily on inductive logic, which is the basic reasoning process of science. Induction is a common mental activity by which we arrive at a general truth by considering specific evidence, whether our own observations or the testimony of others:

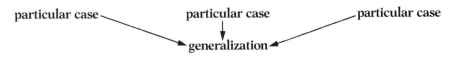

Deduction moves in the opposite direction: it is the process of arriving at a conclusion by *starting* with a general premise instead of a particular case. Deduction most often works through a three-part logical structure known as a *syllogism*, which consists of a general premise, a specific instance, and a conclusion. For example, this is how scientists reason that, as Eric Chaisson puts it, "The experimentalist's 'pulsar' and the theoretician's 'neutron star' are synonymous":

GENERAL PREMISE: Scientists theorize that neutron stars are small, compact, rotating stars that periodically flash radiation toward earth.

PARTICULAR CASE: Researchers have monitored several hundred pulsating stars, or pulsars, that emit short, regular, radioactive pulses.

CONCLUSION: Therefore, scientists conclude that pulsars are synonymous with neutron stars.

Needless to say, essays based on formal logic, such as cause/effect and argument essays, draw on both of these methods of handling evidence. Indeed, as you can see from the essays you have been writing all along, writers most often use deductive order in structuring their essays: they begin by stating the proposition to be defended, and then back up that thesis with a succession of proofs. But our concern at present is with inferential reasoning, and any attempt to draw inferences from observable data is really an exercise in inductive logic.

Detective stories naturally abound with such intellectual puzzles in inductive logic. The following illustration is adapted from a story by Sir Arthur Conan Doyle involving fiction's most famous detective, Sherlock Holmes. Study the situation, and try the classroom activity that follows.

The time: the 1890s; the place: London. One morning after Christmas Dr. Watson, Holmes's assistant, finds the great detective studying (with a magnifying lens and forceps) a very seedy and disreputable-looking hard felt hat. Holmes explains that the hat has been brought to him by a policeman. The facts are these: About four o'clock Christmas morning, the policeman saw a tall man walking with a slight stagger and carrying a white goose slung over his shoulder. The man was then accosted by a gang of roughs, who knocked off his hat; he raised his walking stick to defend himself, and accidentally smashed the shop window behind him. Seeing the policeman, the poor man dropped the goose and ran away.

Here is the intellectual problem: Along with the hat, the policeman has also brought Holmes the goose, which has a small card tied to its leg reading "For Mrs. Henry Baker." The initials "H.B." are legible on the lining of the hat. But there are hundreds of Henry Bakers in London: How is Holmes to return this property to its rightful owner? He must determine the man's identity from this old battered felt hat.

Watson is invited to help solve this problem. This is his report of the evidence:

"I took the tattered object in my hands and turned it over rather ruefully.° It was a very ordinary black hat of the usual round shape, hard and much the worse for wear. The lining had been of red silk, but was a good deal discoloured. There was no maker's name; but, as Holmes had remarked, the initials "H.B." were scrawled upon one side. It was pierced in the brim for a hat-securer, but the elastic was missing. For the rest, it was cracked, exceedingly dusty, and spotted in several places, although there seemed to have been some attempt to hide the discoloured patches by smearing them with ink.

"'I can see nothing,' said I, handing it back to my friend.

"'On the contrary, Watson, you can see everything. You fail, however, to reason from what you see. You are too timid in drawing your inferences.'"

Holmes then observes these additional details, from which he proceeds to draw an astonishing array of inferences:

1. The hat is extremely large.
2. The magnifying lens reveals, under the lining, a great number of hair-ends, which are grizzled,° clean-cut, adhesive, and scented with lime-cream (a hair cream).
3. There are marks of moisture inside the hat.
4. There are five tallow° stains on the outside of the hat.

° **ruefully:** sorrowfully or regretfully.

° **grizzled:** gray.

° **tallow:** animal fat used to make candles.

CLASSROOM ACTIVITY 9.9

You are now invited to try your hand at drawing inferences. Work in groups with your classmates to see what you can infer about the owner of the hat from the set of clues you have been given. When you have finished, compare your results with those of Holmes (reprinted at the end of this chapter).

The previous exercise asked you to make reasonable assumptions, though of course you could not be sure about the accuracy of your "detective work." This kind of inferential reasoning is an automatic, informal, constant process for all of us. But in the essays you write, your capacity to reason objectively depends on your ability to distinguish between facts and inferences. This next exercise, devised by educator Neil Postman, will help you determine how well you are able to separate facts from assumptions.

CLASSROOM ACTIVITY 9.10

Read the brief story below. Assume only that all the information presented in the story is true, and that the grammatical conventions of English hold. Then read the statements following the story. Determine whether each statement is

T—meaning that, according to the information presented in the story, the statement is definitely true.

F—meaning that, according to the information presented in the story, the statement is definitely false.

?—meaning that the statement may be true or it may be false, but on the basis of the information presented in the story, you cannot be certain.

Dr. Darekill, young intern at Blear General Hospital, was in Surgery when a huge electrical storm burst with fury over the city. It was Darekill's first operation, an emergency appendectomy, and the young surgeon was slightly nervous. Darekill's gown clung damply to his body, and his brow was beaded with perspiration. At a critical point in the operation, a crash of thunder shook the room, a huge bolt of lightning split the sky just beyond the window, and the operating theater was plunged into darkness. The instrument nurse standing next to Dr. Darekill flung out an arm for support, and the instrument tray crashed to the floor. Dr. Gallupsie, head surgeon, stepped quickly to Darekill's side and in a low voice told him to remain calm. Dr. Gallupsie reminded the surgeon that the hospital's emergency generator could provide lighting for three hours. In a moment the lights came on again. On the table, the patient was tense with terror. The anaesthetist reported that the patient's pulse rate was 120—far above normal. Dr. Darekill, unnerved by the crisis, looked imploringly to Dr. Gallupsie. Gallupsie told Darekill to try to control himself, and that the operation must continue. Darekill was also reminded that a surgeon must learn to cope coolly with any emergency. The operation was completed in fifteen minutes. As the patient was wheeled from the operating room, Gallupsie praised Darekill for his speedy recovery of self control in a situation which any surgeon would find trying.

1. Dr. Darekill was a young intern at Blear General Hospital. T F ?
2. The emergency appendectomy was the first operation Darekill had performed. T F ?
3. Darekill was slightly nervous about the operation. T F ?
4. Perspiration dampened Darekill's gown and beaded his brow. T F ?
5. The head surgeon was a man named Dr. Gallupsie. T F ?
6. The instrument nurse flung out her arm for support. T F ?
7. A bolt of lightning knocked out the electrical power in Surgery. T F ?
8. A bolt of lightning knocked out the lights in Surgery. T F ?
9. The instrument nurse knocked the instrument tray to the floor. T F ?
10. The patient's terror raised his pulse to 120—far above normal. T F ?
11. The crash of thunder shook the room at a critical point in the operation. T F ?

12. Dr. Gallupsie told Darekill to try to control himself, that the operation must continue, and that a surgeon must learn to cope coolly with any emergency.   T   F   ?
13. The patient died in the operating room.   T   F   ?
14. The operation included removing the patient's spleen.   T   F   ?
15. The emergency generator could provide lighting for six hours.   T   F   ?

Are You Assuming Too Much?

Obviously, the preceding quiz is designed to fool you. The point of the exercise is to make you aware of how automatically we all make assumptions —and how easy it is to make illogical assumptions. The test magnifies the most typical errors writers make in a cause/effect analysis:

FACT VERSUS INFERENCE

As we have noted, *facts* are observable, verifiable bits of information, whereas inferences are guesswork. Yet speakers and writers frequently mistake inferences for facts. Since we have been instructed to assume that all the information in the story is true, the questions are really asking us to determine what is *in the story*, and what we have *added to the story* in our own minds. In other words, what inferences have we assumed to be facts?

Go back to items 1 and 2 on the list of questions. Then compare the corresponding sentences in the selection (the first two sentences) with those questions. What words have been added (inference) that make the questions different from the information in the story (fact)? Since we have been told that the grammatical conventions of English apply in this story, we know that the appositive that follows the subject in the first sentence (Dr. Darekill) *identifies* that subject: Darekill is, in fact, a young intern at Blear Hospital, so the answer to #1 is obviously "T." Question #2 presents a problem, though:

STORY (fact)	QUESTION (inference)
It was Darekill's first operation, an emergency appendectomy . . .	*The* emergency appendectomy was *the* first operation Darekill *had performed.*

The story does not specify the performer of the operation—in fact, the head surgeon, or even another intern not mentioned in the story, might have performed the appendectomy; Darekill might have been observing the operation, as many interns are called upon to do. If you answered "T" to question #2, you inferred an agent in the sentence where there was none. This is a reasonable inference but not a fact.

FAULTY CAUSATION

You have probably noticed that the most frequent connecting word in the reading selection in Activity 9.10 is *and*. In an earlier chapter, we discussed how overuse of this conjunction, the "weak *and*," makes your writing vague and confusing to the reader. The effect of the "weak *and*" in the passage is to show you how we are apt to supply causation where there is none.

This common error in logic is *post hoc*. The full name of this error in causation is the Latin phrase *post hoc, ergo propter hoc*, meaning "after this, therefore because of this." We often think that when one event follows another, the two events must be connected causally. But the fact that one event precedes another doesn't mean it *caused* the second event. If you claimed, "I failed my chemistry test today because I dreamed last night that I was going to fail," you would be guilty of *post hoc*: even if your confidence had been shaken by the dream, your failure wasn't *caused* by it. More than likely, you had the dream because you knew you weren't prepared for the test. In addition, you should be aware of a related error in causation called *non sequitur*, which is Latin for "it does not follow." In this type of faulty reasoning, a speaker or writer arrives at a conclusion that doesn't follow from the premise: "Of course I'll do well on my chemistry test today—after all, I got an A on my math exam."

Similarly, two events that happen at the same time aren't necessarily connected. A person who is walking behind you down the same street at the same pace isn't necessarily following you. Nor, when you read on page 334 that "the instrument nurse . . . flung out an arm for support, *and* the instrument tray crashed to the floor," can you be sure that the two actions are related. What you are observing may be simple coincidence.

Post hoc figures in several of the answers in the quiz you have just taken. For example, compare question #3 with its counterpart in the story:

STORY	QUESTION
It was Darekill's first operation . . . and the young surgeon was slightly nervous.	Darekill was slightly nervous *about* the operation.

The story, as you can see, says nothing about the cause of Darekill's nervousness. Yet the question links the doctor's nervousness to the operation. Can you think of other explanations for his "jitters" besides the operation itself?

THINKING IN STEREOTYPES

One additional kind of error usually shows up in the quiz you've been asked to take. How did you answer question #5 in the quiz? Before you give your reasons for answering as you did—and before you read any further—copy the following sentence in your notebook, and provide punctuation to make the meaning of the sentence clear:

woman without her man is an animal

Now compare your punctuation with that of your classmates. Do you suddenly see other ways of punctuating, and other ways of reading the sentence? What is the difference between the two main ways of reading this sentence? If you only saw one meaning in the sentence, why do you think you and some of your classmates failed to see the other way of interpreting these words?

In the previous chapter, we saw how culture influences our thought patterns, as well as the way we perceive objects and events in our environment. Most students, native and non-native alike, answer "T" for #5; yet the correct answer is "?"—can you explain why? A stereotype is a conventional, oversimplified concept or belief, usually about a group of people. What stereotyped way of seeing things causes most people to respond incorrectly to this question? There is one more question in the quiz that is related to #5 for it elicits the same kind of stereotypical response. Which is it? (The answer appears at the end of this chapter.)

CLASSROOM ACTIVITY 9.11

Go over the remaining questions in the quiz with your classmates, keeping in mind the fallacies noted above.

Citing Multiple Causes

A paper that attributes an effect—say, the rise in gasoline prices—to only *one* cause does not take into account the complexity of most causal relationships. Usually there are multiple causes that have led to the result you observe. The following excerpt from Marie Winn's book *Children Without Childhood* illustrates how the author gathers support for her thesis in a cause/effect analysis. Winn's thesis is that since the 1960s, there has been a profound change in the behavior of American children, and in society's attitude toward these children. As Winn explains, "Once parents struggled to preserve childhood's innocence, to keep childhood a carefree golden age. The new era operates on the belief that children must be exposed early to adult experience in order to survive in an increasingly complex and uncontrollable world." The author suggests a number of reasons for the changes she observes, and this thorough process of investigation keeps her analysis from seeming superficial or oversimplified. Notice, too, that she considers both *immediate* and *remote* causes for the effects she is discussing—for example, she notes changes that began in the 1960s but accelerated during the 1970s.

EXERCISE 9.12

A.) As you read this selection, mark down in your notebook the kinds of evidence Winn uses to support her thesis, such as news reports, interviews, and statistics. These varieties of evidence will be discussed at the end of the selection.

B.) In addition to citing these kinds of reports, Winn makes a number of inferences about causes and effects. See how many of these inferences you can detect, and list them in your notebook. How does Winn indicate to the reader when she is making an inference?

The End of Supervision

At the heart of parental loss of control lies the fact that parents today supervise their school-age children less than their counterparts did even ten years and certainly twenty years ago. A new parental casualness is so much the norm these days that only when one compares contemporary children's lives with those of the 1960s and early 1970s does one realize how much earlier the parental reins are loosened today. There is clear evidence of an overall decrease in parental vigilance about every aspect of children's lives, from the trivial to the life-threatening. Indeed, so universal is children's earlier freedom in today's society that what was once seen as care and nurture is now often regarded as overprotectiveness. Today's children seem to be about two years advanced when compared with children ten years ago. Kids cross the street without holding an adult's hand at four years instead of six. Seven-year-olds ride the bus alone where once they had to wait until they were nine or ten. Bedtime for seven-year-olds is commonly ten P.M., as it once was for fifth- or sixth-graders, while *those* "young adults"—as they are called in the publishing trade—often don't have any required bedtime at all. (A recent informal survey of fifth- and sixth-graders revealed that the majority no longer consider themselves children. When asked "What are you, then?" they answered "Pre-teenagers" or "Young adults.")

What are the reasons for this decline in child supervision? The most obvious are the rising divorce rate and the increase in two-career families.

In each case the parents' attention is inevitably diverted from child supervision to adult matters. Another part of the answer may be that children today, thanks to their new precocity, are simply more difficult to supervise than children were fifteen or twenty years ago. Faced with a steady battle on their hands and with the standard "everybody else can stay out until one A.M." ploy that children have used from time immemorial, faced with kids who may be only eleven or twelve but who "talk sixteen," parents are more inclined these days to capitulate.°

° **capitulate:** surrender.

Winn goes on to discuss the connection between the children's new freedom from adult supervision and their precocious experimentation with drugs and sex:

> Suddenly media attention turned to "children" rather than "teenagers" in articles and documentaries about sex and drugs. A 1980 article in *Newsweek* reported that "young people, especially, are turning on to pot earlier, more often, and in greater numbers than ever." An alarming photograph of two kids looking no older than nine, lighting up joints, accompanies the article. "Pot smoking and dealing have moved down through the school grades and age levels and have become an integral part of the experience of growing up," declares an article in the *New York Times Magazine*.
>
> School personnel began making similar observations in the late seventies. "Several years ago high school students were experimenting. Now we are finding people coming into high school who have started using drugs in fourth, fifth, or sixth grade and who get into a heavy dependence by junior high school," says the dean of students at a Connecticut high school. Even teenagers themselves began to comment on the change, often with a certain indignation. "I started smoking pot in tenth grade, when I went to boarding school," reminisces a college student. "At that time pot hadn't started filtering down to the lower grades yet. It was still a pretty much high school thing to do. But now little *kids* are turning on!"
>
> And yet a decline in supervision is not the entire story. Even in the fifties there were undersupervised children, whose parents were divorced or whose mothers worked, but who nevertheless did not become pregnant at thirteen or even "go all the way" and who did not smoke anything stronger than an occasional Camel or Lucky Strike. The difference is that sex was still in the closet, in those days before X-rated movies and *The Joy of Sex*, and drugs were unavailable outside the lower reaches of society. It took a combination of unsupervised children *and* a permissive, highly charged sexual atmosphere *and* an influx of easily acquired drugs *and* the wherewithal° to buy them to bring about precocious experimentation by younger and younger children. This occurred in the mid-seventies.

° **wherewithal:** the necessary means—usually money—to obtain something.

Finally, Winn maintains, even the strictest, most old-fashioned parents recognize that no matter how much they control their children, there is always the television set waiting to undo all their careful plans:

> Children themselves confirm to an interviewer that their parents can't control what they watch on television or in the movies (often movies on cable TV). "My mother doesn't know," said a childish-looking ten-year-old

girl, "but my younger sister and I watched *Pretty Baby, Ten, The Exorcist,* and *Lipstick* [all movies rated R] on *Home Box Office.*"

"My mom would be shocked to know what I know," an eleven-year-old boy cheerfully admitted. "I wouldn't want her to think I'm perverted or something, so I'm glad she doesn't know the things I watch."

"My parents won't let me watch *HBO*," a twelve-year-old from a stable, protective family informed an interviewer, "but I watch at my friend's house all the time."

It's Not What They Watch

Of course television *is* deeply implicated in the changed image of today's child, and of course television *has* played a crucial role in hastening the end of that protected stage of life that was once known as childhood. But not necessarily in the way most people think. To consider that television's effect on children's lives is primarily a function of its content—of the programs that children watch—is to ignore the medium's real impact. To believe that a nation of eight- or nine- or ten-year-olds could have lost their definition as children and achieved a new integration into adult life mainly as a result of watching *General Hospital* or *Dallas* or sexy commercials or even *Midnight Blue* is to see but the thin top layer of a powerful agent of change.

To be sure, the programs children watch make a difference too. Through television they gain entry into a confusing adult world that cannot help but shake their confidence and trust in those elders who once seemed so omniscient, powerful, and good. But their trust is not diminished all that much—at least not by television itself. Child experts agree that even scary or sexual programs do not deeply affect children who grow up in normal, reasonably happy families. It is when other things go haywire in a child's life—when his parents divorce, for instance—that television's actual images may have a deeper and more negative influence.

True, television programs teach children sophisticated words and phrases and cause them to imitate unchildlike ways of moving, gesturing, dancing, and behaving that create an illusion of maturity not necessarily based on any emotional reality. This too is a factor in childhood's change, but a somewhat superficial one. If a child were to be raised in the way parents reared children in the pretelevision era, it is likely that no amount of sexy imitations he or she might learn, verbal or gestural, would obscure the fact that this was a child imitating a TV program.

But television's very presence in the home has worked to alter children's lives in ways that have nothing to do with *what* they might be watching. Parents' use of the medium as a child-rearing aid is one such way. Its easy availability as a child amuser, baby-sitter, and problem solver has altered long-established child-rearing patterns, allowing parents to coexist with their children without establishing those rules and limitations that parents once had to impose on children simply for survival's sake. Before television, parents had to make sure that their kids could be relied upon to "mind" when necessary, not to interrupt adult conversation, not to demand attention when the parent was busy or instant gratification of their every wish; otherwise nothing would ever get done around the house, and the parents would go crazy. It was crucial for parents who had to live in close proximity with children, to eat with them at the same table, to sit with them in the same living room, that the children learn early how to behave in acceptable, disciplined ways. Television, however, provided an easy alternative to parental discipline. Instead of having to establish rules and limits, an arduous and often frustrating job, instead of having to work at socializing children in order to make them more agreeable to live with, parents could solve all these problems by resorting to the television set. "Go and watch TV" were the magic words. Now mothers could cook dinner in peace, or prepare their briefs for the next day's case, or whatever. No need to work on training the children to play quietly while mothers and fathers discussed a family matter without interruption.

Television brought peace—but at a price. Without establishing firm rules and precise boundaries, parents never defined for the children precisely what the roles of the adults and the children in the family were to be. And without having to take an authoritative position right from the start, parents never gained the control of their children that their counterparts of the past achieved quite inevitably, out of sheer necessity. A new equality between adults and children became possible.

Citing Evidence

In addition to her own observations, Winn cites other experts for corroboration of her thesis. Where do these examples appear, and how do they help the essay? When offering proof for an assertion, writers frequently present not only their own speculations but those of authorities on the subject. This expert testimony adds support to an argument, provided the expert referred to is legitimately qualified to pass judgment on the topic under discussion. Movie-star endorsements are an established advertising technique, but this kind of fallacious appeal to "authority" is not valid proof in an expository essay. Television personalities in ads may be talented actors or actresses, but often they are not authorities on the products being endorsed. They may in fact use the products, but theirs is not impartial testimony, since they've been paid for their endorsements.

Biased endorsements have no place in exposition. If you are conducting a survey on whether Honda Civics get better mileage than Volvos, don't ask Volvo salesmen to testify. Volvo owners will probably be more objective observers than the salesmen, but they still might be prejudiced. Instead, you'll want to question a wide range of Volvo and Honda owners who have tested their cars under a variety of road conditions. This method of gathering evidence by questioning a group of people is known as *sampling*. Naturally, you ought to examine as many examples as possible before making any generalization. Otherwise, you are guilty of the logical fallacy known as *hasty generalization*. To make a fair generalization, you must have sufficient evidence, drawn from a reasonable number of cases. But your examples must be more than plentiful—they must be *representative*.

Consequently, if you are taking a poll of the opinions of a group of strangers, the people you question should be selected carefully and proportionately from different social, economic, and age groups. Make clear to your reader what groups you have drawn your sampling from. And whether you are gathering statistics or expert testimony, guard against selecting some examples and ignoring others just to confirm your thesis. For instance, as background for her study on childhood, Marie Winn conducted hundreds of interviews with children, parents, doctors, and educators. In the preface of her book, she describes how she collected these interviews, and explains the limits she imposed on her sampling:

> Since I live in New York City, my first imperative in studying patterns of change was to branch out, to talk to adults and children in other geographical locations, in suburban and rural areas and in smaller cities. I focused on two diverse communities for extensive interviews. I chose Denver, Colorado, for its Midwestern location and for its nearby isolated mountain area where I might find a more rural population. Since I had once lived in Denver, I was able to make easy contact with a large and varied parent-child network. Scotia, New York, a small suburban area outside Schenectady, I chose for its cozy, small-town feeling, and also because my cousin Helen is a fourth-grade teacher there. This gave me a fortunate access to yet another large network of parents, teachers, and children. In both communities I organized group interviews with children within the public school system, as well as a great number of individual talks with parents, teachers, school administrators, librarians, and child experts. All unattributed quotations in the following pages are taken from these interviews. I have chosen to protect all the parents and children quoted by not using their real names. But virtually every child I interviewed was openly disappointed when I told them of this decision. I promised that I would at least include their names in an acknowledgment section, which I have done.
>
> I made no effort to achieve socioeconomic balance in these interviews—the scope of such a book would have been too unwieldy. Almost without exception the parents and children I spoke to were middle-class. But within that group I found an abundance of differences—occupational, religious, racial, political—enough variety to lead me to believe I was drawing upon a representative selection of that vital part of the American population, average American parents and children.

We've said that induction is the process of reaching a conclusion based on evidence. As in every paper you've written up to now, the strength of your cause/effect analysis depends on your giving evidence, in the form of examples and illustrations, for each general assertion you make. Keep in mind that in a cause/effect paper, you are asking your reader to follow your own inductive reasoning, that is, to see the process whereby you've derived a generalization from examination of concrete evidence. Examples—whether from expert testimony, from your own life, or from your imagination—help clarify your ideas in terms of particular and specific details which your reader can understand more easily. To accomplish this goal, the examples must be relevant and sufficiently detailed to be convincing. The evidence you cite may take any of the rhetorical forms you've practiced so far, such as description, narration, and definition, or may take the form of scientific data, statistics, and lists. Your objective is to present vivid and explicit cases that justify the claims you make.

EXERCISE 9.13

What kinds of evidence might you use to back up the following cause/ effect statements? Be as specific as you can, and strive for a variety of examples:

1. Exams are (or are not) an effective way to make students learn the course material.

2. Dieting isn't enough: you have to exercise, too, if you want to lose weight.

3. Stress can cause high blood pressure.

4. A college degree leads to better job opportunities.

5. Children can benefit from viewing TV.

6. TV viewing can have a negative influence on children.

Writing Cause/Effect Essays

ASSIGNMENT 1

Marie Winn maintains that the most dramatic change in childhood has been the disappearance of old-fashioned childish games, especially among

6-to-12-year-old children. She writes, "In the place of traditional, sometimes ancient childhood games that were still popular a generation ago, in the place of fantasy and make-believe play—'You be the mommy and I'll be the daddy'—doll play or toy-soldier play, jump-rope play, ball-bouncing play, today's children have substituted television viewing and, most recently, video games."

In a brief essay, discuss what the effects of this change in children might be. Do you believe that childhood play and fantasy—especially "make-believe" games—are important to a child's growth? If so, can you foresee any problems that may occur if these games are replaced with TV viewing and video games? On the other hand, can you see how children may benefit from watching TV and playing video games? Make your answer specific: cite examples from what you have read and what you have directly observed among the children you know.

Now observe how one student writer made the final version of his essay far more persuasive by citing evidence for the assertions he made in his first draft of the essay. What's especially noteworthy about this writing sample is that the student *begins* with a first draft that is unusually proficient: the content and organization are exceptionally clear, and the grammar is virtually error-free. Why, then, rewrite? When you read the third and final draft of the paper, you'll see how, over the course of two revisions, the author uncovered a wealth of evidence from his own experience and knowledge of the topic. As a result, he was able to supply the support for his thesis that was missing in the original version.

In his paper, the author analyzes some of the reasons for our stereotypes of Middle Eastern cultures. Stereotypes often have some basis in fact, but serious thinkers and writers try to get beyond these simplistic explanations, and to see more complex reasons for the stereotype. This is one important function of the cause-and-effect essay.

EXERCISE 9.14

A.) The organization of this essay is typical of many cause-and-effect essays. To get a sense of how the author structures his paper and presents his evidence, briefly outline the main points of his final draft in your notebook, and underline the transitions he uses to lead the reader from one paragraph to the next.

B.) In addition, note what kinds of information the writer adds to the final draft—historical anecdote, personal experience, examples, and so forth. Begin with the introduction: what changes does he make in these paragraphs, and what effect does the revision have on you as a reader?

DRAFT #1

Stereotypes about many ethnic groups have been propagated for ages. These semi-truths have been mainly a result of a lack of interaction with that particular group, or perhaps television dramatization. Nonetheless, they have served as a constant source of embarrassment to that particular group. Middle Eastern people have been the subject of a large number of these stereotypes. Among these are misconceptions such as the belief that all Arabs live in the desert, wear djellabas, ride camels, and keep harems. However, as is the case with most stereotypes, these are not true.

Despite what most people believe, life in Middle Eastern cities today resembles that in many modern ones. Modern conveniences such as air-conditioners, dishwashers, and trash compactors are widely used. Large apartment buildings constitute the major form of residence for citizens. Transportation in these metropolises is provided mainly by trolleys, buses, taxi cabs, and private automobiles. Traffic problems also exist as they do in New York City or San Francisco. Living standards in most Middle Eastern cities are relatively high. In fact, the capital of Kuwait, a Middle Eastern nation, has the highest per capita Gross National Product in the world. Although this may not be true of all of them, cities in the Middle East are certainly not slums, ghettos, or deserts.

Another common misconception about the Middle East is that every man has a harem of wives. Most individuals make this understandable mistake because they know that the Moslem religion allows a man to have more than one wife. Although this is true, there are very specific circumstances under which he can do this; there are also stipulations which he must con-form to when he makes the decision to have more than one wife.

In addition to the misconceptions about life in the Middle East and the marriage customs of Arabs, there are also stereotypes about their attire. A large number of people, unfamiliar with Middle Eastern culture, believe that all Arabs dress in djellabas, turbans, and kaftans. Although this may have been true a century ago, it is certainly not true today. The traditional Middle Eastern clothes are worn either by the impoverished, or on very special occasions, such as festivals and celebrations.

Stereotypes about almost every ethnic group have existed for many years, and the Arabs are no exception. Sometimes these misconceptions are based on only a partial understanding or on half truths, but they can only be corrected through knowledge. As a first step, ethnic groups should explain their cultures to each other, and then perhaps some of the problems that exist among them will be eliminated.

DRAFT #3: The Facts Behind the Egyptian Stereotype

"Do Egyptians live in tents in the desert? Do people ride camels down the streets in your village? How many wives did your father have?"

These are the typical questions asked over and over again since I've been in the United States. But where do people get such ideas? Most stereotypes are based on some truth, and these are no exception. At one time in the history of the Middle East, Arabs did live in tents, ride camels, and keep several wives. However, at that time there were practical reasons for doing so.

Some people believe that all Arabs live in tents in the desert, and about a century ago, they were probably right. At that time, tents provided an excellent solution to the lack of building materials and the difficulty of constructing a new dwelling each time the Arabs moved, which was frequent. In addition, tents served as protection from the hot sun during the day and the bitter cold during the night in the desert. So, the Arabs chose animal-skin tents for very practical reasons.

However, life today in the Middle East has changed dramatically. Most people live in large cities such as Cairo and Alexandria. Homes are no longer tents, but small villas or apartments. Apartment buildings help to deal with the crowding problems typical of large metropolises, and modern conveniences, such as air-conditioners and dishwashers, are available. Consequently, living standards are at a reasonable level.

Transportation in the Middle East has been the subject of another misconception, for some people believe that camels are seen on the streets regularly. Years ago, camels did provide Arabs with the best possible transportation in the desert. With their ability to retain food and water and to cross the desert, camels were indispensable to the nomads. Today, however, no one has to travel through the desert in this way. Cars and planes have taken the camel's place. In the cities, trolleys, buses, taxi cabs, and private automobiles provide the major means of transportation.

Another common misconception about the Middle East is that every man has a harem of wives. People make this understandable mistake because they know that the Moslem religion allows a man to have more than one wife. Although this is true, there are specific circumstances under which he may do so, and many stipulations which he must conform to; that is, he must have a very good reason, such as the infertility of his wife. He must also be able to treat each of his wives equally in every way. At one time, it was very important to have many children, so men had harems of wives to insure that many offspring were produced. Today, however, this practice is no longer desirable, and during the time that I lived in Egypt, I never knew or heard of a man who had more than one wife. Certainly, my father had only one wife—as far as I knew. Marriage, in fact, is a very sacred institution in the Middle East, and divorce is looked upon very unfavorably.

Other stereotypes concern the way Arabs dress. Many people think that all Arabs wear djellabas, turbans, and kaftans, perhaps because this is what they see on television shows such as "Saturday Night Live" and in movies like "Lawrence of Arabia." In the past, this traditional attire provided a way to protect the wearer from the heat of the desert sun and the cold of the desert night. But with modern forms of heating and air-conditioning, such clothing is no longer necessary. Western clothes have become the most common form of dress in the Middle East. In fact, the clothes that Arabs wear today while performing their everyday activities are indistinguishable from those of Westerners. Jeans, dresses, slacks, suits, and shirts are as commonplace in the Middle East as they are in the United States, whereas the traditional clothing is worn only by the poor or during festivals and celebrations.

Stereotypes about every ethnic group have been propagated for ages, and the Arabs are no exception. During the nine years that I have been in the United States, I have heard the same ones over and over—especially those about camels and harems. Although I took offense at first, I have tried to correct these misconceptions about Arab life. Perhaps all ethnic groups should do the same, since getting angry does not accomplish anything.

—Ahmed Solieman

ASSIGNMENT 2

Think of a stereotype, or a strong prejudice, held by you, a friend, a relative, or others. In a detailed essay, describe the reasons behind this particular stereotype, and show how this prejudice is either reasonable or illogical. Below we have listed three more possible topics for cause-and-effect essays. Before you begin drafting your essay, however, we suggest you consult the following grammar review, which covers those errors in "grammar logic" that can trip up even the most advanced students of English.

Additional Suggestions for Cause/Effect Papers

- Do you have an unreasonable fear of something? Analyze the roots of this fear: can you, for example, trace it back to a particular incident? What effects has this feeling had on your life?

- What were the reasons behind your selection of your major in college? Discuss the causes for your decision. Then go on to discuss the probable effects of this decision.

- Describe a phenomenon you've recently observed among the students (or teachers) on your college campus—say, a clothing fad, or the popularity (or sudden unpopularity) of the video games in the student lounge. Then discuss the causes and effects of this sociological phenomenon.

THE LOGIC OF GRAMMAR

As we've seen, faulty reasoning often results from assuming that there is a relationship between a particular effect or event and a particular cause when, in fact, there is no concrete evidence for such a relationship. To be convincing, a cause/effect analysis must be firmly grounded in logic, and logic is a system of reasoning that is based on clarity and consistency. When the relationships between facts and ideas are not clear, we are likely to say they don't "make sense."

Similarly, when the relationship between words or groups of words in a sentence is not evident, your reader will assume that the sentence doesn't "make sense." Unclear sentences are *ambiguous*: they wander about, and their meaning is uncertain. Ambiguous sentences are commonly caused by errors in grammar, for grammar is the system of rules that governs a language. And, just as logic connects facts and ideas in a coherent way, so grammar connects the words and phrases that make a sentence coherent. In this section, we'll look at some of the principles of English that lead to clear, consistent, logical sentences.

Problems with Pronouns

CHOOSE THE CORRECT PRONOUN

Although nouns and other pronouns change form only for plurals and to show possession (the *boy's* bicycle, *someone's* umbrella), the *personal pronouns* have different forms, depending on the ways they can function in a sentence. Because personal pronouns must agree—in person, number, and sentence function—with the nouns they replace, it's important to make sure you choose the correct pronoun form. For the sake of review, here are the personal pronouns and the sentence slots they fill:

SUBJECT PRONOUNS: I, you, he, she, we, they, who

OBJECT PRONOUNS: me, you, him, her, us, them, whom

POSSESSIVE PRONOUNS: mine, yours, his, hers, ours, theirs, whose

POSSESSIVE ADJECTIVES: my, your, his, her, our, their, whose

1. Use the *subjective form* of the personal pronoun when the pronoun is the subject of a sentence or a clause, the subjective complement, or an appositive that modifies a subject:

SUBJECT OF A SENTENCE: *She* has been offered an excellent job.

SUBJECT OF A CLAUSE: The man that *he* wants to meet has just arrived.

SUBJECTIVE COMPLEMENT: The biggest fool was *he.*
(You can check this type of sentence by simply turning it around: *He* was the biggest fool.)

APPOSITIVE IDENTIFYING A SUBJECT: Three small people, *he, she,* and *I,* ate four large pizzas.
(To see if you've chosen the correct pronouns for subject appositives, place them in the subject position: *He, she,* and *I* ate four large pizzas.)

Be aware of pronouns that are actually the subjects of *implied* verbs. Implied verbs often occur after *than* and *as*:

> She is smarter than *he* (is smart).
>
> She is as smart as *they* (are smart).

Remember, too, that the indefinite pronouns beginning with *some-*, *any-*, *no-*, and *every-* (listed in Chapter 2) are all singular in form and require singular personal pronouns. What, then, is wrong with this advertisement?

JUST ABOUT EVERYONE who tours Jack Daniel's Distillery wants their photo snapped with Mr. Jack.

2. Use the *objective form* of the personal pronoun when the pronoun is the object of a verb, the object of a verbal, the object of a preposition, or when it is an appositive that modifies an object:

> OBJECT OF A VERB: I like *her* very much. (direct object)
> I gave *them* the package. (indirect object)
>
> OBJECT OF A VERBAL: Finding *him* took hours. (object of a gerund)
> Having found *him*, the police called his parents.
> (object of a past participle)
> The police worked hard to find *him*. (object of an infinitive)
>
> APPOSITIVE MODIFYING AN OBJECT: That dog dislikes only one person, *me*.
> (An object appositive can be checked by placing the appositive in the object position: That dog dislikes *me*.)

3. You know to use *possessive adjectives* before nouns:

> *Her* dog is always chasing *our* cat.
>
> *Her* car is always crushing *our* rosebush.

Remember that *gerunds* are *-ing* verbals that function as nouns, so they also take possessive adjectives:

> INCORRECT: Them joining the club was a wise decision.
>
> CORRECT: *Their* joining the club was a wise decision.

4. Use *possessive pronouns* in noun positions:

> The biggest mistake was *mine*.
>
> *His* is the ugly brown hat with the feather.

5. You'll often hear English speakers making grammatically incorrect statements such as "This is just between you and I," or "My roommate and me love rock music." Unfortunately, compound subjects and compound objects often lead speakers and writers astray: when dealing with compounds, use the same form of the pronoun as you would if it were a single subject or object. To make sure you haven't been misled by the compound, break the sentence into sentences with single subjects or objects:

SUBJECTS: My sister and *I* are going to Paris.
(My sister is going to Paris. *I* am going to Paris.)

Before *he* or *she* arrived, we had decided to leave.
(Before *he* arrived . . . Before *she* arrived . . .)

SUBJECTIVE COMPLEMENTS: Those who suffered most were you and *I*.
(You suffered most. *I* suffered most.)

OBJECTS OF VERBS: The camp director hired Michael and *me* for the summer.
(The camp director hired Michael. The camp director hired *me*.)

OBJECTS OF PREPOSITIONS: She wants to go with *him* and *me*.
(She wants to go with *him*. She wants to go with *me*.)

EXERCISE 9.15

Replace the underlined words in the sentences below with the correct form of the personal pronoun:

1. <u>Mary</u> worked harder than you and <u>Jon</u>.

2. <u>The winners'</u> parents were as happy as <u>the winners</u>.

3. Two students, Mikhail and <u>Peter</u>, were asked to represent <u>Chang, Paul, Alexa, Marita, and me</u> at the meeting.

4. The audience applauded <u>the quartet's</u> singing.

5. The Dean asked Mr. Klein and <u>Ms. Jordan</u> to investigate the theft.

6. The ·guest lecturer will be <u>Dr. Jane Goodall</u>.

7. The Mayor gave <u>the visitors</u> a personal tour of the city.

8. The Awards Committee has to decide between <u>Linda</u> and <u>Rinaldo</u>.

9. Those who struggled hardest were you and <u>Ari</u>.

10. The big black limousine is <u>Ms. Goodman's</u>.

11. Watching <u>the magicians</u> was fascinating.

12. After the woman and <u>the man</u> had testified, the judge announced his decision.

MAKE PRONOUN REFERENCES CLEAR

Because every pronoun you use is a substitute for a noun, your reader must know exactly which noun a particular pronoun refers to. Pronouns must point directly to their *antecedents*, that is, to the nouns that have preceded them.

1. Never use a pronoun that has no antecedent:

In Alaska *they* have a lot of oil.

Who are *they*? Alaskans? Polar bears? The reader can only guess. The sentence, however, is easily corrected: Alaska has a lot of oil. Although we often use expressions like "It says in the dictionary" or "In the South they have" in casual conversation, the indefinite use of pronouns is both unclear and wordy: "The dictionary says" and "The South has" are clear and concise.

2. Make sure that a pronoun refers clearly to its antecedent. In each of the following examples, the reader can use common sense to figure out what antecedent was intended for the italicized pronouns, but the reference is still unclear, and often unintentionally humorous:

George took the cake out of the oven and then he ate *it*. (Exactly what did George eat?)

Whenever my nieces and nephews come to visit, I take them to the zoo to see the elephants. *They* love feeding *them* peanuts. (Who loves feeding whom?)

I saw two movies with my friends last night. *They* were both very violent. (Why do you go out with violent people?)

EXERCISE 9.16

How would you rephrase the previous sentences for clarity?

---

3. A pronoun should be close enough to its antecedent to make the reference unmistakable. Don't use a pronoun to replace a noun that isn't nearby, even if there is no other noun in the sentence or paragraph that it could logically replace:

> Two anonymous donors contributed large sums of money to the school after a fire had destroyed most of the building, and therefore the school was soon rebuilt. Their names were never revealed.

Although *their* in the second sentence can only refer to *donors* in the first, the pronoun and its antecedent are too far apart for the relationship to be clear.

4. Pronouns should not refer to nouns implied by a modifier or another noun or phrase:

UNCLEAR: José always orders chocolate ice cream because it's his favorite flavor. (What does *it* refer to?)

In Hiro's paper, he raises several interesting points. (Who is *he*?)

My neighbor is always discussing good teaching methods, although she's never been one. (*One* what?)

The children were frightened by the dog's loud bark, but it was actually a friendly animal. (What does *it* actually refer to here?)

REVISED: José always orders chocolate ice cream because chocolate is his favorite flavor.

Hiro raises several interesting points in his paper.

My neighbor is always discussing good teaching methods, although she's never been a teacher.

The children were frightened by the dog's loud bark, but the dog was actually a friendly animal.

CLASSROOM ACTIVITY 9.17

With a partner, correct any confusing pronoun references in the following paragraph:

Last weekend I had dinner at a fabulous restaurant with two of my old high school friends. We had decided to go there because it said in the newspaper that it was the best in town. My friends ordered lobsters, and their mouths watered when they saw them. They said they tasted as good as they looked. I had ordered a roast beef platter because it's my favorite meat. Unfortunately, my dinner was delayed because the chef had cut his hand before he started cooking it. When my meal finally arrived, I picked up my fork and devoured it without a pause while they had dessert.

EXERCISE 9.18

Edit the problems with pronouns in these sentences:

1. In the morning newspaper they said it would rain heavily all day.

2. After struggling with my report for an hour, I got up from my typewriter and tore it into tiny shreds.

3. In our history teacher's lectures, he is often funny.

4. When you prepare beef and pork for your children, make sure they are thoroughly cooked.

5. Years ago, a widow started the town library in her basement, and many people donated books and magazines. Today the library is in a large modern building named after her.

Being Consistent

Being consistent means sticking to certain principles, regulations, or ideas. When you are consistent in your thinking or behavior, you do not suddenly change direction without an obvious reason. Similarly, a consistent sentence conforms to logical rules of grammar that provide agreement among sentence elements. Unnecessary shifts in tense, voice, mood, person, or number can cloud the meaning of a sentence and baffle the reader. In this section, we offer some guidelines for consistent sentences.

BE CONSISTENT WITH PERSON AND NUMBER

In grammar, *person* distinguishes the person speaking (the *first person*) from the person being spoken to (the *second person*) and the person or thing being spoken about (the *third person*). *Number,* of course, means singular or plural. All of the sentences below are consistent in person and number:

Students shouldn't watch television while *they* are studying.

A student shouldn't watch television while *she* (or *he*) is studying.

You shouldn't watch television while *you* are studying.

No one should watch television while *he* (or *she*) is studying.

Inconsistent shifts from one person to another, or from singular to plural, are common faults in student writing. Indefinite pronouns account for the most frequent mistakes—remember that these pronouns are singular in meaning.

EXERCISE 9.19

Correct any unnecessary shifts in person and number in the sentences below:

1. A person should not assume that others share their beliefs.

2. One cannot expect to succeed if you aren't willing to work hard.

3. Anybody who didn't have their identification card wasn't allowed to take the test.

4. Students should realize that you have to study in college.

5. A television show can be educational, but they usually are not.

6. One shouldn't buy things they can't afford.

BE CONSISTENT WITH VERB TENSES AND MOODS

Naturally, verb tenses have to change to signal differences in time, but unnecessary shifts from past to present or present to past can bewilder your reader. This problem is especially confusing when a series of events is involved:

UNCLEAR: As I walked into the room, I notice that nobody arrived yet.

CLEAR: As I walked into the room, I noticed that nobody had arrived yet.
OR
As I walk into the room, I notice that nobody has arrived yet.

Another problem occurs when a writer switches the mood of verbs. This is most likely to happen in a set of directions, when the writer alternates between giving commands and making statements:

UNCLEAR: Don't eat desserts or fried foods, and you should also avoid red meat.

CLEAR: Don't eat desserts or fried foods, and avoid red meat.
OR
You shouldn't eat desserts or fried foods, and you should also avoid red meat.

BE CONSISTENT WITH ACTIVE AND PASSIVE VOICE

Sentences that mix the active and the passive voices usually suffer from an awkward shift in subject:

As I left the party, cheers were heard.

The problem here is two-fold: (1) the subject shifts from *I* in the first clause to *cheers* in the second; (2) the main clause is a passive construction that has no agent, so we can't be certain who heard the cheers. Rewriting the main clause in the active voice eliminates both problems:

As I left the party, I heard cheers.

EXERCISE 9.20

Use what you've learned about being consistent with verb tense and voice to edit the following excerpts from student journals:

When I walked into my bedroom, I can immediately see that the place was in shambles. The dresser drawers were all either pulled out or dumped on the floor. As I glanced around in astonishment, I realize that my stereo and my television are missing. My eyes shifted to the desk. My wallet was still there where I left it; it was obvious it wasn't tampered with. Just as I reached for the phone to call the police, a scream was heard outside.

The interior of Radio City Music Hall is luxurious. The high winding staircases leading to the orchestra, mezzanine, and balcony were made of ivory marble, and plush red carpeting descends over their smooth white texture.

"Orchestra to your left," the usher says.

Because my seat was right in the center of a front row, I knew I will be able to see everything that happens on stage. I was never there before, so I was unprepared for the spectacle that was about to be seen.

BE CONSISTENT WITH SENTENCE ELEMENTS: PARALLELISM

In Chapter 8 we showed how correlative conjunctions set up comparisons between items in a sentence, and we observed that the items being compared should have the same grammatical form—nouns, verbs, adjectives, and so on. *Parallelism*, which is simply placing two or more coordinated elements in the same grammatical form, helps to make writing smooth and coherent. As we have seen, classifying members of a group logically calls for describing them in parallel form:

There are three basic body types: *mesomorphic, ectomorphic,* and *endomorphic.* (adjectives)

Any items that are joined by *and, but, or, nor,* and *yet* require parallelism:

The child liked *cake, ice cream,* and *candy.* (nouns)

She never *ate* vegetables or *drank* milk. (verbs)

She was *fat* but *happy.* (adjectives)

Whenever you are comparing or contrasting two or more elements in a sentence—whether words, phrases, or clauses—make sure they are in the same grammatical form:

He prefers *exercising* to *dieting.* (gerunds)

He chose *to exercise* rather than *to diet.* (infinitives)

Over the hills and *through the woods to Grandmother's house* we go. (prepositional phrases)

Because the students were eager to learn and *the teachers were eager to teach,* the program was a success. (clauses)

EXERCISE 9.21

Correct faulty parallelism in the sentences below:

1. He was rich and famous, but without happiness.

2. Whether you like swimming, dancing, exercising, or just to relax and savor gourmet food, you'll enjoy every moment of the cruise.

3. He no longer wanted fame or to have a fortune; he only wanted peace and to have quiet.

4. The boss demanded that I come to work on time and no more leaving early.

5. After struggling for years, fighting for success, and having failed to win, she accepted defeat.

6. To write clearly, be consistent and you should use parallel structure.

7. Traveling through the world, he learned about different places and that people are different, too.

8. Early to bed and getting up early make a man healthy, wealthy, and

full of wisdom.

Problems with Modifiers

Because word order is critical to the meaning of a sentence in English, the way in which we arrange modifiers can determine whether a sentence is clear, confusing, or unintelligible. One common problem arises when modifiers are not joined to the words they are supposed to modify. The modifier may simply be in the wrong place, or it may be modifying a word that is not in that sentence.

MISPLACED MODIFIERS

A *misplaced modifier* seems to modify the wrong part of the sentence, or we cannot be sure what part it was meant to modify. Words, phrases, and clauses should be placed where they will clearly modify the words they are intended to modify:

UNCLEAR: I *almost* studied all night long.
The doctor advised him *regularly* to exercise.

CLEAR: I studied *almost* all night long.
The doctor advised him to exercise *regularly*.

Can you now explain the ambiguities in the following examples? Can you correct them?

Champagne was offered to the guests in elegant, long-stemmed glasses.

I suddenly noticed a man standing by the door wearing a black tuxedo.

DANGLING MODIFIERS

What's wrong with these sentences taken from the rough draft of a student's narrative?

While walking in the jungle with her friend Esmeralda one morning, a large ape jumped from a tree and landed two feet in front of Jane. With hair like a mop, a nose like a squashed berry, and eyes like a rat, they could tell that this jerk was trouble. Pounding his hairy chest and howling wildly, Esmeralda fainted.

Each of these sentences begins with a *dangling modifier.* A dangling modifier hangs loosely onto the sentence because it does not modify anything that is actually in the sentence, or because it is attached to the wrong noun or pronoun. Dangling modifiers are phrases or elliptical clauses that have no expressed subject of their own. Most often, dangling modifiers precede the main clause of the sentence, but they can also appear at the end:

> *While sitting under a tree,* an apple hit Newton on the head.
>
> *Thinking about the falling apple,* an idea came to him.
>
> His theory developed quickly *through reading books on gravity.*

These sentences don't make much sense because the modifiers don't logically describe the words they seem to modify: The apple wasn't sitting under a tree; the idea wasn't thinking about the apple; the theory didn't read books.

An easy way to correct sentences like these is to ask yourself what the *subject* of the modifier is—who was sitting under a tree or thinking about the apple? That subject should either be re-inserted into the modifier, or be made the subject of the main clause:

> While Newton was sitting under a tree, an apple hit him on the head.
>
> Thinking about the falling apple, he had an idea.
>
> He developed his theory quickly through reading books on gravity.

EXERCISE 9.22

Go back to the student sample on page 358 and rewrite it so that its modifiers no longer "dangle."

EXERCISE 9.23

Now see if you can correct the dangling modifiers in these sentences:

1. Racing down the street during the thunderstorm, a massive oak tree crashed to the ground.

2. Having eaten too much already, the table was cleared.

3. Being very hungry, the refrigerator was all I could think about.

4. While cooking the chicken, the kitchen caught fire.

5. Upon getting up, breakfast was always ready.

6. The radio was turned off after listening to the news.

7. When only a year old, my doctor cured me of pneumonia.

8. Having been in a deep sleep, the loud ring of the telephone startled him.

EXERCISE 9.24

The following sentences from student papers and journals all contain one or more of the errors we've discussed in this section on the logic of grammar. Identify the problems and rewrite the sentences.

1. The motorcycle is vastly superior to the car: they are light, quick, and they run cleanly.

2. If a motorcycle rider can't fix their bike, they can take it to the nearest mechanic. You can't do that with a car. Even if the mechanic were far away, he wouldn't have to leave his bike.

3. If a person gets caught driving a motorcycle illegally, he or she can get their license revoked.

4. There are many labor unions that offer equal rights and are giving equal benefits to both their part-time and full-time employees. There are, however, some business chains that don't have unions to fight for them.

5. It's not too much to ask for one day out of the 360 days a year that the store is open off with pay.

6. A few months later, I realize how egotistically I behave toward her when she needed my friendship, and I felt sorry for the way I acted.

7. Some people were listening to the speeches, and others looked at the posters in the store windows. People's faces seemed so different: some were quiet; some were serious; excitement was on others'.

EXERCISE 9.25

In each of its issues, *The New Yorker* magazine reprints amusing errors from periodicals around the country. See if you can identify and correct the problems in the examples below. (*The New Yorker* comments after each excerpt should provide a clue to each error.)

NOON (5) CHEYENNE AUTUMN (1964). James Stewart, Richard Widmark, Carroll Baker, Edward G. Robinson, Ricardo Montalban. Powerful drama of mistreatment of American Indians by the old master, John Ford.—*The Times*.

The dirty rat.

Between 400 and 500 people will fly in or out of the Chemung County airport, the vast majority of them by airplane.—*Elmira (N.Y.) Star-Gazette*.

Noted.

I suppose most of us have our favorite television news teams. Mine is the Channel 2 team. The two main reasons I like Channel 2 news are Jess Marlow and Connie Chung, and another reason is that there are no members of the staff who says things like "It has been a busy time for he and his family."

No one is perfect, though.—*Los Angeles Times*.

No.

DEVELOP interpersonal conversational skills by learning to talk good.—*Adv. in the San Mateo (Calif.) Times*.

Like a conversationalist should.

The Junior Grange had a cookie contest and the winners were Ryan Brown, Kim Quin, Penny Mikkleson, Lincoln Vorse, and Katie Rice. They were all delicious.—*Photo caption in the Blairstown (N.J.) Press*.

How were the cookies?

UH-HUH DEPARTMENT
[*Charles McCabe in the San Francisco Chronicle*]

Apart from talent there was one salient difference between Montaigne and I.

Dobbs wrote a book, Follow a Wild Dolphin, about Donald, the dolphin he befriended. Donald later turned up off the Cornish coast to delight holidaymakers during three summers in the mid-Seventies. He is setting up a research project with a transatlantic yachtsman, James Wharram from Devoran, Cornwall.—*Roy East in the London Sunday Times*.

And what's Dobbs doing these days?

THE OMNIPOTENT WHOM
[*From The Texas Humanist*]

A deep feeling for the land is a characteristic shared by the writers discussed under the rubric of "The Old Order." Addressing the Southern tradition in Texas literature, the session embraced Katherine Ann Porter, born and raised in Kyle; and William Goyen, William Humphrey, George Sessions Perry, J. Mason Brewer, C. C. White, and William Owens, in all of whom's work East Texas figures prominently.

Beverly Whipple's groundbreaking discoveries about female sexuality—delivered to the Society for the Scientific Study of Sex with John D. Perry—placed her immediately in the public eye and made her one of the foremost authorities on a new and controversial area of human sexuality. —*News release from Holt, Rinehart & Winston*.

Where did it place John D. Perry?

The McKoons bought the bench for $50 from the owner of an antique shop in Galveston. After sitting on their porch for two years, Tina decided to undertake its renovation as this year's 4-H project.—*Louise Lambert in the Kokomo (Ind.) Tribune*.

That's Tina for you—careful.

READ, WRITE, & SPELL IT RIGHT. By Samuel Smith et al. Three practical guidebooks in one for anyone who wants to improve their reading, writing, and spelling.—*Adv. from Edward R. Hamilton, bookseller, of Danbury, Conn.*

Three are not enough.

PROGRAMMER/ANALYST

AMERICAN KENNEL CLUB, the national purebred dog registry located in N.Y.C. registers over one million dogs annually and employs over four hundred.—*Adv. in the Times.*

Down, staff, down!

DANISH PASTRY WORKSHOP
(2 sessions)

Learn the fine art of making Danish pastries—those delicious pastries that taste so great! Students will participate in two consecutive two-hour sessions, during which they will be taken home to chill overnight.—*Adult-education schedule for the Montgomery County, Md., public schools.*

So they'll know how a Danish pastry feels.

The stage now is set for a confrontation in the finals of the world championship elimination series between Kasparov and a man who was a chess master before he was born.—*London (Ont.) Free Press.*

But what has he done lately?

Explanation for Exercise 9.5

After writing *Superminds*, Taylor began to realize that he might have been fooled by the children he tested. In 1975, the Amazing Randi, a professional magician, disguised himself as a reporter and visited Professor Taylor in England. Taylor proved quite easy to deceive; his "sealed" tubes were so crudely sealed that Randi had no trouble opening one and closing it up again while Taylor wasn't looking.

In addition, two scientists at Bath University tested Taylor's "shyness effect." They allowed six metal-bending children to perform their amazing feats in a room with an observer who was told to "look the other way" and not pay attention to the children. All sorts of bending immediately took place. None of this was seen by the observer, but the action was secretly being videotaped through a one-way mirror. The film showed, as the disappointed researchers reported, that one youngster put the rod under her foot to bend it, several children used two hands to bend their spoons, and another child tried to hide his hands under a table to bend a spoon.

—*Adapted from Martin Gardner,* Science: Good, Bad, and Bogus

Answer to Exercise 9.9

Sherlock Holmes's "Solution" to the Mystery of the Black Hat

"Then, pray tell me what it is that you can infer from this hat?"

He picked it up and gazed at it in the peculiar introspective° fashion which was characteristic of him. "It is perhaps less suggestive than it might have been," he remarked, "and yet there are a few inferences which are very distinct, and a few others which represent at least a strong balance of probability. That the man was highly intellectual is of course obvious upon the face of it, and also that he was fairly well-to-do within the last three

° **introspective:** given to private thought.

° **foresight:** the ability to anticipate and plan for future events.

° **retrogression:** the act or process of decaying or declining.

° **remonstrance:** words or gestures of protest.

° **sedentary:** characterized by much sitting and little exercise.

° **patent:** obvious; plain or clear.

years, although he has now fallen upon evil days. He had foresight°, but has less now than formerly, pointing to a moral retrogression,° which, when taken with the decline of his fortunes, seems to indicate some evil influence, probably drink, at work upon him. This may account also for the obvious fact that his wife has ceased to love him."

"My dear Holmes!"

"He has, however, retained some degree of self-respect," he continued, disregarding my remonstrance.° "He is a man who leads a sedentary° life, goes out little, is out of training entirely, is middle-aged, has grizzled hair which he has had cut within the last few days, and which he anoints with lime-cream. These are the more patent° facts which are to be deduced from his hat. Also, by the way, that it is extremely improbable that he has gas laid on in his house."

"You are certainly joking, Holmes."

"Not in the least. Is it possible that even now, when I give you these results, you are unable to see how they are attained?"

"I have no doubt that I am very stupid, but I must confess that I am unable to follow you. For example, how did you deduce that this man was intellectual?"

For answer Holmes clapped the hat upon his head. It came right over the forehead and settled upon the bridge of his nose. "It is a question of cubic capacity," said he; "a man with so large a brain must have something in it."

"The decline of his fortunes, then?"

"This hat is three years old. These flat brims curled at the edge came in then. It is a hat of the very best quality. Look at the band of ribbed silk and the excellent lining. If this man could afford to buy so expensive a hat three years ago, and has had no hat since, then he has assuredly gone down in the world."

"Well, that is clear enough, certainly. But how about the foresight and the moral retrogression?"

Sherlock Holmes laughed. "Here is the foresight," said he, putting his finger upon the little disc and loop of the hat-securer. "They are never sold upon hats. If this man ordered one, it is a sign of a certain amount of foresight, since he went out of his way to take this precaution against the wind. But since we see that he has broken the elastic and has not troubled to replace it, it is obvious that he has less foresight now than formerly, which is a distinct proof of a weakening nature. On the other hand, he had endeavored to conceal some of these stains upon the felt by daubing them with ink, which is a sign that he has not entirely lost his self-respect."

"Your reasoning is certainly plausible."

"The further points, that he is middle-aged, that his hair is grizzled, that it has been recently cut, and that he uses lime-cream, are all to be gathered from a close examination of the lower part of the lining. The lens discloses a large number of hair-ends, clean cut by the scissors of the barber. They all appear to be adhesive, and there is a distinct odour of lime-cream. This dust, you will observe, is not the gritty, gray dust of the street but the fluffy brown dust of the house, showing that it has been hung up indoors most of the time; while the marks of moisture upon the inside are proof positive that the wearer perspired very freely, and could therefore, hardly be in the best of training."

"But his wife—you said that she had ceased to love him."

"This hat has not been brushed for weeks. When I see you, my dear Watson, with a week's accumulation of dust upon your hat, and when your wife allows you to go out in such a state, I shall fear that you also have been unfortunate enough to lose your wife's affection."

"But he might be a bachelor."

"Nay, he was bringing home the goose as a peace-offering to his wife. Remember the card upon the bird's leg."

"You have an answer to everything. But how on earth do you deduce that the gas is not laid on in his house?"

"One tallow stain, or even two, might come by chance; but when I see no less than five, I think that there can be little doubt that the individual must be brought into frequent contact with burning tallow—walks upstairs at night probably with his hat in one hand and a guttering candle in the other. Anyhow, he never got tallow-stains from a gas-jet. Are you satisfied?"

—*Sir Arthur Conan Doyle,* "The Adventure of the Blue Carbuncle"

Answer to "Stereotypes" Question on Page 337

The question in the quiz that elicits the same kind of stereotypical response as #5 is #6: "The instrument nurse flung out her arm for support." If you look back to the text, you'll find that the sentence reads, "The instrument nurse standing next to Dr. Darekill flung out an arm for support. . . ." Notice that the gender of the nurse is not specified, although in question #6 it is. Did you assume the nurse was a woman? Why?

unit 6 | Argument

10 | Developing an Argument

The Uses of Persuasion

In an argument paper, more than in any other kind of essay, you are trying to change your reader's thinking, or to encourage your reader to take a certain course of action. The basic line of reasoning in an argument is, "Because X is true, Y must be true," or, "Because X is so, Y should be done." To convince your reader, you must construct a careful case for or against an issue, using sufficient evidence not only to make the reader see your point, but to make him or her adopt your way of thinking. Argument accomplishes this mission primarily through an appeal to reason rather than emotion. The successful arguer avoids preaching, and instead tries to show that the thesis of the essay is logical by offering a sequence of proofs in the body of the paper. Evidence in the argument essay may be presented in any of the rhetorical forms you have practiced in earlier chapters: description, narrative, definition, classification, analogy, or comparison/contrast.

Arguments are a part of both our private and public lives. One student recently wrote in his journal:

> Last night I got into a fight with a close friend. Karen asked me to meet her for dinner at a restaurant, but when I arrived I found out she had already eaten, and had to go to work in an hour. We were supposed to hang out together. That got me angry. We have never had a disagreement like this in the 8 months we've known each other. It was obnoxious of her to pull a stunt like that, though.

We use our persuasive powers to convince this friend that she's behaved badly, to ask a parent for the use of the family car, or to impress a potential employer; we write letters to our representative in Congress; we join special interest groups that protest nuclear arms or advocate the use of solar energy. Arguments can take the form of editorials—

Torturing poor animals for science is inhuman

IN response to Dr. John Suedack, who says animal rights groups have impeded medical research (Letters, Feb. 8), I do not oppose using animals in controlled, necessary medical experiments where the suffering of the animal is kept to a minimum.

I do oppose the totally useless experiments being performed on millions of helpless animals in ludicrous experiments where the answer is already known.

So-called "research laboratories," testing their products, poison, maim and torture animals in experiments that are of no use to anyone.

I suggest the good doctor visit one of these horror houses before condemning animal rights groups.

PAULINE FELICIANO
Island Park, N.Y.

THERE is no question of who is more important — animals or people — in medical research. The question is whether any person has the right to subject a living, feeling creature to the tortures perpetrated in medical laboratories.

In today's technology substitutes can and should be invented so that doctors as well as children in schools do not have to experiment on animals — most of the time with no anesthetic. Many doctors are the first to admit this.

Go back to school, John P. Suedack M.D., and discover a modern way of finding answers to medical problems which should have been solved years ago with all the grants you medical people get.

Better still, offer yourself as a guinea pig. You at least have the option of whether or not your body should be violated.

GEORGIANNA MCKENNA
Queens

ANIMALS DIE SO PEOPLE MAY LIVE

THE actions of animal rights groups have already significantly impeded medical research in our country and elsewhere.

Contrary to what these groups maintain, there are absolutely no substitutes for live animals in animal rights movements should be made to go into hospitals and explain to the sick and dying why lab mice and rats are as important as humans.

They should be made to face the outrage of all of us who will lose loved ones to illness, disease

THE LETTER THAT SPARKED A FUROR

LAST Wednesday Dr. John P. Suedack of NYU Medical Center in a letter on this page defended the use of animals in medical research. Rarely has there been such an outpouring of emotion as has resulted from publication of that letter. Here is a representative sampling. No mail received by The Post so far has supported Dr. Suedack.

Write: The Editor, New York Post, 210 South St., New York, N.Y. 10002. Please sign your name and include your address. NO unsigned letters will be published.

Moral considerations should be based upon the ability to suffer and feel pain, not simply the fact we have power over these creatures.

PATTY ADJAMINE
Manhattan

THE fact that a particular behavior produces benefits to some does not justify the behavior itself. Such "rationalization" has been behind every injustice inflicted on humans over the centuries, from war, to child labor, to slavery, etc.

The fact that some medical progress has been achieved through some animal experiments does not justify all experiments. For example, does the fact that insulin was developed through animal research, justify poisoning millions of other animals per year for cosmetic and household product development?

WHAT gives human beings the right to kill other animals who have lives of their own to live?

Each year, hundreds of animals are burned, shocked, poisoned, blinded, forced to consume alcohol and drugs, etc., and killed in experiments frequently repetitious — and unnecessary for basic research data — to earn PhD's or acquire grant funds.

As animal lovers we will keep fighting and protesting. After all it is our tax money that is being used for these purposes.

GARY & ROSE ANN SMITH
Middle Village, N.Y.

NO ONE HAS A RIGHT TO HARM GOD'S CREATURES

DOESN'T Dr. Suedack know that animals are God's creatures too?

Does he really believe that he, or anyone else, has the right to subject any animal to unbearable torture in the name of scientific research?

Animals have helped man for ages. The dog has aided policeman, blind people, old lonely people, autistic children, firemen, etc.

I recently read where a cat clawed at his owner who was asleep to rouse him when his house was on fire.

The dolphin has aided swimmers in danger of drowning or being attacked by sharks. Is this the thanks we give them?

You speak, dear doctor, of human suffering; you do not mention animal suffering. They, too, cry out.
IRENE PADDOCK
Brooklyn

FOR "the good of humans?" Dr. Suedack left out a lot.

What good was testing Thalidomide on animals when women given this anti-nausea drug during pregnancy gave birth to horrendously deformed babies?

The "Pill" was supposedly tested on animals, yet many women have died of heart attacks, blood clots, or soaring hypertension.

The Air Force hooked up beagles by the score to airplane exhaust hoses until their lungs were destroyed. Their vocal cords were cut, so they died in silent agony. Did this barbaric practice advance the cause of humans in medicine?

Rabbits were held in headlock apparatus by a famous cosmetic firm and had detergent or other harsh chemicals rubbed into their eyes.

An animal is different from a human, therefore the test results are often useless, or dangerously deceptive. **L. ROTTMANN**
Brooklyn

WE need more Albert Schweitzers and fewer John P. Suedacks!
FRANCIS GARCIE
Crestwood, N.Y.

NEW YORK POST, TUESDAY, FEBRUARY 14, 1984

and advertisements—

THIS COULD SAVE YOUR LIFE. BUT YOU CAN'T HAVE IT.

Today people died who shouldn't have. People who would have been saved by air bags.

In an accident, air bags automatically provide a cushioning buffer between you and the car. They protect occupants' necks, heads and faces from flying glass and other debris. They're most effective in front and front-angle collisions, the deadliest kinds of crashes.

Today you can't have this protection. Except for a few luxury imports, cars with air bags are not available.

The auto industry has opposed air bags for years. They claim they would cost twice what the government's independent experts have testified. And they say car buyers don't want

to pay for the extra protection air bags provide.

We think they're wrong.

In the property and casualty insurance industry, we've studied air bags for a long time. Experts tell us they would prevent thousands of deaths a year, and eliminate hundreds of thousands of serious injuries.

How much would air bags actually cost? As standard equipment, they would add about three percent to the price of the average automobile. It sounds like a bargain, and it is.

Right now in Washington, Secretary of Transportation Elizabeth H. Dole is reviewing possible safety requirements for all new cars. And most car companies are trying to keep air bags right where they are

today. Nowhere.

Do something about it while there's still time.

Send for a free copy of our new report, *Air Bags: A Matter of Life or Death*. It sums up the latest facts and tells how you can get involved.

Help save air bags and help save lives. One could well be your own.

| Insurance Information Institute |
| 110 William Street |
| New York, NY 10038 |

Please send me a free copy of *Air Bags: A Matter of Life or Death*.

Name

Address

City   State   Zip   22

 Insurance Information Institute
A nonprofit action and information center

as well as of formal debates, or even songs. In America during the 1960s, "protest songs" that advanced anti-war arguments were an important part of the peace movement. The following stanzas are from a protest song that was especially popular during the period of the Vietnam War. What is the implied thesis of the song, and what kind of support does the author provide for that thesis?

I Ain't Marching Anymore
by Phil Ochs
I marched to the Battle of New Orleans
At the end of the early British war.
The young land started growing
The young blood started flowing
But I ain't marching anymore.

I marched to the battles of the German trench
In the war that was bound to end all wars*
I must have killed a million men
And now they want me back again
But I ain't marching anymore.

I flew the final mission in the Japanese skies—
Set off the mighty mushroom roar.
When I saw the cities burning
I knew that I was learning
That I ain't marching anymore.

It's always the old to lead us to the wars,
It's always the young to fall
Now look at all we've won
With a sabre and a gun
Tell me is it worth it all?

As you can see from this song, writers of arguments do occasionally seek to engage their audience's emotions. It is, of course, important to avoid the dangers of overly emotional appeals and sensationalism in argument. But keep in mind that although the most effective argument is primarily an appeal to rationality, your reader has a heart as well as a mind, and can be stimulated to feel strongly about an issue. Any good lawyer will demonstrate in a court of law that successful persuasion utilizes a combination of logical, emotional, and ethical arguments (an ethical argument appeals to the audience's sense of what is right and wrong). It is often helpful to include examples in your argument that arouse the audience's anger, pity, admiration, or disgust by allowing them to visualize in concrete terms the problem you're discussing. Such examples, however, are never a substitute for logical reasoning, and misuse of this rhetorical technique can turn an argument into mere audience manipulation or propaganda. Before you make a particular argument, ask yourself not only whether it is effective but whether it is logical, fair, and moral as well.

---

* World War I was called "the war to end all wars."

EXERCISE 10.1

A.) Since much of the present chapter will be devoted to a continuation of our discussion of logic, take a few minutes now to test your ability to locate some of the logical fallacies in the letters to the editor on pages 368–369. Which arguments seem to you to be the least effective, and why? Which statements seem to be examples of flawed reasoning or excessively emotional argumentation? Can you explain how they are weak or illogical? How would you argue *against* such statements? Which arguments, on the other hand, seem to you to be most effective, and why? (After you have completed this chapter, you may want to return to this exercise to retest your skills.)

B.) Join in the debate by writing a letter to the editor of the *New York Post*, setting forth your own arguments on the subject of using live animals for medical experiments.

JOURNAL EXERCISE 10.2

During the next week, look for everyday examples of argument—in your own journal, in newspapers, in magazine or television advertisements, in popular songs—and record a few of them in your notebook. Point out effective techniques for argumentation, as well as any logical fallacies you come across.

We've suggested that much of the effectiveness of the protest song quoted above lies in the author's ability to illustrate an abstract concept like *war* in concrete terms. Specifics—in the form of facts, case histories, examples, and the like—provide the necessary support for any argument. Let's look at how this supporting information is incorporated into the three-part structure of the classical argument.

The Structure of Argument

The following format is the traditional approach to an argument essay; it is a basic outline which writers can adapt in a number of ways. This guide should help you to outline the argument essays you'll be writing in this chapter, and will allow you to see more clearly the cause-and-effect relationships between the proposition you're arguing and the proofs you use to back it up.

I.   Introduction—this may consist of one or several paragraphs, and should include one or more of the following items:

   A. *Opening statements* that win the audience's attention and good will by presenting the problem in an interesting or favorable light. A personal reference, anecdote, or description can convince the reader that your paper is of direct interest to him or her.

   B. *Background of the case:* explanation or narration of the history of the problem.

   C. *The proposition* to be proved or defended: the thesis statement of your argument essay.

   D. *Outline of the argument* to show the reader how evidence will be presented in the body of your essay. This step is more important in a speech than in a written argument, since it tells the audience where you are going, and thus makes the argument easier to follow.

II. Body of the Argument

   A. *Confirmation of your case:* here the reasons behind your argument are presented and supported by various kinds of evidence. *Remember that each proof you offer must be directly related back to the proposition of your argument.* Types of evidence include:
1. facts
2. statistics
3. testimony of experts
4. opinions
5. case histories
6. reports
7. definitions
8. examples
9. analogies, comparisons, and contrasts
10. logical reasoning—inductive and deductive

   B. *Refutation of opposing views:* If there are likely to be significant counter-arguments against your proposition, don't ignore them. Instead, mention them, and argue against them by *demonstrating* that they are untrue, illogical, ambiguous, or contradictory. Don't merely make these claims—*prove* them with facts and logical reasoning.

   C. *Concession:* If the opposition has made a valid point, you should in all fairness admit it. Concession is a valuable tactic for the arguer, because it shows that you have calmly considered all important aspects of the issue. After you have conceded the point, however, you should *reply to it by offering an alternate position,* and by showing why your position makes better sense than your opponent's.

III. Conclusion, consisting of a summary of your argument, and a final, heightened appeal for the audience's support.

As we've pointed out, this outline includes all the elements of classical oration. Many modern writers have made good use of this structure; others, while retaining the three-part format, occasionally prefer to eliminate one step, such as the outline of evidence or the concession. Moreover, the sequence of these steps is often flexible. For example, when examining argument essays more closely, you may find that an author has chosen to refute the opposition's views in the opening paragraphs, or has dealt with them one by one in the body of the paper, rather than towards the end of the essay.

Whatever principle of organization you decide on, bear in mind that the key to effective argumentation is to *remember your opposition and your audience.* Accomplished arguers, like good chess players, try to anticipate what the opponent's strategy will be, and plan their offense accordingly. At the same time, they try to imagine their reader's possible comments and objections, and by answering these hypothetical questions make their arguments more persuasive.

EXERCISE 10.3

Re-examine the ads on pages 369–370, and analyze how each handles *refutation* of opposing viewpoints. In each ad, can you name the objections or implied arguments that the writer of the ad is responding to?

Your goal in persuasive essays should be to show the reader that you are clearly on the side of right. Treat the opposing point of view with respect; concede whatever merit your opponent's case may have; then end your essay by showing how your own position has greater merit or makes more sense. For this purpose, many writers like to present their strongest arguments at the end of a persuasive essay.

Naturally, the structure of your essay, as well as the tone of voice you adopt in argument, will depend on your topic and audience. We will consider these questions of subject, audience, and tone in the following section.

Assignment 1: The Personal Argument

In this section, you will be asked to write a letter in which you persuade a friend, parent, teacher, or employer to think or act in a certain way. We have included a number of brief excerpts from student papers that suggest possible approaches to the problem of the personal argument. You may wish to work on several of these topics as journal exercises, in addition to writing a formal essay for this first assignment. The aspects of argument considered in this section include selecting a topic, introducing a thesis, using personal experience to support the thesis, and adopting a reasonable tone.

FINDING A DEBATABLE TOPIC

What issues have been bothering you lately? You may discover the subject for an argument essay in the course of reviewing your journal, as did the student who wrote about his inconsiderate friend. Your journal entries and essays can be vehicles for voicing the complaints and objections you were unable to raise in a situation that provoked frustration or anger. The French have a phrase, *l'esprit de l'escalier,* for those times all of us have experienced when, mounting the stairs to bed after losing an argument, we think of the clever things we might have said. In writing, we can reflect on a particular issue in tranquility, and make the most effective case for our side of the disagreement. This student, for example, might compose an argument essay on an issue he brings up in his journal:

> Last night I saw the movie "Private School." It was one of those "high school" movies and it was really an insult to my intelligence. There were 38-year-olds playing 16-year-olds, and the whole school was made up of some of the most beautiful girls in the world. (It must have been something in their drinking water.) After the movie, I heard an older woman say, "So this is what teenagers do today—it's disgusting." I didn't waste my time replying to her, but her remark made me think about how these exploitation films are influencing the way people think about teenagers.

Then, too, you may find a paper topic in the course of a discussion with a friend, as this writer did:

> Jack, a _____ College student, has decided to get a new car. His old Chevy, which served him well for many years, has died; its engine and other vital parts have burned out. Jack has about seven thousand dollars to spend on a new car, but isn't sure what make or model to get.
> "I want a small car that gets good gas mileage and is dependable," Jack remarked to me. He then asked me if I had any suggestions. I told him to look at a Toyota Tercel. Jack admitted that the Tercel had all of the qualities he wanted in a car, but didn't understand why I recommended a foreign car over an American one. "For your requirements," I answered, "a Japanese car is by far a better automobile than its American counterparts."

The writer went on to present his argument in the form of a comparison/contrast of the Chevy Chevette and the Toyota model, weighing the good and bad points of each car.

Just as often, you may find yourself in friendly debate with a parent—another possible subject for the personal argument paper. Consider this introduction, in which a student expresses her views concerning an ongoing issue in her home. On paper, the writer states her opinion as calmly and coherently as she would like to have done in person:

What is one of the most common arguments a teenager can have with his or her parents? My parents and I rarely fight, but some of the most heated arguments I have had with them concern my use of the family car.

The other day, for example, I asked them if I could drive to school, since my friend Kathy's car was being repaired. Naturally, my mother started in with, "I don't want you driving to school. It's going to rain, and traffic will be heavy." Now, isn't that silly? I know it's more dangerous to drive in the rain, especially with the wet leaves on the ground, but I'm certainly going to have to drive in the rain sometime. Why shouldn't I start getting experience now? And why does Kathy driving make it any safer?

JOURNAL EXERCISE 10.4

Describe an incident that occurred within the past few months in which you disagreed with, or tried to persuade, a stranger, parent, or friend. How successfully did you argue? In retrospect, what might you have said to make your case more persuasive?

Frequently, in the process of writing, writers find that the topic of their argument has changed, or that they have narrowed their thesis as a result of "thinking on paper." For instance, one writer began by writing a draft on the rather dry and over-discussed topic of "Why People Shouldn't Smoke," only to discover that what she really wanted to talk about was "Why Smokers Should Be Considerate of Non-Smokers." The incident that had provoked her first draft, it turns out, concerned an inconsiderate smoker in her Spanish class; yet this incident, and the real thesis of the paper, did not emerge until the second draft. Here is the revised introduction, as well as the paragraph relating the student's experience:

> I don't mind if you smoke. As Roger Moore pointed out in the movie "Cannonball Run," when asked by a girl if she could smoke while in his car, "Go ahead. It's your lungs." I don't smoke but I respect those of you who do. I would like you to respect those who don't smoke, and thus only smoke in designated areas when you are in public. I ask you to remember that when you smoke, you not only endanger your own health, but also endanger the health of non-smokers. . . .
>
> . . . A third example of smokers infringing on non-smokers' rights can be seen in most classrooms of this college. Most of the classrooms have signs stating NO SMOKING. Yet I have found several times that people don't take note of the signs. In my Spanish class, there's a young lady who smokes in the room even though it's designated a non-smoking area. She smokes and exhales that smog over everyone in the room. If the non-smokers are disturbed, as I am, they either have to stop breathing for a moment or leave the room. I usually leave the room, and have never said

anything to her about it, for I am not enough of a reason for her to quit smoking. Indeed, maybe it doesn't bother anyone else in the room. However, it does bother me—a lot—and I wish she would understand my view.

—*Soraya Chang*

JOURNAL EXERCISE 10.5

Do you have a "pet peeve" (a constant source of irritation) like the one described above—something that you'd like to see changed, in your school or your community? If so, write a brief letter to the editor of your school or neighborhood newspaper in which you outline the problem and suggest a solution.

You may choose whatever audience you like for your argument essay, but remember that the issue you are discussing must be subject to debate. There is no point in arguing with easily verifiable facts, or with matters of individual taste, or with the requirements of your school or your profession. It would be a futile exercise indeed to try to convince your math teacher to change your exam grade from D to A, or to ask the College Registrar not to record a failing mark. No amount of argument will alter an inadequate performance.

One enterprising student we know, however, wrote an effective argument essay in which he gently tried to persuade his teacher not to require a revision for a paper he had written much earlier in the course. Since the student had revised most of his other papers, this assignment did in fact seem subject to appeal. He began:

> Dear Dr. _____,
> I am going to try to persuade you that I do not have to revise my narrative paper on _____. I am aiming to have the paper counted for credit in the course in its unrevised state. As you know, I have attended every class and have submitted all my reports and revisions typed and on time. Instead of going backwards and rewriting the narrative paper, which I submitted some time ago, I feel I would do better to concentrate my efforts on future papers. Below are the reasons for my appeal.

We don't recommend that you try this kind of argument very often. But if you do decide to make such a case for yourself, don't fall into the trap of the emotional fallacy.

Avoiding Emotional Fallacies

We've pointed out how an occasional appeal to the audience's sensitivity can bolster a solid argument. Yet an arguer commits an emotional fallacy if his entire case rests on this sort of appeal and plays unfairly on the human frailties of the audience—their vanity, fear, and prejudices. For instance, here's what the *ad misericordiam* fallacy looks like:

> Dear Dr. _____,
>   I am begging you not to ask me to revise my narrative paper. I have attended every class and have submitted all my reports and revisions typed and on time, even though it has taken me four hours to type a page, ever since my accident. None of this work has been easy for me. I have to take care of my six younger brothers and sisters, in addition to working three days a week as a bagger at the local Shoprite store.

Now all of this may be true, but it is not relevant to the matter of required work for an English course. The argument is a sales pitch to *pity* rather than to reason; it is an evasion of the issue. A similar method of evading the issue is called *ignoratio elenchi,* which means ignoring the question under debate—

> Dear Dr. _____,
>   Please don't make me do another revision! I'm already taking nineteen credits, and am way behind in my other courses. This week alone, I have two Art History reports to complete. One of the reports is on the Parthenon in Greece. Page one will discuss the history of the Parthenon. Page two will discuss the temple as the epitome of the Classical Period. Page three and four will describe the sculptural decorations of the Parthenon. . . .

Wise writers avoid becoming sidetracked and arguing off the point. They also steer clear of the emotional fallacy known as the *bandwagon appeal.* It is invalid reasoning to urge your reader to "jump on the bandwagon"— that is, to think a certain way or to do something merely because "everyone else is doing it":

> Dear Dr. _____,
>   I wish you would reconsider the revision assignment. After all, my other professors don't ask me to rewrite my papers.

Remember, too, that a purely subjective thesis isn't debatable, because it can't be supported by evidence. If you say or write to a prospective employer, "You should hire me because I'm the best candidate for this job," you're simply stating a personal opinion; there's no objective way to prove your point. This statement, however, can be turned into an arguable proposition: "I have the right qualifications for the job" is a thesis that can be backed up with proof. Consider, for example, how the writer of the following excerpt uses personal experience as evidence to strengthen his case in a hypothetical job interview:

I Want This Job!

I hate going for job interviews. Employers inevitably ask the same questions: "Why do you want this job and why do you think you should get it?" I always come up with some stupid answer, which I think sounds good at the time, and then they say, "Don't call us, we'll call you!" Whenever they say that, I know I didn't get the job.

Last week, though, I found a perfect summer job in the classified ads. I decided that this time I would be prepared for those infamous questions ahead of time, so I wrote and memorized a great answer that would assure me the job. That way, I wouldn't have to worry about saying something stupid.

I was applying for a part-time job working in a children's nursery. The employer wanted someone young, intelligent, energetic, good with children, and experienced in helping children with their schoolwork problems. The interview went pretty well. I think I persuaded them that I was right for the job. This is what I told the interviewer:

"If you look at my resume, you will see I have excellent recommendations and have had prior experience in this line of work. I was an assistant to a first grade teacher for a year. I helped children solve their problems in reading and mathematics. Some of the children I worked with eventually performed better than many of the supposedly brighter children in the class. The recommendation from the teacher corroborates that fact. I can teach children to apply themselves better, and to make schoolwork fun—not a chore. There were times when things didn't go smoothly, but I never lost my patience. Once you lose patience, the children get discouraged, and when that happens no problems get solved. . . ."

—Glenn Weill

When Glenn read his paper in class, several students questioned him about this last paragraph. They thought the point he was making was effective, but felt he should "prove" the general claims he made for himself by citing personal experience—one specific incident—that would convince his potential employer. As a result, Glenn came up with this expanded version of the paragraph:

"When I worked as the assistant to the first grade teacher, I helped a lot of children. There was one little girl, Lori, who needed my help the most. She didn't like school and since she couldn't get all the attention she wanted from the teacher, she wouldn't concentrate on learning, Lori needed someone to work with her on a one-to-one basis. As I worked with Lori, I saw great improvements in her.

"When I first started working with her, she couldn't read a word. I started from the beginning with her. We did the alphabet until she finally knew it forwards and backwards. After that we went on to words. This took a little more time, but we worked on it until she was able to put words together and read sentences.

"You should have seen the proud look on her face everytime she read a sentence. She was finally enthusiastic about school. She looked forward to working with me and she learned something new every day. As soon as I would walk through the door, there she was with her book and pencil in one hand and her other arm raised over her head waiting for the teacher to say she could work with me.

"As time went on, Lori began to read short stories in her reader and answered questions to show me she understood what she had read. A lot of good things came out of this one. to one basis of teaching and learning: Lori started to excel to levels higher than other children in the class, she began to open up and participate more in class, and I learned that I can teach children."

CLASSROOM EXERCISE 10.6

As a warm-up exercise before you work on your personal argument assignment (see page 374), experiment with a hypothetical issue. Along with your classmates, decide which of the following matters you'd like to argue. Then take 15–20 minutes in class to write a 3-minute speech, to be delivered to the other members of the class, in which you argue your case.

- You have just been informed that a $10,000 grant will be awarded to a student at your college. The grant will not necessarily be given to the student with the best academic record, but to the one who can prove he or she will put the money to the best use. Why should you receive this grant? (Address your speech to the members of the Grants Committee.)

- The administration of your college has recently ruled that class attendance will be averaged in as part of the grade for every course in the school. Argue for or against this rule. (Address your speech to the members of your school administration.)

CLASSROOM EXERCISE 10.7

After you have written the first draft of your personal argument for Assignment 1, read it aloud to the members of your group. Using the writing samples in this section as a guide, you and your colleagues should look for these ways to revise your essay: (1) edit out emotional fallacies; (2) mend any holes in the logic of the paper, and discuss additional material that might strengthen the argument; (3) make sure you are using your own experience as support for your thesis; (4) adopt a tone that is reasonable and judicious, rather than overpowering or hostile. The next section should help you decide on the appropriate tone for your particular essay.

ADOPTING A REASONABLE TONE

Let's say you're fortunate enough to have been hired for the job you interviewed for. You may subsequently wish to request further job benefits or a raise in salary, or you may have to deal with problems that arise during your employment. In situations such as these, the best course of action may be to write a letter to your supervisor or employer. This student, for example, disagreed with the disciplinary policies of her employer, so she composed a letter to the owner of the department store where she had a part-time job:

> Dear Mr. _____:
>
> For the past two years I have been employed as a cashier and salesperson in the sportswear department of your store. Enclosed you will find letters of recommendation from the managers of my department. As they will tell you, I am a capable employee; I work quickly at the register, know the department well, and like my job very much.
>
> I am writing to you to protest the unfairness of the probation system at the store. Two weeks ago, I was called down to the personnel office and told I was to be on probation for one year because I have been late to work several times. Yet I had never received a letter from Personnel telling me that I was about to be put on probation, or that I wasn't doing my job properly. On the contrary, my superiors told me how well I was doing. Along with other employees in the store, I feel that an employee should be warned first, so that he or she may correct the situation; then, if the problem isn't remedied, that worker should be placed on probation. . . .
>
> —*Teresa Marino*

Notice how Teresa establishes her credibility from the outset. Through tone of voice the writer projects a certain picture of herself to her reader. Aristotle advised arguers to convey the impression of "a good person arguing well"; it makes sense in an argument essay to persuade the reader that you are sincere, truthful, and thorough. Naturally, this sort of groundwork is all the more important when you're addressing a reader who doesn't know you personally, as is frequently the case in essays of this kind.

Choosing an appropriate tone is therefore a major concern in argumentation. As you know from Chapter 8, your tone indicates your attitude toward your subjects and your reader. An argument paper should convey the author's respect for the material and for the audience. The writer of the above excerpt resisted the temptation to rationalize or excuse her behavior or to express outrage at what she considered an injustice. If your readers receive the impression that you're too angry to reason clearly, they're unlikely to pay much attention to your argument. After all, few people enjoy being screamed at or bullied. You can, however, sound reasonable without sacrificing a strong sense of conviction, and when your tone is moderate and controlled, people listen.

The tone of your argument can be humorous and casual, serious and formal, or somewhere in between. Obviously, the tone depends on the purpose of the piece and the audience you're addressing. Whatever your subject, avoid the exclamatory, overheated, and melodramatic approach of this student's essay on capital punishment:

> . . . Steps must be taken to stop the terror that sweeps our streets. These facts are hard to deal with. People try to push them out of their minds; but you can't make these horrors disappear. Violent acts are increasing from day to day. FACT: a rape occurs every two minutes. Remember, it can happen to you.
> Don't sit back!
> TAKE ACTION—NOW!

Your *diction*—the vocabulary you use in a particular paper—should reflect your even-handed approach to the topic. Burdening an argument with emotionally loaded words like "tyrant," "beast," or "fascist" will turn off many readers. By the same token, informal diction is usually unsuitable for serious subjects. The following author of a paper on nuclear weapons used colloquial phrases and informal verb and sentence constructions where formality would have been more appropriate. As you read the excerpt, underline any words and expressions that seem out of place in an argument of this nature.

> Playing hand-in-hand with the potential destructive powers of nuclear weapons is the potential destructive power of the minds of some of the leaders of the world. Let's face it, some of them are pretty far gone. What do you think would've happened if Adolf Hitler had gotten his hands on a nuclear bomb? What about the kamikazee pilots in World War II: can you imagine what would've happened if they had had nuclear weapons? And what if the hydrogen bomb the U.S. exploded in Hiroshima had been a nuclear bomb?
> Proponents of nuclear arms say that nowadays, crackpot leaders couldn't get their hands on nuclear weapons. I wouldn't be so sure. Things can always be gotten for the right price. Nuclear weapons can be given to a country in which a revolution then breaks out and the government is overthrown. Now these unstable revolutionaries make the decisions about their arsenal. Terrorist groups can also get their hands on nuclear weapons. The leaders of these terrorist groups aren't too stable to begin with, but with such powerful weapons, they become lunatics.

EXERCISE 10.8

Try rewriting the above excerpt to make its tone more suitable to the topic.

This next section offers you the opportunity to adopt a lighter, more humorous tone of voice—one befitting the problem under consideration.

Assignment 2: Public Argument—The Restaurant Review

Option A: Below is restaurant reviewer Mimi Sheraton's funny and withering report on a restaurant she awarded a rating of "Poor." Imagine you are the owner of this establishment. Your business has fallen off 60 percent since this column appeared. Write a letter to Ms. Sheraton, at the *New York Times*, disputing as many of her assertions as you can. Your goal is to address each of your adversary's main points in a report that is as specific and convincing as hers is.

(Note: Option A may prove more challenging than Option B, on page 386.)

In seven years of reviewing, I have never come across service and food that have been so consistently poor as that found at _____, the well-known _____ discothèque and restaurant. _____ would be considered beneath serious criticism were it not such a highly visible restaurant garnering° much publicity from its fashionable clientele and from its former connections with the talented French chef _____.

° **garnering:** gathering or amassing.

I encountered rudeness and overbearing pretentiousness starting with the man who guards the door right through to checkroom employees who are insolent about the mandatory but unposted checkroom charge and to the maître d'hôtel, captains and waiters.

Arriving with a confirmed reservation for four on a crowded Saturday night, we were met by a maître d'hôtel who said with exasperation, "Oh, I don't know where I'm going to seat you. We're inundated° with royalty tonight." Then, in a stage whisper to a captain, he continued, "The king will be here at midnight with six bodyguards."

° **inundated:** overwhelmed.

We four commoners° were finally seated at an extended table for two, leaving two of us out in an aisle where chairs were kicked every few minutes. It seemed to take forever to place orders for food and wine and even longer to get what we had ordered. When the captain asked how dinner had been and we indicated it had not been very good, he shrugged and said, "Well, you can't fight City Hall."

° **commoners:** those who are not royalty.

The menu opens with desserts because, as a message signed by the hostess says, she is especially proud of that course. But twice we were refused soufflés, once as soon as we ordered because the captain said the chef would make none that night, a second time five minutes after our orders were taken when the captain announced that the soufflé oven was broken. Persisting, we got the soufflés at a third dinner, but the oven may still have been out of whack because not one of the four stodgy and flavorless creations had risen.

Spoiled mussels and stale salmon were only two flaws at a lunch that included many. A mountain of soupy fettuccine with cream and ham tasted like a packaged macaroni-and-cheese dinner, and a shrimp dish arrived in a lobster sauce that could have been achieved with canned lobster bisque. When I complained of slow service, an unshaven captain said: "Well, madame, if you knew how to order properly from a captain instead of from waiters, perhaps you would get things promptly."

On slow nights, staff members stand around in deep conversation, ignoring diners, sipping wine, and non-celebrities are often shown to the worst tables, even when not a single table is occupied. At one dinner we tried to order a fish course, asking to share one of the main course seafoods between appetizer and meat. We were told that could only be done if we paid for an extra complete dinner.

In the course of four recent visits, during which all appetizers and desserts and most of the main courses were tried, I did not find a single dish worth recommending. Shrimp in avocado tasted of iodine, vegetables in an aspic terrine were flavorless, scrambled eggs had been overcooked before being topped with caviar, and quenelles were rubbery on two occasions. The raw beef carpaccio was dark around the edges on one visit, indicating staleness, and on another it was still encrusted with splinters of ice. A metallic flavor overpowered both the duck liver pâté and the hot mussel soup, billi-bi. Smoked salmon, though passable, was hardly worth the surcharge on the dinner.

The most depressing dessert was puff pastry with unripe strawberries. The pastry looked like flaked wet Uneeda Biscuits and the minted cream tasted like toothpaste.

Note: The appointment of a new chef has been announced. Let's hope the change will be for the better.

Don't automatically assume that it is a lost cause for a restaurant owner to fight back against an unfavorable review. Here's what happened when another restaurant owner argued his case against a restaurant reviewer in a court of law:

Restaurant Wins Libel Suit Over Negative Review

by GLENN FOWLER

A Manhattan restaurant owner has won a jury award of $20,005 for libel against the authors and the publisher of a negative review of its food and service in a French-language guide to New York City.

The award was made last week after a four-day trial in Federal District Court in New York.

The jury awarded $20,000 in compensatory damages and $5 in punitive damages to Michael Chow, who owns Mr. Chow's, a Chinese restaurant on East 57th Street, and who also has restaurants in London and in Beverly Hills, Calif.

The review appeared in the Guide Gault-Millau, which is widely distributed in Europe and the United States.

Pancakes Criticized

"We do not know where Mr. Chow recruits his cooks, but he would do well to send them for some instruction some-where in Chinatown," wrote Henri Gault and Christian Millau in their 1981 guide. The review went on to disparage the restaurant's service—"you have to wait 10 minutes to obtain chopsticks instead of forks"—and criticized the pancakes that enclose Peking duck as being "the size of a saucer and the thickness of a finger."

To counter this argument, Mr. Chow sent Stephen Yim, the chef in charge of his noodle-making staff, to roll pancakes before the jury, which apparently found them appropriately paper-thin. Mr. Yim demonstrated how he rolls a 10-foot-long noodle in 60 seconds, a feat for which he was given a place in the Guinness Book of World Records.

The jury and Judge Thomas F. Griesa also saw videotapes of the cooks at Mr. Chow's preparing traditional Chinese dishes, as a means of rebutting the guide's contention that "sweet and sour pork contained more dough (badly cooked) than meat," and that most dishes had "only the slightest relationship to the essential spirit of Chinese cuisine."

"We realized that the only way we could win the case was to convince the jury of the quality and skill of Mr. Chow's kitchen people," said Kenneth E. Warner, the lawyer for the plaintiff. "Obviously we would have had trouble trying to prove to a jury that, on the particular day that the man from Gault-Millau ate there in 1980, the food was not the way it was described in the review."

Richard K. Bernstein, the lawyer for the authors and for Jour Azur, the publishing house, said it was likely that his clients would appeal "because there are important constitutional issues in the case."

Mr. Chow said yesterday that he hoped the verdict would lead to more responsibility in restaurant criticism.

"I think some of them have abused the freedom of the press, and that this will help cause some standards of fairness to be applied to the critics," he said.

Whatever arguments you bring up in your letter to the *Times*, be sure to direct them at the review itself, and not at the person who wrote it. If you attack your opponent, rather than the issue your opponent is raising, you are committing the emotional fallacy of an *ad hominem* argument; you are arguing *to the man* (or to the woman, as the case may be) rather than to the issue. This is one possible response to an unfavorable restaurant review:

> Last week's review of my restaurant was totally inaccurate. I hardly think the author can be trusted to get his facts straight, since most of the restaurant owners I've talked to agree he is a notorious liar. Besides, what does he know about fine French cuisine? In the first place, he was born in America; in the second place, from the looks of his rather ample figure, I'd say he doesn't eat food so much as inhale it.

But this kind of personal attack will never convince your reader of your rationality and fair-mindedness. The characteristics of your opponent's physical appearance or personality are irrelevant: by indulging in name-calling, you're merely avoiding the real issue.

Option B: Instead of writing a rebuttal to Ms. Sheraton, you may wish to write a nasty restaurant review of your own. Choose a restaurant you have frequented—say, a neighborhood hangout or your school cafeteria—that leaves something to be desired in the way of food, service, and atmosphere. Then write a calm, fully documented critique of the restaurant. Your goal is to convince your reader not to patronize this place, though of course you should not come out and state this point. Use details to persuade—but make sure the details are accurate, lest you be sued for libel.

REWRITING SENTENCES

How specific should you be? Let's look at one student's review of a local restaurant that had recently undergone a change in management. In most respects his review is quite specific. But there are several points which might be made sharper and more persuasive with concrete details. Take these sentences, for example:

> The menus were new, as well as the prices on them. Every dish was at least $2.50 more than it used to be. We each ordered our favorite dish. *The waiter was very rude and impatient. It seemed as if he hated his job and everyone in his presence as well.*

Return for a moment to the *Times* article to see how Ms. Sheraton illustrates the rudeness and impatience of the waiters in the restaurant she is discussing. The key, of course, to substantiating matters of opinion like this is to give the reader the opportunity to see and hear the people being described. Quote them directly, if possible. We gave the above-quoted lines about the waiter to the rest of the students in the class, and asked them—along with the author of the sentences—to use their imaginations to make the information more lively and convincing. Here are some of the sentences they came up with:

> The waiter came to take our orders.
> "We're not ready to order yet," I said.
> "Well, hurry up, I don't have all day," the waiter shouted.

> The waiter growled at us, giving us the distinct impression that politeness and patience weren't two of his greatest virtues.

> "Give me those menus," the waiter snapped. "You're taking too long. I'm ordering for you. It really doesn't matter anyway; everything in this dump tastes the same."

> The waiter, tapping his foot and looking at his watch, demanded our orders. When we had finished, he snorted and marched off to unknown regions.

> We knew the waiter wanted to be anywhere else but in this restaurant when we saw him making paper airplanes out of his order pad.

> "I'm Vinnie, your waiter, but don't bother me," he said, "because I'd sooner beat you up than wait on you."

The point of a rewriting exercise like this one is not to encourage students to lie or exaggerate, but to remind you that a specific report, providing it is accurate, lends support to a thesis—in this case, that the service of an establishment is substandard.

CLASSROOM ACTIVITY 10.9

When you have completed one of the assignments in this chapter, try a sentence-revision exercise like the one above. Your teacher may ask members of the class to write some general statements from their papers on the blackboard and then have the other members of the class rewrite these sentences to make them more concrete.

We have been discussing ways to use details to make your argument more credible. But detailed is not the same as wordy. On the following pages, we offer some tips on how to trim wasted words from your essay.

Vocabulary Reducing: A Few Words on Being Concise

We've all experienced monetary inflation—spending more but getting less. Just as common is a kind of word inflation that creeps into undisciplined writing. *Wordiness* means using many words when a few will do the job. Wordiness not only wastes the reader's time, but can also obscure a writer's meaning.

On the other hand, being *concise* means expressing much in few words, and concision aptly describes a prose style that achieves clarity and compactness by eliminating all unnecessary words and phrases. Concise prose is powerful. The writer has discovered exactly what he or she wants to say and is able to say it forcefully.

Concise writers are usually ruthless editors of their own work: exactness and economy are rarely the marks of unrevised writing. With this editing goal in mind, we'll look at a few of the most common causes of wordiness and consider the ways in which diligent rewriting can clean up a cluttered sentence.

UNNECESSARY WORDS AND PHRASES

In everyday speech, most of us use unnecessary words and phrases because they fill empty spaces in our conversations and give us time to struggle with undeveloped thoughts. But writing is not simply recorded speech: a good paragraph or essay expresses fully developed ideas in a precise and economical manner. This doesn't mean that a sentence is concise simply because it's short, or that it's wordy because it's long. It does mean that every word fulfills a function or contributes significant information.

Observe, for example, that each of the common phrases listed below can be replaced by a single word:

Because of the fact that	
For the reason that	because
Due to the fact that	
At this point in time	
At the present time	now
Until the day that	until
By means of	by
In the event that	if
In the final analysis	finally
For the purpose of	for

Other phrases can be cut without losing anything: expressions such as "as far as I'm concerned," "by way of response," "for all intents and purposes," "it goes without saying that," and "all things considered" add nothing but flab to a sentence. And words like *frankly, honestly,* and *truthfully* as sentence modifiers can usually be eliminated: the only way to impress your readers with your honesty is with facts, not assertions of your sincerity.

EXERCISE 10.10

Make the following sentences concise by cutting useless words and phrases:

1. Due to the fact that many writers use ten words to do the job of just one word at this point in time, their sentences—and indeed all their writing—is full of wordiness.

2. Until the day that writers learn to be concise for the purpose of clarity, their work will be weak as far as I'm concerned.

3. For all intents and purposes, good writing is, in the final analysis, concise.

4. Frankly, it goes without saying that because of the fact of wordiness a piece of writing is often unclear.

5. In the event that your essay is wordy, cut out unnecessary words.

"REPETITIOUS REDUNDANCY"

As you know, words can be repeated for emphasis or for the sake of parallel structure, but careless repetition of words or ideas undermines the effect of any sentence. Be on the lookout for *redundant* phrases, such as *a pair of twins,* which say the same thing twice—like the title of this section.

EXERCISE 10.11

In his best-selling book on the state of American English, *A Civil Tongue,* author Edwin Newman compiled an assortment of redundancies culled from political announcements, newspaper articles, and television shows. We've used some of the redundancies he noted to compose the sentences below. Your task is to eliminate the repetitious words. Use your dictionary to help you with any word you're unsure of.

1. After the operation, the patient got tired and fatigued very easily.

2. The newspaper headline announced that a fatal slaying had taken place in the public library.

3. The sign said "No trespassing without permission."

4. The three triplets were identical and looked exactly alike.

5. My parrot is very unique.

6. The two nations reached a mutual agreement.

7. My birthday present was an unexpected surprise.

8. We must work together cooperatively if we are to successfully achieve our goals and objectives.

9. Philosophers are known to be deeply profound thinkers.

10. There were no solid facts to prove that he was guilty.

11. The landlord is planning to renovate the building so that it looks brand new.

12. There was loud shouting in the audience when the candidate explained his hopes, aspirations, and plans.

EXERCISE 10.12

On November 19, 1863, President Abraham Lincoln delivered one of the most famous speeches of modern times. The occasion was the dedication of a national cemetery in Gettysburg, Pennsylvania, where one of the greatest battles of the Civil War had been fought. Below, we've taken the opening of Lincoln's speech, a model of economy and a powerful piece of persuasive writing, and weighted it down with useless and redundant words and phrases. Edit our version carefully, and then compare your results to the original speech, which appears in its entirety on the last pages of this chapter.

° **four score:** 80 (1 score = 20). Lincoln did, in fact, say "four score and seven" rather than 87. Why do you think he used this "wordy" phrase here?

Sometime around four score° and seven years ago, our fathers who came before us brought forth on this very continent a fresh new nation, conceived in freedom and liberty, and dedicated to the proposition that all men are created equal and the same.

At this point in time we are engaged in a great vast civil war; testing whether that identical nation, or for that matter any nation so conceived and dedicated, can long continue to exist and endure. Because of the fact of the war, we are met together on a great immense battlefield of that war. For all intents and purposes, we have come to dedicate a portion of that field as a final last resting place for those who here gave their lives that the nation might live. In my personal opinion, it is altogether fitting and proper that we should do this.

PROBLEMS WITH SENTENCE STRUCTURE

As you've discovered, skillful sentence combining not only helps to clarify the relationships between ideas, but also reduces the number of words needed to express these ideas. Because wordiness often results from a lack of subordination or from faulty use of coordination, sentence-combining skills are essential to concise writing. Whenever you are revising a paper, look for more effective ways to join ideas, as well as to eliminate unnecessary or repetitious words and phrases.

EXERCISE 10.13

Test your editing power by revising the following paragraphs. Use what you've learned about both sentence combining and wordiness to make these paragraphs clear and concise:

It was my very first time away from home. I was excited, scared, and a little bit frightened. I was in a strange country. I didn't speak the language well, and I didn't know my way around, and I didn't understand the culture. I was surprised. I learned quickly. Now I feel comfortable here. Life has become easier. My English has improved. I sometimes give directions to tourists. I know what is expected of me.

I recently read an article in the newspaper. The death penalty may soon be re-established in our state again. The reporter also interviewed several citizens. He asked them their opinion of capital punishment. Some said it would help to reduce the crime rate, and others said it would have no effect, and a few said they objected to capital punishment, and they think society should value every human life. Who is right? A person murders intentionally and deliberately. Is the innocent victim who has done nothing wrong totally insignificant and unimportant? Is the life of the murderer more important than the life of the victim?

Writing a Précis

In every chapter of this book we've emphasized the importance of details. But there are times when what we need is a brief outline of a subject rather than a detailed account. Scholarly publications, for example, frequently provide short summaries, called *abstracts*, of full-length essays so that readers can quickly decide if a particular essay is likely to contain the information they're looking for.

Learning to write a *précis*—a summary of something you've read, seen, or experienced—is an effective way to practice concise writing and sharpen your ability to spot the main ideas in any selection. You may not realize it, but giving summaries is a routine part of your life. When you come home from work or school, you're likely to tell a family member or a friend what has happened during the day. Obviously, you don't recount every event. (Of course, we all know people who don't summarize but chatter on about pointless details. We've all felt our eyes glaze over as we suppress a yawn when someone like this makes us his captive audience.) Instead, you mention anything important, funny, disturbing, or interesting that will give your listener an idea of the kind of day you've had.

Similarly, when you write a letter to someone you haven't seen for a while, you summarize what's been going on. And when you are talking about a movie, a book, a sports event, you focus on the main events: you condense by concentrating on the significant features and eliminating unnecessary information. News reports and reviews of books, plays, and films are all summaries. In fact, the resume you worked on in Chapter 3 was also a summary, for it provided an overview of your experience and education. Most applications for jobs and schools, too, call for a summary of your background or your reasons for seeking a place there.

Being able to summarize skillfully will help you to write reports, take notes and prepare for tests, incorporate information into papers, and handle essay questions on exams. Your first step in preparing any summary is, of course, a careful reading of the material under consideration. After you've read the selection at least once, go back and find its thesis or controlling idea, which is usually suggested in the opening paragraph. Proceed by jotting down the main ideas and important facts included in the piece. You should now have a brief outline on which to base your précis.

Remember that your goal is to give someone who has not read the selection a clear idea of its content in a limited number of words: your précis should condense all of the main ideas and essential facts into as few words as possible. By restricting your summary to, say, 100 words, you force yourself to focus on the essential content and to omit all unnecessary words and phrases. Review your notes for any minor details or non-essential information before you start to compose your summary.

At this point, you're ready to write your précis. Open with a clear statement of the writer's thesis or conclusion, and then go on to the essential points which support that thesis or lead to that conclusion. Record only information from the selection—a précis is no place to express your own opinions. When you've finished, check your work by asking someone who isn't familiar with the selection to read your summary. Does it give your reader "the heart of the matter"?

JOURNAL EXERCISE 10.14

To prepare for an upcoming test in one of your courses, write a ten-minute summary of a chapter in the textbook for that course. At the next class meeting, ask a classmate who hasn't read the chapter to read your summary. Does your reader understand the main points presented in the chapter after reading your summary? What items need clarification?

CLASSROOM ACTIVITY 10.15

Turn back to Chapter 9, to the excerpt from *Children Without Childhood* entitled "It's Not What They Watch" (pages 340–341). For a practice exercise in précis-writing, see if you can summarize the excerpt in 50 words. When you have finished, compare your précis with those of your classmates. Did you include all of the main ideas and essential facts? Have you left out minor details?

Before we move on to other assignments in précis-writing, you may find it helpful to go over the following section on noun clauses—another tool for reporting statements and combining sentences in your summaries.

Noun Clauses

Noun clauses are especially useful to précis-writers because a précis usually involves *paraphrasing,* or reporting an author's statement in your own words, and this type of clause lends itself naturally to reporting facts and speech. Noun clauses do exactly what nouns do—they serve as subjects, objects, and complements. Noun clauses replace a noun in a main clause and can be adapted from statements, questions or requests, commands, and exclamations. They are introduced by the relative pronouns *that, who,* and *which,* or by *how, if, when, where, whether,* and *why.*

When a noun clause is derived from a statement, it begins with *that.* Let's take an American proverb as the basic sentence to be transformed in the following examples:

> *The early bird catches the worm.*

That the early bird catches the worm is often true. (Subject)

People believe *that the early bird catches the worm.* (Object of a verb)

My belief is *that the early bird catches the worm.* (Subjective complement)

It is said *that the early bird catches the worm.* (Subject after *It*: This use of the passive is a method to avoid citing the source of a statement.)

EXERCISE 10.16

Here is a proverb: *Honesty is the best policy.* Use the patterns in the examples above to turn this statement into a noun clause that functions as (1) a subject, (2) the object of a verb, (3) a subjective complement, (4) a subject after *It.*

Noun clauses that are derived from questions begin with *whether (or not), if, who, what, which, when, where, why,* and *how:*

> *Will the early bird catch the worm?*

Whether or not the early bird catches the worm is unimportant. (Subject)

I don't know *if the early bird will catch the worm.* (Object of a verb)

The question is *how the early bird catches the worm.* (Subjective complement)

I am thinking about *why the early bird catches the worm.* (Object of a preposition)

EXERCISE 10.17

Respond to the following questions with sentences that turn the questions into noun clauses. (For example: "Where does the early bird catch the worm?" "*Where the early bird catches the worm* doesn't interest me.")

1. When will you write your composition?

2. Where are you going on your vacation?

3. Will you be able to pay your rent this month?

4. Why do people eat junk food?

5. What do you want for your birthday?

Noun clauses are also derived from exclamations:

What an early bird you are!

The worm doesn't know *what an early bird you are.* (Object of a verb)

Notice how noun clauses are used to transform direct quotations into reported speech:

The Governor said, "I will work to end poverty."
The Governor said *that she would work to end poverty.*

Remember that word order is reversed when a question is turned into a statement:

Is the universe expanding?
No one knows *if the universe is expanding.*

"Do you take vitamins?" the doctor asked.
The doctor asked *if I took vitamins.*

EXERCISE 10.18

Change the first sentence in each pair below into a noun clause that will fill the blank in the second sentence:

1. Smoking is dangerous to your health.

   _____ has been proven.

2. I suspect that you are lying to me.

   My suspicion _____ is getting
   stronger.

3. Virtue is its own reward.

   It is often said _____.

4. What a fool I am!

   I have discovered _____.

5. How will we finish our work?

   We are worried about _____.

6. What will I be doing in ten years?

   I wonder _____.

7. The teacher said, "Late papers will be penalized."

The teacher said _____ .

8. "When did the plane land?" he asked.

He asked _____ .

EXERCISE 10.19

Correct the errors in the following sentences:

1. I don't know why didn't I study harder.

2. They wondered where did he get all that money?

3. She didn't understand why was he so upset.

4. I called him to ask is he going to the party.

5. We want to know what are you doing?

EXERCISE 10.20

Later on in this chapter, you'll be reading and writing about the much-discussed question of how to improve U.S. schools. What follows is an excerpt from a newspaper article about this issue. First, write a fifty-word summary of these three paragraphs. Then go back to the article and transform each of the direct quotations into reported speech. (For one or two of these quotations you may wish to *paraphrase*—that is, to rewrite the statement in your own words.)

Educators insist that few reforms confront a basic reality—that many students are not motivated and have no support at home. "Kids coming to school today bring all sorts of emotional and family problems with them," said Mary Futtrell, president of the National Education Association. "And, like it or not, the teacher has to deal with these." Carolyn Swinney, who teaches social studies at James Monroe Junior High School in Tampa, Fla., spoke of dealing with students who drop out because they are pregnant. One of her students has been absent half the term because she is too tired to come; her mother works as a janitor at night and takes the youngster to work rather than leave her home alone. "I also have a student who has been in five different schools this year alone because she is being shuffled among members of the family," Mrs. Swinney said.

What many students need, according to their teachers, are counselors, psychologists, social workers and other support personnel. That's not what they are getting, said Rachel Tompkins, executive director of the Children's Defense Fund, who noted that "out-of-class needs go almost unrecognized," which increases the likelihood of children falling behind and dropping out.

Schools need abler teachers, studies have concluded. To get them, Tennessee is offering career ladders, Iowa has adopted higher certification standards and New York is instituting teaching internships. Several states have proposed scholarships for those who want to enter the profession. There is little mention of improving working conditions or significantly boosting salaries, which average $22,032. Yet, "60 percent of college-bound students cite low pay as the main reason they are not interested in becoming teachers," said John Mangieri, dean of Texas Christian University's school of education, who surveyed students in six states for the American Association of Colleges of Teacher Education. Said Gerald Grant, a Syracuse University professor of education, teacher dissatisfaction today lies in having "increased responsibility while suffering a loss of authority."

EXERCISE 10.21

Now try your hand at summarizing a longer piece. Compose a 150- to 200-word summary of the article on pages 400–401 in the next section on policewomen. When possible, use appropriate alternatives for "said"—verbs such as *stated, mentioned, warned, indicated, commented,* and *noted*—to enliven your précis.

Assignment 3: Public Debate on Policewomen

Representation of women in law enforcement in the U.S. has increased from less than one percent at the beginning of this century to more than three percent in 1980. In addition, the role of female police officers has changed significantly: no longer confined to the women's and juveniles' bureaus, these officers are increasingly assigned to the same kinds of jobs as male officers, including the tougher patrol duties.

The question asked in this section is, "Do you think women can perform as ably as men in police patrol work?" Your teacher may decide to assign this issue as a paper topic, or as an informal classroom debate, to be written up in essay form later on. In either case, we have provided a variety of sources for you to look at in preparation for your assignment. The source materials include a feature story from a newspaper; an article from a specialized periodical (*Police Studies*); an abstract of an article; a summary of a report; and a review of relevant legislation regarding equal opportunities for women and minorities. You will note that only one of these sources—the *Police Studies* article—is presented in the form of an argument; the other three selections provide the raw material for an argument essay. We'll start off with the newspaper article, and your assignment.

The article on pages 400–401 from the *Boston Globe* describes the gradual acceptance of women onto the Massachusetts police force. Read it, and after you've written your précis of it according to the directions in Exercise 10.21, decide your position on this issue:

Are you in favor of or against increasing the number of women who serve as police officers? If against, put yourself in the situation faced by the 700 Newton residents who, according to the *Globe* article, signed a petition in 1974: draft your own present-day version of the petition, setting forth the arguments you would use to block the hiring of women to patrol your neighborhood. Address the petition to the Chief of the Newton police force.

Alternatively, write a speech, to be delivered by Roger MacLeod of the Massachusetts Commission Against Discrimination, in favor of recruiting female officers. Your speech will be addressed to those police administrators who are still resistant to hiring women.

Before you begin drafting your position paper on this issue, read all the material in this section. In addition, it will be useful for you to discuss the issue with your classmates before debating or writing.

Should your class decide to conduct a debate on this topic, here are a few guidelines for organizing an informal debate:

- Divide into two teams: the *pro* side (in favor of . . .) and the *con* side (against . . .). For 15–20 minutes at the beginning of the session, the members of each team will brainstorm, trying to think of strong arguments to support their position, as well as to anticipate the other side's arguments. Elect three or four spokespersons on each team who will do the actual debating, and make sure they jot down the team's main ideas.

- Traditionally, the *pro* side in a debate speaks first, followed by the *con* side. Each team will have five or six minutes to present its arguments to the class. It's a good idea to divide the arguments among the spokespersons for each team, and then let each of these debaters speak for a minute or two.

- After each side has spoken, reassemble with your teammates for ten minutes to prepare a *rebuttal* (like a refutation in written argument) to the arguments the other team has raised. Then each side will have an additional six minutes to present this rebuttal to the class.

FEMALE POLICE

Women slowly gaining acceptance on forces in Massachusetts

By R.S. Kindleberger
Globe Staff

It's been a decade since women began winning jobs in Massachusetts as full-fledged police officers, strapping revolvers around their waists and venturing into the night side-by-side with the men to face everything a cop has to face.

Until Boston hired 11 women for regular patrol in 1972, the few females in police departments were kept off the front lines. They were called policewomen or matrons, and they watched over female prisoners, investigated juvenile cases or performed other jobs in which their superiors thought they could not get hurt.

Acceptance of the new female officers has often come slowly; their numbers are still low and some people still question their ability to do the job. But police officials and the women are emphatic in declaring that female officers are here to stay.

In Newton, Chief William Quinn had this to say recently: "I haven't heard anything about a male officer not wanting to ride with a woman officer for years."

Nine years ago 700 Newton residents signed a petition in an unsuccessful effort to block the hiring of 12 women officers. The controversy has long since died, according to Quinn. Six of the 12 are still on patrol duty, he

said, and other women have replaced some who left the force. In Quinn's view, the experiment of nine years ago is a success.

In Boston, females now are welcomed by the Boston Police Patrolman's Assn. "They've proven they can do the job," vice chairman Donald Murray said. "They can get shot just like we can."

The number of female officers in Boston has risen to 103, or 5.6 percent of the uniformed force. Although the number still seems small, it's far greater than that of most other communities in the state. As of the end of 1982, the state's 351 cities and towns employed 290 female police officers, 2.5 percent of the total, according to the state Department of Public Safety. Most were employed by cities, and 246 communities reported no female officers.

SANDRA O'BRIEN
A chilly reception

ans to the top of Civil Service hiring lists, has limited the opportunities for women.

The law, however, applies only to veterans with wartime service, defined for the Vietnam war as ending in 1975.

"As fewer and fewer veterans are eligible or interested, opportunities for women have to increase," explained Michael Gardner, former Boston Police personnel director.

Some departments still resist hiring women, according to Roger MacLeod of the Massachusetts Commission Against Discrimination, "but the number of departments where that is true is being reduced year-by-year."

Sheryll Pichon, a Boston officer who is president of the Massachusetts Assn. of Women Police, notes few women have been promoted above the rank of patrol officer. She says, however, that because of budget constraints there have been fewer promotions generally in recent years.

Pichon's organization was formed five years ago to offer support to women in a job where they face both physical danger and recurrent questions about their role as women in what is perceived as a man's world. Some male officers doubt their usefulness in a fight, and some civilians look on them as a curiosity.

SHERYLL PICHON
Injured on duty

Thousands of women are attempting to become officers. Of the 13,000 persons who took the Oct. 1 Civil Service test for entry police jobs, a preliminary count showed 2156, or 17 percent, were women.

Many of the old barriers have fallen. Strength tests and height requirements were done away with in the mid-1970s, but a major stumbling block remains. Absolute veterans preference, the state law° that lets qualifying veterans skip ahead of higher-scoring nonveter-

The Federal Veterans' Preference Act of 1944 covers almost all persons who served in the military before 1976. The federal government and all states maintain civil service systems that give hiring and/or promotion preference to veterans, of whom few are women.

LYNDA COSTA
"Learning fast"

Questions of more stress

Edward Donovan, director of the Boston Police stress program, believes women leave police jobs earlier than men, in part because of the additional stress. No nationwide studies have been done, according to Peggy E. Triplett, consultant to the Police Foundation in Washington, but she suspects "there is no difference or very little difference in attrition rates."

Anecdotal evidence suggests female officers are showing the same vulnerability to alcoholism, drug addiction, heart disease and suicide that plagues their male colleagues, Donovan said in an interview. Their divorce rate appears even higher, he claims.

But despite the difficulties and the occasional failures, many female officers report a high level of satisfaction with their jobs.

– Sandra O'Brien is 5 foot 2, soft-spoken, happily married, and the mother of three. She is also an unusually able police officer. One of two detectives on Wayland's 24-officer force, she investigated all four of the town's armed robberies last year.

"Because of her perserverance, she was able to clear all the armed robberies and obtain convictions and jail sentences on the subjects responsible," Lt. Gerald Galvin said recently. "Excellent" is his one-word summation of her abilities.

When O'Brien was assigned to patrol duty, some of her colleagues were decidedly chilly. They were uneasy at her backing them up on trouble calls, and felt they had to be especially vigilant in backing her up, O'Brien said. She says the tension passed after they saw she could handle herself.

She is small, but O'Brien has not shrunk from getting physical with troublemakers when the situation demanded. Responding once to reports a man was threatening neighbors with a knife on a dark road, she dropped the six-footer on his back when he moved to put his hand in his pocket. It was nothing special, she said later, just "a technique I learned at the police academy."

– Waneda Jordan graduated from Boston's Girls' High School in 1955 with a yen to get into police work. What seemed like a reasonable ambition was not to be fulfilled until 19 years later, when she was sworn in as a Cambridge police officer.

Jordan remembers sitting down in 1972 to take the first Civil Service police exam open to men and women. One of the first questions had her laughing aloud: "Do you like tall women?" The test-preparers apparently were as slow reacting to the idea of a sexually integrated police force as were some departments.

When Jordan was hired two years later, she was 36 and one of the city's oldest recruits.

A friendly woman with an easy manner and occasional flashes of impish humor, Jordan spoke during an interview at the station of how she enjoys "working with people, helping people." But she strives to leave her work behind when she goes home. As a woman, she said, "I enjoy having doors opened for me."

Now assigned to the records bureau, Jordan has also worked communications, and she spent her first six years on patrol.

"She's an effective police officer," said Lt. Timothy Toomey, executive aide to the chief. "She knows her job and she does it well."

Battle to gain job

– In her three years on the New Bedford police force, Lynda Costa has been kicked, bitten, spat on and thrown-up on while subduing suspects or answering disturbance calls. She and her male partner patrol the city's tough North End on the night shift, when trouble is routine.

Costa might be a nine-year veteran by now if she were two and a half inches taller: she was rejected in 1974 because she missed that margin the 5 foot 6 height then required. The city repealed its height requirement a few months later, but because of official preference for veterans and minorities, her subsequent applications were rejected. She finally was hired under court order in 1980. Her lawyer, Thomas McKenna of Boston, has asked the Supreme Court to hear her bid for nearly seven years of back pay.

Costa, now 33, was 20 minutes late for an interview at her New Bedford ranch house recently. She had been in court all day to testify on an arrest. The charges were armed robbery, kidnaping, assault and battery and illegal possession of a firearm. She and her partner were the arresting officers.

Her platoon commander, Lt. Jack Sylvia, said in an interview that Costa, while still comparatively new on patrol, is "learning fast" and likely to mature into a fine officer.

Michael Costa, her husband of nine years and Costa's biggest booster, said the key to her effectiveness is "guts and brains." He predicted, only half humorously, that given the chance, she'll end up chief. – "that's how smart she is."

Injuries 'part of the job'

– George A. Moran's attempt to flee police in a high-speed chase through Cambridge and Boston two months ago came to an abrupt end on Mercer street in South Boston. It was there that the convicted armed robber and escapee from Walpole state prison ran his car into the cruiser of two police officers, both women.

News accounts said the officers had blocked the street with their car. In fact, Sheryll Pinchon said recently in an interview in her Dorchester home, she and partner Mary Evans had become lost and were on their way back to their Area D station house when Moran's car came speeding at them.

Both women were injured and have been on leave recuperating since. For Pinchon, who has been receiving therapy for a neck injury, it wasn't the first time she's been injured on duty. "It's part of the job," she said with a shrug.

As you can see, the *Boston Globe* article begins with a history of female police in Massachusetts, and goes on to relate a number of anecdotes about individual officers interviewed by the reporter. This next article presents its case in the form of a comparison/contrast of males and females and their suitability for patrol work. Here, the author develops her topic with generalizations made on the basis of research (quoted throughout the article). Notice that the title of the piece is ironic: the author reverses the usual question about whether women make good police officers, and considers instead whether male officers can do the job properly. What are the advantages and disadvantages of males and females on the police force?

EXERCISE 10.22

Read the following article and write a précis of it in your notebook. In addition, as you read, jot down in the margin the components of van Wormer's argument as they correspond to the outline on page 373.

Are Males Suited to Police Patrol Work?

Katharine van Wormer
Assistant Professor of Criminal Justice, Kent State University

The more one reads of police officers the more one wonders about the suitability of the male person for this very important and demanding task. Information for the present analysis is drawn from comments of knowledgeable male observers and from data gathered by government sponsored commissions concerning sex differences in patrol performance.

Females today are occupationally on the defensive. Of the host of articles to appear recently on the subject, none has questioned the roles that men are best able to play in police work.

Not until 1972 (Washington, D.C.) and 1973 (New York City) were women sent out on street patrol. The literature to date asks questions like, "How Well Are Policewomen Doing a Man's Job?" "Whatever Happened to Lady Cops?" The answers are implied in other articles with titles like "Women Make Good Cops" and "Female Police Officers Measure Up in Stress Situations." One finds not a single article or treatise with the title, "Should Males be Placed in Patrol Work?" Or, "Are Males Doing a Good Job?"

It would simply never occur to anyone to ask. Surveys on the subject would be difficult. A survey of police chiefs in 42 cities asked respondents to list advantages and disadvantages of using women on patrol. Imagine that the all-male police chiefs were sent questionnaires on male effectiveness. Such an approach would in all probability bewilder the average police administrator.

Fortunately, further studies are not necessary in light of the volumes of data on all-male patrol units and how they have functioned. Looking at the literature as a whole, findings concerning male as opposed to female recruits can be categorized into advantages and disadvantages of being a male police officer.

Advantages of Using Men on Patrol

1. Looming above other advantages mentioned is the superior physical strength of the male combined with the stamina to subdue a suspect. An experiment with cadets made by a police trainer indicates the physical superiority of the male in making a physical arrest ("Women in Blue," 1976). According to a survey of police chiefs across the country, to those who perceived distinctive sex differences in performance, men prove themselves more physically rugged than women (Edmiston, 1975).

2. It is easier for a male to handle night work, rotating shifts, and long hours. The male has a wife at home cooking for him, caring for the children. For the female, especially a mother, adjustment is sometimes difficult ("Women in Blue," 1976).

3. If you hire a man, aggressiveness under the call of duty can be taken for granted. If you hire a woman, resocialization, assertiveness training is required. Milton (1974) points up a sex difference in a study of police executives—men were more persistent than women when obstacles were encountered. Male officers are likely to emerge as the dominant partners in mixed situations; they make more arrests than females and participate in strenuous physical activity more often (Sichel et al., 1978).

4. Males are more apt than females to have had related job experience. Some are veterans who have been military police; others have worked in security. On the other hand, women recruits rarely have had suitable background experience. (Milton, 1974, deplores the practice of preference for veterans; nevertheless, there is a preference, and males are likely to be veterans.)

Disadvantages of Using Men on Patrol

1. That male police officers are more likely than female officers to generate complaints or provoke violence is commonly mentioned in the literature. In dangerous situations, while the female presence is said to have a disarming effect, inasmuch as women do not carry a threatening, violent image, the presence of policemen is often provocative. According to the psychologist Sherman's study (1973) of the police, society expects the use of force by a policeman; we get what we expect. It is Sherman's observation that America's police forces remain bastions of male supremacy and American style machismo. His recommendation is for women to be hired because a "decrease in muscularity often leads to an increase in efficiency."

As Horne (1975) states, policemen are often attacked because "it is heroic." While women might avoid such assaults and produce a calming effect on aggressive behavior, male officers actually tend to stir up violence. An anonymous male officer quoted by Milton (1974) had this to say:

> My chances of getting hurt, in actuality, are much more with him (a man). She's not going to—force an issue . . . We can usually talk our way out of situations.

2. Related to the previous disadvantage is poor public relations. Studies show that men are more likely as a sex to become involved in serious

unbecoming conduct which can damage community relations. They are more likely to be involved in police car crashes (Block, 1970). Reports indicate that men do not relate as well to the public generally as women do, that it is harder for them to get essential cooperation (Sherman, 1973).

3. In regard to resorting to physical brutality, males are the winners by a long shot. The government study edited by Winslow (1977) points up the kind of police practices that exist which cannot be justified. Among these is abusive treatment of minority groups and the poor. Ramsey Clark (1971) decries the amount of force currently used in junior high schools and high schools and on college campuses. Sherman (1973) sees the police brutality among males as a vicious cycle in that initially it is expected of them. The cop is first and foremost masculine, and to be masculine in America is to be two-fisted, strong, and aggressive.

In the Washington, D.C. study (1970), the following incident is described:

> Another policewoman was handling an incident "beautifully" in the words of the observer, as she worked to persuade a drunk to go home with his wife. Then a male officer interceded, putting his hands on the drunk, and starting some pushing and shoving. The patrolman ended up arresting the man and getting credit for an arrest.
>
> Block and Anderson, 1970:19

4. Male officers are reluctant to accept females; they do not want to share the power and security of the position. This attitude is destructive of good inter-police and community relations. With the police, resistance to hiring women is a matter of male fears about their image. Most police departments operate under a masculine value system in which the favored image is that of an armed man of action (Milton, 1974). Accordingly, it is not surprising that in the Washington, D.C. report, police officials and male officers stated a definite preference for patrolling with a male rather than a female partner.

5. Male officers tend to overprotect female partners. Then they complain that women are a handicap (Edmiston, 1975). In failing to relate to policewomen on an equal basis, they put them down. Joint decision making, according to Sichel et al. (1978) is still a rarity. The Sichel study of 41 male and female police officers, using a matched sample, indicates a relative lack of female assertiveness in mixed partnership that disappeared when female subject officers were assigned female partners.

6. Educational differences are reported between male and female officers with females having the higher education. Education is a significant factor because of the high correlation between low education and social class and authoritarian attitudes. Horne's evaluation of policewomen in California and St. Louis (1975) and the report published by the Police Foundation (1974) acknowledge the tendency for police departments to require college for women applicants.

An official (Block and Anderson, 1970) gives his observations on male educational level: "I find that a great many male officers are of substandard quality in the areas of intelligence, fundamental knowledge, commitment to community, work habits and dress."

Female report writing is mentioned throughout these studies as of a higher quality than the male. Male officers are described as not only being sloppy in their writing but also as paying less attention to important detail than female officers. Radelet (1977) sees the fact that police are recruited largely from the undereducated, typically conservative working class as related to their toughness and hostility. When you recruit from lower class levels you run the risk of getting people who have built-in violent reactions (Blum, 1967).

The finding of a social class difference between male and female officers would be expected on the grounds that the salary and even social status of being on the police force would be comparatively higher for a woman than a man in our society. At the present time, women in our society are generally less educated and ambitious than men. So it can be speculated that the police field would attract more middle class than working class women and more working class than middle class men.

7. Policemen have acquired a poor reputation. The literature on battered wives and their families confirms this dismal assessment. Police Commander James Bannon of Detroit made the following statement on the field of law enforcement today:

> Of all the nonathletic occupations, none is so absorbed with the use of physical coercive force as that of the police officer. None are any more thoroughly socialized in their masculine role images. This . . . suggests to me that traditionally trained and socialized policemen are the worst possible choice to attempt to intervene in domestic violence.
>
> Quoted in *Ms*, 1976

Sherman's psychological view of women in policing says that in domestic violent situations a woman can empathize with another woman, thus cooling the conflict. Battered wives rarely expect to get psychological support from a male officer; all too often they don't.

8. The matter of questioning rape victims is another area that is tough for a male—by virtue of being male—to handle. Books devoted to the subject of rape, such as Brownmiller's (1975), invariably bring this shortcoming up with the recommendation that female officers be the ones to interview the victims and escort them to the hospital and so on. Policewomen in Britain have fulfilled this function for some time.

Male police and detectives, according to Schurr (1971), victimize the victims, and make women feel more guilty than the accused. Police equate submission with consent. The difficulty may not be relating so much to a certain type of victim as toward troubled females in general. According to Niederhoffer (1967), the precinct has about it a "locker room" aura, pervaded by a strong erotic quality. An ambivalence toward and vague distrust of women are characteristic.

All the studies under consideration overwhelmingly mention the disadvantage of being a male officer when it comes to interviewing the female victim of a sex crime.

The Question

The question we are pondering is, "Are Males Suited to Police Patrol Work?" After looking at the advantages and disadvantages we would have to say they have a role, although a qualified one. Hopefully, the female influence will modify the machismo aura of the police department; thus, long-held and counterproductive attitudes will come to shift. Special training for males in the sensitivity area would be a positive first step; different criteria for selection of police officers would be another.

A real as opposed to token integration of male and female police officers would have some unforeseen positive effects:

> I believe in some instances the female officers shame their male counterparts into doing some work, cleaning up their appearance, improving their vocabulary.
>
> Official, quoted by Block, 1970:45

Similarly, from *The Police Chief*:

> In almost every case, the attitude, enthusiasm, behavior and general performance of the field training officer improved markedly.

Regarding criteria for selection of new recruits, we must recognize that the strength of law enforcement cannot come from the club and the gun. It must come from devotion to duty executed with high skill (Clark, 1971).

In short, many of the males presently employed by the police department are not suited to police work. But more careful hiring practices and the positioning of females in positions of leadership as well as on patrol duty would do much to alleviate the overmasculinized police image that currently exists.

— From Police Studies, *Volume 3 (Winter 1981), pp. 41–44.*

Professor van Wormer's article surveys the research of a number of writers concerned with the capabilities of female and male police officers. The following paragraph describes a different kind of survey—one that was conducted by the administration of the police force to evaluate women officers among its ranks. This paragraph is an abstract of an information packet containing the results of performance evaluation surveys of policewomen conducted in the police departments of eight American cities:

ABST: Six of the studies summarized evaluation of patrol capability and were conducted in Washington, D.C., St. Louis County, Mo., New York City, Denver, Newton, Mass., and Philadelphia. All six studies found that performance and results, when interacting with angry or violent citizens, were similar for men and for women police officers. Some other findings include: Male police officers felt generally negative toward women officers as partners on patrol; women officers performed less aggressively than men, made fewer arrests, and used preventive activity less often than males; and women officers were less likely to damage community relations (males received more community complaints) and, in fact were more likely to enhance such relations. The study on police officer heights and selected aspects of performance lacked sufficient data to establish a clear estimate of the relationship between the variables of height, seniority, and officer performance. However, findings showed that height differences had no statistically significant effect on police officer performance, officer assaults, auto accidents, department complaints and commendations, or duty injuries. The report on women traffic officers by the California Highway Patrol found both men and women performing critical tasks acceptably (making high-risk and felony vehicle stops, effectively using firearms, taking charge at accident scenes, lifting and carrying prisoners or victims, preparing written reports, administering first aid, communicating well verbally, and recognizing drunk drivers). It also found that academy grades were highly correlated with performance in the field by both men and women. Footnotes are included throughout.

> —*Summary of information packet published by the National Information and Research Center on Women in Policing Performance Evaluations, by R. D. Townsey. (The summary appears in* Topical Search: The Most Representative Documents on Policewomen, *National Institute of Justice, August 1982, p. 9.)*

And here is a more detailed summary of the study of policewomen in the Denver, Colorado, Police Department, conducted in 1977. Also included (on page 408) is a table showing the distribution of women and minorities on the Denver police force according to rank. What facts can you gather from this chart?

Summary

Between 1953 and 1978 the number of women among Denver's sworn personnel grew from two to 67, making up a relatively high complement of 4.9 percent. Largely in response to a 1972 minority sex discrimination lawsuit, which revised recruiting and hiring practices, the number of female officers increased more than 40 percent between 1973 and 1978. Highly indicative of the impact of the resulting 1975 consent decree is the specific increase in the number of minority women, which between 1970 and 1978 grew from a total of one (.1 percent) to a total of 31 (2.3 percent). However, the most current rates of application (19.4 percent) and representation (4.9 percent) of women in the Denver Police Department do not accurately reflect their presence in the local civilian labor force (39.4 percent). Specifically, the complement of white female officers is far below the presence of white women in the labor force—2.6 percent compared to 33.8 percent. Similarly situated are black women: .9 percent of the female officers but 1.8 percent of the female labor force. Hispanic women maintain a similar dichotomy: 1.1 percent of Denver's female officers but 3.8 percent of the female labor force.

Since 1968 the Denver Police Department has been involved in a number of minority recruitment efforts which culminated in the hiring of significant numbers of women. The Denver police officer selection process is conducted

Distribution of Full-Time Sworn Personnel
by Gender, Ethnic Group and Rank
1978

| | FEMALE* | | | | | | MALE** | | | | | | | | Total | |
| | White | | Black | | Hispanic | | White | | Black | | Hispanic | | | | | |
Rank	No.	%	No.	%	No.	%	No.	%	No.	%	No.	%			No.	%
Police Officer	26	72.2	11	84.6	15	100.0	464	43.3	58	76.3	115	75.0			689	50.5
Detective	6	16.6	2	15.4	—	—	250	23.3	8	10.5	21	14.0			287	21.0
Technician	2	5.6	—	—	—	—	121	11.2	3	4.0	9	6.0			135	9.9
Dispatcher	2	5.6	—	—	—	—	26	2.4	—	—	1	.65			29	2.1
Sergeant	—	—	—	—	—	—	133	12.4	5	6.6	2	1.3			140	10.3
Radio Engineer	—	—	—	—	—	—	10	.91	—	—	2	1.3			12	.90
Supt. of Radio Engineer	—	—	—	—	—	—	1	.1	—	—	1	.65			2	.15
Lieutenant	—	—	—	—	—	—	43	4.0	1	1.3	—	—			44	3.2
Captain	—	—	—	—	—	—	17	1.6	1	1.3	—	—			18	1.3
Division Chief	—	—	—	—	—	—	5	.5	—	—	—	—			5	.40
Chief	—	—	—	—	—	—	1	.1	—	—	—	—			1	.07
TOTAL	36	100.0	13	100.0	15	100.0	1071	100.0	76	100.0	151	100.0			1362	100.0

* Excluded are one Oriental and two American Indian policewomen.
** Excluded are six Oriental officers, one a ranking lieutenant; and five American Indian police officers.

by the Denver Civil Service Commission and certain aspects of it are being validated for selection purposes. One device undergoing validation is the Oral Interview Board, which was authorized by the 1975 consent decree. Presently, the Denver Police Department does not employ a physical agility test in appraising the suitability of police applicants. However, a physical agility test as well as a psychological examination are currently under consideration as selection criteria. Unlike the continued use of an oral interview board or use of a psychological examination, the use of a physical agility test may adversely affect the selection of female applicants as demonstrated across the country.

Of note are the department's remedial training provisions for recruits who perform poorly in academics and/or physical training, and its use of field training officers. It is reported that women experience a very low wash-out rate, although they experience at least one major physical training problem, push-ups, which is corrected with remedial training. One female officer functions as a field training officer and this is credited as having a positive influence upon women, particularly during their probationary° year.

° **probation:** a trial period in which a person's fitness for membership in a working or social group is tested.

—From Progress Report on Women in Policing, *by Cynthia G. Sulton and Roi D. Townsey, Police Foundation, 1981.*

Finally, below are some of the significant acts of legislation that have been passed in this country to guarantee equal opportunities for persons regardless of race, religion, or gender. We have also indicated how these laws have affected the rules governing the hiring of female police.

- *The Equal Pay Act of 1963* prohibits discrimination in the payment for services on the basis of sex.

- *Title VII of the Civil Rights Act of 1964* prohibits all employment activities (terms, conditions, hiring, recruitment, promotion, termination, classification, layoff, benefits, etc.) that discriminate on the basis of race, color, religion, sex, or national origin. *The 1972 amendments* authorize the Equal Employment Opportunity Commission (EEOC) to file suit against private employers, while the U.S. Department of Justice is authorized to sue public employers charged with employment discrimination.

- *The Pregnancy Discrimination Act of 1978* prohibits discrimination on the basis of pregnancy, childbirth, or related medical conditions. The Act also prescribes that pregnancy be treated as any other temporary disability by employers in the provision of employment benefits.

These laws have had the following effects, among others, on the hiring practices of police departments in the United States. Again, we quote from the Sulton/Townsey *Progress Report*:

- Height and weight requirements traditionally used by police agencies as selection criteria have been challenged as discriminatory when they result in the exclusion of a disproportionate number of women and other groups of applicants. Defendant police departments have argued that minimum height requirements identify candidates for patrol officers who have physical strength and ability, and who are free of any psychological disorder bred of small stature. Recent legal battles concerning the use of height and weight requirements have been won by plaintiffs alleging past, present, and future disproportionate impact. Success has rested largely upon defendant police departments' failure to show that the employment practices were justified (as a matter of law) as business necessities.

- In their interpretations of Title VII, courts have ruled that all applicants for a position requiring physical strength and agility must be given an opportunity to demonstrate their ability to perform the work in question without regard to their sex. Further, EEOC Guidelines on Sex Discrimination prohibit the refusal to hire women based on characteristics attributed to them as a class.

In writing up your speech for either side of the policewoman issue, remember to take into account not only what you have read in the sources reprinted here,* but what you have learned from your own experience as well. What have you observed about the requirements and responsibilities of police officers in the U.S., and in your own country? How can you use these observations to strengthen your side of the debate? As one final aid to your argument, we offer the following discussion of three more logical fallacies that often tempt debaters.

Additional Logical Fallacies

The either/or argument: Most questions worth debating are multifaceted. It would be oversimplification to reduce a complex issue to two choices— for example, "Either we reinstitute height and weight requirements for our police officers, or we'll wind up with a weak and puny police force!" When two conditions are falsely presented as the only alternatives, the argument is weakened by superficiality. Your argument will be more persuasive if you recognize all possible choices, and then advocate your own position.

---

* Be sure to credit the source of any information you cite: for example, "According to a 1983 *Boston Globe* article by R. S. Kindleberger on female police, ..."

Hypothesis contrary to fact is illustrated by this cartoon:

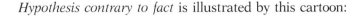

The computer in this fanciful cartoon has arrived at an illogical deduction because it began with a false hypothesis, or thesis. You can't start with an untrue hypothesis and then draw any supportable conclusions from it. If, in the debate on policewomen, you were to argue, "If the majority of police officers were women rather than men, we wouldn't have so much crime in our city streets," you'd be advancing a hypothesis contrary to fact.

A related fallacy is called *begging the question*. This error in reasoning occurs when you present a debatable proposition as absolute fact, and then base the rest of your argument on that questionable premise. A premise that is really an opinion requires factual support: you can't build an argument on a premise that has yet to be proved. This statement from a student paper shows its author begging the question (and stereotyping as well):

> Most male emotions are aggressive, so when a male police officer loses control of his emotions, he reacts physically. Females, however, take longer to lose control of their emotions, and are less aggressive, so they never resort to police brutality.

Use what you have learned about logical fallacies in this chapter, as well as in Chapters 8 and 9, to point out illogical statements in the following paragraphs taken from student papers on the policewomen issue. How would you disprove or counter each of these statements in a debate?

1. "One problem is that females would get too emotionally involved with the victims of crimes. For example, if a woman is raped, the female officer might become so obsessed with finding the rapist or helping the victim in some other way than in the capacity of a policewoman that all other crimes would become secondary to the female officer. These other crimes won't get solved. In police work, there is no room for both crime-solving and emotional involvement."

2. "Granted, we are now in the years of the 'liberated woman,' but we the people feel that women are pushing themselves into places where they don't belong. They don't want this work as a profession. They just want it so they can try and show up the men. They are interested only in competing with men, not working with them."

3. "Members of the police department who are resistant to hiring women are conservative and childish in their thinking. They should open their eyes to the world we live in and work in."

4. "It's the same with women who want to be firefighters. Firefighters who don't have great strength are completely ineffective at their jobs. Women, of course, are 'the weaker sex,' and therefore would be poor firefighters. Clearly, they would be just as ineffective as police patrol officers."

5. "Women are not physically equipped for the job. The height and strength tests were done away with because of them. Now, if they can't pass the same tests as men, how can they do the same job? No matter how much they know about self-defense, women will have no chance against a criminal who is twice their size. Also, criminals won't feel intimidated by a woman, even if she is a police officer."

6. "If women weren't capable of handling demanding jobs such as police work, then they wouldn't be holding high positions such as doctors, lawyers, and supreme court judges."

7. "It is not a good idea for women to become patrol officers. If they want to work for the police force, they should settle for desk work or work as meter maids. It is not only men who feel this way. There are women, even some liberated women, who agree with the arguments presented in this petition. We are not saying that all women should

stay home and be housewives. We are just saying that they should not be hired to serve on the police force."

CLASSROOM ACTIVITY 10.24

Now, with the other members of your group, edit your own argument paper to eliminate logical fallacies such as those discussed in Chapter 9 and this chapter.

The next assignment in argument will give you the option to write your response as a timed essay examination, to be written in class. Below, we have suggested some steps to help you prepare for this common type of college assignment.

Suggestions for Taking an Essay Exam

Many students despair when a teacher announces that an exam will include "essay questions": they would much prefer taking their chances with a multiple choice or true/false test. Yet an essay question actually offers you the opportunity to show not just what you know, but also how you use this knowledge to support your ideas. The essay exam tests your ability to make connections between facts and ideas, and to select those details that best support your thesis.

Essay questions characteristically use terms that should be familiar to any reader of this book. Most often, they will ask you to *identify, describe, define, explain, analyze, compare, contrast, agree or disagree, discuss causes and effects,* and so on. Although most of these terms do not suggest argument, the essay exam is usually argumentative in that it requires the careful marshaling of evidence to support the main ideas you've chosen to write about. For example, a question such as "Discuss the causes of the Crimean War" is actually asking you to select what you believe to be the main causes of the war and to use facts, details, and examples to convince your reader that these reasons are significant. Indeed, all of the skills that you've developed as you've worked your way through this text will come to your aid during any essay exam: your job in this type of test is to show your mastery of the material by providing the concrete "proof" that will make your ideas more powerful and convincing.

Ideally, preparing for a test begins on the first day of a course. If you take careful notes in class, keep up with your homework, and go over your notes regularly, you're on your way to a fine performance. Following these additional steps should help:

BEFORE THE TEST

1. Several days before the test, begin by systematically reviewing all the materials you've compiled. Your outlining skills will come in handy here, because outlining your notes will give you an organized overview of the course material, and help you to see connections among the facts you've amassed.

2. After looking carefully at your outline, try to anticipate the kinds of questions the teacher may ask. Use our list of typical essay question terms to compose your own sample questions.

3. Now practice writing essay answers to the questions you've come up with. Start by making a rough outline of your answer, and then compose a clear, direct response. Your opening statement should address the question immediately, and in the rest of the essay that statement should be illustrated with facts, details, and examples. Because the time you'll be able to spend on each question is limited, remember what you've learned about being concise and writing summaries.

4. It's often beneficial to have a study session with some of your classmates. You can compare notes and discuss possible questions and answers.

5. On the day before the test, go through a final review—and then relax and get a good night's sleep.

TAKING THE TEST

1. Arrive early.

2. Read the entire test carefully—especially the directions—before you attempt to answer any of the questions. Make sure that you understand exactly what the question is asking before you write anything.

3. Figure out how much time you can spend on each question. If some questions are worth more points than others, you'll obviously give them more thought.

4. Identify those questions you know most about and address them first.

5. We've all experienced the nightmare of "drawing a blank" in the middle of an exam. There's an easy way to prevent this from happening: in the first five minutes, throw down on paper everything you can think of that has bearing on the question. Then, organize your line of reasoning and your information by making notes or a rough outline: first jot down your main ideas and then sketch in the supporting facts, examples, and quotations before you begin composing your answer.

6. After you've completed the questions you feel most confident about, move on to those that are more difficult. Don't waste time on a question you know little about.

7. Finally, leave some time to proofread your test before the exam period is over.

Mixed Sentences and Incomplete Constructions

When you're writing quickly, whether you're working on a rough draft or taking an essay exam, incomplete or mixed sentences and thoughts are likely to crop up because your mind is working more rapidly than your pen. Being able to recognize these problems should help you to correct them when you proofread your work.

A *mixed sentence* often results when a writer begins a sentence with one grammatical pattern in mind but unintentionally switches to another pattern before finishing the sentence. The example below illustrates what happens when a writer starts a sentence with a modifying phrase and then treats that phrase as the subject of the sentence:

> By working days and going to school nights is how some students pay for their education.

The problem here is that prepositional phrases can rarely act as subjects. One way to correct this error is simply to drop the preposition *by*, which leaves a gerund phrase acting as the subject:

> Working days and going to school nights is how some students pay for their education.

Similarly, adverb clauses cannot function as subjects:

> *Although I have chocolate icing on my face* does not mean I ate the cake.

This problem is easily solved by adding a necessary subject word:

> Although I have chocolate icing on my face, *that* doesn't mean I ate the cake.

Be careful, too, not to follow a subordinate clause with a coordinating conjunction that introduces the independent clause. In English, we don't mix *although* and *but*, or *because* and *therefore*:

> MIXED: Although my sister ate the cake, but she won't admit it.
>
> CORRECT: My sister ate the cake, but she won't admit it.
>
> CORRECT: Although my sister ate the cake, she won't admit it.

The preceding sentences are mixed because their parts don't work together grammatically, just as a car won't work if one of its parts doesn't fit mechanically. Another kind of problem sentence doesn't work because one of its parts is missing a necessary word or words:

> I waited all week for the money, *but no check.*

Make the contrast complete by adding the second verb:

> I waited all week for the money, *but no check arrived.*

Incomplete comparisons can also create ambiguity:

> He loves the dog more than his wife. (Does he love his wife less than he loves the dog? Or does his wife love the dog less than he does?)

Can you think of two ways to correct the above sentence?

EXERCISE 10.25

Correct the mixed sentences and incomplete constructions below:

1. After eating the entire box of pretzels was probably the cause of her stomachache.

2. We've been buying lottery tickets for years now, yet no luck.

3. When the lights go out is usually the result of a power failure.

4. Although we spent days trying to solve the puzzle, but we couldn't do it.

5. Our teacher seems to enjoy grammar more than his students.

6. By eating moderately and exercising regularly is the best method of weight control.

7. Even though he was lazy and dishonest, yet he was able to make others admire him.

8. My mother likes ice cream more than my father.

9. Because he hadn't practiced, therefore he couldn't play the song.

10. I see my mother less often than my brother.

Assignment 4: The Essay Exam—Education at Risk

In April of 1983, the National Commission on Excellence in Education published *A Nation at Risk,* the result of an 18-month study of U.S. public schools.* Warning that "the educational foundations of our society are presently being eroded by a rising tide of mediocrity that threatens our very future as a Nation," the report has led to a national discussion of what can be done to improve education in America. In this section, you are invited to join in the debate.

In Chapter 8, we asked you to draw upon your background as a student to write a comparison/contrast of different school systems or different levels of education. Your next task is to use your own experience in schools here and abroad, and the information in the pages to come, as the basis for two in-class essays and a longer essay to be written at home. In each assignment you'll have the opportunity to address a different aspect of the crisis in the nation's public schools. There are several factors involved in this issue, but much of the debate has focused on what is required of the students in U.S. schools and on what many observers believe to be problems in the teaching profession. Before we ask you for your recommendations for improving teaching and learning in the public schools, let's look at some of the facts.

PART ONE: THE BACKGROUND

The Students

The graph on the following page shows how students have been performing on the Scholastic Achievement Tests** that are required of most college-bound students in the United States (this graph and the graphs on pages 419 and 420 are adapted from an article called "What to Do About America's Schools," by Peter Brinelow, that appeared in the 9/19/83 issue of the business magazine *Fortune*):

---

*   The term "public schools" refers to elementary and high schools that are publicly funded.

** The Scholastic Achievement Test (SAT) is a standardized examination that measures mathematical and verbal ability. Scores on each of the two sections range from 200 to 800.

SCHOLASTIC APTITUDE TEST SCORES

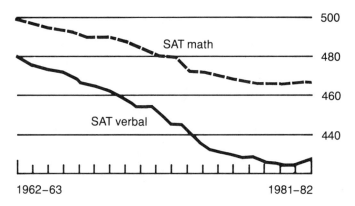

The SAT Slump
After some gains in the late 1950s, SAT median scores
declined continuously until 1982 — despite the fact
that the test seems to have gotten easier.

Among other facts that point to the problems in U.S. schools are these,
quoted from the National Commission on Excellence in Education study:

- Many 17-year-olds do not possess the "higher order" intellectual skills
  we should expect of them. Nearly 40 percent cannot draw inferences
  from written material; only one-fifth can write a persuasive essay; and
  only one-third can solve a mathematics problem requiring several steps.

- There was a steady decline in science achievement scores of U.S.
  17-year-olds as measured by national assessments of science in 1969,
  1973, and 1977.

- Average achievement of high school students on most standardized
  tests is now lower than 26 years ago when Sputnik was launched.

- Between 1975 and 1980, remedial mathematics courses in public
  4-year colleges increased by 72 percent and now constitute one-
  quarter of all mathematics courses taught in those institutions.

- Average tested achievement of students graduating from college is
  also lower.

- International comparisons of student achievement, completed a decade ago, reveal that on 19 academic tests American students were
  never first or second and, in comparison with other industrialized
  nations, were last seven times.

- Some 23 million American adults are functionally illiterate by the
  simplest tests of everyday reading, writing, and comprehension.

- About 13 percent of all 17-year-olds in the United States can be considered functionally illiterate. Functional illiteracy among minority youth may run as high as 40 percent.

- Over half the population of gifted students do not match their tested ability with comparable achievement in school.

JOURNAL EXERCISE 10.26

To many observers, the preceding facts prove that U.S. schools are no longer doing a satisfactory job of educating students. Others point out, however, that the student population taking standardized tests has changed over the past twenty years. Before the mid-sixties, for example, a much smaller percentage of U.S. high school students took the SATs, and far fewer students went on to college. In your journal, discuss why this change in the student population might explain the decline in achievement test scores. Then compare your response to those of your classmates.

The Teachers

Let's shift our attention from the students to the teachers and examine the following graphs:

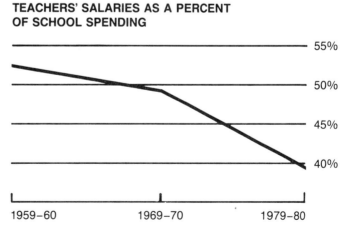

TEACHERS' SALARIES AS A PERCENT OF SCHOOL SPENDING

55%

50%

45%

40%

1959–60   1969–70   1979–80

Symptom of Bureaucracy
Teachers' salaries are a decreasing proportion of current per-pupil expenditure. One reason for heavier administrative costs: complying with federal regulations.

AVERAGE ANNUAL SALARIES

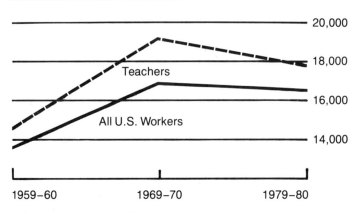

Salary Slide
When adjusted for inflation, teachers' pay fell during the
1970s. It is now barely above the U.S. average — but
remember, teachers only teach about 180 days a year.

And this excerpt from *A Nation at Risk* summarizes the Commission's findings regarding the teaching profession in America:

> The Commission found that not enough of the academically able students
> are being attracted to teaching; that teacher preparation programs need
> substantial improvement; that the professional working life of teachers is
> on the whole unacceptable; and that a serious shortage of teachers exists in
> key fields.
>
> • Too many teachers are being drawn from the bottom quarter of grad-
>   uating high school and college students.
>
> • The teacher preparation curriculum is weighted heavily with courses
>   in "educational methods" at the expense of courses in subjects to be
>   taught. A survey of 1,350 institutions training teachers indicated that
>   41 percent of the time of elementary school teacher candidates is
>   spent in education courses, which reduces the amount of time avail-
>   able for subject matter courses.
>
> • The average salary after 12 years of teaching is only $17,000 per year,
>   and many teachers are required to supplement their income with
>   part-time and summer employment. In addition, individual teachers
>   have little influence in such critical professional decisions as, for ex-
>   ample, textbook selection.
>
> • Despite widespread publicity about an overpopulation of teachers,
>   severe shortages of certain kinds of teachers exist: in the fields of

mathematics, science, and foreign languages; and among specialists in education for gifted and talented, language minority, and handicapped students.

- The shortage of teachers in mathematics and science is particularly severe. A 1981 survey of 45 States revealed shortages of mathematics teachers in 43 States, critical shortages of earth sciences teachers in 33 States, and of physics teachers everywhere.

- Half of the newly employed mathematics, science, and English teachers are not qualified to teach these subjects; fewer than one-third of U.S. high schools offer physics taught by qualified teachers.

In-Class Essays

In-Class Essay #1: Use the information above and on the preceding pages and your own experiences and observations to agree or disagree with one of these statements:

a. The quality of the teaching profession cannot be improved without raising teachers' salaries.

b. Too many teachers are not qualified for their jobs. Until teacher training programs and requirements for certification are made more rigorous, the quality of the teaching in U.S. schools will not improve.

In-Class Essay #2: Now consider the additional facts that follow, as well as your own knowledge of schools here and abroad, to discuss one of these topics:

a. the courses you believe high school students should have to take and why these courses should be required.

b. the amount of time high school students should spend in school and the amount of homework they should be expected to do. Be sure to justify your recommendations.

Here is the additional data, from *A Nation at Risk*:

- The amount of homework for high school seniors has decreased (two-thirds report less than 1 hour a night) and grades have risen as average student achievement has been declining.

- In many schools, the time spent learning how to cook and drive counts as much toward a high school diploma as the time spent studying mathematics, English, chemistry, U.S. history, or biology.

- A study of the school week in the United States found that some schools provided students only 17 hours of academic instruction during the week, and the average school provided about 22.

- One-fifth of all 4-year public colleges in the United States must accept every high school graduate within the State regardless of program followed or grades, thereby serving notice to high school students that they can expect to attend college even if they do not follow a demanding course of study in high school or perform well.

- In England and other industrialized countries, it is not unusual for academic high school students to spend 8 hours a day at school, 220 days per year. In the United States, by contrast, the typical school day lasts 6 hours and the school year is 180 days.

- In many other industrialized nations, courses in mathematics (other than arithmetic or general mathematics), biology, chemistry, physics, and geography start in grade 6 and are required of *all* students. The time spent on these subjects, based on class hours, is about three times that spent by even the most science-oriented U.S. students, i.e., those who select 4 years of science and mathematics in secondary school.

- A 1980 State-by-State survey of high school diploma requirements reveals that only eight States require high schools to offer foreign language instruction, but none requires students to take the courses. Thirty-five States require only 1 year of mathematics, and 36 require only 1 year of science for a diploma.

- In 13 States, 50 percent or more of the units required for high school graduation may be electives chosen by the student. Given this freedom to choose the substance of half or more of their education, many students opt for less demanding personal service courses, such as bachelor living.

- About 23 percent of our more selective college and universities reported that their general level of selectivity declined during the 1970s, and 29 percent reported reducing the number of specific high school courses required for admission (usually by dropping foreign language requirements, which are now specified as a condition for admission by only one-fifth of our institutions of higher education).

PART TWO: THE RECOMMENDATIONS

In Part Three at the end of this section, we'll ask you to write your own proposal for bettering the quality of education in U.S. schools. Below, we have listed some of the proposals for improving the teaching profession that are now circulating throughout the country. Read these recommendations and the argument that follows them, to prepare for your own proposal:

- In September of 1983, the governor of New Jersey called for a starting salary of $18,500, a merit-pay system for distinguished teachers, an emphasis on classroom discipline, and an alternative system of teacher certification that would not require education courses.

- The governor of Tennessee has endorsed a sweeping merit-pay plan that would create four career stages similar to the ranking system of university faculty. At the top would be "master teachers," who would make as much as 60 percent more than the base salary.

- To attract the most qualified people into the teaching profession, the governor of New York has proposed the creation of a State Teachers Corps, which would provide loans to college students who pledged to teach in the state's schools. Teachers who fulfilled their service commitment would not have to repay their loans.

- In Houston, Texas, a bonus program is already underway in the Houston Independent School District. Its teachers are able to make as much as $6,000 in bonus pay a year by teaching in the rougher neighborhood schools, missing no more than five school days a year, and teaching areas in which there are critical shortages of qualified instructors—areas such as bilingual education, math, science, and special education.

EXERCISE 10.27

In the following selection, Albert Shanker, president of the American Federation of Teachers, explains his reaction to three other popular proposals for improving the teaching profession. Before you begin to work on your own proposal, use the following questions to analyze the structure and techniques of Shanker's argument:

1. How does the opening paragraph suggest the thesis?

2. How does the second paragraph narrow this discussion of educational reform?

3. What three popular ideas for improving the quality of teachers does Shanker address? How does he argue for or against each of these ideas?

4. In outlining this brief essay, refer back to page 373 to see which of the elements of argumentation appear in each paragraph. Can you point to anything on the list that Shanker doesn't include which might strengthen his argument?

Shouldn't We Retest Doctors, Too?

Old 'Cures' Floated for Incompetence

Every wave of education reform brings with it some good ideas and others which are attractive but not well thought out. The current reform wave is no exception.

One of the great virtues of the current wave is that it recognizes the classroom teacher as the key to a good education. (It's hard to believe that only a few years ago an earlier generation of reformers pinned their hopes on the creation of "teacher proof" educational materials.) Many of the recent reports list recommendations designed to retain our teaching force and attract new talent, but it is inevitable that any discussion of teacher quality will also deal with the question of how to get rid of incompetents.

All of us were at one time students, and while we were lucky enough to have one, two or three great teachers who inspired us, the chances are good that we had just as many teachers at the other end of the quality spectrum. Of course, there are differences in judgment, and there are occasions when a given teacher rated as incompetent by one student or principal would be deemed satisfactory or even outstanding by others. Still, there's no doubt that teaching has its share of incompetents, as does every other field, and the reform wave has resurrected some old "cures."

Most popular is the idea that tenure should be abolished so that teachers thought to be incompetent by their principal or superintendent may be dismissed without the protection of tenure—the right to know why the discharge is being sought and to challenge it before an impartial body which has the opportunity to hear both sides of the case. Somehow the public thinks that tenure gives teachers something that no one else enjoys—a special protection. It's just not so. What teachers have is no better than, and usually weaker and worse than, that enjoyed by other professionals—doctors, dentists, lawyers, pharmacists—and millions of workers in both the private and public sectors who can only be dismissed for "just cause."

But the real question is, would abolishing tenure lead to better teaching, better results in school? We don't have to abolish tenure in order to find out. Since at least two states do not have tenure—Mississippi and Texas—if tenure were the big stumbling block to improving education by easily removing incompetents, someone should be able to demonstrate the superiority of education in these two states. Anyone with the evidence ought to produce it. And if there is no evidence, it's time to put this idea back into mothballs.

A second idea is recertification. Even people who were really good 5, 10, 15 years ago get worn out—everyone knows that. Why require a "trial" to get someone out? Why not have all teaching certificates terminate after a specific period of time, such as five years? Most teachers' licenses would be renewed after five years, but some would not, thus avoiding messy disputes and arguments. The idea is appealing, but why apply it only to teachers? Why not to doctors, dentists, lawyers, pharmacists? Any of these whose performance deteriorates is likely to do at least as much damage as a teacher. If recertification were imposed on all of these and other job categories (and I don't mean a *pro forma* recertification but one which really reviews the desirability of granting another five years), it would be hard to ask that teachers be exempt, but it's just as unfair to subject teachers to this when no one else's certification is up for review. Also, we'd be sending a message to many who are now in college: In addition to having low pay and low prestige, the profession they're preparing to enter can easily be taken away from them every five years. We'd thus be adding exceptional insecurity to the other disadvantages of the job.

Third is the idea of retesting teachers. I've been a strong advocate of giving teachers tests before they're hired and requiring high pass marks in the subject matter to be taught. But why give a pencil-and-paper test to a teacher after 5 or 10 years, when you can spend a few hours in his or her classroom and find out by direct observation whether the teacher knows the subject and knows how to teach it? Of course, knowledge in a given field is always expanding. Shouldn't teachers be tested again to make sure they're keeping up with the latest advances? Again, the answer is yes—but only if they're not singled out. The knowledge explosion in medicine, dentistry and pharmacy is much greater than new developments in the teaching of Shakespeare, Dickens, irregular French verbs, high school algebra or fourth grade arithmetic. Here, too, if we're going to retest teachers to protect the public, it's going to be hard to convince teachers that they and only they should be retested.

You can't blame teachers for feeling that they're being scapegoated when these proposals are floated by officials who are trying to hire teachers at $12,000, $13,000 and $14,000 a year; who don't bother giving teachers a test before they're hired, and who don't follow a policy of granting tenure only to those who meet very high standards during their probationary period.

Does all this mean that nothing can be done? Not at all. In the near future I'll deal with how one school district and its teachers' union are dealing with the problem of incompetence in a very different way.

PART THREE: THE ASSIGNMENT

Below are three possible topics for a longer essay exam, to be completed at home. Choose the one you feel you can address most convincingly. Before you start to write, go back to the suggestions for taking an essay exam on pages 413–415 to help you organize your ideas, your experiences, and those facts you've culled from the preceding pages that will best support your argument.

Whether you quote from outside sources directly or paraphrase, remember to introduce the source of the idea. Using what you learned about appositives in Chapter 8 will help you to identify a source for your reader. For example:

> DIRECTION QUOTATION: *A Nation at Risk*, a government report on U.S. public schools, warns that "not enough of the academically able students are being attracted to teaching."

> PARAPHRASE: *A Nation at Risk*, a government report on U.S. public schools, warns that too few good students are becoming teachers.

Finally, make sure that you allow ample time to revise your argument before you submit it.

Option A: One of the major questions to emerge from the debate on education is how to attract the most capable people into the teaching profession. Your job is to draft a plan, to be presented to the members of the American Federation of Teachers, that will draw the best people into the field.

Option B: The issue of merit pay for outstanding teachers has aroused vigorous debate. Many observers believe that there is no fair way of determining which teachers are superior, while others contend that treating all teachers as if they were equal is in itself unfair. Write an editorial for your campus newspaper in which you argue for or against merit pay. Be sure to anticipate and address the possible objections of your opponents.

Option C: Take any of the other problems indicated by the facts that appear on the previous pages, and compose your own recommendation for solving the problem you have chosen. Your goal is to try to convince a group of concerned parents that this proposal should be implemented in their children's school. (You may want to return to one of the in-class essays you've already written and expand it for this assignment.)

Source for Exercise 10.12

Address at the Dedication of the Gettysburg National Cemetery

Four score and seven years ago our fathers brought forth on this continent, a new nation, conceived in Liberty, and dedicated to the proposition that all men are created equal.

Now we are engaged in a great civil war; testing whether that nation, or any nation so conceived and so dedicated, can long endure. We are met on a great battlefield of that war. We have come to dedicate a portion of that field as a final resting-place for those who here gave their lives that that nation might live. It is altogether fitting and proper that we should do this.

But, in a larger sense, we cannot dedicate—we cannot consecrate—we cannot hallow—this ground. The brave men, living and dead, who struggled here have consecrated it, far above our poor power to add or detract. The world will little note, nor long remember, what we say here, but it can never forget what they did here. It is for us the living, rather, to be dedicated here to the unfinished work which they who fought here have thus far so nobly advanced. It is rather for us to be here dedicated to the great task remaining before us—that from these honored dead we take increased devotion to that cause for which they gave the last full measure of devotion; that we here highly resolve that these dead shall not have died in vain; that this nation, under God, shall have a new birth of freedom; and that government of the people, by the people, for the people, shall not perish from the earth.

Appendices

Appendix 1: Principal Parts of Irregular Verbs

BASE	PAST TENSE	PAST PARTICIPLE	BASE	PAST TENSE	PAST PARTICIPLE
awake	awaked, awoke	awaked, awoke, awoken	fly	flew	flown
			forbid	forbade	forbidden
be	was, were	been	forget	forgot	forgotten, forgot
bear	bore	borne	freeze	froze	frozen
beat	beat	beaten, beat	get	got	gotten, got
become	became	become	give	gave	given
begin	began	begun	go	went	gone
bend	bent	bent	grind	ground	ground
bet	bet	bet	grow	grew	grown
bind	bound	bound	hang (an object)	hung	hung
bite	bit	bit, bitten	hang (a person)	hanged	hanged
bleed	bled	bled	have	had	had
blow	blew	blown	hear	heard	heard
break	broke	broken	hide	hid	hidden, hid
breed	bred	bred	hit	hit	hit
bring	brought	brought	hold	held	held
build	built	built	hurt	hurt	hurt
burst	burst	burst	keep	kept	kept
buy	bought	bought	kneel	knelt, kneeled	knelt, kneeled
catch	caught	caught	knit	knit, knitted	knit, knitted
choose	chose	chosen	know	knew	known
come	came	come	lay (put)	laid	laid
cost	cost	cost	lead	led	led
creep	crept	crept	lean	leaned, leant	leaned, leant
cut	cut	cut	leave	left	left
deal	dealt	dealt	lend	lent	lent
dig	dug	dug	let (allow)	let	let
dive	dived, dove	dived	lie (recline)	lay	lain
do	did	done	light	lighted, lit	lighted, lit
draw	drew	drawn	lose	lost	lost
dream	dreamed, dreamt	dreamed, dreamt	make	made	made
			mean	meant	meant
drink	drank	drunk	meet	met	met
drive	drove	driven	pay	paid	paid
eat	ate	eaten	prove	proved	proved, proven
fall	fell	fallen	put	put	put
feed	fed	fed	quit	quit, quitted	quit, quitted
feel	felt	felt	read	read	read
fight	fought	fought	rid	rid, ridded	rid, ridded
find	found	found	ride	rode	ridden
fit	fitted, fit	fitted, fit	ring	rang	rung
flee	fled	fled	rise	rose	risen

BASE	PAST TENSE	PAST PARTICIPLE	BASE	PAST TENSE	PAST PARTICIPLE
run	ran	run	spread	spread	spread
say	said	said	spring	sprang, sprung	sprung
see	saw	seen	stand	stood	stood
seek	sought	sought	steal	stole	stolen
sell	sold	sold	stick	stuck	stuck
send	sent	sent	sting	stung	stung
set	set	set	strike	struck	struck, stricken
shake	shook	shaken	swear	swore	sworn
shine	shone, shined	shone, shined (trans.)	swim	swam	swum
			swing	swung	swung
shoot	shot	shot	take	took	taken
show	showed	showed, shown	teach	taught	taught
shrink	shrank	shrunk	tear	tore	torn
shut	shut	shut	tell	told	told
sing	sang, sung	sung	think	thought	thought
sink	sank	sunk	throw	threw	thrown
sit	sat	sat	wake	waked, woke	waked, woke, woken
sleep	slept	slept			
slide	slid	slid, slidden	wear	wore	worn
speak	spoke	spoken	weave	wove	woven
speed	sped, speeded	sped, speeded	weep	wept	wept
spend	spent	spent	win	won	won
spin	spun	spun	wring	wrung	wrung
split	split	split	write	wrote	written

Appendix 2: Two- and Three-Word Verbs

Two-Word Verbs

Two-word verbs consist of a verb and a particle (a preposition or an adverb acting like a preposition) that combine to create a meaning different from the usual meanings of the individual words. Most of the words that make up two-word verbs are short and frequently used. A given verb, however, may take several different prepositions, and each of these combinations will have a distinct meaning. *Get*, for example, combines with a number of particles: *get up*; *get over*; *get through*; *get around*; *get along*; *get by*; *get back*.

Two-word verbs function like normal verbs, but because they are idiomatic, they can create special vocabulary problems for non-native speakers. An ESL student who tries to decode a sentence such as "I ran across my doctor on the street yesterday" will come away with a strange image indeed if the ordinary definitions of *ran* and *across* are applied. In this case, *run across* is a two-word verb that means "to meet by chance." Yet *run* and *across* often do not constitute a two-word verb. "To run

across a street," for example, carries the usual meanings of the individual words, so one must be able to use context to distinguish between the possible meanings.

Furthermore, two-word verbs fall into three categories: separable, inseparable with objects, and inseparable without objects. The following lists of common two-word verbs include brief definitions and rules for their structures.

Separable Verbs

Separable two-word verbs can take objects, and the noun or pronoun object may come between the verb and its particle. However, if the object is a personal pronoun, it is always placed before the separable particle:

CORRECT: I can't *figure out this puzzle.*
CORRECT: I can't *figure this puzzle out.*
CORRECT: I can't *figure it out.*
INCORRECT: I can't figure out it.

blow up	cause to explode
break in	use something new until it is comfortable
break off	end, stop suddenly
bring about	cause to happen
bring on	cause to happen
bring up	raise from childhood
call off	cancel
carry out	accomplish, complete a plan
count in	include
count out	exclude
cross out	eliminate
cut down	reduce in amount
cut off	stop, interrupt
cut out	stop, eliminate
figure out	understand, solve
fill out	complete a printed form
find out	discover
get across	make understood
hand in	submit
hand out	distribute
hand over	give control of
have on	be dressed in
hold up	delay; rob using a weapon
leave out	omit
let down	disappoint
let out	free from confinement
look over	examine
pick out	choose
pick up	take or lift
point out	show or indicate
put off	postpone, delay
put away	put in proper storage place
rule out	eliminate
see through	complete
take out	remove; escort
think up	invent
throw away	discard, put in garbage
try on	put on an article of clothing to see if it fits
try out	test
turn down	reject or refuse; lower the volume
turn in	submit, hand in
wear out	use something until it is no longer usable
wind up	finish, bring to an end

Some two-word separable words can occur with or without objects:

NO OBJECT: The crowd finally *calmed down.*

OBJECT: She *calmed the baby down.*

calm down	become calm; make calm
close down	close permanently
close up	close temporarily
get back	return; recover something
give up	give in; surrender
keep up	continue
quiet down	become quiet; make quiet
save up	accumulate or collect
take over	take control of
work out	resolve

Inseparable Verbs Followed by Objects

These two-word verbs are always followed by their objects. For example:

CORRECT: A nurse *cared for the patient.*

INCORRECT: A nurse cared the patient for.

care for	like; attend to the needs of
come across	meet or discover unexpectedly
get over	recover from
get through	complete or finish
go over	review
hear from	receive spoken or written communication from
look for	try to find
run across	find unexpectedly; meet by chance
run into	meet by chance
see about	attend to; consider
take after	resemble

Inseparable Verbs Without Objects

Some two-word verbs do not take objects:

The storm *blew over* quickly.

The car *broke down* on the highway.

blow over	pass without doing damage
break down	stop working or functioning properly
break out	appear or develop suddenly
come by	visit
come through	succeed or recover despite problems
come to	regain consciousness
die away	fade, disappear
die down	fade, diminish
die out	disappear
fall off	lessen
fall through	fail to happen
get up	arise
give in	surrender
go on	continue

grow up	mature
hang up	put a phone receiver on its hook
hold out	resist; persevere
let up	diminish or lessen in intensity
pass away	die
pull in	arrive
pull out	depart
pull through	survive or recover despite difficulties
show up	arrive, appear
stand by	be ready to help
stand out	be evident; excel
stand up	be durable, last
wear off	fade, disappear

Three-Word Verbs

In addition to two-word verbs, there is also a smaller group of three-word verbs. They are usually followed by nouns and they are all inseparable:

The baby *came down with* a cold.

We must *face up to* our failures.

Here are some common three-word verbs:

come down with	become ill with
come out with	declare; state publicly
come up to	be equal to
come up with	propose; produce
do away with	destroy, eliminate
face up to	accept or acknowledge something unpleasant
feel up to	feel able to do something
get along with	have a friendly relationship with
get away with	do something wrong or unconventional without penalty
get rid of	eliminate or discard
go back on	break a promise; betray
go through with	complete despite difficulty
live up to	fulfill a promise; meet a standard
look back on	remember
look forward to	anticipate eagerly
make up for	compensate for a mistake or shortcoming
measure up to	meet a standard
put up with	tolerate
run out of	become used up; exhaust the supply of
stand up for	defend
stand up to	face up to; resist opposition

Appendix 3: Forming Comparative and Superlative Adjectives and Adverbs

Adjectives and adverbs have different forms to indicate different degrees of the qualities they name. The *comparative* form shows a greater degree—*larger, faster, more economical*—while the *superlative* form indicates the greatest degree—*largest, fastest, most economical*. As you can see, there are two ways to form the comparative and superlative: some words add -*er* and -*est*, and others use *more* and *most* before the base form of the adjective or adverb.

When only two things are being compared, the comparative form is used:

The U.S. is *larger* than Greece.

Writing is *more difficult* than speaking.

The superlative form singles out a member of a group larger than two:

The Soviet Union is the *largest* nation on earth.

Is Paris the *most beautiful* city in the world?

Some Rules for Comparing Adjectives and Adverbs

1. Adjectives and adverbs with only one syllable take -*er* and -*est*:

small, smaller than, the smallest

2. Adjectives and adverbs with two syllables that end in *y* or *le* take -*er* and -*est*. Notice that if a word ends in *y*, the *y* changes to *i* before the suffix is added:

happy, happier than, the happiest
little, littler, littlest

3. Adjectives and adverbs with three or more syllables use *more* and *most* instead of -*er* and -*est* because "interestingest" would be clumsy indeed:

interesting, more interesting, most interesting

4. For the same reason, adjectives and adverbs with two syllables that end in -*ed*, -*ful*, -*ing*, -*ish*, -*less*, or -*ous* use *more* and *most*:

more dangerous, most stylish

5. Some two-syllable adjectives can take *either form*:

   a) adjectives ending in *-er, -ow, -some*:

   clever, cleverer, most clever

   narrow, more narrow, narrowest

   handsome, more handsome, handsomest

   b) the following words:

   common, cruel, pleasant, polite, profound, quiet, severe, sincere, stupid

6. Finally, here are some spelling tips for adding *-er* or *-est*:

   a) If an adjective ends in a consonant plus *y*, the *y* is changed to *i*:

   lazy, lazier, laziest   sloppy, sloppier, sloppiest

   b) If an adjective ends in a single vowel plus a consonant, the consonant is doubled:

   hot, hotter   big, biggest

   c) If an adjective ends in *e*, simply add *-r* or *-st*:

   pale, paler   large, largest

All but a few adjectives and adverbs use one of these two ways of showing comparison. Make sure you're familiar with those that don't:

IRREGULAR ADJECTIVES

bad	worse	worst
far	farther	farthest
good, well*	better	best
little	less	least
much, many	more	most

IRREGULAR ADVERBS

badly	worse	worst
well*	better	best

* *Well* can act as both an adjective and an adverb:
   He is not a *well* man, but he still works *well*.

Appendix 4: Spelling Guidelines

As you've discovered, the complex history of the English language has created a number of irregularities, one of which is its complicated spelling system. We offer these general rules to help you with common spelling problems:

ie or *ei*?

Many American schoolchildren are taught this rhyme: "*I* before *e* except after *c*, or when it sounds like long *a* as in *neighbor* and *weigh*."

I BEFORE E:

believe	chief	friend
grief	hygiene	thief

EI AFTER C:

ceiling	conceive	deceit
deceive	perceive	receive

EI PRONOUNCED AS LONG A:

beige	eight	freight
sleigh	vein	weight

Unfortunately, there are exceptions to this useful rule. The following words are spelled with the *ei* combination but do not follow *c* and are not pronounced like long *a*:

either	forfeit	leisure
neither	heir	seize
foreign	height	seizure

the silent *e*

The silent *e* is the unpronounced final *e* in words like *bite, use, surprise,* and *love.* When you add a suffix that begins with a vowel to a word with the silent final *e*, drop the *e*:

bite, biting	use, usable
surprise, surprising	love, lovable

But keep the final *e* if the suffix begins with a consonant:

   lovely, useful, forceful, careless

EXCEPTIONS: Dropping the final *e* before a suffix that begins with a vowel would, in some cases, cause confusion or incorrect pronunciation; in these cases, it is kept. For example, *dye* becomes *dyeing* to distinguish it from *die/dying. Change* becomes *changeable* so we don't pronounce the soft *g* or *j* sound as a hard *g*.

Another exception is that the silent *e* is sometimes dropped before a suffix beginning with a vowel if the *e* is preceded by another vowel:

   argue, argument   true, truly

the final *y*

When you add a suffix to a word that ends in *y*, change the *y* to *i* if it follows a consonant:

happy, happier   beauty, beautiful
merry, merrier   worry, worries

Don't change the *y* when it follows a vowel or when the suffix is *ing*:

day, days   fly, flying
obey, obeys   study, studying

doubling consonants

Some words that end in a consonant double the consonant when a suffix is added:

1. One-syllable words double the consonant when a single vowel precedes the final consonant: *stop, stopping*; *trip, tripped*; *fat, fatter*. But do *not* double the consonant when two vowels or another consonant precedes the final consonant:

hear, hearing   fair, fairly   bark, barking

2. Words of more than one syllable double the final consonant *except* when the consonant is preceded by two vowels or another consonant, or when the accent does not fall on the last syllable of the stem when the ending is added:

repeat, repeated   invent, invention   infer, inference

forming plurals

1. Most nouns add -*s* to form plurals:

girl, girls   horse, horses

2. Nouns and verbs that end in *s, ch, sh,* or *x* add -*es* to form the plural:

boss, bosses   lash, lashes
church, churches   fox, foxes

3. Nouns that end in *o* preceded by a vowel usually add -*s*:

radio, radios

4. Nouns that end in *o* preceded by a consonant usually add -*es*:

potato, potatoes   hero, heroes

5. Nouns and verbs that end in *y* preceded by a consonant change the *y* to *i* before adding -*es*:

baby, babies   cry, cries

Exceptions to this rule include

decoy, decoys   play, plays
delay, delays   ploy, ploys

6. Some nouns that end in *f* or *fe* form the plural by changing the ending to *ve* before adding -*s*:

wife, wives   wolf, wolves
leaf, leaves   thief, thieves
knife, knives

7. Some nouns that come from Latin, Greek, Italian, and French have retained their original plural forms:

analysis, analyses   larva, larvae
criterion, criteria   hypothesis, hypotheses

8. A small group of irregular plurals comes from Old English:

child, children   woman, women
foot, feet   tooth, teeth
man, men   goose, geese

9. Some fish and animal names have the same form for singular and plural:

bass   deer   salmon   sheep   trout

adding prefixes

Attaching a prefix to a word does not change the spelling of the original word:

un + happy = unhappy
mis + spell = misspell

Appendix 5: Punctuation Review

The Apostrophe

Apostrophes indicate omitted letters in contracted verb forms:

1. Contraction of modals or the verbs *have* and *be* with *not*:

is + not = isn't   will + not = won't
can + not = can't   have + not = haven't

2. Contraction of verbs with subjects:

It is ready.   It's ready.
Who is there?   Who's there?
They are here.   They're here.
The plane has landed.   The plane's landed.

Apostrophes indicate the possessive case of nouns and indefinite pronouns:

1. Add *-'s* to singular words, even if the word ends in *-s*:

The *dog's* leash is missing.

My *neighbor's* flowers are blooming.

Someone's coat was left in the classroom.

Mr. *Jones's* daughter is a lawyer.

Charles's tape recorder doesn't work.

2. Exceptions to this rule include a few singular nouns that end in an *s* or *z* sound and the possessives of ancient proper names. In these cases, add only an apostrophe:

For *conscience'* sake

Moses' tribe

Ulysses' wife

3. Add *-'s* to irregular plural words that do not end in *-s*:

The *children's* parents are here.

The *people's* votes were counted carefully.

4. Add only an apostrophe to *plural* words ending in *-s*:

The *boys'* fathers took them camping.

We bought the *Lawrys'* house.

5. Add *-'s* to the last word of a compound word or phrase:

My *mother-in-law's* purse was stolen.

This is *someone else's* umbrella.

6. To show joint possession of the same item, place the apostrophe after the final noun:

George and Martha's business is doing well.

(one business jointly owned)

7. To show individual possession, place apostrophes after each noun:

George's and *Martha's* businesses are doing well.

(two separate businesses)

8. The apostrophe is usually used only for living creatures. However, apostrophes are used with nouns that express time, political entities, and natural phenomena:

a *week's* wait

Italy's government

the *sun's* rays

9. No apostrophe is used with the possessive forms of personal pronouns:

The dog is always wagging *its* tail.

The mistake was *yours* (*his, hers, ours, theirs*).

The Period*

Use a period to end sentences that are statements, mild commands, or indirect questions:

*See Chapter 1 for a discussion of the exclamation point (!) and the question mark (?).

We hold these truths to be self-evident.

Please fasten your seatbelts.

The child asked where her father was going.

Use periods with most abbreviations:

M.A.	Ms.	B.C.
A.M.	e.g.	Dr.

NOTE: When an abbreviation falls at the end of a sentence, use only one period: We traveled throughout the U.S.

The Comma

1. Use a comma before a coordinating conjunction linking independent clauses:

He knew what he wanted, and he was determined to get it.

NOTE: If the clauses are short, the comma may be omitted:

They were bored and so was I.

2. Use a comma to set off introductory phrases and clauses:

If I were you, I'd exercise more caution.
(subordinate clause)

Fortunately, the missing necklace was found.
(sentence modifier)

Terrified, the cat backed into a corner.
(participle)

To gain the lead, the sprinter picked up speed.
(infinitive phrase)

From now on, I promise to study harder.
(prepositional phrase)

3. Use a comma to separate words, phrases, or clauses in a series (that is, three or more items of equal importance):

June's sister, brother, and mother planned the surprise party.

You'll get a promotion if you work hard, meet your responsibilities, and get along with your peers.

We ate supper at midnight, we danced the night away, and we sat on the beach until sunrise.

4. Use commas to set off nonrestrictive phrases, clauses, and appositives in a sentence. (A nonrestrictive element gives added information but does not limit the meaning of the sentence):

The child, looking for attention, threw her food onto the floor.

My neighbor, who is a grouch, banged on my door.

Jonathan Miller, a writer and physician, wrote *The Body in Question.*

5. Use commas to set off contrastive phrases or parenthetical expressions*:

The meeting is on Monday, not Tuesday.

It's a good idea, moreover, to show up on time.

The proceedings, I suppose, will last for several hours.

6. Use a comma to set off tag questions, *yes* and *no*, words of direct address, and mild interjections:

It's sweltering in here, isn't it?

Yes, it is a bit stuffy.

Will you open the window a crack, Ralph?

Oh, the window seems to be painted shut.

7. Use a comma to set off absolute phrases. (An absolute phrase is a noun or noun phrase followed by a modifier; it modifies a whole sentence rather than a particular word or phrase in the sentence):

Their job finished, the house painters took a lunch break.

8. Use commas to separate introductory, concluding, and explanatory words from quotations**:

Who said, "Home is where the heart is"?

"Ms. Baker is in a meeting right now," said the receptionist.

"But if you'd like to wait," he continued, "please have a seat."

9. Use commas with dates, addresses, place names, and long numbers:

James Joyce's book *Ulysses* takes place on June 16, 1904, in Dublin, Ireland.

The sweepstakes winner collected $10,000—or was it $10,000,000?

10. Use a comma to prevent misreading:

CONFUSING: Those who can do.

CLEARER: Those who can, do.

The Semicolon***

1. Use a semicolon to separate main clauses not joined by a coordinating conjunction:

He wanted to go; we begged him to stay.

2. Use a semicolon to separate main clauses joined by a

conjunctive adverb (such as *indeed, besides, still, thus, besides, therefore,* and so on):

I've eaten too much already; still, I'll have another piece of pie.

3. Use a semicolon between coordinate elements with internal commas, as in the following sentence:

Normally you would use a comma with the coordinating conjunctions *and, but, or, nor,* and *for;* but placing a semicolon between long clauses with internal commas makes the sentence easier to read.

4. Use a semicolon between items in a series when the items themselves contain commas:

Among the other people at the dinner party were my brother, Jeff, an investments analyst; my sister-in-law, Miriam, an advertising executive; and my husband, Steve, a business writer.

The Colon

The colon is used to introduce and to separate.

1. Use a colon between two independent clauses to introduce explanations and statements preceded by *the following* or *as follows*:

There is something I must tell you: you're bothering me.

My advice to you is the following: leave me alone.

2. Use a colon to introduce an appositive that ends a sentence:

The Declaration of Independence upholds these freedoms: life, liberty, and the pursuit of happiness.

3. Use a colon after the salutation of a formal or business letter:

Dear Mrs. Garcia:

4. Use a colon to introduce a long or formal quotation:

The book of Ecclesiastes in the Bible reminds us: "To every thing there is a season, and a time to every purpose under heaven."

5. Use a colon to separate the parts of biblical quotations; for example, the quotation above comes from verse 1 of Chapter 3 in the book of Ecclesiastes, and would be written thus:

Ecclesiastes 3:1

6. The colon is used to separate hours and minutes:

1:45 P.M.

7. The colon is used to separate titles and subtitles:

Garry Wills wrote *Inventing America: Jefferson's Declaration of Independence.*

---

*Dashes and parentheses are also used to set off parenthetical elements in a sentence. (See page 435.)
**See Chapter 7 for rules regarding punctuation of quotations.
***The semicolon and colon are also discussed in Chapter 4.

The Dash

The dash is used to indicate sudden changes in tone or thought, and to set off certain sentence elements.

1. Use a dash—or double dashes—to show a sudden interruption in tone or thought, or a hesitation in dialogue:

> She exclaimed—though we could scarcely believe it—that she had been robbed.

> He wondered what would have happened if—but he was too tired to think.

> "I was hoping—if it wouldn't be too much trouble—could you—" he paused a moment to catch his breath.

2. Use a dash or double dashes to set off an appositive or a parenthetical expression:

> All the elements of the summer night—moonlight, soft breeze, silence—contributed to the romantic encounter.

> They saw an oasis—or was it a mirage?—far off in the distance.

3. Use a dash to set off an introductory series or brief summary:

> Firecrackers, picnics, flag-waving—we associate these things with the Fourth of July.

Parentheses

Parentheses are used to enclose nonessential elements in a sentence.

1. Use parentheses to set off nonessential facts, explanations, minor digressions, and examples:

> When he graduated from college (in 1970) he decided to apply to graduate school.

> All of the schools refused him (though one put him on the waiting list).

> The great apes (orangutans, chimpanzees, gorillas) are classified as Primates.

NOTE: When the parenthetical expression comes at the end of the sentence, place the period outside the parenthesis. If, however, the parentheses enclose an entire sentence, place the period inside the parenthesis:

> All of the schools refused him. (One, however, put him on the waiting list.)

2. Use parentheses to enclose letters and numbers in lists within sentences:

> Parentheses can be used to set off (1) facts, (2) explanations, and (3) examples.

Brackets

Use brackets to enclose editorial corrections or your own additions to a quotation:

> The lawyer asked him [the defendant] his whereabouts on the day of the crime.

> The defendant responded, "I was home [on Elm Street] all day."

NOTE: The word *sic* (Latin for "in this manner") in brackets indicates that an error appeared in the original quotation and was not made by you:

> According to the newspaper, "The defendant lives on Elk [*sic*] Street."

The Ellipsis Mark

Use the ellipsis mark, which consists of three spaced periods (. . .), to indicate that something has been left out of a quotation:

1. Omission of part of a sentence:

> Two nights before the Derby, she was at a big party in town, when one of her rushes of anxiety about her boy . . . gripped her heart till she could hardly speak. She fought with the feeling . . . for she believed in common sense. But it was too strong. She had to leave the dance and go downstairs to telephone to the country.
>
> —D. H. Lawrence

2. Omission of two sentences:

> Two nights before the Derby, she was at a big party in town, when one of her rushes of anxiety about her boy, her first-born, gripped her heart till she could hardly speak. . . . She had to leave the dance and go downstairs to telephone to the country.

NOTE: When the ellipsis mark follows a sentence, as in the above example, *four* spaced periods are used: one to end the sentence, and the three periods of the ellipsis.

Ellipsis marks may also be used to indicate unfinished statements in quoted speech:

> "If only . . ." he began; then he stared into space.

The Hyphen

1. Use a hyphen to divide words *of more than one syllable* at the end of a line. Try to hyphenate in the middle of a word, and do not set off single letters. Consult your dictionary to determine where the syllable breaks occur in a word:

> CORRECT: conju-gation   osteo-pathy
>
> INCORRECT: smarm-y   lea-ve

2. Hyphenate spelled-out compound numbers from *twenty-one* through *ninety-nine*.

3. Hyphenate a compound of two or more words when it is used as a modifier before a noun:

COMPARE: He was a middle-class suburbanite.

He was of the middle class.

NOTE: Do not use a hyphen when the first word of the compound is an adverb ending in *-ly*:

COMPARE: She handed in a half-finished assignment.

She handed in a partly finished assignment.

Appendix 6: Rules for Capitalization

1. Capitalize the first word in a sentence:

Every sentence, including this one, begins with a capital letter.

2. The pronoun *I* is always capitalized:

I told him I'd be back by six o'clock.

3. Proper names, and nouns used as proper names, are capitalized. (*Common nouns* name general classes of persons, places, and things. *Proper nouns* name specific persons, places, and things.)

a. Names of people and races:

George Gissing
Oriental
Negro
Caucasian

b. A title preceding a proper noun:

Professor Sandra Carpenter
Princess Grace
Prime Minister Margaret Thatcher

c. Specific geographical locations, streets, and buildings:

Amazon River
New Jersey
Mount Everest
Venezuela
Empire State Building
Fifth Avenue
Notre Dame Cathedral

d. The words *north, south, east,* and *west* when they refer to a specific section of the country rather than a direction.

the Midwest
the East

BUT: Her aunt lives thirty miles *south* of Dallas.

e. Nationalities and languages:

German
Korean
Urdu
British

f. The specific names of high school and college courses (as they would appear in a school bulletin):

I'm taking Latin, Computer Science 110, and Introduction to Biology.

BUT: I'm taking courses in computer science and biology.

g. Names of religions, religious figures, sacred terms, and religious books:

Krishna
Moslem
Protestant
the Ten Commandments
the Bible; the Koran

h. Days of the week, months, and holidays:

Monday
September
Independence Day

BUT: Do not capitalize the names of the seasons—spring, summer, autumn, winter.

i. Titles of books, articles, periodicals, songs, poems, movies, plays (the first word and all important words of the title are capitalized; as a rule, articles and prepositions are not):

"I'm in the Mood for Love"
Time Magazine
The Right Stuff
Death of a Salesman

j. Names of ships and trains:

the *Queen Elizabeth II*
the Orient Express

k. Names of documents, historical events or periods, and organizations:

the Declaration of Independence
the Franco-Prussian War
the Middle Ages
the League of Women Voters

Index

About the Authors

Amy Tucker is Director of the ESL Composition Program at Queens College of the City University of New York. She received her B.A. from Barnard College and her Ph.D. in English literature from New York University. Her teaching interests and publications range from American literature to ESL and composition theory.

Jacqueline Costello is Director of the Writing Skills Workshop at Queens College of the City University of New York. She received her B.A. from William Paterson College and her Ph.D. in English literature from New York University. She has taught ESL, composition, and English literature at William Paterson College, LaGuardia Community College, and New York University. From 1978–1980 she was a lecturer in English at Lingnan College in Hong Kong, and she has written articles for various Asian magazines.